Other books in the series

GLEN DUDBRIDGE: The *Hsi-yu Chi*: A Study of Antecedents to the Sixteenth-century Chinese Novel

STEPHEN FITZGERALD: China and the Overseas Chinese: A Study of Peking's Changing Policy 1949–70

CHRISTOPHER HOWE: Wage Patterns and Wage Policy in Modern China, 1919–72

RAY HUANG: Taxation and Government Finance in Sixteenth-Century Ming China

DIANA LARY: Region and Nation: The Kwangsi Clique in Chinese Politics, 1925–37

CHI-YUN CHEN: Hsün Yüeh (A.D. 148–209): The Life and Reflections of an early Medieval Confucian

DAVID R. KNECHTGES: The Han Rhapsody: A Study of the Fu of Yang Hsiung (53 B.C.–A.D. 18)

J. Y. WONG: Yeh Ming-ch'en: Viceroy of Liang Kuang (1852–8)

LI-LI CH'EN: Master Tung's Western Chamber Romance (Tung hsi-hsiang chu-kung-tiao): a Chinese *Chantefable*

DONALD HOLZMAN: Poetry and Politics: The Life and Works of Juan Chi (A.D. 210–63)

CAMBRIDGE STUDIES IN
CHINESE HISTORY, LITERATURE AND INSTITUTI[

General Editors
PATRICK HANAN & DENIS TWITCHETT

YEH MING-CH'EN

兩廣總督葉名琛

黃宇和著

劉敬之署耑

Yeh Ming-ch'en during his imprisonment at Fort William
(L/PS/5, Vol. 167, Herbert–Beadon, 5 April 1858)

Yeh Ming-ch'en

VICEROY OF LIANG KUANG
1852–8

J. Y. WONG

Department of History, University of Sydney

CAMBRIDGE UNIVERSITY PRESS

CAMBRIDGE

LONDON·NEW YORK·MELBOURNE

Published by the Syndics of the Cambridge University Press
The Pitt Building, Trumpington Street, Cambridge CB2 1RP
Bentley House, 200 Euston Road, London NW1 2DB
32 East 57th Street, New York, NY 10022, USA
296 Beaconsfield Parade, Middle Park, Melbourne 3206, Australia

© Cambridge University Press 1976

Library of Congress catalogue card number: 75-18119

ISBN: 0 521 21023 2

First published 1976

Printed in Great Britain
at the
University Printing House, Cambridge
(Euan Phillips, University Printer)

IN MEMORY OF G. F. HUDSON

CONTENTS

Contents

Part six: *Yeh's last days*

FIGURES AND MAPS

TABLES

ACKNOWLEDGEMENTS

My greatest debt is to the man to whom this book is dedicated, and who wrote the foreword to this book shortly before he died. The late Geoffrey Hudson was much more to me than a scholarly and solicitous supervisor. His constant encouragement and gentle kindness gave me the strength and will to carry through my work and overcome many setbacks.

Other friends have devoted many hours to helping me to think and write in a foreign language, as together with them I have written, rewritten, reconstructed and clarified the text of this book. Any clarity of thought and expression which may be shown in this book has been painfully extracted from me by the labours of Richard Miller, Andrew Purkis and Gordon Clack. Janet Hunter, Diane Elson and Kennon Breazeale have put far more time into assisting me with checking my manuscripts, typing and proof-reading than I had any right to expect, even of such good friends. Without the friendship and moral support of all these, this book would not have been written at all.

I have drawn only slightly less extensively on the time and effort of a veritable army of friends. Chief among them are Stephen Gibbs, Stephen Hickinbotham, Claudia Elliott, Brian Powell, T. S. Gregory, Susumu Takiguchi, Hilary Kilpatrick, Toru Koroiwa, Susan Flood, Rose Barugh, Dr A. Smith, Mrs Templeton, Jane Burden, Linda Tsang and Sim Kung.

Many librarians and archivists have given me their kind assistance and consideration: Adrian Roberts of the Bodleian Library, Oxford; Jeffrey Ede, Kenneth Timings, Norman Evans and Michael Roper of the Public Record Office; Dr F. Taylor and Miss Matheson of the John Rylands University Library of Manchester; Messrs Owen and Gantrey of the Cambridge University Library; Miss F. Ranger of the Royal Historical Commission; John Lust, Angela Castro and David Chibbett of the Library of the School of Oriental and African Studies, London; Howard Nelson of the British Museum; Messrs S. C. Sutton, Bingle and Myer of the India Office Library; and Miss Anne Abley of St Antony's College Library, Oxford.

I have been fortunate enough to have comments and suggestions from several distinguished scholars who have read my manuscript: Professors D. C. Twitchett, J. K. Fairbank, W. G. Beasley, R. Carr, G. R. Storry, and Dr Mark Elvin.

The Chinese title of the book is written by my former teacher, Mr Lau King-chi. The frontispiece is a photograph by Mr Robert White of a portrait of Yeh; this portrait has been painted by Mr S. K. Choi from a sketch by courtesy of Oxford University Press.

I am indeed fortunate to have met such good friends and teachers as those I have mentioned. I am profoundly grateful to all of them.

The faults of this book are all my responsibility. All quotations other than those from English sources are my translation from Chinese sources.

Finally, I am deeply indebted to the Warden and Fellows of St Antony's College, Oxford, for having provided me with the means to do my work since 1968, and to Sir John Keswick and Mr John Swire for having jointly financed a Research Fellowship at St Antony's College for me for the last two years.

J. Y. WONG

Oxford
1974

FOREWORD
by G. F. Hudson

In the modern history of China the eighteen years from the signing of the Treaty of Nanking in 1842 to the entry of the British and French forces into Peking in 1860 form a distinct period, intermediate between the old time before the Opium War, when the seclusion of the Ch'ing Empire was unbroken, and the later age, when the Legations of the Western powers were established as of right in the capital of the empire and China was involved willy-nilly in the web of global international relations. In this intermediate period the Chinese political system was already confronted with problems of a kind for which previous experience provided no satisfactory precedents; trading communities of the maritime barbarians were now firmly lodged in five of China's main seaports under the protection of their formidable warships, and the influence of their intrusive religion combined with local discontents of a traditional kind to produce the great Taiping rebellion which shattered the authority of the Ch'ing dynasty over a large part of the country. Yet the basic institutions and mental outlook of China remained intact as they had existed a century before; foreign nations had still no right of diplomatic representation in Peking or of travel or residence in the interior of China, and even the Taiping rebel leader, when a British consul visited him in Nanking, showed an attitude towards foreign relations hardly different from that of the Manchu emperor whom he sought to supplant.

It is because this period differs in such degree from those which preceded and followed it that there is a special interest in a biography of a great official personage of the Chinese empire who reached the climax of his career in these years. Yeh Ming-ch'en was born in 1807, but the important part of his life was his service in Canton from 1847 to 1858, when he was taken prisoner by the British forces which captured the city in the course of the Second Anglo-Chinese War; he died a year later by self-starvation in captivity in Calcutta. As a major figure in the provincial administration of China in the middle of the nineteenth century, he belonged to the last generation of Chinese imperial civil servants to grow up in a world on which Western influence had not yet begun to impinge; born into a family of scholars and himself of high educational attainment in the Chinese classical tradition, his mental formation was broadly typical of the old scholar-official class as it had existed since the time of the Ming dynasty, with a continuity of cultural and political development going back to the Han, when the Chinese imperial system first acquired its specific character. As governor-general of Kwangtung and Kwangsi he had to deal with problems and tasks not so very different from those which would have confronted a predecessor in the same region in the first century B.C. or the fifteenth A.D., and his approach to them was on very similar lines. But as Imperial Commissioner in charge of relations with the foreign powers trading by sea with China he had to cope with the unprecedented situation created by the Treaty of Nanking, and it is in this capacity that he figures not only in Chinese, but in British, history, as adversity in the *Arrow* War and a protagonist in a story involving Palmerston and Clarendon – an issue in a British General Election. The outcome of the conflict was dramatically appropriate, for the difference between the old order that was passing away and the new age that was beginning was symbolically represented by the contrast between the outstanding success of Yeh Ming-ch'en as an old-time mandarin in a traditional setting and the utter disaster which overtook him in his efforts to deal in diplomacy and defence with a European power.

The great value of Dr Wong's biography of Yeh is that for the first time it presents to the British or Western reader a major figure on the Chinese side in the crucial period of China's early political contact with the Western world as a fully substantial historic personality, a man of his own time and country, with his own background of education, endeavour and achievement, and not merely as he was seen from London or Hong Kong, a figure symbolic of Chinese obstruction of British purposes and existing only in relation to them. Such an all-round biography can naturally only be written by using the available Chinese sources as well as what can be discovered from the British side, and this is what Dr Wong has done, with a thorough examination of the Chinese material. By a curious irony of history, however, it was the British, the enemies of Yeh, who unintentionally preserved a collection of Chinese documents without which we would have relatively little information about him. When they occupied Yeh's official residence in the capture of Canton in 1858, they took possession of all papers they found there, including both administrative documents and private correspondence; this collection was retained even after the conclusion of peace with China and deposited in the British Legation in Peking, where it served as a file of intelligence material which gradually became obsolete. Eventually it was sent to London and finally came to rest in the Public Record Office where it is known as the Canton Archive. Having been thus preserved as it was originally found, it is uniquely comprehensive as a record of provincial administration in the middle of the nineteenth century, because it was customary in provincial offices to relieve pressure on space by periodic clearances of less important papers and thus great quantities of documents of interest to the historian have perished, not to speak of the havoc wrought in China by war and revolution over many years. By arduous work on the Canton Archive, which had not previously been used by any historian, Dr Wong has been able not only to bring Yeh himself to life as a man and as a statesman, but to provide an exceptionally detailed account of the administration of a Chinese province in the sixth decade of the nineteenth century.

It was not surprising that Yeh was regarded by the British as the villain of the piece in the story of Anglo-Chinese relations in the period which ended in the Second Anglo-Chinese War. He was certainly a hard-liner in foreign policy in so far as he was determined to resist all foreign encroachments going beyond the letter of the treaties; in this he differed from Ch'i-ying, who had followed a policy of appeasement. Yeh's atitude was regarded as one of obstruction by the British and other Western powers who did not consider the Treaty of Nanking and similar agreements of the 1840s as a permanent settlement, but as mere preliminaries to far more drastic terms to be imposed on China by minatory pressures. It might be supposed, however, that Yeh's strength of purpose in standing up to Western pressures would at least have earned him in retrospect the approval of contemporary Chinese historians, who apply standards of national patriotism in judging the record of Ch'ing statecraft. Yeh's reputation, however, has suffered on account of the dominant fashion of glorification of the Taipings as revolutionaries who would have saved and regenerated China if they had not been prevented from doing so by a corrupt combination of Chinese feudal reactionaries and foreign imperialists. Nobody who fought against the Taipings can get fair treatment as a statesman from historians under the influence of the Taiping cult, and one of the important facts about Yeh is that he not only fought against the Taipings, but was decisively successful in keeping them out of Kwangtung, and even financed the campaign against them in other provinces from resources of his own. It is possible to argue that it would have been better for China if the Taipings had been victorious and the new Heavenly Kingdom established in Peking, but the dubious hindsight of the late twentieth century has very little relevance for the conduct of a high official of the Ch'ing empire who was confronted with rebellions – and the Taiping was only one among several – in the provinces committed to his charge. For Yeh there was never any crisis of conscience or ideological dilemma; he took it for granted that it was his duty to serve the monarch who had appointed him to high office, and that the empire which he helped to administer was worth defending against both internal and external enemies. In his time it was a more viable concern than is now commonly recognised; if the cowardice and incompetence of high officials in some provinces which were overrun by the Taipings is taken as proof that the Ch'ing political order was in a state of collapse, the vigour and efficiency of men such as Yeh must also be accepted as evidence of its continuing vitality. The insurrection of the Taipings was suppressed, as that of the White Lotus had been half a century earlier, essentially as an episode in Chinese domestic politics, though this historical fact has been obscured by the foreign intervention in the last stage of the civil war, undertaken to counter a disruption of trade when the Taipings were already a declining force. In any case there was no foreign support for the imperial government when Yeh fought against the Taipings and other rebels in Kwangtung, and his success in dealing with them was entirely due to his own efforts. On the one occasion when he suggested joint action with British warships against a rebel naval force which was interrupting trade in the Canton estuary, he was so far from being ready to purchase aid with political concessions that Sir John Bowring had to report that 'even the straits to which they are reduced and the dangers with which they are surrounded have so little abated their obstinate pride and unteachable ignorance that they still turn a deaf ear to my well-meant proposals'.

When in January 1858 Canton was captured by the invading British and French forces, Yeh allowed himself to be taken into captivity rather than put an end to his life as custom would normally have required in such a situation, because he believed that he would still be needed for the negotiation of a settlement to end the war, and that he could use his captivity to acquire a first-hand knowledge of Britain and its institutions such as no Chinese official of that time possessed. But the British had no intention of dealing any more with the Governor-General of Canton as representative of the Chinese central government for foreign relations; they were determined to go north and deal directly with the Court in Peking, a policy which after many months of negotiation and fighting was to bring the British and French armies into the streets of the capital. Yeh was taken, not to London, but to Calcutta, and gradually came to realise that the British government was no longer interested in negotiating through him. When he was thus disillusioned in his expectation that he could still be of service to the emperor in a diplomatic capacity, like Su Wu, who had been a captive of the Hsiung-nu in the time of the Han dynasty, he decided to end his life and, the provisions he had brought with him from China having run out, he starved himself to death rather than eat the food of his captors. The British were quite unaware of his intention and were puzzled as to the cause of his death; it has hitherto been assumed by historians to have been due to natural causes, but Dr Wong, by a careful comparison of British records relating to Yeh's captivity with poems which he composed shortly before his death, has shown beyond any doubt what actually happened. It was a tragic, but honourable, end to a career which had long been a success story within the traditional setting of Chinese public life and had appeared to be leading to the highest eminence attainable by a subject of the emperor.

He did not treat, nor made defence,
Nor yielded, nor showed fight;
He did not die a soldier's death,
And did not take to flight.
A statesman of such policy,
A general of such might
Was never seen in yesteryear
And seldom comes to light.*

* Hsieh Fu-ch'eng. 'Shu Han-yang Yeh-hsiang Kuang-chou Chih pien', *Yung-an hsü-pien*, 2 (Shanghai, 1897), 14a–21a. Translation by the present author.

Part one
Yeh's background and his time

---

1 Early career

Family background

The Yeh family originated in the Yellow River region. Nomadic invasions of northern China drove them southwards, as they drove many other Han Chinese, and they migrated to different areas of the Yangtze valley. Yeh Ming-ch'en's ancestors settled at Li-shui in Kiangsu, in which province the Yangtze River flows into the sea. One of Yeh's ancestors in the mid seventeenth century was a famous medical doctor. He travelled widely in the Yangtze area and tended poor patients even if they could not pay him. When a plague broke out during the Manchu conquest, he became an army doctor for the Manchus. He saved so many lives that it came to be believed that his patients invariably recovered.

Yeh Ming-ch'en's great-great-grandfather (1685–1750) was a merchant doing business in Han-yang, a commercial centre in the neighbouring province of Hupeh. He died there and left his property, which was in Han-yang, to Yeh Ming-ch'en's great-grandfather, Yeh T'ing-fang (1726–79), who consequently moved there and was thus registered as a native of Han-yang. According to family records, Yeh T'ing-fang was the first of his family for a very long time to achieve the status of *sheng-yüan* (lit. 'government student'). This was regarded as a great honour to the family, and his success was considered to be heaven's reward for the altruistic virtues of his grandfather, the medical doctor.[1]

Yeh T'ing-fang was reported to be a very serious scholar. He would not read books by any authors but Confucius, Mencius, and neo-Confucianists such as the Ch'eng brothers and Chu Hsi. His scholarship must have had an important influence on his son Yeh Chi-wen (1755–1830), who subsequently acquired sufficient education to qualify himself for the degree of *kung-sheng* (lit. 'tribute student'),[2] in 1777. For the next twelve years he served as a state teacher (*chiao-yü*) in various places in Hupeh, one of which was Ch'i-shui, but he continued to educate himself in his spare time and eventually passed the metropolitan examination in 1790, thereby becoming a *chin-shih* (lit. 'advanced scholar'), holder of the highest academic degree in the empire. With this degree, he was appointed secretary (*chung-shu*) first in the Grand Secretariat (Nei Ko), then the Grand Council (Chün-chi Ch'u), and in 1804, the Imperial Clan Court (Tsung-jen Fu). From 1811 till his retirement in 1822, he held posts of higher responsibility in the Censorate (Tu-ch'a Yüan), and in the Ministries of Finance, Justice and Rites.[3] During this period of more than thirty years of service in the imperial administration at Peking, Chi-wen held in addition the post of compiler in the Hui-tien Kuan and Yü-tieh Kuan, which gave him access to rare books and manuscripts about the history, institutions and rites of the past. Consequently he became very learned and developed a special taste for antiquities. He wrote commentaries on the *Book of Rites* and on Chu Hsi, the famous neo-Confucianist of the Southern Sung dynasty (1127–1278), and also poems which were highly regarded.[4]

His son, Yeh Chih-shen (Yeh Ming-ch'en's father [1779–1863]), was even better known as a scholar. Brought up in Peking, Chih-shen managed to read widely under the instruction of his father, who was reported to have possessed one of the best private libraries of the time. Later, he specialised in the study of ancient inscriptions in stone and bronze, and subsequently became an expert on the antiquities of the Hsia, Shang and Chou periods. The works he published in this field were regarded as authoritative.[5] He also produced works on history, litera-ture and poetry. His official career, on the other hand, began as an archivist in the Imperial Academy of Learning (Kuo-tzu Chien), then as a corrector (*chiao-lu*) in the National College of Historians (Kuo-shih Kuan); and afterwards he served for fourteen years in the Ministry of War (Ping Pu), rising to the position of director of the Department of Selections (*Wu-hsüan Ssu*). In this capacity, he had a reputation of outstanding ability. He retired in 1839, when he was sixty.[6]

There is no record of where Yeh Ming-ch'en was born, but the fact that both his father and grandfather were officials at Peking at the time of his birth may suggest that his mother's confinement on 21 December 1809[7] took place at the imperial capital rather than Han-yang. The scholar-gentry tradition of the first three generations had an important effect on the fourth. It is only natural that Chi-wen and Chih-shen, both well established academically, but neither of them rising beyond the rank of 5a during their life-long political services in Peking, should be very eager to see that the next generation, of which Yeh Ming-ch'en was the eldest, had much more success in the career of an official, which was the most esteemed profession in the empire.[8] The young Yeh Ming-ch'en was described as being 'solemn and taciturn, he seldom spoke or laughed; obedient to family rules, he was industrious in his studies.'[9]

Education

Born to a family of established standing in Peking, Yeh Ming-ch'en had the enviable opportunity of being educated at the capital, gaining access to library facilities and moving in high circles denied to students of the provinces. Favourable environment together with industriousness and high talents helped to produce an outstanding *curriculum vitae*. Yeh Ming-ch'en was quite a well-known scholar even in adolescence. He received his first major degree, the *kung-sheng*, with second rating, when he was only eighteen, in 1825. He displayed such refinement and excellence of style in this test that the examiners thought that he was an aged scholar. Until he became a *chü-jen* (lit. an 'elevated man'), holder of the second highest degree, in 1831, he served as a corrector in one of the Throne Halls, Wu-ying Tien, which prepared books for the use of the imperial court. This gave him a chance to read even more widely, and in 1835 he was awarded the highest academic degree, the *chin-shih*, with second class honours, and subsequently was among the 54 of the 272 *chin-shih* of his year selected to be bachelors (*shu-chi-shih*) of the Han-lin Academy.[10]

This academy was a unique post-graduate institute for producing an administrative elite for the empire. Competition for entry into it was very keen, as places were limited; but once admitted, a bachelor was given a generous scholarship, free accommodation, and every privilege at the capital where the academy was situated. He studied under the supervision of two professors specially appointed by the emperor to teach the post-graduates; at the same time he had plenty of leisure to look around, make friends, and observe how the government was run, thus gaining some knowledge of politics and useful contacts. The curriculum of the academy involved sending its members to preside over examinations in the provinces. These journeys were expected to broaden the minds of the young scholars, and acquaint them with the geography, customs and politics of the country. This post-graduate course lasted for three years, at the end of which an examination was held, and those who passed creditably would be appointed compilers at the institute. Yeh Ming-ch'en passed this literary examination after only one year, and spent the rest of his two years as a compiler.[11] Had he not been so actively involved in politics afterwards, he might have become one of the leading lights among Chinese scholars. However, once he was appointed a compiler at the Han-lin Academy, the way lay open to administrative positions of great authority in the empire, and his life took a very different course. In 1838, he was appointed to the post of prefect of Hsing-an,[12] in the province of Shensi. At this point, it is necessary to explain briefly how the local government of China was organised, and then to discuss how much training in administration Yeh had received so far.

The Chinese empire at this time was divided into provinces, each ruled by a governor (*hsün-fu*).[13] Above the governors were governors-general (*tsung-tu*), who supervised the administration of one, two or three provinces.[14] In administering his province, the governor was assisted by a provincial treasurer (*pu-cheng-shih*),[15] a provincial judge (*an-ch'a-shih*) and a salt comptroller (*yen-fa-tao*). A province was divided into circuits (*tao*), each governed by an intendant (*tao-t'ai*). A circuit was subdivided into prefectures, each headed by a prefect (*chih-fu*). A prefecture consisted of magistracies, which were the lowest units of local government, and whose officials – the magistrates (*chih-hsien*) – were the real administrative officials (*chih-shih chih kuan*, lit. 'officials in charge of affairs'); their superiors – prefect, circuit intendant, provincial judge, provincial treasurer, governor and governor-general – were the supervisory officials (*chih-kuan chih kuan*, lit. 'officials in charge of officials'),[16] who merely gave or transmitted orders from above and saw to it that the orders were carried out. In Chinese official life, there were no separate professions as such; the posts from magistrate to governor-general as listed above represented merely a ladder of promotion in the civil hierarchy.[17] Yeh Ming-ch'en's early political career, as set out in Table 1 (p. 9), provides an illustration of this point.

According to this table, Yeh went through all the stages of a Chinese administrator's career. This raises a second question: how much training in government had he received before he took up his first official appointment? Furthermore, what did he know about specialised subjects such as salt administration, law and finance? One may safely say that the answer is nothing: these subjects were not included in the syllabus of the civil service examination of Yeh's time, and Yeh himself frankly admitted that he never studied them.[18] To pass the civil service examination, a candidate was required to have only a good knowledge of the classics and the ability to write a good essay – the so-called eight-legged essay (*pa-ku wen*)[19] which demanded a high degree of literary refinement. A further question which naturally follows is: since a scholar well-versed in literature does not necessarily make a good administrator, how could Yeh be expected to carry out his official duties efficiently? One can answer by comparing the Chinese civil service examination system with that of the British at that time. In Great Britain, students of Greek and Latin classics were frequently recruited into the civil service; they too were not taught economics or politics, but the study of classics was supposed to have given them a good training of the mind so that they could handle affairs intelligently. The study of Chinese classics was meant to serve the same purpose, and the very demanding nature of the eight-legged essay provided an objective, though rigid, standard for selecting only the most intelligent to serve the government.[20]

On the other hand, it is not true that Yeh was entirely out of touch with politics until he actually became a prefect. As already mentioned, the Han-lin Academy was a unique institution for producing an administrative elite for the empire. Yeh, of course, had the additional advantage of having been brought up in Peking and born into a family in which both the father and grandfather were officials in the central government. Through them he must have acquired a good knowledge of the customs and practices of the imperial administration.

Furthermore, a junior official would often receive instructions from his superiors as to how the government was usually run. For example, when Yeh took up his first official appointment, as prefect of Hsing-an, he received a document from the provincial judge specifying his duties, pointing out the peculiar geography of the district and the problems in governing it, and explaining how he could most effectively supervise his junior officials and foster an efficient administration.[21] When he was promoted to the post of salt comptroller of Kiangsi, with the additional duty of supervising the administration of three prefectures, he received an order from the governor to write comments on the prefects and magistrates under his jurisdiction, filling in standard forms which would be bound into a book which the governor could place on his desk to be studied whenever he was free to do so.[22] Of all the documents which Yeh had handled during his early political career, these two were among the very few which travelled with him from one post to another and eventually found a place in the Canton Archive. This shows the degree of importance which he attached to these instructions, which were indeed 'lecture notes' for his early political training.

Moreover, all officials of the Ming and Ch'ing periods, from magistrates to governors-general, were assisted by administrative experts, namely private secretaries (*mu-yu* or *mu-pin*, lit. 'friends or guests serving in a tent').[23] These were educated men who had failed the higher civil service examinations or successful candidates who could not find an official post who then specialised in administrative matters, especially law and taxation, and served as professional advisers to officials. In the Canton Archive there are numerous written suggestions to Yeh as regards policy-making. Very probably, these were prepared by his private secretaries, but since few of them bear any signature, and the one or two that do cannot be identified, there is no way of knowing who they were. However, there are some clues to his employment of private secretaries. Chang Ching-hsiu, the provincial judge of Kwangsi, who was dismissed in 1855 because of a military reverse at Hsün-chou,[24] was later employed by Yeh in a private capacity to assist him in handling foreign affairs.[25] Again, when he was on his way to his exile in India in 1858, Yeh told W. Cooke that he paid his private secretaries about 100 taels a month (the salary of an official of the fourth rank was only 105 taels)[26] and that they made 300 or 400 more by perquisites.[27] The annual income of private secretaries in Canton, reported in 1800 to be between 1500 and 1900 taels, was believed to be the highest in the empire,[28] but even this bore no comparison to that of the 4,800–6,000 taels of Yeh's *mu-yu*. Although both examples belong only to his term of office at Canton, they nevertheless give us some idea of the quality of his private secretaries.

Finally, Yeh himself was said to have had a talent for administration. Even before he took up the prefectship of Hsing-an in 1838, a scrutiny of the ability of metropolitan officials carried out by the Censorate graded him first class, when he was a compiler in the Han-lin Academy.[29] Graced with a favourable family background, outstanding administrative ability and the assistance of capable private secretaries, he was to become one of the most prominent figures in the history of modern China.

Friends at court

As shown in Table 1, except for a brief period in 1846, Yeh's political life was spent in the provinces. It was important that he should have friends and, above all, influential friends at Peking, who would be in a position to protect him from court intrigues and party strife. The most desirable friend was of course the emperor himself, whose favours the Yeh family had enjoyed from the time of Yeh Ming-ch'en's grandfather. Yeh Chi-wen was brought to the notice of the court by reason of his filial piety, for centuries the most praised virtue in China. The sadness caused by the death of his mother,[30] was aggravated by the accidental overturning of the boat which was carrying her to burial. Clutching the floating coffin he cried out in a voice that 'shook the banks of the river'. Though he was eventually saved from drowning, his hair had all turned white. It was said that during the subsequent three years of mourning, the trees in his garden all withered, but revived when the period of mourning was over. The court came to learn of these phenomena and invited him to join the Imperial Service.[31]

Later it was academic distinction that put the Yeh family in direct contact with the emperor. When he was a secretary in the Grand Secretariat, Chi-wen was responsible for most of the important ceremonial and palace essays. Those of the Imperial Secretaries and officials of the Imperial Clan Court most endowed with poetic talents could expect to be called upon to produce adulatory compositions for major state occasions and celebrations at which the emperor presided. Customarily these consisted of paeans addressed to the Son of Heaven, rhapsodising on the prosperity in which the empire basked under his enlightened rule. They would be read during the celebration, and were the artists to display sufficient literary skill and ingenuity to impress both emperor and revellers, they could expect some token of imperial pleasure, perhaps a piece of rare silk, an embroidered purse, or some curiosities. In 1801, Emperor Chia-ch'ing interviewed the examiner to be sent to Shantung and said, 'Your assistant is Yeh Chi-wen, a good Han-lin.' Once a palace essay was presented to the emperor who, impressed by its quality, inquired about the author. The Grand Secretary having forgotten the name, the emperor said, 'He must be Yeh Chi-wen', who was accordingly rewarded. Again, a memorandum to the king of Vietnam was once drafted, and the emperor remarked, 'This must have been written by Yeh Chi-wen.'[32] As for Chih-shen, his ceremonial essays, pictures, paintings and poems also earned him many special imperial rewards.[33] When Yeh Ming-ch'en was a compiler in the Han-lin Academy, he wrote a 'Petition to Heaven for Rain', which was 'granted'. The emperor, Tao-kuang, was extremely pleased and ascribed this success to 'Ming-ch'en's filial piety towards his parents having moved the Divine Heart to grant his request'.[34]

For the emperor to have learnt who Yeh Ming-ch'en was through his family and academic distinction was obviously of great advantage to the latter's official career. Of course, ability was decisive for a successful career – many newly appointed officials were indeed stripped of their offices immediately after an interview with the emperor, who concluded that their 'ability and knowledge cannot match such a post'.[35] It was also true that many promising young officials must have been denied the opportunity to exercise their genuine ability in the traditional clumsy bureaucracy, where normally they had a chance of promotion only once in every three years, when a censorial scrutiny would be carried out to decide whether they should be promoted, demoted, or remain where they were. Yeh's annual promotion as shown in Table 1 was extremely unusual in the history of China, and may be accounted for both by his considerable capabilities and the fact that the emperor knew him personally. Hu Feng-tan remarked that 'the accomplishments of Yeh Ming-ch'en's ancestors had an important bearing on his career'.[36] This was indeed true in the sense that they paved the way for the emperor to notice his ability and put him in suitable positions of responsibility, so that in less than ten years he rose to a governorship. Emperor Tao-kuang certainly took a great interest in him, expecting him to uphold the empire which had already begun to show signs of weakness and instability (see chap. 2). He even wrote a paternal letter to him after he had appointed him governor of Kwangtung, specifying his duties and encouraging him to be a good official.[37]

The next emperor, Hsien-feng, who came to the throne in 1850, also had great faith in Yeh's ability, and apparently much affection for him too. Even after Yeh's defeat and capture by the allied forces in 1858, he merely removed him from the post of imperial commissioner for foreign affairs. He did not degrade him from the rank of upper first class (1a) official, nor strip him of his honorific titles of Junior Tutor of the Crown Prince, and Grand Secretary. There was no mention either of depriving him of his status as First Class Baron.[38] Yeh, when he had the opportunity to read the imperial edict himself, remarked with apparent relief with regard to his punishment, 'Henceforward then, I have nothing to do with foreign affairs.'[39] An English contemporary also observed that the edict was 'much milder than was anticipated – milder than the translation which went to Europe would lead us to think; for the translator has interpolated some words of censure not in the Chinese'.[40] One of the censors did insist that Yeh should suffer more heavily, at least the confiscation of all his property. For, he maintained, Yeh's offence called for capital punishment.[41] The emperor, however, reiterated that Yeh's dismissal from the post of imperial commissioner for foreign affairs was already most fair and appropriate.[42] Indeed, the imperial edicts could give one the impression that the primary concern of the emperor in dismissing Yeh was to make him of little value as a hostage.[43] 'Yeh has been tenderly dealt with. He has evidently some great protecting interest in Pekin, and will probably become again a great power in China.'[44] Indeed, if Yeh had been able to return to China instead of dying after a year in captivity, it was probable that he, like his predecessor Lin Tse-hsü, would have regained his importance as a Chinese statesman.

Apart from the emperor, Yeh had a wide circle of friends in Peking. Of these, by far the most influential was Ch'i Chün-tsao, a powerful figure in the Grand Council (the cabinet of the emperor) from 1841 to 1854.[45] Ch'i had been a colleague of Yeh's father, when Ch'i was minister of war (1840–1), and Yeh referred to himself as Ch'i's nephew when he wrote to Ch'i.[46] Other important courtiers with whom Yeh maintained friendly relations included Grand Councillers Mu-chang-a, Wen-ch'ing and P'eng Wen-chang, and ministers such as Wo-jen and Cho Ping-t'ien. To these and other officials and his relatives in Peking Yeh sent presents at Chinese New Year, to keep up his connections at the capital.[47]

Early political career[48]

Yeh's first post with real governmental powers, as prefect of Hsing-an in Shensi province, entailed duties which were by no means simple. Hsing-an was, as described by a governor of the province, 'situated at

Table 1
The political career of Yeh Ming-ch'en,[a] *1838–58*

Year	Post	Rank
1838	Prefect of Hsing-an, Shensi	4b
1839	Intendant of Yen-p'ing circuit, Shansi	4a
1840	Salt comptroller of Kiangsi	3b
1841	Provincial judge of Yünnan	3a
1842	Provincial treasurer of Hunan[b]	2b
1843	Provincial treasurer of Kiangsu and then of Kansu	2b
1844–6	Observed the 3 years of mourning for the death of his mother; stayed at Han-yang	
1846	Acting metropolitan governor[c]	2b
1847	Provincial treasurer of Kwangtung	2b
1848	Governor of Kwangtung	2a
1852	Governor-general of Kwangtung and Kwangsi	1b
1856	Appointed Grand Secretary of T'i-jen Ko,[d] but ordered to keep his post and continue his functions as governor-general[e]	1a

[a] Information for this table is drawn largely from *Ch'ing-shih lieh-chuan*, 40. 45ff.
[b] Cf. *Hu-nan t'ung-chih*, 2512.
[c] Cf. *Shun-t'ien fu-chih*, 82.22a.
[d] There were four Grand Secretaries (*ta-hsüeh-shih*) in the Grand Secretariat (Nei Ko), two Manchu and two Chinese, each belonging to one or the other of the Throne Halls or Pavilions of the Imperial Palace, i.e. Pao-ho Tien, Wen-hua Tien, Wu-ying Tien, T'i-jen Ko, Wen-yüan Ko and Tung Ko. The selection of a particular hall or pavilion depended on the will of the emperor (H. S. Brunnett and V. V. Hagelstrom, *Present Day Political Organization of China*, pp. 43–4).
[e] The appointment did not relieve him of his post as governor-general. It was in practice an honorary appointment since the emperor did not expect him to perform the duties of Grand Secretary while he specifically ordered him to continue his functions as governor-general.

the foot of the Nan Mountains, bordering on the turbulent provinces of Szechwan and Honan, to which the scum of the earth flock from everywhere else. It is vital for the safety of the empire to keep peace in this area, but it requires exceptional ability, skill and knowledge to do so.'[49] Yet it was in this very place that Yeh first won for himself a reputation for efficiency.[50] This reputation he was to carry to all the areas he subsequently served. 'Everywhere he went', recorded a local gazetteer, 'he initiated and expanded good things and systems and did away with the bad; he kept a strict eye on his juniors and kept the people contented; hence high praises in his name proliferated throughout the provinces.'[51] The next year he was promoted to the post of intendant of Yen-p'ing circuit in the province of Shansi. His task was mainly financial, with the additional title of military intendant (*ping-pei-tao*).[52] In the following year, 1840, he became the salt comptroller of the province of Kiangsi, and he had the additional title of director of water works (*shui-li*). Later, he was appointed acting provincial judge of the same province.[53]

In 1841, he rose to the position of provincial judge of Yünnan, where he was in charge of the judiciary, postal services and the conduct of officials in the whole province. He also supervised the provincial examinations and assisted in the general running of the provincial government. The next year he was promoted to be the provincial treasurer of Hunan, where he was responsible for administering the finances and organising the census of the province. He also had to inspect all junior officials and supervise the provincial examinations, besides sharing the administrative burden of the provincial government.[54] It is here that we first begin to glimpse some of his political concepts, in a document which he issued to his subordinates, giving instructions to hunt down vigorously any forged official documents that might exist so as to establish a reputation for efficiency and trustworthiness in government.[55]

In 1843 he was transferred to the more important post of provincial treasurer at Nanking in the rich province of Kiangsu. It will be recalled that Yeh's great-grandfather was originally a native of Kiangsu, and since the law forbade any official to serve in his native district, Yeh had to exchange posts with the provincial treasurer of Kansu. The next year his mother died, and he observed the customary three years mourning. Once this was over, in 1846, he was offered the post of provincial treasurer of Kwangtung, but was obliged to stay in Peking because of his temporary appointment as acting metropolitan governor (*Shun-t'ien fu-yin*). During this short term of office at the capital, he presided over the metropolitan military examination, but was censured for the use of defective equipment in the examination.[56] Later in the year he proceeded south to take up his post in Kwangtung, which will be the subject of discussion in the ensuing chapters.

Several conclusions may be drawn from this brief description of Yeh's early political career. First, his experience as an administrator governing turbulent peoples would be very valuable to him when he went to Canton, where the people were even less peaceable. His achievement at Hsing-an has already been noted. Shansi was also full of bandits and agitators when he was intendant there, yet he passed this test, too, with flying colours, and gained further promotion. Again, as provincial judge of Yünnan, he had to deal with both disgruntled native Chinese and ethnic minorities, as well as with refugees, vagrants and adventurers from neighbouring, more densely populated, provinces. The conflicts between these different interests often developed into clashes with the government. In fact, a serious rebellion broke out in Yünnan five years later, in 1848, which led to the demotion of the governor-general and many of his junior officials.[57] There are no known records which relate similar disturbances during Yeh's incumbency, and this suggests that either he was lucky or that he managed to preserve order. In any case his promotion ten months later means that his superior had written good reports and that the emperor was pleased with his work.[58] Hunan presented the same problems, though on a smaller scale, as did Kansu, where secret societies were very active.[59] Yeh's early career saw him working hard to control law-breakers and the discontented, and from this he gained useful experience which was to be of benefit to him in Canton. Ten years of experience in dealing with the turbulent hardened into an iron will and a policy of severe reprisals, by which tens of thousands were to die.[60]

Secondly, he developed a close relationship with the army from the beginning of his career (or even before, as his father had served in the Ministry of War for fourteen years right up to 1839). As intendant of Yen-p'ing, he was granted the title of military intendant. When he was salt comptroller of Kiangsi, he was accorded merits for helping to prevent the invasion of the province by rebels of neighbouring provinces.[61] His appointment to preside over the metropolitan military examination in 1846 signified the fact that he was not just a bureaucrat, but also a military organiser.

Thirdly, he had ample experience of financial affairs, with which he had been dealing from his initial appointment, and which were often connected with the army; hence he was financial intendant and at the same time a suppressor of rebellions. Again, an important part of his task as provincial treasurer of Kansu was paying the frontier and river guards and supplying their necessary provisions. Indeed, when he was governor and then governor-general at Canton, he won unprecedented favour from the court in acting as paymaster-general to the troops of the empire engaged in suppressing the Taiping Rebellion.

However, Yeh's office at Canton involved not only administrative, military and financial matters, but also foreign relations. His education did not include the study of foreign languages or international law,[62] nor in his early political career did he have any experience in dealing with foreigners. His superiors and predecessors were almost as ignorant in this respect, and could not have offered him such appropriate advice or instructions as they did in matters of government. It is true that he had served for years in the so-called frontier provinces of China, Shensi, Shansi, Yünnan and Kansu, which had constant trouble with neighbouring national minorities (see Map 1);[63] but at Canton, he would encounter an entirely different kind of alien. He would have to probe in the dark. His concepts, and subsequently his style of diplomacy, were gradually formulated during the initial years of his incumbency at Canton. This, of course, is not to say that he was unaware of the problem of foreign hostility. In fact his attention was called to this matter quite early in his career. Part of his memorandum to the emperor in 1842 reads, 'When I

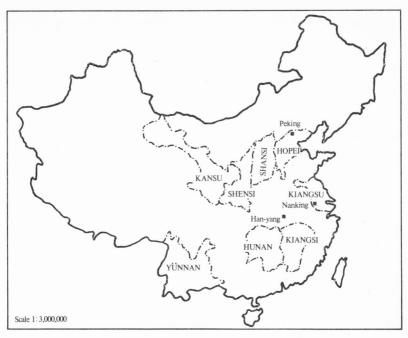

Map 1. Yeh's early political career, 1838–46

hurried to Peking in the fourth month of this year, I was four times granted audience with Your Majesty.'[64] The audience took place at the time when the Ch'ing dynasty was forced by its defeat at the hands of the British troops to sign the first humiliating treaty in its history. While all the memoranda and edicts of the time were filled with reports, suggestions and orders dealing with the Opium War, it is highly unlikely that Provincial Judge Yeh Ming-ch'en would have been summoned to the court from Yünnan, one of the southern provinces farthest away from Peking, and interviewed four times by the emperor, to discuss anything but the burning issues of the day. There are no known records revealing the nature of the talks, what proposals Yeh made, or the reaction of the emperor, but the fact that he was sent to serve at the earliest practicable date[65] at Canton – the centre of diplomatic relations – may suggest that the emperor had confidence in his ability to deal with such a difficult situation.

Yeh the man: some aspects

It may be illuminating to make some conjectures on the kind of influence Yeh's father and grandfather might have had in shaping his character. To begin with, a few words have to be said about Confucianism, one of the dominant influences on Chinese official thinking, whose texts formed the curriculum for education and the syllabus for state examinations. Among the attitudes and patterns of behaviour desirable for a Confucianist, the first five were: submissiveness to authority – parents, elders, and superiors; submissiveness to the mores and norms (*li*); reverence for the past and respect for history; love of traditional learning; esteem for the force of example.[66] Confucianists taught by parable and example, while 'living exemplars had an equally important part in the formation of character. Submissiveness of the young to the old, of the unlearned to the learned, reinforced the imperative to pattern oneself after an approved exemplar. This might be a father or an uncle, but it was more often a teacher.'[67]

In the Yeh family, Chi-wen was both teacher and grandfather, and Chih-shen, teacher and father, to the young Yeh Ming-ch'en. The two elders were highly esteemed scholars as well as officials in the imperial administration, ideal examples for Yeh to model himself on. It is even probable that after his retirement in 1824 (when Yeh was seven), Chi-wen spent the rest of his life, until his death six years later,[68] giving personal tuition to his grandson. As mentioned, Yeh Chi-wen was very interested in the famous neo-Confucianist Chu Hsi, and had written commentaries on his life (*Chu-tzu wai-chi*). Chu Hsi advocated strict self-discipline as regards behaviour and studies.[69] As far as studies were concerned, we have seen that Yeh was very solemn and industrious. As for his behaviour, W. Cooke had this to say: 'Yeh is in his private life a very respectable Chinaman. He is entirely free from all suspicion of those detestable habits common to his countrymen, and for which even the virtuous Keying [Ch'i-ying] was but too notorious. He smokes no opium; his ordinary drink is only warm tea.'[70] Therefore one may safely assume that the way Yeh Chi-wen educated Yeh was very much influenced by the teachings of Chu Hsi. However, it is not certain whether Chi-wen's enthusiasm for Chu Hsi carried him to the extent of actually practising Chu's teachings about meditation – Chu taught his disciples to study for half a day and meditate for the other half.[71] Very possibly Chi-wen did, and therefore one might assume that Yeh became familiar with the practice throughout his youth and adolescence. In fact, Yeh pursued a very similar practice when he was detained on board the *Inflexible* in 1858. Cooke wrote:

His devotions consist of sitting in the posture of a Chinese idol, his legs crossed, and his face to the east. He remains in an abstracted state for about ten minutes, and the act of devotion is accomplished. When he first came on board he retired into this contemplative state several times a-day. He afterwards became much more remiss, and once a-day appeared to suffice him. . .We asked him what Taoli this was, 'Confucian?' 'Yes.' 'Buddhist?' 'Yes.' 'Taoist?' 'Yes. It is more ancient even than Confucius. It is the ancient ceremonial of China.'[72]

Hu Shih once described neo-Confucianism (*li-hsüeh* or *tao-hsüeh*) as a mixture of Zen Buddhism (*Ch'an-tsung*), Taoism (*Tao-chia*), popular Taoism (*Tao-chiao*), Confucianism (*Ju-chia*) and popular Confucianism (*Ju-chiao*), under the cloak of Confucianism.[73] Yeh's answers to Cooke's questions may be regarded as a statement of Ch'ing neo-Confucianism. Yeh must have worked very hard during his early years to earn himself the exceptional annual promotion, and judging from the scale of the tasks he had to deal with at Canton, as will be apparent in the ensuing chapters, it is important that his philosophy led him to regular periods of complete relaxation. Furthermore, if he could sleep 'the sleep of infancy – an unbroken slumber'[74] when he was a prisoner of war on board the *Inflexible* moored in the harbour of Hong Kong, it may have been possible for him throughout his political career to forget all about his administrative, military and financial problems at night, have a good rest, and be energetic and efficient when the day came. Perhaps this may have contributed to the success of his official career.

As for Yeh's father, most Chinese accounts reported that he was very fond of divination.[75] As mentioned, Chih-shen was an expert on inscriptions on antiquities, and these inscriptions were often records of divination and important events in prehistoric or ancient times. It is hardly surprising that someone who spent his lifetime studying divination should have practised it himself. The same accounts went on to say that the dutiful Yeh built a Taoist temple called Ch'ang-ch'un hsien-kuan in Canton, where his father might live and pursue his hobby.[76] It was said that in this temple his father worshipped two demigods, the Taoist Lü Tung-pin and the famous poet Li Po.[77] This is also probable because there is a plan of such a building in Yeh's archive. Cooke also reported that 'among the tiers of temples which cover the Magazine-hill[78] stands the only house in Canton city which an English gentleman would think inhabitable...It is called Yeh's House, and was yet unfinished when the city was taken [in February 1858].'[79]

The accounts went further and asserted that Yeh's military moves during the *Arrow* War were all decided by the casting of oracles in this temple. This accusation sparked off a series of questions by Cooke,[80] which may prove illuminating as to Yeh's character and beliefs. First, did Yeh believe in oracles? He answered, 'I can't tell you. Sometimes I believe in them, sometimes I do not.' Secondly, did Yeh himself cast any oracles to foretell political events? He replied, 'No. I was always busy with official duties; how could I have the time for such things?' Thirdly, there were divination queries among Yeh's captured papers. Where did they come from? How much importance did he attach to them? Yeh answered, 'It is true that fortune-tellers have been sent to me on various occasions; such things have been, but they never influenced public affairs.'[81] Yeh may have been telling the truth. In fact, augury was

Table 2
List of divination queries in the Canton Archive

Date	Subject	Ref. no.
1 1851	When would the rebellions in Kwangsi be suppressed? The oracle was cast in Kiangsi by a state teacher and the result enclosed in a report from the deputy salt intendant of Ch'ao-chou to Yeh	324.1
2 (1851)	When would the rebel leaders at Ch'ing-yüan be captured?	68.4.17
3 (23 July 1853)	Would Nanchang, provincial capital of Kiangsi, survive the siege by the Taipings? The query was written in Kiangsi and enclosed in a letter to a person called Li Fan.	378B.1.63
4 29 Nov. 1855	Could Hsün-chou survive the siege?	391.3.53
5 29 Nov. 1855	When would be the auspicious time to send troops to lift the siege of Hsün-chou?	68.4.16
6 15 Feb. 1857	When would all the rebellions of the empire be suppressed?	378B.7.4

as much a part of the cultural inheritance of the time as was Confucianism.[82] Cooke himself could not come to any conclusion after his conversation with Yeh, but observed earlier that Yeh 'undoubtedly does consult his Chinese almanack for the lucky day to shave his head, but it is not easy to ascertain from him whether he does so attaching any belief to such superstititions, or whether he merely follows popular custom.'[83] There is certainly little evidence to prove that Yeh cast oracles himself. All but two of the divination queries found in his archive are written in different hands,[84] and the Chinese accounts accused only Yeh's father, not Yeh himself, of extreme superstition. As to the extent to which Yeh's decisions were influenced by super-stition, it will be useful to make a list of the divination queries and the documents connected with them that are in the Canton Archive.

As shown in Table 2, there are only six divination queries over a period of seven years. Of course, similar queries could have been lost in the course of time; the same must have happened to other documents of the Archive. If a numerical comparison is valid, the fact that these six manuscripts constitute only a tiny fraction of the voluminous Canton Archive may give us an idea of the very insignificant role divination played in Yeh's government. Furthermore, all six queries dealt with the suppression of rebellions, which may suggest that superstition did not intrude upon other aspects of his career. After all, the accusations in the Chinese accounts referred only to the *Arrow* War. The same can be said

Table 3
*List of manuscripts in the Canton Archive
connected with superstition*

Date	Subject matter	Ref. no.
1 (1853)	Report recommending that two tombs built in 1850 in one of the hills in the immediate north of Canton be removed because they were the source of all the trouble (i.e. rebellions) since then.	325.3.2
2 (1853)	Report stating the progress of the work of extending the rear part of Yeh's *yamen* and making changes in certain buildings in such a way as to improve the fortune of the Liang Yüan (over the rebels).[a]	378B.7.4
3 (1855)	Draft memorandum from Yeh and Po-kuei to the emperor listing various critical moments when the god of war, Emperor Kuan, revealed himself and dispersed the rebels, and requested an additional title to be conferred on the god as a token of gratitude.	391.4.36
4 (Oct. 1856)	Part of a draft proclamation, referring to a recent attack by the British on the river forts near Canton, stated 'At that time the sky was bright and it was windy but cloudless. Consultation of astrology showed that it was inauspicious for the attackers and auspicious for the defenders.'	327.5.40

[a] *Yamen* was a Chinese term for a government office. Liang Yüan was a combined term for the governor-general and governor, representing in this particular case Yeh Ming-ch'en and Po-kuei.

of Table 3, although the last item needs some elaboration. The proclamation was meant for the edification of the general populace; here again, it is not easy to say whether the part about astrology was included because of any genuine belief attached to it or for the sake of the audience.[85] Indeed, if one wants to compare popular beliefs in China with those of the west, the incident in which Yeh and Po-kuei requested the emperor to confer an additional title on the god of war, when their troops reported to them that the god had fought at the head of the army and dispersed the rebels, is not very different from the story of the angel of Mons. Thus, Yeh's own account of his attitude and belief may be regarded as an honest one.

Cooke also had the following observations to make about Yeh:

In his personal appearance Yeh is a very stout and rather tall man, about five feet eleven, with the long thin Chinese moustache and beard, a remarkably receding forehead, a skull in which what the phrenologists call 'Veneration' is much developed...

The eye – that round slit Mongolian eye – is the most expressive feature of the man who is sitting opposite to me...

He does not wear long nails. He says he has been too busy all his life to do so...

There is strong will, there is dogmatic perseverance, there is immovable inert resistance...

He boasts that he has worn his outer coat for 10 years, and its appearance justifies his assertion...[86]

Yeh's outer coat, like his brother's vegetarian breakfast (see page 18), provides us with some insight into the frugal nature of the man. When he was in exile in India, $3,000 (silver dollars) were sent to him, with the object of placing 'within his reach at the request of his relatives in China, the means proper to a prisoner of war of his rank for smaller necessities'.[87] This sum he never touched until the day he died.[88] When the *Inflexible* anchored at Hong Kong, Cooke asked him if he would like to go to the horse-races. 'He answered, just as the father of a serious family might answer, that it never had been the custom of his family to go to the races.'[89] The Bishop of Hong Kong went to see him, and Cooke remarked that

if there is any profession for which a proud Chinese literate entertains a supreme contempt, it is for that of the priesthood of all faiths, Buddhist emphatically included...

Yeh said he had long ago read the Bible; it was a good book – all books of that kind were good – they tend to purify the heart, as do the Buddhist and Taoist books.[90]

As regards Yeh's attitude towards medical science, Cooke wrote:

Report says...that the Viceroy's father was an apothecary. The son manifests great interest in European surgery...

'But do you think it objectionable?'

'My individual opinion is, that dissection for knowledge sake is not wrong.'[91]

This remark by Yeh, who was fully aware that 'the people would not endure such a thing in China',[92] helps to illuminate yet another aspect of his personality, that he was perhaps not so bigoted a mandarin as he is so often depicted.

Finally, Yeh was sufficiently calm and detached to be insulated from the vicissitudes of political life. While his career was threatened by the siege of Canton, he betrayed no signs of fear or nervousness (see chap. 6). When he was captured by the British forces, he 'exhibited great self-possession and remained perfectly quiet while his boxes of which the room was full were opened and examined for papers.'[93] Similarly, he received the edict which degraded him with great equanimity: 'I am neither glad nor sorry. It was at the emperor's command I took them up, and at his command I lay them down.'[94] This answer to Cooke's inquiry about his reaction to the edict clearly indicates his detachment. It also shows his Confucian loyalty, like that of Lin Tse-hsü,[95] towards the emperor; he left no will, and his last words were simply

> I have disappointed His Imperial Majesty;
> I shall die with my eyes wide open.[96]

Family life

Yeh Ming-ch'en's great-grandfather broke from the Yeh lineage[97] at Li-shui in Kiangsu. The fortune of the new family grew with the success of the next three generations in official life, and its social position became eminent enough for it to adopt a title, namely, *Yeh Chia-hui-t'ang*. Property began to be acquired under this title, and over a period of twenty years (1822–42), fifteen items, including small pieces of land and building and burial sites in Han-yang, were bought.[98] When Yeh began his official career by serving in the provinces, he maintained close links with the other members of the family by a regular correspondence entitled *Chia-hui-t'ang p'ing-an chia-hsin* (lit. 'Family letters of *Chia-hui-t'ang* reporting that all is well'). One of these letters still exists in the Canton Archive. It was addressed to Yeh Ming-ch'en by his younger brother Yeh Ming-feng. The envelope was marked *Chia-hui-t'ang p'ing-an chia-hsin* No. 10. The date was 19th of the 10th month (year unspecified, possibly 1856). The letter was written on sheets of red paper, and began with formal inquiries made by Yeh Ming-feng and his wife, of the health first of the father, Yeh Chih-shen, and then of Yeh Ming-ch'en and his wife. The rest of the letter contained personal matters concerning the two brothers. It began with an acknowledgement of the receipt of Yeh Ming-ch'en's *an-hsin* No. 11, dated 11th of the 10th month. Then Ming-feng discussed with his brother the prospects of his future career, and how he was progressing with his post as a secretary in the Grand Secretariat. He also remarked that he was in good health, and that during the past year he had acquired the habit of having vegetarian breakfasts. After dark, he used to enjoin his son to sit by him when he read, and was delighted that the child seemed intelligent enough to appreciate what he was reading. The letter concluded with a few remarks about the weather in Peking, and the postscript included news of the movements of some officials in the capital.[99]

From this letter, one can see that the Yeh family was a closely-knit unit and, in a sense, disciplined. Furthermore, the way Yeh Ming-feng taught his son was perhaps not different from the manner Yeh Ming-ch'en was educated when he was young. It has been reported that

Yeh and his brother had great affection for each other.[100] The intimate nature of the letter reinforces the report. The two brothers were well-known scholars even in adolescence, but Ming-feng was far less successful in his official career. He became a *chü-jen* in 1837, and was later appointed one of the secretaries of the Grand Secretariat, which position he held until 1857, when he was promoted to be an assistant reader (*shih-tu*, rank 6a) in the same office.[101] Since he served in Peking most of the time, he was able to supply his brother with useful information about the political atmosphere at the capital, as he did in the postscript of the letter. Although he was not notably successful in his official career, his reputation as a scholar continued to grow; his poems, in particular, were highly regarded. He lived sparingly, though there was no need to do so. He loved his brother, and news of Yeh's death in 1859 seemed to have hastened his own end later in the same year, at the age of 48.[102]

Numerous acts of charity and welfare work by the Yeh family were recorded in the local histories of Han-yang and Hupeh. In 1848 and again in 1849, for example, floods from the Yangtze threatened to drown the whole of Han-yang; Yeh Chih-shen took the lead in organising the gentry for contributions and strengthening the dykes, which successfully prevented disaster.[103] Consequently these local histories were high in their praises of the Yeh family, and demonstrated the goodwill of the native inhabitants. The family was also reported to have maintained very friendly relations with members of the Yeh lineage at Li-shui, and in the Canton Archive there is a letter from a high official in Kiangsu thanking Yeh Ming-ch'en for a donation (out of Yeh's own purse) of 5,000 taels for relief purposes in the province which had recently been badly hit by a natural disaster. In fact, Yeh had made a donation of 10,000 taels, the other half going to Hupeh, which was hit by the same flood; and the letter praised Yeh for making no distinction between the two places, both of which were considered his native province.[104]

Finally, let us examine Yeh Ming-ch'en's married life. His first wife was surnamed Li. She died young, and Yeh married a girl from a Wang family resident in Peking. His father-in-law, Wang T'ing-chen,[105] was a prominant scholar and was at some time tutor to the crown prince (the future Tao-kuang) as well as director of the Yü-tieh Kuan, where, as mentioned before, Yeh Ming-ch'en's grandfather held the additional post of compiler. Wang T'ing-chen also had a long and outstanding record of service as the head of various Ministries in Peking; because of his merits, his son Wang Pao-yüan was given, through *yin* (lit. 'hereditary privilege'), the post of an assistant department director (rank 5a) in the Ministry of Justice (Hsing Pu), and his second son, Wang Pao-jun, the prefectship of Nan-an in Kiangsi.[106] The Yeh and Wang families probably came to know each other in the Yü-tieh Kuan, and there may also have been scholarly links. It is unlikely that politics could have been a cause for closer ties between the two families because Wang T'ing-chen died in 1827 (when Yeh Ming-ch'en was only 14) and his two sons were relatively unimportant officials. After the marriage, the only information we have about the relationship between the two families was a letter written in the 1850s by Wang Pao-jun to Yeh Ming-ch'en, thanking the latter for having despatched troops from Kwangtung to Kiangsi to prevent a complete collapse of the provincial government and asking for more money to pay the troops.[107] It was Yeh's policy to help the neighbouring provinces as much as he could therefore his assistance to Wang should not necessarily be construed as an act of favouritism, although his relationship with Wang by marriage might have given the case higher priority.

The records do not indicate that Yeh's first wife gave birth to any child, but his second wife produced three daughters and no son. Consequently, he adopted a son called Yeh En-i from his brother Yeh Ming-feng. Apparently he left his adopted son to be educated by his brother in Peking; when Wang Pao-jun wrote to Yeh, he inquired after his sister and nieces, but made no reference to the nephew; again, when Yeh was captured by the allied forces early in 1858, Yeh En-i was reported to be still in the capital pursuing his studies and was hence spared the fate of captivity. Yeh's wife and three daughters also escaped because he had sent them back to Han-yang under the care of his father, immediately before the city fell.[108]

One wonders how much attention Yeh gave to his own family. There is no information in the records, but indirectly, one may draw a picture from numerous documents in the Canton Archive. Most of the draft memoranda to the emperor had been corrected by Yeh before they were properly copied out again. The calligraphy of these corrections looks most immature; the explanation lies probably in the fact that it was winter and Yeh was lying in bed or by a fire (to keep warm) when he corrected the drafts at night.[109] Judging from the amount of work he had to deal with at Canton, as will be apparent in the ensuing chapters, it is not surprising that his evenings were also taken up by official matters, and consequently very little time was left for his own private life. Even his arch-enemy Sir John Bowring paid tribute to him by saying that he 'was a most industrious administrator, wrote his own despatches, which, like those of Lin, were much admired for their correctness of style'.[110] His wife was said to be a virtuous woman,[111] presumably in the sense that she was capable, and was able to run the family and bring up the children almost single-handed, so that her husband could concentrate on his official duties. On the other hand, it might be argued that, had his children been boys, he might have taken a more active interest in them – in a society where the man dominated public life, it is not difficult to imagine that much prejudice should exist against female offspring. If this were the case, then ironically, the fact that Yeh had no sons of his own might have made him feel relieved from many of his family concerns. Thus he was able to pay more attention to public affairs, which might be taken as yet another explanation of his success in official life.

2 The Canton period 1847–58: a general survey

The most important period of Yeh Ming-ch'en's political career, his eleven years at Canton from 1847 to 1858, will be studied in detail in the ensuing chapters. It may be useful, before analysing more closely the various aspects of his administration, to give a brief introduction to the political condition of the Manchu Empire in 1847 and its social and economic unrest, and then discuss it in the context of local conditions in Kwangtung and Kwangsi of which he was to become governor-general. A short history of the relations with western powers, especially with Great Britain after the Opium War (1840–2), will also help us to understand Yeh's role in this respect from 1847 onwards. Finally, a chronological survey of the important events of this decade may provide a guideline to make the analytical chapters easier to follow.

The state of the Empire in 1847

Founded in 1644, the Ch'ing dynasty reached the climax of its power under the fourth emperor, Ch'ien-lung, who reigned for sixty years (1736–96). He was a very ambitious man, and used the wealth and strength of the nation to engage in as many as ten military expeditions against the so-called 'rebellious peoples' in the border areas.[1] These expensive wars overstrained the economic structure of the nation, and gave rise to malpractices. Instances of official corruption began to multiply, among which the case of Ho-shen (1750–99) was perhaps the most notorious, and, as pointed out by historians, seriously undermined the efficiency of the government from Ch'ien-lung's time onwards.[2] One may add that Ho-shen's crimes were in fact made possible by an already weakening administrative system.

Internal decay was accelerated by the importing of opium on an ever-increasing scale. The Portuguese had initiated the trade in this drug in the sixteenth century. The detrimental effects, moral and physiological, of drug addiction quickly became known, and an imperial edict by Ch'ien-lung in 1729 prohibited the sale and consumption of opium. However, the trade was so lucrative that contraband traffic continued unabated. In 1773, the British East India Company joined in the trade, and quickly managed to monopolise it. The annual importation of opium steadily increased, from about 200 chests (a chest weighed approximately 140 lb) in 1729 to 1,000 chests in 1767, to over 4,000 chests by the turn of the century, 8,000 in the 1820s, 17,000 between 1828 and 1835, and 30,000 between 1835 and 1839.[3] Until 1826, the balance of foreign trade had always been favourable to China, because of the export of tea and silk, but the phenomenal increase in the importing of opium reversed the situation. The constant drain, and in ever-increasing quantities, of silver from China to pay for the drug resulted in a chronic inflation. Silver was a precious metal and was used as a measurement of large sums only, such as government revenue and expenses, while the medium of exchange among the ordinary people was copper cash. The outflow of silver inevitably put up its rate of exchange against the copper cash. A tael of silver was worth about 1,000 copper cash in the eighteenth century; in the 1830s, it was worth twice as much. Between 1831 and 1834, the Chinese spent yearly over 20 million taels on opium, a sum equivalent to half the annual national tax revenue of the same period.[4] Peking's decision to take drastic action against opium smugglers and addicts sparked off the Opium War (1840–2). China was defeated, and among many concessions, she had to pay an indemnity of 21 million taels. The peace treaty did not however settle the question of opium. According to Chinese law, its sale and smoking was still prohibited, but the government was powerless to enforce the law; in addition the drug, not having been legalised, was not taxed as a foreign product. Thus, the government was put in a very embarrassing position, while opium continued to devastate the moral, physical and economic health of the nation. Indeed, a well-known Chinese historian described his country in the 1840s as declining, defeated and impoverished.[5]

Severe inflation made life very difficult for ordinary people. As mentioned, their medium of exchange was copper cash, but the tax they had to pay was fixed in terms of silver. The doubled exchange rate between copper coins and silver in the 1830s meant that they were taxed twice as much. Moreover, large landowners continued to take advantage of the temporary difficulties of individual peasants to annex more and more arable land. Worse still, they were often influential enough to pay only nominal taxes. Consequently, the peasants were forced by local officials to pay all kinds of illegal charges in an attempt to cover up the deficit.[6] This was the thin end of the wedge, as local officials were quick to create more and more illicit charges so that they, too, might benefit. These officials knew that they were making excessive demands, and they often found it necessary to bring troops with them when they went to the countryside to urge the delivery of taxes. Brutality was not uncommon; the peasants retaliated, and the murder of tax collectors from the early nineteenth century onwards was not uncommon.[7]

Another factor which greatly aggravated the situation was the phenomenal increase in the population, which was estimated at about 143 million in 1741, 286 million in 1784 and 430 million in 1850.[8] This increase was not accompanied by a paralled expansion of the national economy. According to Ho Ping-ti's analysis, China had reached her optimum condition – the point at which a population produces maximum economic welfare at the technical level of the time – between 1750 and 1775.[9] Thereafter, further increases in population led only to a lowering of the standard of living. Mark Elvin, on the other hand, has suggested that as early as the fourteenth century Chinese technology was already subject to severe constraints; further progress required a discontinuous shift in the technological ceiling, necessitating heavy investments.[10] Basically, what this amounts to is that China was continually experiencing the problem of population pressure and food shortages. By the nineteenth century, after decades of rapid population increase, the problem was becoming particularly acute, causing grave social problems one of which was unemployment. The redundant drifted into secret societies, which had their origin in antiquity and which had been the champions of the poor in times of distress.[11] Social unrest produced rebellions. As early as 1773, while Ch'ien-lung was still on the throne, several thousand members of a secret society called the White Lotus rebelled. In 1783, the Moslems in Kansu province rebelled. The secret societies in Taiwan staged an uprising in 1786, and held out until 1788. In the last year of Ch'ien-lung's reign, 1796, the White Lotus again rose in revolt. They attacked the city of Lin-ch'ing, in Shantung. This city was of great strategic importance. It controlled a key point along the Grand Canal which supplied Peking with most of its provisions. If a hostile force occupied this city, the lifeline of Peking would be cut. The Manchus of course recognised the importance of the Grand Canal and deployed a strong force under the command of a governor-general to guard it. Lin-ch'ing nevertheless fell to the rebels, and it was some time before they were driven out. In each case the number of rebels amounted to tens of thousands, proclaiming that they had been forced to rebel by the oppressive officials, and that their aim was to overthrow the Ch'ing and restore the Ming.[12] Rebellions had become endemic.

The situation was made worse by natural calamities, not the least of which were the floods of the Yellow River. At its source the river is clear, but it flows through what is known as the Yellow Soil Plateau where the earth is loose, and thus carries down-stream large quantities of yellow soil, which gives the river its name. The silt settles in the river bed, so that the river becomes shallower and shallower. It would be impossible naturally to dig up the silt; what the Chinese did was to try to contain the river water by building higher and higher dykes along the banks, until the river bed was above ground. Thus the North China Plain became vulnerable whenever any section of the dykes showed signs of collapsing in a typhoon. All Chinese governments had to devote much of their resources and manpower to keeping the dykes in good condition – indeed, the Yellow River was always regarded as a barometer of the efficiency of a Chinese government at any time. Between 1796 and 1820, floods burst out of the dykes seventeen times.[13] Worse was yet to come in the 1830s, 1840s and 1850s, when critical study of local histories shows that there was an unusually large number of natural disasters.[14]

Thus, in brief, Yeh lived at a time when general bureaucratic incompetence, economic depression, over-population, chronic famines and increasing social unrest were compromising the very existence of the Ch'ing dynasty.

Kwangtung and Kwangsi

Kwangtung

Geography. Kwangtung is a maritime province in South China, with a coastline of about 1,560 miles (nearly 23% of the entire coastline of China). Seventy per cent of the province is composed of highlands, situated mostly in the north, and communication with the northern provinces is through steep mountain passes. Of its two main river systems, the Han River in the east is the smaller. The Pearl River, much longer, is considered one of the three main river systems (the other two being the Yellow River and the Yangtze) and has three tributaries, the East, North and West Rivers, of which the last is the longest, starting in Yünnan and Kweichow and flowing across Kwangsi before entering Kwangtung. The average annual rainfall is 63 inches, some three-quarters of which falls between April and September. Both the West and East Rivers are situated almost on the same parallel of latitude, and thus receive at more or less the same time heavy rains which they cannot easily drain. The North River and the Han River run from north to south, their upper section receiving heavy rainfall in May, the middle section in June, and when the swollen waters of both reach the lower section, it is the rainy season there. Worse still, the North, East and West Rivers converge on the Canton Delta. As the river system cannot cope with sudden rises in the volume of water, floods are commonplace,[15] and the proper maintenance of dykes is essential.

History. Kwangtung developed relatively late in the History of China. It was not until the Han period (206 B.C. – A.D. 220) that the Han Chinese began to migrate south into the North River region and the Canton delta, hitherto inhabited only by non-Han Chinese tribes. Migration was accelerated by the prolonged disorder in central China after the fall of the Han dynasty. The building of the Ta-yü road in the T'ang period (A.D. 618–907) greatly facilitated communication with, and the migration into, Kwangtung. However, large-scale development of the province did not take place until the Southern Sung dynasty (1127–1278).[16] The Manchu conquerors encountered much resistance from Kwangtung when they tried to subdue it in the seventeenth century: A Ming prince fled to Canton in 1647; the gentry of the area rallied to his support and helped him to establish his court there. Canton fell, but the gentry made spirited attempts to drive the invaders from their city. Many of the leaders were captured and executed, but their example inspired the formation of secret Ming loyalist groups. In 1648, the head of the Ch'ing forces occupying Canton, a Han Chinese called Li Ch'eng-tung, reversed his allegiance and invited another Ming prince to return to Kwangtung as emperor. His opportunism may be partially explained by the strength of anti-Manchu feeling in the province. He was defeated in 1649, and in the following year Canton was once again surrounded by Manchu troops. The city fell after a prolonged siege of eight months, and 100,000 inhabitants were reported to have been put to the sword.[17]

The loyalists of Kwangtung, like their counterparts in the maritime provinces of Fukien, Chekiang and Kiangsu, emigrated in large numbers to Taiwan to continue their struggle under Cheng Ch'eng-kung (Koxinga). The Manchus, accordingly, ordered the removal inland of the population within 50 *li* (about 13 miles) of the coast, and the prohibition of any vessel, mercantile or fishing, from going out to sea. This caused great hardship among the coastal populace.[18] In 1673, the Han Chinese military leaders of Kwangtung, Yünnan and Fukien staged a rebellion – the so-called San Fan Rebellion, which was not suppressed until 1681.[19] This 'left the Manchus with a lasting suspicion of the loyalty of the south'.[20] Open resistance and rebellion had been subdued, but the anti-Manchu movement was carried on underground by secret societies with the avowed purpose of 'overthrowing the Ch'ing and restoring the Ming'.[21] The Manchu policy of upholding the traditional privileges, political, social and economic, of the Chinese elite broadly referred to as the gentry, and of adopting almost wholesale the Chinese system of government slowly won the support of the gentry, but the secret societies continued to be the champions of anti-Manchu (anti-government) elements, especially the disaffected peasantry in times of distress.

Demographic pressure. After the suppression of the San Fan Rebellion in 1681, Kwangtung enjoyed a long period of peace and prosperity. Consequently, its population swelled rapidly, reaching the 16 million mark in 1787, and 28 million in 1850.[22] These are only official figures which might be considered smaller than the real ones, since the gentry often bribed local government underlings to evade registration and because of the rise of 'a restless or otherwise marginal and mobile section of the population'.[23] The increase in population was not, however, accompanied by a comparable increase in arable land, and migration was very much in evidence. The Cantonese had been moving up the North River and forced the aboriginal peoples deeper and deeper into the mountains, until one of them, the Yao, decided to make a last determined but futile attempt at resisting the invasion – the so-called Yao Uprising in the 1830s. The Hakka (lit. 'guest people') who had settled in the northeast of Kwangtung, in Chia-ying-chou, not long before, also found that their numbers had outgrown the resources of the land, and the surplus population began a large-scale migration into the centre of the province, which was already densely populated by the Punti (lit., 'local people', in this case, the Cantonese). Constant friction between the two groups led to widespread fighting in the mid-nineteenth century in areas west of Canton – the so-called Hakka–Punti War. The Hakka finally concluded that they could not oust the local people, and resumed their massive migration further west, into Kwangsi, Kweichow and Szechwan.[24]. Even those Hakka who had settled in the Canton region earlier and had roots there found that there was not enough land to satisfy their needs. The pretext which Feng Yün-shan (one of the early Taiping leaders) used to persuade his family in Hua-hsien (north of Canton) to join him in Kwangsi was that there was plenty of arable land after the suppression of a local rebellion. Consequently his wife and children, his brother and family all decided to leave Hua-hsien in search of a better world.[25]

The Yao rising and the Hakka–Punti conflicts were thus symptoms of fundamental demographic problems, and heralded a coming major social upheaval.

Social structure. In China, villages were basic units of rural society. In Kwangtung and Fukien, the lineage and village tended to coincide.[26] This meant that a village could act promptly and unanimously in case of any land dispute or the vital question of water supply to the paddy fields. Indeed, armed conflicts among villages were commonplace in Kwangtung, so much so that a prominent anthropologist has come to the conclusions 'that lineage alignments were the key to organized fighting and that it cannot be an accident that the part of China where local fighting was carried to a pitch unknown in the rest of the country was also the seat of Chinese lineage organization in its fullest form'.[27] This helps to explain why the people of Kwangtung, including the gentry, who 'dominated the scene in clan feuds as in other activities of the kinship groups' were so bellicose.[28] Since the gentry were the leaders of clans, commanding respect and exercising power over their fellows, they constituted a force which no governor could afford to ignore.

The lineages were the largest landowners of the province. One

Chinese scholar estimates that 50–70 per cent of the land was in their hands,[29] although his Japanese counterpart has not put it as high (33 per cent).[30] Mark Elvin has suggested that since A.D. 1000, manorial landlordism had, for various reasons, been slowly replaced by small holdings in many regions in China. However, this is a general statement which does not apply to Kwangtung, and Elvin has indicated that his study excludes the development in that province. Indeed, his brief reference to the Canton delta confirms the fact that arable land in that area was concentrated in a few hands.[31] The revenue from the 'clan fields' (*kung-t'ien*) furnished members of the clan with schools, scholarships, subsidies to degree-holders and candidates taking public examinations, as well as funds for welfare purposes such as relief for the poor, the sick and the disabled, and finally, for financing clan wars and paying compensation to those wounded in the clashes.[32] Thus, a clan was a focus of economic and political power, whose members, 'enjoying the bounty of their land and contented with their customs',[33] rarely abandoned it. On the other hand, the concentration of landownership in a few hands (the clans and powerful gentry), meant that the majority of the farmers were tenants.[34] The pressure of population and the shortage of arable land had, by the early nineteenth century, considerably raised the price of land as well as rentals,[35] and the tenants were badly affected: 'there are such hereditary tenants [of fellow clansmen]...who, in addition to farming the fields assigned them, render service as labourers, servants, watchmen.'[36] It is not surprising then, that these tenants should 'harbour deep resentments against the clan leaders who enforced high rents or usury'.[37] More and more began to join secret societies, which had been champions of the oppressed since their creation, and which transcended the clan.[38]

The *pao-chia* system, in which families were organised in units of ten for mutual surveillance, had been conceived as an important tool for rural control by instilling mutual fear and suspicion so that no one 'dared to venture into seditious schemes'. However, 'the government often found it difficult to enforce its operation; it was unable even to establish uniformity in its structure'.[39] In 1814, the emperor was jubilant about the fact that, thanks to the *pao-chia* system, some criminals were arrested in Kwangtung; but Hsiao Kung-ch'üan remarked that such 'favourable reports...may have exaggerated the results attained if any results actually were attained'.[40] In any case, from 1821 to the end of the Ch'ing dynasty, little reference had been made to the *pao-chia* in official records, and when the emperor did so in 1850, it was to lament its decay.[41] The *hsiang-yüeh* was also designed for rural control: villagers were supposed to assemble twice a month to listen to local scholars expounding the tenets of Confucius. By the nineteenth century, this system seems to have broken down too; but Yeh shrewdly revived it in

Kwangtung as a means of alliance among villagers for local self-defence against the Red Turban rebels (see chap. 3).

Economy. Since the time of the Sung dynasty, Canton had become the centre of commerce, the handicraft industry and foreign trade. The sugar industry was highly developed, Canton, Ch'ao-chou and Lien-chou being the main centres of manufacture. By 1700, the sugar thus produced was sufficient to meet the demands of Kwangtung and certain of her neighbouring provinces, with some export to South East Asia. The introduction of cotton into Kwangtung at the end of the Sung dynasty paralleled the already flourishing silk industry in the province. Fo-shan, Shan-t'ou (Swatow) and Ch'iung-chou sprang up as centres of the textile industry. Fo-shan was also important for the production of ironware, fireworks and parasols. Other industries like porcelain flourished at Ch'ao-chou and Tung-kuan, and embroidery at Canton, Hui-chou and Shao-chou. Other centres of commerce and handicraft industry included Lien-chou, Lei-chou and Kao-chou (see Map 2). As regards foreign trade, the Portuguese were the first Europeans to come to China, in the sixteenth century, followed quickly by the Spaniards, Dutch, British and French. In 1757, the Manchu government closed the whole of China except Canton to foreign traders. Canton prospered even more under this monopoly, exporting the tea and silk of central and eastern China, and importing silver, copper, arms and other foreign goods. This foreign trade was handled exclusively by a group of Chinese firms called the Co-hong, and the entire establishment has been referred to as the Canton System.[42]

As a result of China's defeat in the Opium War, the Canton System was abolished; in addition, four other ports, namely, Amoy, Foochow, Ningpo and Shanghai were opened for foreign trade. Though the new ports, especially Shanghai, drew off much of the trade from Canton, sufficient remained. Silk from Kiangsu and tea from Anhwei and Chekiang naturally found their way to the nearest market, but those from Kiangsi, Hupeh and Hunan continued to go to Canton. As regards imports, 'the new ports only created new markets and caused no diminution of the Canton trade'.[43]

Rice was the main agricultural product of Kwangtung, with two or even three crops a year. However, the importation of rice from abroad – mainly Thailand – and from neighbouring provinces began as early as 1723.[44] This was partly due to an ever-increasing population and a shortage of arable land, such as led to a rice shortage throughout China.[45] This factor was particularly important in hilly Kwangtung, where only 16 per cent of the land was cultivated as late as 1955,[46] and where much of this cultivated land was used to grow commercial crops instead of rice. In 1727, the governor of Kwangsi protested to the

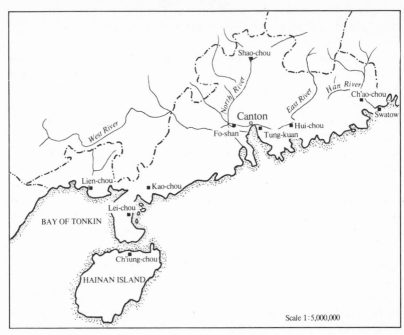

Map 2. Centres of commerce and handicraft industry in Kwangtung

emperor about the 'extensive purchase of Kwangsi rice by the people of Kwangtung', and 'attributed the rice shortage in Kwangtung to the fact that a considerable portion of its good farmland had been devoted to such commercial crops as fruits, sugar cane, tobacco and indigo'.[47] Whereas such crops undoubtedly added to the wealth of the rich landowners and merchants, the plight of the common folk was aggravated by the rapidly rising price of rice.

Kwangsi

A spine of mountains, rising in stages, runs northwest through the province from Kwangtung towards Yünnan. The highest ground, at 2,000–6,5000 feet, is in the west of the province, but the whole of Kwangsi is a criss-cross of mountains and canyons, and level ground is to be found only in narrow valleys in the southeast, along the lower branches of the West River system (see Map 3)[48] As late as 1933, life in northern and western Kwangsi was described as primitive, and fixed landownership was almost non-existent. These parts were inhabited mainly by aboriginal minorities, such as the Miao, Yao and Chuang, with whom the Han Chinese had a long history of trouble. The Han Chinese lived in the southeast, which was more developed; Wu-chou

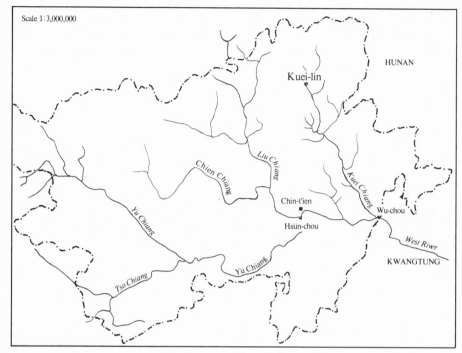

Map 3. Kwangsi province

was the most important commercial centre, occupying a key position on the West River, the only major line of communication with Kwangtung. Business was largely controlled by the Cantonese; as a result, Kwangsi has been described as a 'colonial market' of the Cantonese. Commerce yielded profit, which was often invested in land, and consequently, landownership in this region was concentrated in a few hands. There was very little industry except some silver mining.[49]

Thus the southeast part of Kwangsi was in a rather unusual position. It was sandwiched between the rich east (Kwangtung) and the very poor west. The high mountains and deep valleys provided a natural haven for outlaws, bandits, river pirates and secret societies. The situation was aggravated by the effects of the Opium War. The Treaty of Nanking opened four ports in addition to Canton to foreign trade. This inevitably changed the trade routes within China, and large numbers of porters in Kwangtung were laid off. Displaced adventurers and desperadoes around Canton moved west into mountainous Kwangsi. Furthermore, the provincial government of Kwangtung began a rigorous programme in 1847 to clean its coast and the Pearl River delta of the pirates. Consequently, bands of pirates migrated up the West River to the high mountain country. Hence by 1850, southeast Kwangsi contained an extraordinarily high concentration of outlaws of all descriptions.

Far more serious was a polarisation of the population in this area. The inhabitants here were Han Chinese, but they were divided, as mentioned above into the so-called Punti (lit. 'local people', including many Cantonese) and the so-called Hakka (lit. 'guest people'). The Hakka were migrants from north China, who began to appear in Kwangsi only in the seventeenth century, and continued to come in large numbers throughout the eighteenth century. By the nineteenth century they had become so numerous that much tension had developed with the local people, or Punti. The Punti were relatively rich and powerful. Many of them were members of the gentry, merchants and large landowners. The Hakka, as late-comers, had to eke out a meagre living by becoming tenants, labourers and silver miners. Many of them were so destitute that they had to resort 'to banditry to supplement their income'.[50] As tenants and labourers, they were heavily exploited by the local people, as bandits, they came into direct armed conflict with them. Thus the feuds between the two groups intensified with the passage of time and by 1850 bloodshed was commonplace. The local people represented the Hakka to the government as bandits and asked it to take action. The Hakka requested protection in turn from a secret society called the God-worshippers, many of whose leaders were themselves Hakka. Thus, the feuds between the two groups of people became a confrontation between the government and a powerful secret society, marking the beginning of the so-called Taiping Rebellion.

Hence, by the end of the 1840s, rebels and bandits saturated Kwangsi, and as will be seen in chap. 4, made frequent incursions into Kwangtung from 1849 onwards.

A brief survey of China's relationship with the West

In East Asia, the age, size, civilisation and wealth of China made her the natural centre of this part of the world. Her relationship with her neighbours was one which has been described as the 'tribute system', whereby the heads of these states sent envoys to pay tribute to the Chinese emperor and thus recognise his suzerainty, in return for very generous gifts and the privilege to trade (during the envoy's stay in China). Thus, when European countries came into contact with China, 'They were expected and when possible obliged to do so as tributaries.'[51] However, the Europeans, first the Portuguese and the Dutch, and later the British and Americans, were only interested in trade; diplomatically, they wanted to be treated as equals. Thus the expansion of trade in the eighteenth century was accompanied by an increase in conflicts. Moreover, the activities of the early merchants and sailors were typified by a combination of trade, piracy, drunkenness and violence. Not surprisingly, China eventually decided in 1757 to close to foreign trade all her ports except Canton. Even in Canton, the foreigners were subject to restrictions which gave rise to much complaint. In an attempt to mitigate the restrictions and exactions, and to expand the trade to other ports in China, England despatched Lord Macartney in 1793 and Lord Amherst in 1816 to Peking for negotiations, but without success.

Meanwhile, the so-called triangular trade between China, India and England flourished. China exported tea and silk to England, for which the British merchants paid by exporting opium to China from India. As we have seen, Chinese prohibition of the smoking and selling of opium sparked off the Opium War, and the subsequent Treaty of Nanking removed the restrictions at Canton and opened four more ports for foreign trade. Whereas this treaty has been regarded by most historians as 'the dawn to the New', J. K. Fairbank believes that it 'only began the twilight of the Old'. For, he suggested, the Ch'ing rationale in accepting this and subsequent treaties with America and France had been an application of the traditional concept of *chi-mi* (lit., 'bridling and reining in'): 'The materialistic foreigners were granted certain benefits and privileges that would grow into vested interests, for which they would depend upon the emperor and by which he might therefore control them.'[52] This is an illuminating interpretation, which is in fact supported by innumerable imperial edicts in the *Veritable Records* of the late Tao-Kuang and Hsien-feng periods. One may perhaps add that the same documents as well as many writings by contemporary Chinese officials[53] show that their authors, far from consciously adopting a new policy, resented the concessions of the treaty. It is true that for a period after the conclusion of peace, the Ch'ing government did adopt a kind of appeasement policy,[54] but its hand was forced. The emperor eventually spoke his mind when, after the Chinese triumph over the so-called Entry Crisis of 1849,[55] he decreed that for nearly ten years he had quietly suffered humiliation by foreigners, and that his joy over the recent diplomatic victory was beyond description; the officials were also jubilant, and one even wrote that he was 'twittering' with joy.[56] Therefore, Yeh's task when he assumed office as imperial commissioner, was to keep the peace with foreigners through abiding strictly by treaty provisions and to prevent further loss of face through more concessions. Shortly after the *Arrow* incident, for example, the emperor decreed that if the British repented and sued for peace, Yeh should still use *chi-mi* to avoid war, but should never yield any ground because this would only lead to further demands.[57] Later, after the battle of Canton and Admiral Seymour's withdrawal from that city,[58] the emperor again decreed: 'Yeh Ming-ch'en should have long-term plans to settle the dispute. He must not yield any ground in the hope of avoiding the present conflict, nor should he be aggressive, which would inevitably result in war. I am sure that with his experience, he knows how to perform his duty.'[59]

The Canton Period 1847–58: a chronological survey[60]

Yeh Ming-ch'en was appointed to the provincial treasurership of Kwangtung in 1846. On 2 April 1847, Sir John Davis, governor of Hong Kong, forced his way to Canton with a number of gunboats and intimidated the then Governor-General Ch'i-ying into promising to grant permission, after two years, for foreigners to enter the city of Canton. The year had hardly passed before Ch'i-ying suffered another humiliation at the hands of Davis over the Huang-chu-ch'i incident, in which six Englishmen were killed in a fight with Chinese villagers. Then in 1848 Governor Hsü Kuang-chin was appointed to replace the inept Ch'i-ying, and Yeh was promoted to the post of governor. On 6 April 1849, the deadline set by Ch'i-ying had expired. Hsü and Yeh, convinced that fulfilment of this promise would lead to open rebellion by the Cantonese, had decided to resist it at all costs. Troops were mobilised and the militia assembled. The situation was so grave that the incident has always been referred to as the Entry Crisis. However, England was not prepared for war at this stage, and decided to let her demands remain in abeyance. This was regarded as a great diplomatic victory by the Chinese; Hsü was made a viscount, and Yeh a baron.

The external threat had barely disappeared before internal unrest took on a very serious aspect. The excitement caused by the abovementioned incidents might, in fact, have encouraged the disaffected elements, who began to gather in large numbers in the North River region (Ch'ing-yüan and Ying-te) in 1849, and ambushed a detachment of government troops. The provincial commander-in-chief of the land forces had to be sent to the area to suppress the uprisings. This was only the beginning; the local rebels were reinforced by large numbers of outlaws from Kwangsi in 1850, and the commander-in-chief appeared quite incapable of controlling the situation. Yeh himself had to go to the scene to assume command, and to engage in hard fighting for a year before the rebellion was finally quashed. Lien-chou, a prefecture in the extreme west of Kwangtung, was also affected by incursions from Kwangsi after June 1850, and was not pacified until two years later. The worst happened in Kwangsi itself, when the Taipings gathered at Chin-t'ien and formally declared their rebellion on 4 November 1850. Meanwhile, Sir George Bonham kept up the pressure by going to Shanghai in September and tried to communicate with Ch'i-ying and Mu-chang-a at Peking about the entry question.

In 1851, the revolts increased in number and scale. In addition to those at Ch'ing-yüan, Ying-te and Lien-chou, two more broke out, in Hainan Island and in Kao-chou. That in Kao-chou was particularly serious, and Hsü had to go there to direct the campaign in person. In Kwangsi, the government forces had little success against the Taipings, and Imperial Commissioner Chou T'ien-chüeh, specially appointed to suppress the rebellion, was replaced by Sai-shang-a.

Severe fighting continued throughout the year of 1852. Hsü's war effort against Ling Shih-pa in Kao-chou made little headway and Sai-shang-a proved himself militarily quite incompetent, by allowing the Taipings to besiege the provincial capital, Kuei-lin, in April. In June, therefore, the emperor ordered Hsü to go into Kwangsi, and Yeh took over command in Kao-chou. Within two months, Yeh defeated Ling Shih-pa, by which time, however, the Taipings had fought their way into Hunan and were threatening to descend on Kwangtung from the north. Immediately, Yeh went to Shao-chou and warded off the threat. Before the year ended, he was appointed governor-general of Liang Kuang and imperial commissioner for foreign affairs in place of Hsü, who had become imperial commissioner to suppress the Taipings.

By far the most significant event that took place in 1853 was the capture of Nanking by the Taipings on 19 March and the establishment of this city as their Heavenly Kingdom ten days later. The whole empire was shaken, and Yeh was ordered to send more and more troops to central China to fight the Taipings. However, the rebels were not satisfied merely with the capture of Nanking, but soon began sending expeditions north to attack Peking and secret agents south to Kwangtung to stir up large-scale uprisings. Yeh might expect a major storm, but either because he was unaware of the threat or, more probably, because his hand was forced by the emperor, he was busily assembling and then despatching large bodies of troops and huge quantities of supplies to central China to fight the Taipings. Nor was he left alone to attend to his internal problems; soon after taking office as the new British Plenipotentiary in April 1854, Sir John Bowring demanded an interview with him, and he had to decline on the grounds that he was too busy conducting campaigns in several provinces.[61] Bowring persisted, but when Yeh finally agreed to see him and suggested the Bogue[62] or a pack-house just outside the city of Canton as a meeting place, he declined as he insisted on seeing Yeh within the walled city. Then he went to Shanghai in September to demand treaty revision. He was told to return to Canton. Distracted by Bowring's requests and weakened by the exigencies of the situation in the interior, Yeh found himself ill-prepared and without his best troops and most of his money when the storm finally broke in Kwangtung in July 1854. Many thousands of members of secret societies rose in revolt and quickly besieged the provincial capital. Yeh had to fight for his very survival. He worked steadily and resolutely towards beating off the rebels. The courageous and determined campaign which he waged against them and which finally enabled him to break out from Canton was the climax of his career, and won him a formal appointment to the Grand Secretariat, one of China's highest honours.

The years 1855 and 1856 were marked by severe fighting as the government forces tried to regain control of the Pearl River region. Slowly but steadily, the main bands in the West River area were driven into Kwangsi, those in the North River area into Hunan, and those in the East River area into Kiangsi. The flight of the more substantial rebel groups did not, however, mean a return to peace. Remnants of the rebel armies continued to terrorise the countryside, and the rural areas were kept under control only with the greatest difficulty. The vigorous campaign of rural recovery continued throughout 1856 and 1857. At times, the main rebel groups who had left Kwangtung were on the point of breaking through Yeh's frontier defences and descending on Canton once more along the three tributaries of the Pearl River. To forestall this, Yeh had to send large bodies of his troops across the border to keep the most formidable groups away from Kwangtung. It was at this very juncture that a second war with England was sparked off by the so-called *Arrow* incident of 8 October 1856. Yeh was now confronted with an almost impossible situation. He could not recall the troops he had sent out to central China before and after the siege of Canton in 1854, because they were still badly needed there by the emperor. Indeed, the demand on the soldiers and supplies of Kwantung continued unabated even after the outbreak of foreign hostilities.[63] His other troops were tied down fighting in the countryside and defending the provincial frontiers, and the withdrawal of these troops would probably have to the rebels to converge once again to besiege Canton, this time together with the British; the provincial government would then stand little chance of survival because provisions would not be forthcoming either from abroad or from the countryside. Therefore, Yeh had to settle the foreign dispute while deprived of most of his regular troops. He tried to bring his enemy to reason first by words and then by stopping their trade. When both failed, he attempted a war of attrition and employed guerilla tactics, using such troops and militia as were available. In this way, the *Arrow* war dragged on for fourteen months, until the British suddenly turned up with large reinforcements and French allies. Yeh was caught unprepared; on 29 December 1857 Canton, and on 5 January 1858 Yeh himself, fell into the hands of the allied forces.

Part two
The administrator

3 The administrator I: the scholar-gentry class

The civil government in theory and in practice

Late in 1846, Yeh Ming-ch'en arrived at Canton to take up the post of provincial treasurer of Kwangtung. In July the following year he was promoted governor of the same province. In 1852, he was appointed imperial commissioner for foreign affairs and governor-general of Liang Kuang (Kwangtung and Kwangsi), which position he held until his capture by the British in January 1858. To clarify his role in these four different posts, it is necessary to define them institutionally; and, more important, to show how they actually functioned when held by him.

The imperial commissioner and the governor-general

The office of imperial commissioner for foreign affairs was created as a result of the Nanking Treaty of 1842, and was concurrently held with the office of governor-general of Liang Kuang, with full power from the emperor to deal with foreign affairs. The first imperial commissioner for foreign affairs was Ch'i-ying, who was well known for his conciliatory policy. He fared quite well until Governor Hsü Kuang-chin and Provincial Treasurer Yeh Ming-ch'en, both strongly opposed to his style of diplomacy,[1] came to serve at Canton in 1847. Eventually Hsü replaced Ch'i-ying and Yeh became governor the following year. Ch'i-ying attached more importance to his work as imperial commissioner than as governor-general, as can be inferred from the fact that he always worked in the imperial commissioner's office, and sent a copy of each diplomatic document to the office of the governor-general for reference.[2] When Hsü became acting imperial commissioner, his clerks replaced those of Ch'i-ying, but he followed Ch'i-ying's practice for some time.[3] Then he decided to work in the governor-general's office, and that of the imperial commissioner decreased in importance, until Yeh's time, when the office probably disappeared altogether. This development seems compatible with the growing predominance of dangerous internal problems during Yeh's years of incumbency.

The governor-general and the governor

The function of a governor-general was originally military in nature – he was the supreme commander of the forces maintaining order in his viceroyalty; the civil responsibilities belonged, strictly speaking, to the governors of the respective provinces.[4] However, the governor-general frequently took advantage of his superior position to interfere with the civil administration, and more often than not, came to serious conflicts with the governor should they both reside in the same city, as was the case in Canton. Indeed, despite conflicting evidence, it seems that in 1847, Governor Hsü and Provincial Treasurer Yeh may have conspired to wrest the control of foreign policy from Governor-General Ch'i-ying by inducing his removal from Canton.[5] Therefore it is of some importance to determine how Yeh himself got along first with his superior, Governor-General Hsü Kuang-chin, and later with his inferior Governor Po-kuei. His relations with these two men might determine his success or failure as an administrator.

Cordiality among colleagues may depend, in the final analysis, upon their sharing the same views and attitudes about policy-making and methods of administration. Hsü and Yeh were in agreement about these subjects: 'the Governor General and the Governor not only transact their business in strict good faith,' reported Po-kuei to the emperor in 1849, 'but in all cases without disagreement...[I have] never witnessed so much concord between the Governor General and the Governor.'[6] On foreign policy, for example, both were convinced that a firm line should be adopted. During the Entry Crisis of 1849, they both sent strongly worded memoranda to Peking advising against permitting the British to enter the city of Canton, even though the emperor had granted temporary admittance, and to the British they sent the so-called False Edict, which continued to close the gates of Canton to foreigners.[7] In doing so, they risked their careers, but the crisis passed, and both were honoured with titles of nobility. From then on, they had the reputation of 'always working secretly together, alone in the council hall, devising plans to handle the British'.[8] The two, having gone through so much together, became the closest of friends.

Foreign threats were not their only problems. Internal unrest began to demand their attention from their early days of office at Canton. Contemporaneously with the Entry Crisis, rebellions broke out in northern Kwangtung and soon after in the west as well. When the commander-in-chief of the land forces of the province was unable to suppress them,[9] circumstances dictated that the Liang Yüan[10] should be on the spot to direct the campaigns personally, although their heavy administrative duties could not be neglected. Hence they arranged to take turns to stay at Canton to head the government, Hsü in 1851 when Yeh went to north Kwangtung, and Yeh in 1852, when Hsü left for Lo-ting in the west. They bridged the distance thus created between them by extraordinarily frequent correspondence, with an average of a letter every two or three days,[11] where they discussed politics, finance, the merits and failings of their subordinates, the subjects about which they were to inform the emperor, and when they should do so. They also exchanged military intelligence and enclosed confidential reports. In one letter Hsü said, 'We must report about the capture of the rebel Li Pei-she promtly to His Majesty so that no one[12] shall bring this news to him before us.' In another he said, 'Concerning Prefect Liu, I agree with what you said in your last letter, that the matter must not be mentioned in our memoranda until the rebellion here in Lo-ting is put down.' In others he said, 'I enclose these reports which I have just received. Please return them to me when you have read them.' 'Now that I have read your letter, my previous proposal should be dropped.' 'Colonel Ch'ing is really too weak; when Colonel Chao returns, I want to put him in Ch'ing's place; what do you think?'[13] Because of the incompleteness of these letters, the subjects of discussion are obscure. But these extracts at least serve to show how closely the two men worked together, and that Yeh exercised far more power than that of a mere governor from 1848 onwards. These extracts cannot but lead to the conclusion that Hsü and Yeh were in charge of the Liang Yüan as one man. Therefore it is perhaps not too excessive to describe Yeh as imperial commissioner and governor-general from 1848 onwards.

The two men's affection for each other increased with time. Hsü's wife fell ill when he was away fighting at Lo-ting. Yeh went twice to see her and then reported to his friend about the doctor's prescriptions and her progress. When Hsü wrote to Yeh, he always concluded by saying, 'My respectful regards to your father, my uncle.'[14] Hsü had spent nearly a year in Lo-ting without much success, when the rapidly deteriorating military situation in Kwangsi decided the emperor to send him there.[15] Someone had to take over the unwelcome task of directing the campaign at Lo-ting, in which the chances of failure and loss of favour of the emperor were great; nevertheless Yeh decided to go. In gratitude Hsü wrote to him: 'Loyalty to the emperor and love of your friend have persuaded you to take this burden from me...True friends have no need to speak of gratitude, yet how can I remain silent with so great a debt?'[16]

By the end of 1852, Hsü was appointed imperial commissioner to fight the Taipings; Yeh took place as governor-general and Po-kuei became governor. Very soon, Hsü found it impossible to finance this expensive war. In serious difficulty, he appealed to Yeh for help. The Kwangtung treasuries, however, had been emptied the year before. Knowing too well that if Hsü's troops remained unpaid, his friend would face disaster, Yeh, at great risk to himself, re-directed to Hsü an important part of his own indispensable military budget, totalling 400,000 taels (see pp. 124–5). But Hsü failed to show the necessary qualities of generalship and eventually he was stripped of all his titles and position. There is no information about the relationship of the two friends hence,[17] but there is plenty of evidence to show that before this happened, they were exceptionally good friends, a friendship which offered Yeh immense political opportunities as administrator when he was only titular governor.

Let us now examine the relations between Yeh and Po-kuei, who, until 1858, constituted the new Liang Yüan. There was a vast difference between the two men. Yeh, though only one step higher on the bureaucratic ladder, was imperial commissioner, junior tutor of the crown prince, governor-general and first class baron, Po-kuei was plain governor. Moreover, Yeh was much younger and far more energetic. These differences in status alone were sufficient to make Po-kuei acutely conscious of his inferiority, apart from the fact that he had been accustomed to receive orders from Yeh in the Hsü–Yeh era, first as grain intendant of Kwangtung in 1848, than as provincial judge in 1849, and finally as provincial treasurer from September of the same year. He was Mongol, and Yeh was Han, which may have added to the differences between them. Certainly Po-kuei found that Yeh, being 'solemn and serious, industrious and a hard task-master, stern and taciturn, striking fear into his subordinates,'[18] as a critic put it, was not easy to approach as a superior. It is clear that responsibility and control were firmly in Yeh's hands. When he left for Lo-ting in June 1852 to direct the campaign there in place of Hsü, he reported to the emperor that

numerous additional stations have now been set up on the way between Canton [where Po-kuei remained, officially to head the government] and Lo-ting, so that in case of emergency, any official despatch may arrive at its destination in a matter of ten days. In this way I am in control of the entire situation, although I am stationed in a corner of the province.[19]

When Po-kuei received an imperial edict, he had to send a copy to Yeh;[20] but the reverse was not always the case unless the edict also concerned Po-kuei directly. In October 1855, Yeh was appointed deputy, and shortly afterwards promoted to full 'grand secretary still in office as governor-general in Kwangtung'.[21] Po-kuei was still simply governor. The difference in status between them was so great that, although as a matter of course the Liang Yüan jointly reported to the emperor on important events like a major military victory, Yeh's chief office clerk in

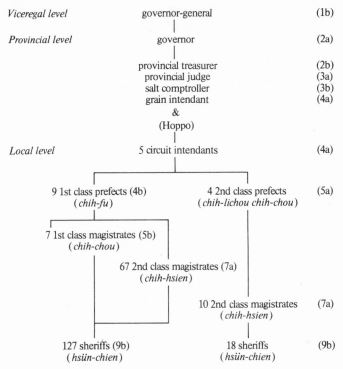

Fig. 1. The official hierarchy of the province of Kwangtung

1857 attached a note to a draft report, which Yeh was to send to Peking, entitled 'Complete victory over the rebels in Ch'ing-yüan and Fo-kang areas', saying, 'Last time Your Lordship made the report alone; shall we ignore the governor yet again?'[22] This shows Yeh's tendency for a long time to prepare the more significant memoranda alone. Po-kuei was no mere puppet, and most of the paperwork of civil and military administration fell to his responsibility and to the clerks of his *yamen*;[23] but Yeh certainly enjoyed supreme power in most affairs. When Yeh fell in the *Arrow* War, Po-kuei and his colleagues despatched a joint memorandum to the emperor, accusing Yeh of conducting diplomacy autocratically, without due reference to his colleagues.[24]

Officials of the provincial level

There were four officials of provincial level, the provincial treasurer, the provincial judge, the salt comptroller, and the grain intendant; a fifth, the Hoppo (*Yüeh hai-kuan chien-tu*),[25] was quite independent of the others, at least institutionally.

The main task of the provincial treasurer was to make sure that the magistrates collected and delivered in time the full amount of land tax and miscellaneous taxes according to quotas.[26] When Yeh held this post in 1847, he sent his own agents, in addition to urging the prefects and intendants, to speed deliveries.[27] His promotion to the governorship did not free him from this responsibility. Indeed he was fined three months of salary (a total of 38.75 taels) for having failed to complete the tax quotas of 1848 by less than 10 per cent. Again, he was demoted two grades in his salary (an annual reduction of 37.5 taels) for having failed by 20 per cent to complete the tax quotas of 1852.[28] This duty was beneath the governor-general, but in the interest of sound finance, Yeh made sure that his subordinates did all they could to collect the fullest possible amount of taxes in the turbulent years of the 1850s. He continued to send his own commissioners to put pressure on the magistrates to do their job properly, and required the provincial treasurer to send him a report every ten days.[29] When the rebellions made it impossible to satisfy the time limit, as they did as early as 1852, he asked the emperor to have it extended.[30]

The provincial judge, as the name might suggest, was in charge of the legal administration of the province, although this does not mean that he alone dealt with legal cases, nor that legal duties were his sole responsibility.[31] He could, for example, be called upon to perform military duties. In fact, the Kwangtung provincial judges of the 1850s spent most of their time fighting battles. Ch'i Su-tsao fought shoulder to shoulder with Yeh in north Kwangtung in 1850 and 1851. Shen Ti-hui was a formidable general who fought the major campaigns for Yeh in the critical years of 1854–6. During this period judicial administration was carried out by a separate body called the Special Court (*yen-chü*), an emergency institution set up by Yeh to cope with the masses of captured rebels streaming into Canton. The provincial judge was of course only the figurehead of this organisation, and Yeh commanded it to submit a report to him every ten days, stating the total number of rebels executed, serving sentences, released, and still under detention.[32] Very often Yeh personally interrogated captives who, he thought, could give information of vital importance,[33] and he claimed that 'no individual was put to death without being previously examined by him'.[34]

The salt comptroller looked after another significant source of revenue, salt, of which Kwangtung was one of the principal producing areas. Here, as elsewhere, the salt administration had experienced many changes in the past, but an imperial edict ruled that it was to be headed by the governor-general,[35] a law still in force during Yeh's years of office. Because of the extreme financial straits of the time, Yeh asked the salt comptroller to write for him a daily balance-sheet of taxes collected and money disbursed.[36] The distance between Ch'ao-chou and

Canton made it difficult to have as frequent reports from the deputy salt intendant but monthly reports describing the weather, the production and sale of salt reached Yeh regularly.[37]

The grain intendant took care of the grain transportation,[38] civilian colonies,[39] and irrigation of the province.[40] More important was the shipment of grain tribute to Tientsin, which was undertaken by merchant vessels. Yeh personally supervised the details[41] of this transaction because it involved Peking, and therefore was a matter of special concern.[42]

The four above-mentioned officials had their respective *yamen*, but were all stationed at Canton; and although they performed their duties separately, Yeh, as we have seen, was deeply involved with each of them and did much more than the usual supervision of a governor-general who wrote a report about them to the emperor at the end of every year.[43] Indeed, he was an administrator and not merely an inspector which his position warranted. More important still, when the scattered revolts from 1849 onwards flared up into a full-scale rebellion in 1854, he incorporated the four officials, for the sake of unity of action, into one body called the Military Supply Bureau (*chün-hsü-chü*) in June 1854, to form a government on an emergency basis, dealing in fact less with civil matters (as there was little or no civilian life) than with planning campaigns, organising militia, arranging provisions and everything connected with the suppression of rebellion.

The fifth official, the Hoppo, was quite independent of the provincial hierarchy. The duties he collected on foreign trade went, unlike that from other taxes, directly to the Ministry of Revenue and the Imperial Household and not through the provincial treasury. Moreover, the correspondence between him and the provincial government took the form of a *tzu* (inter-departmental memorandum) rather than a *pin* (report or petition), although he was much inferior in rank to the governor-general.[44] With the onset of the Taiping Rebellion and its astronomical cost to the central government, however, imperial edicts could no longer specify from what source Kwangtung should give financial support to fight the war; they would simply demand a certain sum from any source. This gave Yeh control over all resources, including those of the Hoppo. From the early 1850s onwards, the Hoppo had to send Yeh a financial report every five days.[45]

Officials of the local level

The highest local officials were the circuit intendants, of whom there were five.[46] As they were entrusted with power over vast sections of the province, the Liang Yüan could take no chances. In 1851 for example, both Hsü and Yeh personally interviewed the newly appointed intendant

Table 4
Salaries and subsidies of officials and officers[a]

	Salaries (taels)	Subsidies (taels)	Subsidies (rice)
A Kwangtung			
Governor-general	180	15,000	nil
Governor	155	13,000	nil
Provincial treasurer	155	8,000	nil
Provincial judge	130	6,000	nil
Salt comptroller	130	6,000	nil
Deputy salt intendant	105	2,000	nil
Grain intendant	105	3,400	nil
Hoppo	—	2,500	nil
A circuit intendant	105	3,000	nil
Tartar general	605	1,500	120 *shih*
A deputy lieutenant-general	511	700	105 *shih*
Commander-in-chief of land forces	605	2,000	nil
Commander-in-chief of marines	605	2,000	nil
A brigadier	511	1,500	nil
B Kwangsi			
Governor	155	10,000	nil
Provincial treasurer	155	6,000	nil
Provincial judge	130	4,920	nil
Salt intendant	105	2,200	nil

[a] Information for this table is drawn from a document (F.O. 682.377), the date of which is believed to be 1865. This date is slightly later than that of Yeh's term of office; the document nevertheless gives some general idea of what the salaries and subsidies were like in Yeh's time.

of Hui-ch'ao-chia circuit, Ts'ao Li-t'ai, when he arrived at Canton from Peking. After Ts'ao took up his post, Hsü and Yeh sent their secret agents to gather information about the new intendant, until they were satisfied with his performance.[47] When Yeh was provincial treasurer, the acting intendant of Chao-lo circuit, Liu Hsün, was impeached for tyranny and corruption. Yeh took advantage of his trip as examiner in 1847 to Ch'ao-chou, where Liu was previously prefect, to investigate the charge. Next spring the same duty caused him to pass through Chao-lo circuit on his way to Kao-chou, so that he was able to gather more information about the intendant. The evidence convinced him of Liu's merit, and he submitted a memorandum to the emperor in his defence.[48] At the end of each year, Yeh wrote a report of the merits and faults of each individual intendant, as he did with senior officials, to serve as a guide-line for promotion or punishment.[49] If an intendant was

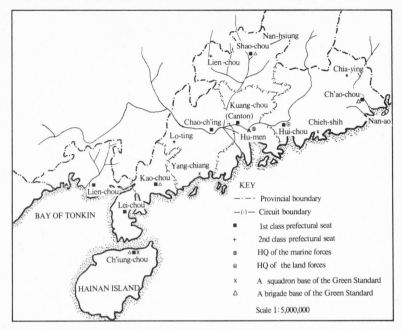

Map 4. The five circuits of Kwangtung (showing the
brigades and squadrons of the Green Standard)

promoted, as in the case of Tsung Yüan-shun in 1851, the imperial edict
to this effect would reach the Liang Yüan first. Hsü and Yeh then
transmitted the message to Tsung, who in turn had to thank the emperor
in writing through the Liang Yüan.[50]

The prefects served as intermediaries between the magistrates and
the intendants. Among them, the prefect of Kuang-chou enjoyed special
prestige and power; since the provincial government was situated in his
prefectural capital, Canton, he was frequently involved in politics at the
provincial level. When Yeh was provincial treasurer, for example, he
asked the prefect of Kuang-chou to prepare him a list of all prefectures
and magistracies that were in arrears in the payment of taxes, and
continued to do so when he was governor.[51]

The magistrates formed the lowest stratum of administration, but Yeh
was by no means out of touch with local administrative problems. In
1856, for instance, piracy along the coast revived on a large scale
because most rebels, defeated on land, took to the sea. Peace and order
could be maintained only by a joint effort of the magistracies along the
coast, each sending an appropriate number of boats to patrol the seas.
Partly owing to the devastating effect of the rebellion, which plunged
most magistracies into abject poverty, the officials concerned could not

come to any agreement as regards joint patrol. In despair, the principal official responsible for fostering such co-operation appealed to Yeh for help, suggesting that Yeh issue a writ ordering the officials to co-ordinate action. Short of such a writ, the principal official said, nothing could be done.[52] Such was Yeh's prestige and power, and his indispensable role in even the lowest stratum of administration.

The military role of the magistrates is revealed by the following incident. In 1850, the provincial treasurer of Anhwei, Chiang Wen-ch'ing, suggested to the emperor that the intendants and prefects of all the provinces follow the example of their counterparts in Taiwan, who were allowed to command troops and fight battles. The emperor enjoined Hsü and Yeh to consider the suggestion, whereupon they replied that in Kwangtung, not only were intendants and prefects allowed to mobilise troops, but the magistrates, as a rule, personally led soldiers into the countryside to capture law-breakers, a fact made necessary by the unusually militant nature of the inhabitants.[53] The magistrates of Kwangtung were so accustomed to military life that they were great assets to Yeh during the rebellion of the 1850s. In contrast to the many incidents of mass flight of officials before the Taipings in the Yangtze area, officials of the Pearl River region rarely deserted their cities, but fought hard to defend or recapture them. This is not to say that a frail scholar would become a capable army commander overnight once he was in Kwangtung. His superiors had to take pains to train him. An example may be found in a report to Yeh by the acting prefect of Ch'ao-chou, Wu Chün, in June 1853. He remarked that the indecision of the magistrate of Hui-lai was encouraging subversion and restlessness, but that since he was young and intelligent, he should be transferred to a less demanding area to gain experience, as other magistrates had been for similar reasons.[54]

Yeh began his career as a prefect, and therefore must have been familiar with the rules regarding the promotion and transfer of prefects and magistrates. Furthermore, he was trained by his superiors in his early career to know his subordinates intimately, and to keep on his desk records of their merits and faults to be studied constantly. It is also clear that Yeh was not an aloof governor-general, but took an active interest in local matters. This makes it less likely that he would have recommended the wrong person for a post. However, there is a document in his archive which listed the number of cases in which he was fined for making recommendations against regulations;[55] but these same officials whom he recommended against regulations, such as Wu Ch'ang-shou and Ch'e Jen-chung, proved outstanding in the suppression of rebels at a later date. Yeh was determined to try to put the right person in the right position, and to disregard the cumbersome bureaucratic rules which might hinder efficient government.

The law decreed that any official who lost his city to rebels was to lose his head too. Peking was eager that this law be strictly enforced, without fully realising what could be involved in a rebellion. Yeh, being on the spot, had a better understanding of the situation. Whenever a city was lost, he used every means of finding out what had actually happened: reports from the principal official responsible, from the various members of the gentry, from his own agents, or from an official he specially commissioned to investigate; and private letters of eye-witnesses addressed to their friends or relatives if Yeh managed to get hold of them.[56] The evidence might be conflicting, but once Yeh was convinced of the innocence of a subordinate, he fought hard to defend him, against pressure from Peking,[57] and he always had his way if his subordinate was able to recapture the city. In this way many of his officials managed to keep their heads and also their posts.[58] The policy he adopted was not only reasonable but necessary. If he had had executed every official who had lost his city, the war effort would have broken down completely, for in times of emergency officials could not be easily replaced. Besides, officials often tried to avoid appointments to disturbed provinces, or if they were none the less appointed, endlessly delayed their date of departure.[59]

On the other hand, the death of an official or officer in action was no simple matter for administration either. As a case study, we may take for example the death of Ma Pin, acting magistrate of Ho-shan. In 1854, his city fell despite the gallant defence he had organised. Ma Pin was captured. Instead of yielding to the demands of the rebels, he continued to upbraid them and was killed for his pains. Yeh learnt of the case and ordered an investigation by the prefect of Kuang-chou,[60] who in turn entrusted the mission to Magistrate Hua T'ing-chieh of Nan-hai. When Yeh received the report from Hua, he transmitted it to the Ministry of Personnel for consideration for rewards. The ministry agreed to propose to the emperor that Ma should be granted a posthumous honour and his son an hereditary title and stipend. The emperor gave his consent, and the order to this effect was transmitted through Yeh and the prefect of Kuang-chou to Hua, who then proceeded to secure from Ma's son a signed declaration to the effect that he was the eldest male offspring of the late magistrate. This declaration Hua also signed as witness. These documents had to go through the same official channels to Peking before the grants were made.[61] Yeh had to work his armies of clerks very hard to cope with the numerous cases of officials and officers killed in the rebellion. At the same time, to preserve morale, he had to take care not to leave deserving candidates unrewarded.

Kwangtung and Kwangsi

The two provinces constituted the viceroyalty of the governor-general, and one would have expected him to treat them both equally. The governor-general might have supposed that he did give them equal consideration,[62] but his subordinates in Kwangsi often believed otherwise. In connection with a certain military reverse involving officials of both provinces, Hsü found that some officials of Kwangsi feared that he might be prejudiced against them and give preferential treatment to their counterparts in Kwangtung.[63] The two provinces were separate, linked to each other only by the artificial superstructure of the viceroyalty; the governor-general had always been stationed in Kwangtung, which was far richer and more important than Kwangsi and consequently occupied more of his time. The additional responsibility imposed on him since 1844 as imperial commissioner for foreign affairs must have left him with even less time for Kwangsi. The distance between the two provincial capitals presented yet another difficulty; when, in March 1852, the emperor asked Hsü as governor-general of Liang Kuang to ascertain the merits of individual officials and officers of the two provinces who jointly put down the revolt led by Ho Ming-k'o, Hsü replied that he would readily comply with the request as regards Kwangtung, but would prefer to leave Kwangsi to Imperial Commissioner Sai-shang-a (who was commissioned to suppress the Taipings) and Governor Chou of Kwangsi.[64]

The division was perhaps even greater when both were absorbed in the suppression of their own local insurrections, as they were under Yeh. The difference between them stood out even more clearly when, eventually, Kwangsi became so impoverished that its authorities proposed to tax Kwangtung salt. The fury that this suggestion provoked among officials of Kwangtung showed that they regarded Kwangsi as a separate and unfriendly province like any other.[65]

The two provinces were indeed distinct, not to say alien, and Yeh's main concern was Kwangtung; furthermore, he never visited Kwangsi. It is true that he was required by law to write an annual confidential report to the throne about each official of the two provinces down to those of the prefectorial level; with this injunction he fully complied. However, he was chiefly responsible for commenting on officials at provincial level, from whom he obtained information about officials beneath them,[66] and it is inconceivable that Yeh could have known the prefects of Kwangsi intimately since he had never been there. Not surprisingly, when the rebellion in Kwangtung was subsiding, and Yeh sent his troops up the West River into Kwangsi to help suppress the uprisings there, these forces were regarded as purely alien (see chap. 6). Certainly it is nearer the truth to describe Yeh as administrator of Kwangtung rather than of Liang Kuang.

Yeh's relationship with Peking[67]

Family connections at Peking, and better still, with the emperor, were essential for any administrator, especially for one residing at Canton, which was very distant from the capital. Officials of the central government were often out of touch with local conditions and issued to the provinces orders of dubious relevance to the situation. The difficulties created by such orders had to be carefully smoothed over in order to avoid giving offence. To do this required high political skill and powerful connections at Peking. Both of these Yeh possessed. In 1852, for instance, when a massive campaign for donations from the rich to finance the militia was being successfully organised by Yeh at Canton, an unexpected order from the Ministry of Revenue placed so many obstacles in its way that the campaign was brought to a standstill. Instead of complaining to the emperor or writing to Ch'i Chün-tsao, a powerful figure in the Grand Council, Yeh asked Wang Han-ch'iao, who was a former student of Ch'i and who was directly involved in the campaign, to write to Ch'i analysing at great length the difficulties caused by the order. Naturally Ch'i referred to Yeh for the details; Yeh then took advantage of the opportunity thus created to convince Ch'i of the necessity for the order to be withdrawn. In fact Ch'i was a former colleague of Yeh's father, and Yeh referred to himself as Ch'i's nephew when he wrote to Ch'i. He could well have written to Ch'i directly about the order in question; the fact that he did not indicates a certain political shrewdness and subtlety.[68]

Education and examinations

On the whole little attention has been devoted to the role of the Liang Yüan in education, and the administration of public examinations within the province. Indeed, it may seem at first sight somewhat irrelevant to discuss this in detail. There was after all a director of education (*hsüeh-cheng*) whose specific responsibility was to look after such matters; and the Liang Yüan had apparently more important affairs to attend to, especially in times of crisis. However, Yeh was very active in the field of education and public examinations, which indicates that he attached great importance to these subjects; and the history of his administration at Canton suggests that in so doing he showed political insight of a high order. He could not have survived the insurrections without the loyal support of the gentry (see chap. 5 and 6). A Chinese became a member of the gentry, not by birth as in Europe, but by passing the lowest public examination (*t'ung-shih*) or so-called entrance examination. The institutions that prepared the candidates for this high public examination were the schools and academies. By maintaining his patronage of these institutions in difficult times, and by upholding justice in the public examinations, Yeh not only ensured that the supply of graduates did not cease,[69] but secured their unswerving loyalty. Hence, far from educational matters being irrelevant, it is hardly an exaggeration to say that they were, in importance, second to none.

Education

There were two kinds of educational institutions in a province in the Ch'ing period, the schools (*hsüeh-hsiao*) and the academies (*shu-yüan*). The schools had their origins in ancient times; they provided supervision and conducted internal examinations, but did not give instructions. Hence academies with the actual responsibility of teaching were founded as private institutions in the Sung and Ming periods to supplement the schools.[70] As foreign trade brought in large quantities of capital, academies in Kwangtung began to multiply. During the Ch'ing period, however, the state took control of these academies. With government patronage, they continued to prosper. Up to 1847 as many as 298 academies were either established or rebuilt; during Yeh's years of office, the number was increased by thirty.[71]

The academies may be divided into two kinds, those giving lectures only, and those performing the additional function of forming villages into associations for police purposes and the 'promotion of amity' (*hsiang-yüeh*).[72] The former 'produce scholars whose influence brings harmony and refinement to the lives of the people, and who form the basis of a prosperous state'.[73] Thus they served as a useful agency of propaganda, and their students as stout defenders of the existing regime. As a wise administrator, when the country was in turmoil, Yeh ensured that the academies were little affected, by taking pains to see that urgent military expenditure did not jeopardise education. He made sure that the budget of the academies was not cut and that the teaching staff were paid their full salaries. It was the practice in Ch'ing times to assign certain sources of income to meet certain expenditures. The academies were one of many organisations (including, to some extent, the army and the navy) financed partly from the interest derived from sums of money deposited with the money lenders. The yield from this source dwindled during the rebellion and all the organisations dependent on it for their income were affected; but Yeh, determined that education should not suffer more than was inevitable, refused to re-direct its revenue to meet military expenses,[74] as he considered education just as important as, if not more than, feeding the soldiers. When the prefectural city of Nan-hsiung was in danger of falling to the rebels in 1854, for instance, the local officials and gentry agreed that they should appropriate a large part of the annual income of the prefectural academy, some six hundred taels, for the defence of the city, but this emergency measure was not repeated, since they knew very well the policy of their governor-general.[75]

With sufficient money, Yeh was in a position to choose his lecturers, who had to be his fervent supporters. Even in 1857, the last and perhaps the most difficult year of his rule in Kwangtung, he had a report made to him about the employment of lecturers in the principal academies of the province and a list made of those who had not sent in their quarterly reports.[76] Most of the students received maintenance grants, which constituted the largest item of expenditure in the academies. This again enabled Yeh to decide what kind of students he wanted, to carry out the edict of 1745, part of which read: 'Let all governors-general and governors co-operate with the directors of education to examine carefully the students, who should be of good conduct as well as learned.'[77] Yeh had a good opportunity to do so once every year, during the entrance examination of the acadmies. Those who were already students had to take the same test if they wished to continue, and failing this meant leaving the academy they had been attending. The examination procedure and the inaugural ceremony of each academic year involved the governor-general in elaborate details of supervision and etiquette,[78] but Yeh none the less seemed to have attended these regularly and appeared to have achieved much more than just keeping watch over the students. When the British shelled his *yamen* on 28 December 1857, he sought refuge in Canton at the Yüeh-hua Academy.[79] He might not have done so had he not known the surroundings of the academy well, or been on friendly terms with the staff and students. Such knowledge and friendship could only have been achieved through regular patronage of the academy and attendance at its ceremonies. In this Yeh was unusual. After more than two hundred years of peace and stability, officials had become accustomed to devote themselves either to pleasure or to securing promotion by currying favour with their superiors; they had little time for attending tedious academic ceremonies, which did not further their ambitions. Yeh, however, probably realised that the performance of formal duties was important in pleasing public opinion (that is, the opinion of the gentry), particularly in time of crisis. The time, money and energy that he expended on the academies ultimately paid dividends, when the students and gentry sold land and property and sometimes sacrificed their lives to help him suppress the rebellion.

The second kind of academies, *hsiang-yüeh*, were better known as *she-hsüeh*. They combined education with administration, and the political character of this kind of academy was more pronounced and direct than the first. They formed effective self-governing bodies in the lowest stratum of the political organisation, helping to resolve disputes and instil a sense of social responsibility.[80] In 1854, when full-scale rebellion caused all institutions to be put on a military footing, thousands of *she-hsüeh* were set up through the province at the instigation of Yeh. They by no means deserved the name of academy, for they only served to organise the villages into local militia units for self-defence; lectures were out of the question. What happened in the shrievalty[81] of Mu-te-li, in the magistracy of P'an-yü, may serve as an example. To this place Yeh sent a commissioner to organise, with the help of the local gentry, the 360 villages of the area into 17 *she*, with the function of raising militia and collecting money to finance it.[82]

The schools were similar to the academies in function and curriculum – they prepared candidates for the civil service examinations – but as mentioned, they provided supervision but not instruction; if their pupils wanted to join the lectures given in an academy, they had to pass its entrance examination and become its members. The schools required their students to hold the diploma of the first public examination (*t'ung-shih*) which conferred the official title *sheng-yüan* (government student). Their teachers were civil servants, holding official rank. In short, the schools were a government department, under the Ministry of Rites; as such, the provincial schools came under the control of the governor-general. Some, like Yeh, took a serious interest in them, keeping a record of the careers of both teachers and pupils, and decided (in collaboration with the director of education of the province) on the promotion of teachers on a three-year basis. Reports on the students were submitted to him four times a year, in order that he might check on each individual, or help them if they were in difficulty, and issue certificates if they died.[83] The total number of government students in Kwangtung in the middle of the nineteenth century was estimated to be 39,116;[84] if the schools had by Yeh's time produced far more graduates than there were posts, it certainly could become a great problem for the government as the number of unemployed gentry, and hence their frustration, continued to climb. It was to Yeh's credit that he was able to harness their excess energy to serve his cause by appointing them as commissioners or leaders of militia. Instead of violently protesting about their unemployment, they flocked to Yeh's office asking for extra work, unpaid or paid very little, so that they had an opportunity to prove their value in the hope that an official appointment might eventually be forthcoming.

The examinations[85]

A public examination was considered one of the most important aspects of administration, because it was the channel through which the government recruited its officials. It was imperative that it should not be conducted haphazardly. Thus in 1854, when several Fukien magisterial

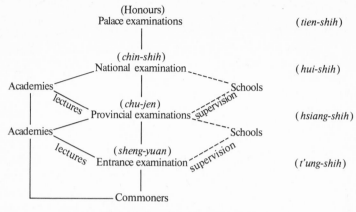

Fig. 2. The relationship between the schools,
academies and public examinations

Note: This figure is adapted from the one given by Liu Po-chi, *Kuang-tung
shu-yüan chih-tu,* p. 435. When the government was in financial difficulties, the
degrees were sometimes sold to rich people, in which case the term *chuan-shu*
('by donation') was prefixed to the name of the degree.

capitals bordering on Kwangtung were besieged by rebels, and appeals
for help were sent to Prefect Wu Chün of Ch'ao-chou. Wu, fully
appreciating the serious consequence of his decision, turned down the
request, on the ground that he had to pay full attention to the prefectural
examination then in progress.[86] Similarly, in 1856, while the acting
prefect of Hui-chou, Hai T'ing-ch'en, was busy fighting the rebels in the
Lung-ch'uan and Ho-p'ing areas, the time for the prefectural examination had come. Had he been able to stay longer, his victory would have
been decisive; yet he had no choice but to report to Yeh on the state of
affairs and then withdraw to the prefectural capital to preside over the
examination. Inevitably, the situation rapidly deteriorated after his
retreat, but he continued to ignore the urgent appeals for help.[87]
Eventually Yeh had to decide whether it was wise to proceed with
provincial examinations due to be held in 1855 at the expense of the war
effort. Canton had just recovered from the dangerous siege of 1854,
while the rest of the province was still torn by the rebellion. Candidates
would possibly not have survived the journey to Canton. Taking all
these reasons into consideration, Yeh finally asked permission of the
emperor to postpone the examinations to the following year.[88]

Officials at provincial level were often sent to preside, jointly with the
prefects, over the prefectural examinations. In 1847, when Yeh was
provincial treasurer, he went for this purpose to Ch'ao-chou in the
extreme east of Kwangtung, and early next year he went on the same

mission to Kao-chou and Lien-chou in the extreme west of the province.[89] In 1849, as governor of Kwangtung, he presided over the provincial examination, while in the first year of Emperor Hsien-feng's reign (1851), there was an extra provincial examination, over which he again presided.[90] Although institutionally the governor was responsible for the provincial examinations, the promotion of Yeh to the governor-generalship did not put him out of touch with such matters. During the examinations of 1856 (postponed from 1855), Yeh had a prominent share in their administration and supervision from behind the scenes, personally criticising the papers set and supervising their printing, and following closely the daily procedure of the examination.[91] However, it was in his capacity as governor that he remedied most of the irregularities of the provincial examination in Kwangtung.

The year 1849 saw the new governor's policy at work: in the course of the provincial examination, his agents were scattered throughout the city of Canton, collecting information about malpractices. On the basis of this information a list was compiled of candidates suspected of bribery, of exercising illicit influence, of hiring others to sit the examination for them, of competing under a false name and the like. His subsequent measures wrought such havoc among the offenders that even the most daring smugglers of question papers decided to lie low, and the 'professionals' who used to sit the examination for others declined offers of whatever value. 'Poverty-stricken candidates', reported an intelligence agent, 'are profoundly grateful for the curbing of corruption.'[92] This, perhaps, helps to explain the overwhelming support for Yeh from the scholar-gentry class in his efforts against the rebellion.

Yeh's remedial measures were not limited to matters outside the examination hall (kung-yüan),[93] but extended inside the building as well. After careful investigation, several proposals were made to him. Usually question papers were distributed very early in the morning, the candidates having been admitted into the hall in the previous evening. The darkness offered an excellent cover for smuggling the papers out of the hall. It was proposed that a hundred or so papers should be posted in the various apartments of the hall, in order that the candidates could read them first, and the rest distributed the next morning.

Cribs for the illicit use of candidates were often smuggled into the hall by servants who brought in meals from the kitchen, and between the two divisions of the hall by porters who brought water from the wells. It was proposed that the servants should be searched before they were allowed to fetch the meals and the number of water tanks doubled so that there might be no need to carry in water during the examination. It was hoped that in this way candidates would be more effectively incommunicado. If cribs none the less found their way into the hall, the answer would be a transfer of guards: before, there had been cases of suicide because, owing to a change of guards, the cribs had gone astray; if all guards were immediately transferred after the hall was closed, this would help to prevent cribs reaching their destinations. The walls around the hall were double, leaving some space between. Tunnels were often dug linking this narrow space with the neighbouring houses, thus offering, with the help of the guards, yet another means of communication between the candidates and their collaborators outside; therefore, watch over these walls should be intensified. Finally, the invigilators should be confined to the hall the day before and during the examination, and the number of servants cut to the bare minimum. In this way, it was hoped that illicit traffic between the hall and the outside world would be effectively severed.

Candidates were searched before they entered the hall. However, guards were often bribed either to smuggle in printed model answers beforehand or to carry out the search perfunctorily. Moreover, workmen who repaired the hall were also bribed to smuggle in similar booklets. As these models gave the same answers, the examination authorities did not need to trouble about them.[94]

His investigation of the cases of malpractice and the detailed proposals for preventing either the question papers leaking out of the hall or the cribs filtering in, showed that Yeh treated his duties very seriously. By making the provincial examination a fair competition, he hoped to win the good will of the gentry. Throughout his tenure of office, he was eager to see to it that examinations in Kwangtung were properly conducted, that they were just, and that their budgets were not jeopardised because of some urgent military need.[95]

The role of the gentry[96] in Yeh's government

The gentry constituted only a minute portion of the population of Kwangtung (38,638 in 21,000,000[97]), but they were the traditional leaders in their clans and in clan feuds. As mentioned, the gentry in Kwangtung were different from the gentry in other parts of China: they were the leaders of violent feuds and hence of disorder rather than keepers of the peace. Such feuds were so commonplace in Kwangtung that in 1823 the Ministry of Justice had to make an exception in the law for this province, ordering that in the case of conflicts involving the loss of lives, a distinction should be made between crimes committed by individuals and large-scale fighting between clans.[98] Yeh's task in the 1850s was to decide, not whether any violence was personal or communal, but whether it was communal or rebellious. It is evidence of his political shrewdness that he was able to make such a distinction. For he had no previous intimate knowledge of the peculiar temperament of the people of Kwangtung, having been born and brought up in Peking. Had he treated outbreaks of communal violence as directed against his authority, he might well have forced the warring clans to actual rebellion. As it was, he was able to distinguish, in the very confused and violent rebellions of the 1850s, between sedition and, for example, the Hakka–Punti warfare. The scale of devastation was the same, perhaps even worse in the latter case because the attacks aimed at the wholesale extinction of villagers, so that the victors could take possession of their property and land. If he had blindly sided with the Punti, as the Kwangsi authorities had done, it is possible that the Hakka would have taken refuge in the secret societies *en masse*, swelling the ranks of the rebels. However, Yeh attended first to those who raised their banners against the government. Until 1856, when he had the rebellions under control, he did not devote much of his attention to the violence of a non-political nature which was prevalent along the West River. When he did, he first ordered an investigation in the causes of the conflict, the villages and clans involved, the number of battles and warriors, the casualties, the number of villages burnt down or destroyed, and above all, whether the fighting was of a temporary or a permanent nature. Then he sent his formidable general, Provincial Judge Shen Ti-hui, to lead a large army into the area, not intending to fight, but to cow the warring parties into obedience, into settling their disputes and giving up the ring-leaders.[99]

In fact Yeh was able to harness the energies of the gentry (who did not need to be paid) in the service of his administration. As the clouds of rebellion were gathering, he received lists from the gentry of unruly members of their village (clan) who were plotting to rebel. During an uprising, they were instructed to restrain members of their clan from joining the rebels; he also attempted to revive the *pao-chia* system by ordering the gentry to collect registration cards from Canton, register the number of inmates of each household and affix to each house the completed card, so that constant checks on the movement of the inhabitants could be made.[100] They also helped him in one of his important measures to crush the rebel bands. The gentry were instructed to act as guarantors for any peasant of their village who was forced into a rebel group against his will, in order that an official certificate sparing his life (*mien-szu chih-chao*) could be issued to the unhappy victim. In this way many misled peasants were given the opportunity to become law-abiding villagers once more. When an uprising was subsiding and the rebels were slowly returning to their villages, the gentry were again entrusted with the task of making a list of suspects for Yeh, tracking down the ring-leaders, and resettling those unwilling rebels whose lives they had spared.[101] In the case of exceptionally turbulent villages, Yeh would have his own agents to report on the situation. We may take Ssu-ma village in the magistracy of

Tung-kuan as an example. The agent reported on conditions within thirty *li* (about ten miles) of Ssu-ma, listing the nineteen villages in this area, the number of clans (usually one, sometimes two or three) in each village, its population and the agitators. He commented on the gentry and elders (or elders alone if that village had no gentry), in particular upon their degree of authority over their clansmen. Finally, he assessed the distance of each village from the trouble spot.[102]

If a clan were discovered to be harbouring some 'undesirable' members, the authorities, by threatening to unearth their ancestral graves and raze their shrines to the ground if they did not co-operate, compelled them to make some effort to arrest these. This happened in the case of the town of Chiu-chiang, which a native ring-leader by the name of Kuan Chü had made his headquarters for plunder and from which he had just fled because of the recent intensification of government efforts to arrest him. Yeh's attitude was that since the Kuan gentry did nothing to Kuan Chü when he was there, they were guilty of connivance, and the impressive reward they put up afterwards for his arrest was only an attempt to conceal their crime. This did not necessarily represent the real intentions of the Kuan gentry, but it made no difference as far as Yeh was concerned; they might have been powerless against the outlaw, but again this was immaterial. From Yeh's point of view, passive support was not enough. The gentry must be actively and totally committed to him, even to the point of dying for him; and if they were not they must be compelled to change . Hence he ordered the perfect of Kuang-chou, who was commanding a fleet in Kuan Chü's pursuit, to make a list of the names of the Kuan gentry so that he could strip them of their titles and seal up their shrines, and, should they still delay handing over the ring-leader, to arrest them and send them to Canton to be severely punished.[103] In other words, Yeh's principle in his administration at village level was to make the gentry live up to their ancient ideal of setting an example to and taking responsibility for the commoners, which was tantamount to governing the rural populace on behalf of the authorities.

Above village level, Yeh persuaded the gentry to organise their clans into self-financing militia units for policing purposes, to foster 'family feeling within the clan in order that we may live together in peace and happiness; and friendship with our neighbouring clans in order that we may make a concerted effort against the rebels in defence of our homes.'[104] These organisations mushroomed during, and particularly after, the large-scale uprising of 1854–5. In descending order of size the units were the *Huan, chia* and *she*. The smallest units, the *she* (*she-hsüeh*), were, as mentioned, in origin educational institutions but were always less concerned with public lectures than with providing a meeting-place for people from different villages. By the 1850s, they gave practically no public lectures but devoted all their time to keeping the peace. As a result, newly created institutions of this type could rather be called *chü* (*kung-chü*), which meant a local council, in no way connected with education. This is evident from numerous documents in the Canton Archive, in which both the *she* and *chü* referred to the same kind of organisation. Thus, although they sprang from different roots, both *she* and *chü* came to perform the same function in an age of turmoil, namely, recruiting men and raising money to help the government in the war effort. They also policed their localities, interrogated travellers and arrested defeated rebels who returned to their villages, and brought them to justice. More importantly, they acted on Yeh's instructions to pacify and resettle the wandering population who had been either press-ganged into the rebel camps or made homeless by them.[105] Thus they performed the vital function of ruling the rural areas on behalf of the authorities, who were fully occupied with the rebels.

Such a policy was, however, not without its side-effects. The gentry had so much power entrusted to them in the field of local administration that the already difficult problems of localism became almost impossible for later governments to contain; but that was for Yeh's successors to face, although even in his time he had to deal with gentry who wielded their powers illegally. This was a delicate task because the gentry, having been entrusted with the mission of organising a militia and financing it, could easily turn their forces against the government, as happened for instance in the magistracy of Hsiu-jen in Kwangsi.[106]

Whenever Yeh heard of any misconduct on the part of a member of the gentry, he first sent a secret agent to investigate the matter. If there was evidence of any crime, he instructed his agent to flatter the offender and to recommend him to wait upon Yeh at Canton to be rewarded for his supposed merits. Once that particular petty warlord was lured out of his power base, Yeh could make him an example of what would happen to a member of the gentry who misbehaved. In 1855, for example, a new prefect, Chang Ch'ung-k'o, was appointed to serve in Lien-chou, in the extreme north of Kwangtung. Before his departure from Canton, he waited upon Yeh to receive instructions. During the interview he gave Yeh a report on the grave misconduct of the two sons of Major Ch'e, who was responsible for the defence of that area. Yeh enjoined him to do what he thought was appropriate, or to try to send the Ch'e brothers to see him at Canton. On Chang's arrival at Lien-chou there began an intensive investigation. The results showed that the Ch'e brothers, after the fall of the prefectural capital to the rebels on 22 September 1854, gathered under the name of militia gangs of unemployed vagrants from the circuit of Hui-ch'ao-chia and indulged in reckless plundering and kidnapping of people for ransom and blackmail. After the recovery of the city on 2 April 1855, their crimes increased in both scale and gravity, being committed under the cloak of immunity by their claim that they had helped to pursue the fleeing rebels. Chang eventually made a list of their collaborators and lured them and the Ch'e brothers to Canton, where, presumably, they tasted the justice of a harsh governor-general.[107]

Unfortunately, although Yeh could punish the gentry and utilise them effectively in furthering his own policy, he could not prevent them from enforcing their traditional rights, the exercise of which inevitably involved the exploitation of the peasantry. What happened at the magistracy of Po-lo may serve as a good example. In the summer of 1854, numerous uprisings induced Magistrate Hsieh Yü-han to order the inhabitants of the magisterial city and the neighbouring nine villages to organise themselves into militia units for self-defence. The gentry in the city also organised a local council for the same purpose, helping to organise the militia and run it. As a result, the rebel group that threatened the city was beaten off. However, the financing of the militia constituted a great strain on the resources of the nine villages; in addition, the year's crop was a bad one. Consequently, the villagers requested their landlords (who lived in the city), of whom the Han clan was the wealthiest and most influential, to accept for the time being 60 per cent of the rent for that year. The Han clan, headed by a *kung-sheng* by the name of Han Shih-wen, refused, and demanded that Hsieh should help them force the villagers to pay the full amount. Hsieh was of course aware of the difficulties of the peasants and advised Han Shih-wen to accept the offer, promising to make the villagers pay the rest after the rebellion was suppressed. Far from satisfied, Han first came to an understanding with the rest of the landowners and then executed in the name of the local council of the city the leader of the tenants who resisted Han's demands, on the pretext that he was keeping back the 40 per cent to support the rebels. Thus, when the magisterial city was again beseiged by the rebels at the end of the year, the nine villages refused to send any reinforcements, and the city fell. After it was recovered on 11 February 1855, the only resource at the disposal of the government was the grain stored for emergency relief purposes. Out of this had to be paid the expenses of repairing the city wall and feeding the refugees. The Han clan, who had long cast a covetous eye on the grain, demanded that it should come under the control of the gentry for paying the mercenaries hired by the local council. When their demand was refused, they signed a petition and sent it to Canton accusing Hsieh of embezzlement. They also asked a member of their clan, who was a censor at Peking, to impeach Hsieh for the same crime.

Yeh ordered an investigation and, having satisfied himself that Hsieh was an innocent victim of the avarice of the Han gentry, he successfully defended his subordinate. As regards the rent dispute of 1854, a compromise was reached whereby the tenants paid 70 per cent for the time being; but in 1855, the Han clan again threatened to arrest any tenant as a rebel if he failed to pay full rent for that year in addition to paying the 30 per cent arrears of the previous year. It is not clear how this dispute was finally settled; perhaps another compromise was reached since it was certainly beyond the ability of the heavily exploited tenants to meet the demands of their landlords.[108]

The relationship between the gentry and the people thus remained one basically of exploitation and constant conflict. Even in a time of such unrest, the privileged position of the gentry was not seriously jeopardised because of the new powers entrusted in them by a vigorous governor-general for the sake of peace and order.

4 The administrator II: the non-scholar-gentry class

Social welfare

As mentioned in chap. 2, Kwangtung is very vulnerable to floods because of the peculiar timing of the rainy season and the geography of the province. Worse still, typhoons occur every summer and flooding is very common. As a result crops were very often destroyed. Preventive measures such as the building and maintenance of dykes along the rivers were therefore vital for the well-being of the local population. The gentry traditionally took care of this task, but in the early Ch'ing period, the government assumed this responsibility. Apparently the Manchus as conquerors did not wish to see any kind of voluntary action on the part of the gentry, particularly if it was organised. Their putting the private academies under state control seems to be a result of the same suspicion. Consequently the gentry no longer concerned themselves with the problem of maintaining the dykes but relied entirely on the government to do so. Inevitably the condition of the dykes deteriorated with the decline of the empire. It is ironic that in 1743 the emperor complained that without the co-operation of the gentry, the officials were unable to maintain the dykes properly, and flooding was becoming worse and worse every year.[1]

When Yeh became governor of Kwangtung, he travelled widely throughout the province and realised that the dykes needed immediate attention. In 1851, his request for permission to repair the dykes of the most vulnerable area, Nan-hai, in the delta, was granted by the emperor.[2] With a considerable sum donated by Howqua, a member of the merchant-gentry, Yeh embarked on the project without delay. It was completed just in time to avert disaster as a result of an unusually violent thunderstorm in the following year, but the rest of the province was caught unprepared.[3] Consequently, 'the rice crop near Canton', observed a Chinese merchant, 'will not suffer much from the rains but up the country it has been severely injured and many lives have been lost.'[4] Worse was yet to come. The summer of 1853 witnessed such ruinous flooding that numerous villagers were made homeless and crops destroyed. Yeh launched a massive campaign for contributions from the official hierarchy, and set the example by donating 3,000 taels from his own income.

Table 5 shows how the money from contributions was spent. The sum assigned to repairing dykes was almost three times as much as that used for immediate relief. Indeed Yeh paid great attention to maintaining the

Table 5
Donations by officials for relief, 1853[a]

Income

Donors	Amount (taels)
Governor-general Yeh	3,000
Governor Po-kuei	1,000
Hoppo Tseng	3,000
Acting provincial treasurer Ts'ui	3,000
Acting provincial judge grain intendant Wang	3,000
Salt intendant Chao	3,000
Prefect of Kuang-chou Chang	3,000
Acting magistrate of Nan-hai Feng	1,000
Magistrate of Nan-hai Hu (sum not yet delivered)	2,000
Magistrate of P'an-yü Li (sum not yet delivered)	1,000
Gross total	23,000
Actual total	20,000

Expenditure

Magistracies	Relief (taels)	Magistracies	Repair of dykes (taels)
Nan-hai	1,500	Kao-ming	700
San-shui	2,000	San-shui	10,000
Ch'ing-yüan	500	Kao-yao	1,000
Ta-pu	280	Ssu-hui	
Yao-p'ing	210	Hai-yang	2,300
Feng-shun	210	Ch'eng-hai	
Total			18,700
Remainder			1,300

[a] This table is drawn according to the information given in 253A.3.110. The 1,000 taels expended on repairing dykes in Kao-yao and Ssu-hui was originally meant for relief. However, the magistrates and the *wei-yüan* (who conveyed the money there) reported later that no relief was necessary and the sum was subsequently allocated to the repair of the dykes of the two magistracies.

dykes, appointing commissioners to measure the amount of damage inflicted on them by the floods, and distributing the appropriate amount of money for repairs. The gentry were also called upon to help.[5]

It is highly arguable whether Yeh made the right decision in giving a higher priority to the repair of dykes than to the feeding of starving refugees. However, he took a long-term view of the matter. In his estimate it was more important to try and ensure good harvests in the following years by repairing the dykes; otherwise there was a danger that expenditure on relief might become a permanent feature. Indeed Hsü and Yeh showed great concern about the weather, lest it should jeopardise agricultural production. In one of his letters to Yeh, Hsü wrote, 'There was a rainstorm yesterday, bringing the rain necessary for a good harvest.'[6] They also composed a song, which was printed and meant for the edification of the peasants, describing the happiness and joy a good harvest brought, and exhorting everybody to work hard to attain a rich and peaceful life.[7] There was also a system by which old peasants were rewarded with buttons signifying official ranks.[8] These were long-term measures encouraging agriculture and, like the repairing of dykes, were calculated to ensure good harvests rendering social relief unnecessary. Unfortunately, few starving peasants could see much beyond the immediate future. As early as 1852, the magistrate of Ch'ing-yüan, Ch'eng Chao-kuei, expressed his secret fear that the prevalent starvation might result in a revolt.[9]

Another source, besides contributions, from which Yeh could have drawn relief was the government grain stores (ch'ang-p'ing ts'ang) in the various magistracies. A general survey of these stores made before the rebellion showed that most of them were in fairly good condition, and the total amount of grain actually in store was 2,135,165 shih out of a provincial quota of 2,964,538 shih.[10] If Tseng-ch'eng may be taken as an example of what happened in a magistracy in general,[11] one cannot but come to the conclusion that very little grain was taken out of the stores to help the starving. Yeh might have been misled by some of his subordinates into thinking that the disaster was not as serious as it really was.[12] He might not have been completely free to dispose of this grain because at least in peace-time Peking had a say in such matters;[13] possibly Peking or Yeh himself decided that since there was an acute shortage of government funds (see chap. 5), it was safer to keep the grain where it was as a provision against further emergencies.[14] Whatever the reasons, it was undoubtedly a grave miscalculation from both the political and humanitarian points of view not to have released the grain for relief. Consequently, Magistrate Ch'eng's fear proved well-founded, and the sporadic revolts which had broken out since 1849 culminated in full-scale rebellion in 1854.

This is not to say that there was no social welfare of any kind:

> Under Yeh,[15] right well
> Orphans, old, lame, ill,
> Widowed, single still
> All are helped, we see;
> Simple folk, should we
> Think it rain and dew
> Giving life anew,
> Nor should we rebel.[16]

This is an extract from a piece of work by a member of the gentry, meant for the edification of the masses. Social welfare of a kind did exist under Yeh. One or two examples may illustrate this. In one of the reports by the salt treasury, the money expended daily by the infants' home of P'an-yü was given as 1.6 taels; meanwhile, 51,430 taels, possibly an annual sum, were donated by the Kwangtung Customs Office (Yüeh hai-kuan) to a charity organisation called P'u-chi T'ang, and 1,943.135 taels to meet the expenses of a certain infants' home. The total expenditure (time unspecified) of two similar organisations at Chao-ch'ing was quoted as 400 taels, and there was also a home for the aged at Nan-hsiung. The provincial treasury too, had a fixed amount allotted to help the 'single and abjectly poor' in the magistracies of Nan-hai and P'an-yü every season.[17]

The judiciary

In an age of turmoil Yeh found it necessary to reform the judicial system and simplify its proceedings. On 25 June 1854, he established a special court to deal with the large number of captured rebels pouring into Canton. He personally supervised its functions, and required it to send him different kinds of periodic reports about the number of captives who had arrived, their names and origins (sometimes with a précis of their history), a description of the court hearing, the number of captives who died before trial, those executed, and those still in custody.[18] As time went on, these reports began to take two standard forms. The first was a report to him every ten days,[19] listing the number of captives dealt with in this period, the number of executions, sentences, releases and of those waiting for re-trial. The second was an overall report, also made every ten days and classified in the same way, but always dating from 3 September 1854.[20] The reason why the overall reports should date from 3 September, rather than the day on which the special court was instituted, is not clear; possibly the first forty days or so of the existence of the court represented the formative period, before the procedure and the form of the reports were eventually standardised.

Table 6 derives its information from one of the overall reports which dated from as late as 9 November 1855. It will be seen in this table that between the latter part of the fifth and the beginning of the seventh month of HF5, there was a sudden drop in the number of captives dealt with. This does not mean that their number decreased; on the contrary, it swelled beyond all expectations and the court was so congested that during this period of 64 days, a temporary branch had to be established in the *yamen* of the prefect of Kuang-chou (Table 7).

One would expect that to staff and finance a busy institution such as the special court would have put a heavy strain on the manpower and

Table 6
Proceedings of the special court[a]

HF	Mth	*Hsün*	Prose-cutions	Execu-tions	Re-leases	Deaths due to illness	In custody for Sentences	Re-trial
4	Inter.	2nd	109	39	53	16	—	1
		3rd	164	76	56	28	1	3
	8th	1st	149	92	34	18	2	3
		2nd	129	78	37	13	—	1
		3rd	142	92	25	19	1	5
	9th	1st	148	78	52	15	1	1
		2nd	139	105	15	19	—	—
		3rd	112	71	30	7	—	4
	10th	1st	254	95	27	28	3	1
		2nd	137	108	10	12	3	4
		3rd	134	82	32	15	—	5
	11th	1st	261	111	118	31	1	—
		2nd	220	107	76	34	—	3
		3rd	194	127	28	33	4	2
	12th	1st	401	190	113	88	3	6
		2nd	408	280	54	66	5	2
		3rd	468	332	48	78	8	2
5	1st	1st	442	345	40	51	3	3
		2nd	636	516	62	52	0	6
		3rd	1,361	1,207	26	110	11	7
	2nd	1st	1,280	1,188	12	64	11	5
		2nd	618	556	12	43	1	6
		3rd	690	589	5	73	16	6
	3rd	1st	498	442	9	38	2	7
		2nd	512	445	14	44	3	4
		3rd	705	630	14	50	1	10
	4th	1st	1,379	1,284	15	64	5	10
		2nd	1,856	1,684	5	148	9	10
		3rd	904	830	3	56	15	—
5	5th	1st	1,056	1,009	1	40	5	1
		2nd	1,225	1,158	4	48	7	8
		3rd	943	890	3	38	3	9
	6th	1st	908	733	20	130	15	10
		2nd	768	702	6	42	7	11
		3rd	999	935	4	38	19	3
	7th	1st	1,658	1,579	4	54	19	2
		2nd	1,612	1,490	3	70	37	12
		3rd	963	909	1	40	6	7
	8th	1st	1,393	1,319	9	37	24	4
		2nd	754	703	3	34	11	3
		3rd	880	795	6	37	32	10
	9th	1st	772	688	—	32	32	20
		2nd	690	583	2	35	54	14
		3rd	426	359	—	25	31	11

[a] This table is adapted from 289.3A.3. Proceedings of Special Court (1855).

Table 7
Proceedings of the special court (Kuang-chou-fu branch)

HF	Mth	*Hsün*	Prose-cutions	Execu-tions	Re-leases	Deaths due to illness	In custody for	
							Sentences	Re-trial
5	4th	2nd	779	717	3	32	23	3
		3rd	793	712	3	40	30	6
	5th	1st	926	856	1	37	27	4
		2nd	948	880	2	39	19	3
		3rd	748	692	3	25	22	4
	6th	1st	820	775	1	18	24	1
		2nd	586	545	1	21	19	—

Tables 6 and 7
Proceedings of the special court

HF	Mth	*Hsün*	Prose-cutions	Execu-tions	Re-leases	Deaths due to illness	In custody for	
							Sentences	Re-trial
Grand total:			35,097	30,808	1,105	2,225	575	263
Total no. in custody								838

Note: HF means the year of reign of Emperor Hsien-feng, Mth = month in the Chinese calendar; and inter. = intercalary month; *hsün* = the three ten-day periods into which each month was divided.

resources of any government. However, it was again Yeh's policy of employing the cheap labour offered by the careerist gentry that carried the day. In a list of members of staff of the special court recommended for rewards, all were, strictly speaking, members of the gentry on the waiting list for offices; and the recommended rewards consisted of either honours and titles, or promotion to the waiting list for higher posts. Even the head of the special court, who was reputed to have tried more than 25,000 cases, was only promoted from the waiting list for a second-class prefectship to that for a first-class prefectship.[21] One large item of expenditure of the special court would have been that on food for the captives, and Yeh avoided this by making the magistracies from which the defendants originated meet their expenses.[22]

The total number of executions ordered by the special court was 33,200 by 13 May 1856 (see Fig. 3). This must represent only a small part of the total number of executions throughout the province, since only rebels who were likely to give information of strategic value, or who were captured near Canton, were sent to this court. Shao-chou, for

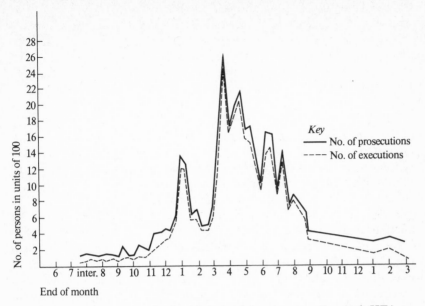

Fig. 3. Prosecutions and executions between the seventh month HF4
and the fourth month HF5

Note: This figure is drawn from 289. 3A.3 Proceedings of Special Court (1855).
HF means the year of the reign of Emperor Hsien-feng. Inter. means
intercalary month.

example, had its own court and sent only important captives to Canton.
Moreover, even this regional court found it difficult to cope with the
volume of captives. To avoid unnecessary deaths caused by the heat of
the summer and overcrowding, many of them were returned to their
magistracies of origin (within Shao-chou) to be tried.[23] As there is no
mention in Yeh's archive of any of the rebels captured in Ch'ao-chou
having been sent to Canton, one may assume that because of the
distance and difficulty of transport, the officials of the Han River region
dealt with their prisoners independently. If prefectures like Shao-chou
sent only important captives to Canton, and Ch'ao-chou sent none at all,
the number of executions at Canton must therefore have constituted a
small proportion of the total. Furthermore, regular magistrates conducted their own courts; in peacetime, cases of capital punishment had
to be referred to Canton, whence they were transmitted to the Ministry
of Justice in Peking. However, this procedure was for practical reasons
abolished in the 1850s, and a local official was empowered to execute
any rebel arrested.[24] A certain magistrate (who cannot be identified)
reported to Yeh that during the first fifteen months of his office, he had
captured 10,744 rebels: of these, he had executed 8,757, sent 631 to

Canton, released 386 and detained, pending trial, 211; 468 had died of natural causes in custody.[25] There were more than eighty magistracies in the province at this time, and although the example just quoted does not necessarily represent what happened in an average magistracy, one wonders how many lost their lives through judicial channels alone in these troubled times.

The policing units (militia units) run by the gentry, the *she-hsüeh* and *kung-chü*, also played an important role in the judiciary of the province during the rebellion. For instance, the T'ung-jen she-hsüeh, which consisted of thirty-two villages, was ordered by Yeh to execute summarily any rebel they captured, and to send the ears of the victims to the Military Supply Bureau at Canton.[26] However, as the rebellion subsided, and the task became one of rounding up defeated rebels rather than suppressing rebellion, these units were instructed to hand over the captives either to Canton or to their local authorities for proper trial.[27]

Most of the executions were carried out in the summer of 1855, when the government regained control of much of the province. The place of execution at Canton was by all accounts horrific: filled with headless corpses and flowing with rivulets of blood; the soil all turned red, and in the air a sickening stench.[28] Indeed similar sights were to be found outside Canton, in all the places of execution of the prefectures and magistracies. Eventually, 'orders have now been issued', wrote a British consular official, 'that all but important criminals shall suffer punishment wherever taken.'[29] Still, the executions were numerous enough to earn Yeh a special title, 'Yeh the Great Executioner'.[30] However, governments were rarely, if ever, lenient towards rebels. It was exactly his efficiency and severity which won Yeh the supreme favour of the Manchu government and his importance as 'The second man of the Empire' (see chap. 5).

It is important to point out that if the gentry testified that a man was a rebel, it was sufficient to cost him his head. Indeed Provincial Judge Shen Ti-hui remarked at the beginning of 1855 that since the establishment of the special court more than 10,000 rebels had been tried and executed, all on the evidence of the testimony given by the gentry and village elders.[31] The punishment of the rebels was extended to their ancestors. Yeh always sent his secret agents to locate the ancestral graves of prominent rebel leaders and then appointed a commissioner to exhume the bodies and burn them. The ancestral graves (up to three generations) of Chou Tou-p'i-ch'un, for instance, were desecrated.[32] Those of Hung Hsiu-ch'üan were not spared either.[33] This affront to the dead was in itself a punishment for the living; there was also a superstition that destruction of the ancestral graves brought misfortune and extinction of the clan.

Against the rebels, the judiciary reigned supreme; but it ran into serious difficulty with the army. It will be seen in the next section that morale in the army was very low indeed. Many of the soldiers were members of secret societies and defected to the rebel camp in 1854 when the government seemed in peril, then reverted (at least on the surface) to the government side when the rebels were losing ground. The execution of these soldier-rebels reflected upon the officers, who were held responsible for the behaviour of their rank and file. What happened at Fo-shan may serve as a good example. On 25 May 1855, three suspects were arrested during a house-to-house check. A first trial was conducted by a *wei-yüan*. The suspects confessed that they were soldiers from a company stationed in the neighbourhood, but at the same time they were members of a secret society and had joined the forces of Ch'en K'ai, who occupied the town the year before. The principal official of Fo-shan, Hsieh Hsiao-chuang, conducted a second hearing and, being convinced of their guilt, sentenced them to death. According to Hsieh, the head of the company, Acting Lieutenant K'ung Chi-an, came to his office the day after the execution and said that the dead soldiers had previously been dismissed. Three days later (29 May 1855), however, he received a note from K'ung saying that the three soldiers had been arrested by mistake and requesting that they should be returned to their base. K'ung referred to his superior for action and this subsequently sparked off conflict between the civil and military hierarchies, which demanded Yeh's attention. Meanwhile, 51 members of the gentry, who were responsible for organising the militia of Fo-shan, jointly signed a petition testifying that the three executed soldiers were truly rebels; they also brought eye-witnesses who gave evidence to the same effect.

Yeh charged the provincial judge and some intendants with the duty of studying the case. After careful deliberation they found the judicial system facing a dilemma. If the civil proceedings, which ruled that the three soldiers should be executed because they had been rebels, were adopted, the military hierarchy would be in serious trouble. The officers directly responsible would have to be executed if they were aware of the fact that their rank and file had joined the rebels but helped to cover it up; if on the other hand, through negligence they were unaware that some of their soldiers had become rebels, they would have to be dismissed, their higher officers not directly involved demoted two ranks and transferred elsewhere, and the commander-in-chief demoted one rank. However, should the accusations of the military hierarchy be accepted as true, Hsieh and the leader of 51 members of the gentry who signed the petition would have to be executed, and the rest exiled. The provincial judge and the intendants could not come to any decision as to how the case should be settled, but hinted that it was a common practice to treat soldiers who had committed crimes as having been previously dismissed in order that the officers might be spared the punishments. As will be apparent in the next chapter, Hsieh was eventually transferred out of Kwangtung to fight in Kwangsi, which shows that Yeh followed the hint and acted accordingly. Certainly it would have been unwise to antagonise the whole of the military hierarchy, nor could he afford to lose the support of the gentry by punishing 51 of their members.[34]

The armed forces

In Yeh's time, the armed forces of China may be divided into four categories: the Eight Banners, the Green Standard,[35] the mercenaries and the militia. This section will analyse his relationship with these four groups.

The Eight Banners

It had been widely assumed that a governor-general had power over the Green Standard, and was not in any way connected with the Banners.[36] In fact this was not the case, at least in the days of Hsü and Yeh at Canton. In 1850 for example, Hsü was appointed imperial commissioner to inspect the armed forces of Kwangtung and Kwangsi, of which he was governor-general. Together with the Tartar general (*chiang-chün*, rank: 1b) of Canton (the sole commander of the Banners, who garrisoned the city) and two brigade-generals (*fu-tu-t'ung*, rank: 2a), Hsü went in person to the parade ground to inspect the Banner forces and subsequently made to the emperor several recommendations for promotion and demotion. He then joined Governor Yeh to inspect the regiments of the Green Standard stationed at Canton. Again he made the appropriate recommendations.[37] Three years later, in 1853, Yeh assumed the same duty and dismissed several officers who were unskilled in either archery or fighting.[38] In 1857, when once more it was the turn of the forces of Kwangtung to be inspected, Yeh, who was again appointed imperial commissioner for this purpose, asked the emperor to postpone this function because most of the troops were mobilised to fight the rebels and hence were not ready for inspection. His request was granted.[39]

Regular inspection of the troops was not the only means whereby Yeh had authority over the Banners. During the Entry Crisis of 1849 he was chiefly responsible for the defence of the city of Canton, obviously with the power to command the Banners in addition to the Green Standard, mercenaries and militia.[40] When Canton was beseiged by the rebels in 1854, he assigned the defence of different gates of the city to the different Banners.[41] Again, when the allied forces attacked Canton during the *Arrow* War, one of the brigade-generals of the Banners, Shuang-ling, addressed his request for reinforcements to both his superior, the Tartar general, and Yeh.[42] Furthermore, the Banners were not as independent of the civil government as is generally supposed; their expenses had to be met by the resources of the latter. Their salaries and wages, their pensions, their ration of rice, the money to buy horses, uniforms and so on, were all paid by the provincial treasury and the salt treasury, over which Yeh had absolute control. In 1855, some of the less important items such as allowances for travel and uniforms were over four years in arrears,[43] because Yeh decided that the money was more urgently needed elsewhere.[44] Another factor which contributed to Yeh's control of the Banners was that these forces were all stationed at Canton, and any misconduct on their part could hardly have escaped the notice of a vigorous governor-general. Finally, the standard of living of the average Banner soldier had declined considerably by the mid-nineteenth century.[45] Groups of idle young Bannermen wander about the city of Canton, provoking trouble wherever they could, became a serious problem for both Yeh and the Tartar general, who were jointly responsible for settling any dispute between the Bannermen and the civilian population. As a result, it was suggested to Yeh that he should take advantage of the urgent demand for soldiers during the siege of Canton in 1854 to recruit the jobless Bannermen into a mercenary force attached to their own Banners to strengthen the defence of the city.[46] However, to have done this would have been to violate the sacred laws laid down by the emperor regarding the status of the Banners. According to these laws the Bannermen were a separate elite and the traditional way in which they functioned could not be altered. The mere fact that Yeh and his advisers dared contemplate such a step says much for their courage, or their predicament.[47]

The Green Standard

There were two divisions of the Green Standard in Kwangtung, the land forces and the marine forces, each under a commander-in-chief (*t'i-tu*), who was in turn under the supreme commander, the governor-general. In addition, the Liang Yüan had their own troops called respectively the governor-general's regiment (*tu-piao*) and the governor's regiment (*fu-piao*). The commander-in-chief of the land forces was stationed at Hui-chou. His troops consisted of four brigades (*chen*), namely, Shao-chou, Ch'ao-chou, Kao-chou and Ch'iung-chou, policing areas corresponding roughly to the five circuits of the province (see Map 4, page 45). Hu-men, on the other hand, was the headquarters of the marine forces, which consisted of four squadrons (also called *chen*), two on each side of Hu-men along the coast. Since the Green Standard was scattered all over the province, it was impossible for Yeh to look into every detail of its administration. However, maps were drawn up for him for each *chen* (brigade or squadron), and the regiments, battalions and companies into which it was subdivided, describing the geographical environment of the place it policed and the number of soldiers it contained.[48] In addition, he probably also had periodic reports sent to him as he did with the civil government. He certainly took action when serious misdemeanours were committed,[49] but otherwise, the routine administration was left to the officers. One exception was, of course, his own regiment, which he inspected every spring and autumn,[50] and whose details of administration he examined down to the smallest unit. There was, for example, a report to him from the sergeant of the squad stationed at the fort at She-t'ou Bay, naming the two corporals (*ping-mu*) and 27 soldiers on duty, the 5 soldiers recently returned from their special duties at Canton and the two privates from their services in other units. In each case the name of the individual soldier, not only that of the officer, was given.[51] It is a matter of speculation whether Yeh actually knew the names of the rank and file in his regiment, or whether names were merely required in reports of this kind.

As in the civil government, general censorial scrutinies (*chün-cheng*) were conducted.[52] The department within Yeh's *yamen* that dealt with this was the east document office (*tung-chüan-fang*), headed by Liu Sheng. When it was time to scrutinise the governor-general's regiment (six battalions) and the governor's regiment (two battalions) for instance, Liu drafted forms for this purpose and presented them to Yeh, who returned them to him when he was satisfied with them. Liu then distributed them to the clerks of the various battalions to fill in the details of the birthplace, age and early career of the officers concerned. The forms, when completed, were sent back to Liu, who again presented them to Yeh to verify the information they contained. Finally, Liu made a fair copy of the forms and bound them into a book, ready for Yeh to put down his comments on each officer.[53]

The censorial system certainly gave Yeh the means to keep the military officers in check, but in times of crisis something more than a routine check was necessary. Indeed, the need then was not so much to supervise the officers as to instil in them the spirit of initiative; this required flexibility and good judgement on the part of the governor-general. Yeh seems to have possessed these qualities. In July 1854, he saw that a serious insurrection was about to erupt, and accordingly asked the emperor to empower him to fill any post that should fall vacant without having to refer to the Ministry of War. The imperial edict granting permission did not reach Canton until 12 April 1855,[54] obviously because the siege of Canton had severed communications with Peking. By this time, however, the rebellion had begun to subside, and Yeh had almost regained control of the province, particularly the area around Canton. Yeh could not have achieved this without having made the vital decision of replacing on his own initiative officers who were either incompetent or killed in action with those of his own choice. For example, the acting first-captain of the regiment at Chao-ch'ing was killed in action in 1855. Immediately Yeh appointed a lieutenant to the post, which meant promoting a man of 6a rank to 4a. He then notified the governor, the Tartar general, the commander-in-chief of the land forces, the provincial treasurer and the Ministry of War of his decision.[55] In this Yeh arrogated to himself the power of the emperor, but of course with the rebellion at its height, there was no time left for conferences and bureaucratic delay. In fact, to be able to make decisions like this on the spur of the moment, Yeh, like any good administrator, must have known intimately, or have kept a very detailed and up-to-date record of, officers even below the rank of 5b, the lowest rank which the censorial system required him to scrutinise.

Few are born with the ability to command an army; most have to acquire it. In the case of Yeh, his interest in military affairs was fostered by his family background and his experience of handling turbulent peoples in his early career. His office at Canton also gave him plenty of opportunities to learn to deal with military officers, both through practical experience and through his friend Hsü, who was much older and more experienced in dealing with people. For instance, Yeh once remarked to Hsü that two *wei-yüan* were not very active in war. Hsü explained that they probably needed incentives from their superiors, and that he had just sent them a note in which reprimand was mixed with soft words. This note Hsü also showed Yeh, adding that Yeh would no doubt see through the tricks in it.[56] Yeh himself was exceptionally gifted in human relationships; and with two years' experience as governor-general he was able to write a letter, in reply to Commander-in-chief Hui-ch'ing of Kwangsi, which clearly testifies to the great skill he had achieved in the management of military officers. Apparently Hui-ch'ing wrote to Yeh expressing despair at the state of affairs in the extremely impoverished province, because the armed forces, whose wages had not been paid for months, were on the point of mutiny, and were certainly not willing to suppress the widespread revolts.[57] Yeh's reply was full of sympathy, concern and reassurance. He pointed out that the only answer to the long-standing arrears of wages was the eventual suppression of the rebellion. 'Grain comes from the land, and the land has to be cultivated by the peasants; if the army fails to restore peace, the peasants would not be able to cultivate the land. Besides, assistance from Kwangtung will definitely be forthcoming once communications between the two provinces are restored.'[58]

The ability to say the right thing at the right time to the right person was one of the important factors which made Yeh a successful administrator, indeed so successful as to inspire awe in his subordinates. In 1854, for instance, there was an armed conflict between the marines at Hu-men and the neighbouring villagers. Commander-in-chief Hung Ming-hsiang was very worried that Yeh might look into the matter and wrote to his contact at Canton enjoining him to 'be as calm and indifferent as if nothing had happened at all, should his lordship inquire about the incident'.[59] Ironically, Yeh's intelligence network was so efficient that even this letter fell into his hands, and after a full-scale investigation,[60] Yeh decided that Hung should retire 'because of his old age'.[61]

In Chinese military terms, a differentiation is made between the ability to command officers (*chiang-chiang chih ts'ai*) and the ability to command soldiers (*chiang-ping chih ts'ai*). We have seen that Yeh no doubt possessed the former. With regard to the administration of the rank and file, he adopted the same policy as in governing the masses; he induced the gentry to rule the peasants and similarly he put pressure on the officers to keep their soldiers in check. Yet this policy, which appeared the only one open to him, was never very successful. Instead of the officers keeping control over the soldiers, the soldiers often intimidated the officers into giving them what they wanted. There was a case, for example, in which a sub-lieutenant of Lieh-chou battalion conspired with twelve soldiers to intimidate the officer in charge and tried to control the administration of the battalion. In the end the intendant of the circuit of Lieh-ch'iung, who was basically a civil administrator, was called in to investigate and settle the matter.[62] Nor were the marine officers any more capable. The marines at Hu-men, for instance, were in the habit of intimidating villagers of the area. This had become such a part of everyday life that any restraint put on them led to violent protests, sometimes to the point of mutiny. In one such incident they assaulted the lieutenant-colonel who, fearing even more serious consequences, such as his own dismissal for failure to control his rank and file, decided not to punish the offenders. Such an action only succeeded in emboldening the marines still further.[63]

The incompetence of officers as administrators was only part of Yeh's problem; the real trouble lay in the soldiers themselves. Instances of soldiers such as the three executed at Fo-shan joining secret societies were not uncommon.[64] Statements made in the same case provided evidence of the soldiers smoking opium,[65] and indeed the aftermath of the executions gave further insight into the gravity of Yeh's problems with those under his command. The mothers of the executed men caused alarm by going around to government offices making serious charges against the gentry of the Ninety-six Villages (see below). Out of fear that their position might eventually be jeopardised, the gentry agreed to let the women continue to receive the executed soldiers' income from betting and prostitution.[66] Drug-addiction, gambling,

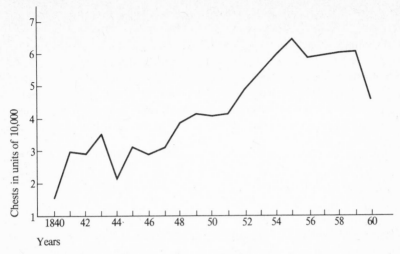

Fig. 4. Estimated opium consumption, 1840–60

Source: Drawn from Morse, *International Relations*, Table G (p. 556).

prostitution, illicit dues, secret societies – in all these the troops had a hand. Their greed certainly weighed more heavily than military discipline. They relished the opportunity to collect the loot of the rebels for themselves, and during the battle against Ch'en Chi of Shun-te, for example, they immediately fell on the booty left by the rebels who were routed, despite the order to pursue the rebels and wipe them out.[67] There was perhaps nothing Yeh could do to change the situation, which was deeply rooted in the society of his time. What was urgently needed then was an effective army to suppress the rapidly spreading rebellions, not a change in society. Dictated by circumstances, Yeh might have had to turn a blind eye to some of the evils among his soldiers.

The mercenaries: government-hired

All mercenaries have one feature in common – with but a few exceptions, they are fighting purely for money, and their greed could be a source of much embarrassment for those who hire them. However, Yeh had to use mercenaries because the regular troops were insufficient to deal with the uprisings. Since regulars and mercenaries were fighting side by side, the misconduct of the former communicated itself to the latter, and mercenaries could become an even greater problem to control. Yeh kept a check on them by recording their addresses and professions, so that they knew that if they misbehaved, retribution would visit their families.[68] He also offered them high pay, higher than that of regulars, and disbanded them once their particular mission was completed, before they found time to become entrenched in stubborn resistance to authority. Very often a report listing the number of mercenaries disbanded contained the same number of fresh recruits.[69] But there were some exceptionally good and indispensable mercenaries who at the same time were extremely lawless. In such cases, he came to the conclusion that the war effort had to take priority, and instead of disbanding these, he sentenced the offenders to severe punishments which he suspended on condition that they became law-abiding soldiers again. This policy he applied, for example, to a group of mercenaries who helped to recover the city of Fo-shan: a name-list was made and the offenders were ordered to expiate their crimes by gaining merit in ensuing battles. They did so, and were eventually pardoned.[70]

It is hard to assess how successful Yeh's measures were, but a comparison with what happened in neighbouring provinces may be instructive. An official in Kwangsi, for example, remarked that the mercenaries there were completely out of control, using the threat offered by the rebels as capital to blackmail authority; they were cowardly in battle and restless out of it, even to the extent of collaborating with the rebels.[71] Indeed, cases of mercenaries arrested as rebel suspects were not rare.[72] As regards Kiangsi, about 4,000 mercenaries were hired and went to north Kwangtung to help lift the siege of Shao-chou laid by the rebels in 1854. Claiming that they had suppressed the major rebel groups in Kwangtung and lifted the siege of Canton as well (which was absolutely untrue), they demanded payment of 146,000 taels which they claimed to have disbursed, and threatened to cut communications between the two provinces by seizing all the ferries along the river.[73] The mere fact that the mercenaries in Kwangtung had more, if not total, respect for authority, and appeared to be braver in battle, than their counterparts in other provinces, seems to indicate that Yeh's administration was more efficient than those of his colleagues in neighbouring provinces.

Mercenaries: gentry-hired

Yeh employed numerous mercenaries at the beginning of the uprisings, but as the war wore on, there was an acute shortage of government funds, and the gentry were induced by him with the promise of honours, titles or even offices to use their own resources to hire their clansmen as mercenaries. For this purpose, certificates were issued empowering these gentry to lead their own troops to fight alongside the regulars. Most of these mercenary units were also run on a temporary basis, and the certificates had to be handed back to the authorities once the troops were disbanded.[74] Speaking the same dialect as, and commanding the traditional respect of, their clansmen, the gentry often made excellent commanders and administrators of mercenaries of this kind.[75] The most successful mercenary group of this sort was that led by Lin Fu-sheng, of the magistracy of Hsiang-shan. Lin was indeed so successful that he was promoted from an ordinary member of the gentry to the rank of prefect. His administration of his men may serve as an example of how bodies of troops of this kind were run. He imposed strict discipline on his soldiers. He required them, during combat, to obey his orders to the letter, and when encamped, to weapon-train constantly. Any men found guilty of quarrelling, gambling, consuming wine or opium, or bullying or defrauding the natives would be summarily discharged. Any soldier who committed rape or robbery, or betrayed intelligence to the rebels or spread vicious rumours would be court-martialed. Each man had to carry his identity card at all times, and apply for special leave to return home.[76] The fact that these regulations were observed is demonstrated by the efficiency and high reputation of this particular body of troops and by the military success enjoyed by Lin.

On the other hand, there were also cases of mercenaries whose only interest in the exercise of their craft was to achieve financial gain for themselves. Those led by Ch'en Chao-ch'ing for instance, were, because of the limited resources of their employer, paid no wages but only a sum of money for food for a certain period. The mercenaries used this lump sum to fill their boat with illicit salt which they hoped to sell at a profit at their destination. Ch'en was aware of this, but there was nothing he could do about it unless he abandoned the mission and thereby his hopes of gaining official favour. He decided to proceed with his original plans to sail up the North River to fight the rebels. However, his vessel was stopped on its way for investigation. The mercenaries all jumped into the river and escaped. Ch'en was arrested.[77] It could be more serious if, when fighting far from home, the gentry ran out of money and could not even pay for the food of their men. This happened to a certain member of the gentry called Chung Ju-ch'i, who led his troops to fight at Wu-chou in Kwangsi; the starving soldiers resorted to plunder.[78] Instances such as these were not uncommon, but Yeh's main concern was the suppression of rebellion, and minor cases of mismanagement had to be regarded as inevitable evils of any policy.

The militia[79]

Prompted by the siege of Canton in 1854, Yeh revived the use of local militia units for regional defence.

The siege was jointly carried out by several groups of rebels from different districts around Canton. After their defeat, they dispersed into the countryside, roaming and plundering. Sending large units of troops to chase them in wild country was both ineffective and wasteful in terms of resources and manpower. Besides, there was always the danger that these gangs would regroup to form another formidable force to overthrow the government. Furthermore, the villagers who were made homeless by the plundering rebels could easily become outlaws themselves in order to survive. In view of this situation, Yeh ordered the gentry of each village to arm their clansmen and organise them into militia units. Several villages of one area formed a *she*; a certain date in each month was fixed for the militia from several *she* to meet for training in military tactics.[80] These organisations at the village and multi-village levels have been discussed in detail above, from an administrative point of view. It need only be added here that they not only policed their native areas and defended them when threatened by rebels, but helped to block the routes by which the rebels retreated before the victorious government troops; thus the army were often spared the frustration of a wild goose chase.

The militia flourished most in the magistracies north of Canton, where the rebel forces concentrated to besiege the city, and whither most of them retreated. As the rebels lost ground, more of them sailed down the Pearl River to take to the sea, preying on the villages along the coast. While mobilising the marines to suppress them, Yeh summoned the gentry of these villages to his office and ordered them to organise militia both for self-defence and to help the marines in their campaigns. When such an order was received, the gentry would gather together and elect as their leaders members who were known to be upright and just. There was often a division of labour in which the scholar-gentry were charged with the administration of the militia, and the military gentry were responsible for training the militia and commanding them in battle.[81]

The most famous and powerful among the militia units was one called the Ninety-six Villages; these villages were situated somewhere between Canton and Fo-shan. They were so well organised and efficient that Yeh interviewed their gentry several times and gave them cannon and ammunition to fight against Ch'en K'ai of Fo-shan. As a result, they not only successfully defended their own homes, but brought Ch'en K'ai's troops, who were advancing on Canton, to a halt. This was vital for the survival of Canton because it prevented Ch'en joining forces with the rebels besieging the city.[82] As a whole, the militia did not venture far from home. Nevertheless, their contribution towards the suppression of rebellion and policing of the rural areas was considerable.

Conclusion

In this and the previous chapter, Yeh's work in the fields of civil government, education, and judicial and military affairs has been reviewed. His relationship with, and use of, the gentry, have also been discussed. What may one conclude?

> Active alike in war and in debate,
> In thee the emp'ror trusts to guard the state.
> The fruits of peace and law thou plantest far;
> The people hail in thee their guiding star.[83]

This assessment is found in a private letter to Yeh, which, despite its note of flattery, nevertheless expressed what some of his contemporaries thought of him as an administrator. It is apparent that Yeh was very hard working and vigorous; and beside being painstaking, he was also a flexible administrator, refusing to sacrifice efficiency either to bureaucracy or tradition, but always adapting his policies to suit the needs of the situation. This was unusual since most high government officials were more concerned with sticking to the rules and being on the safe side than with good government. Yeh was full of initiative and was not afraid to use it. He was not, however, a reformer. His interest was in making the existing system effective rather than in changing it. In this he was to a large extent successful, as shown in his implementation of the examination system and the way he trained his subordinates to be efficient officials and officers; his measures were shown to be effective during the rebellions which, as we shall see in the next chapter, were resisted more effectively in Kwangtung than they were elsewhere in South China during the 1850s.

It is impossible to say that his government was free from corruption. Perhaps the lower the hierarchic level, the more corrupt were the officials. When Yeh was provincial treasurer, he discovered magistrates who put into their own pockets portions of the taxes collected. His severity may have remedied some of the worst aspects of such embezzlement, for later reports from his prefects contained fewer complaints about the misconduct of magistrates than about the difficulty of collecting taxes because of the rebellion;[84] the murder of local tax-collectors for extortion in villages continued to occur, however.[85] It would have been impossible for one man to eradicate the age-long practice of extortion by *yamen* runners, even if Yeh had wished to do so. Furthermore, his attention was rapidly taken up by the rebellions and finding the means to finance his expensive campaigns. In view of the extreme economic straits of his regime, he would have been more than satisfied to see some taxes collected, without bothering to ask whether they were collected by force, torture or consent.

It was a similar situation with the armed forces, the evils of whose behaviour were deeply rooted in the system; with great determination and steadfastness, he made the best of what was at his disposal, and he and his government survived the rebellion. The same applies to the gentry. He could execute those who rebelled; he could punish those who abused their privileged position; he could compel the indifferent to commit themselves totally to his side; he could tempt the careerists to spare no efforts in serving his cause; but there was little he could do to prevent the gentry from enforcing in full their privileges, which were prescribed by the political system of the time at the expense of the common folk, however harsh the results might be.

Despite such shortcomings in Yeh's government, perhaps the most telling point about him as an administrator is that he not only managed to maintain his official position, but also to improve it, gaining honours and titles at a time when other governors-general were falling into disgrace one after the other because of their failure to be flexible in this age of great change. It was possibly against this background that the rhyming couplets above quoted were written.

Part three
The military organiser[1]

It has been observed that Yeh's interest in military affairs was fostered by his family background, and that his ability to manage military officers was achieved through his own practical experience and the subtle influence of his friend Hsü. However, to be a successful military organiser demanded something more than these qualities. He had to be familiar with the theory and practice of military strategy. Moreover, since each campaign possessed its peculiar characteristics, reliance on theory or on past experience was not sufficient. Good military judgement was also called for. In this part of the book, Yeh's record as a military organiser will be examined. He was called upon to exercise his skill in dealing with the sporadic uprisings of 1850–3 and the general insurrection of 1854–8.

5 The revolts, 1850–3

Kwangtung had always been a particularly unruly province. The turbulence increased with the internal decay of the Ch'ing dynasty. When, in 1849, the government was also under external pressure, the outlaws were further emboldened. They formed large bands and were active in the mountainous areas separating the prefectures of Kuang-chou and Shao-chou, namely in the magistracies of Ch'ing-yüan and Ying-te. The first captain who was sent against them was killed, and many of his troops and the magistrate who went with him were wounded. Hsü and Yeh regarded this as rebellion rather than banditry, and they sent the commander-in-chief of the land forces, Hsiang-lin, and the provincial judge, Chao Ch'ang-ling, to suppress the uprising.[1] The presence of such a powerful force of government troops temporarily subdued the rebels.

Subsequently, however, the rebels received reinforcements from Kwangsi, where disturbances were widespread and more violent. Not only outlaws were involved: disaffected peasants and rural workers, such as miners and charcoal burners, joined them. One of the groups

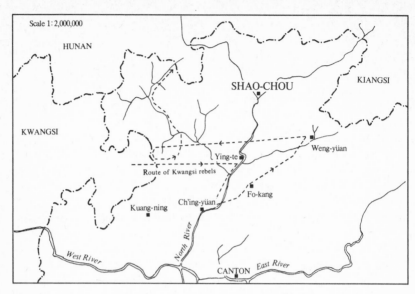

Map 5. The campaign at Ch'ing-Ying

formed at this time was that of the Taipings. Many of them had connections in Kwangtung; some, indeed, were migrant workers with families still living in Kwangtung. By the early 1850s they were infiltrating Kwangtung and joining forces with the local outlaws, laying siege to cities, and ambushing army detachments. This section will deal chronologically with Yeh's response to these disturbances – disturbances which may more appropriately be characterised as invasions from Kwangsi.

Ch'ing-Ying,[2] May 1850 – April 1851

The first of these incursions came in May 1850, followed in August by a rebel group of 4,000 strong, who first ambushed a government detachment in Ying-te,[3] and then divided themselves into guerrilla groups among the mountains. From these highlands the rebels planned, with the co-operation of local outlaws, surprise attacks on the cities; and in September, they routed a strong force sent against them.[4] Thus established, some of them infiltrated back to Kwangsi and returned with thousands of reinforcements. The rebels were only regrouping and waiting for an opportunity to overthrow the existing regime. The situation was indeed grave, so much so that the major responsible for the defence of the area became ill with anxiety and eventually committed suicide.[5] Yeh decided to take personal command of the military campaign and went to Ying-te. First of all, he deployed his troops to contain the rebels in the mountains and sealed off all possible routes of retreat back to Kwangsi. Then he sent his *corps d'élite* into the mountains to eliminate any rebel group it might find. For more than ten days, however, this strategy proved futile and Yeh immediately changed it. He instructed his troops to stop chasing the rebels, and to lure them to attack the cities, where he could deploy an overwhelming number of fresh troops to fight them in pitched battles. Unaware of this stratagem, the rebels attacked the magisterial city of Ch'ing-yüan, whose defence they believed to be weak. They were met by more than 3,000 government troops, who inflicted heavy losses upon them.

The rebels were disheartened by this and several further defeats, and there was a split among them, especially between the infiltrators from Kwangsi and the natives. The former decided to return home, only to find that their routes of retreat were heavily guarded by Yeh's troops. They then tried to escape into Kiangsi through the north of Kwangtung. Again they were stopped at the frontier by large bodies of troops guarding it, and were unable to escape a surprise attack by Yeh's troops who were in swift pursuit. This group of rebels was thus effectively dispersed by February 1851.

To deal with the local rebels, Yeh redirected many of his troops from the frontier back into the interior of Kwangtung and tightened the circle around the rebels. From various strongholds, he led his troops into the mountains, to search for and destroy them. The difficulty of communication, however, posed many problems. The first was to obtain sufficient food to feed his 6,000 troops, who were fighting deep in the mountains beyond the reach of ordinary transport. Provisions had to be obtained locally. Therefore he issued to his men strict orders to trade with the natives on a fair basis, and secured the rice he wanted.[6] The second was the difficult terrain and sometimes the absence of tracks in the wilderness, in which the dangers of his soldiers losing their way or being ambushed were great. Accordingly he asked the local gentry to provide him with detailed maps of the area and used these in deploying his troops.[7] Within two months, the remaining 2,000 rebels were either killed or captured.

The campaign thus ended in complete victory for Yeh. He had won seven major battles; more than 6,000 rebels had been killed or dispersed, and none of the rebel leaders had managed to escape.[8] The emperor issued this decree: 'In recognition of his tireless labours at the head of our forces, and of his final victory over the rebels in the areas around Ying-te, let the title of Junior Tutor of the Crown Prince be bestowed on our loyal servant Yeh.'[9] This exceptional honour enhanced further Yeh's prestige and power. The experience he had gained through conducting the campaign was even more significant.[10] When the campaign

Table 8

The various rebel leaders active in Lien-chou-fu,[a]
July 1850–June 1852

Name	Active	Followers	Result
1 Li Shih-k'uei	vii–viii. 1850	—	Captured in action
2 Fang Wan	vii–x. 1850	—	Captured in flight
3 T'ao An-jen	x. 1850	1,000	Killed in action
4 Liu Pa	viii. 1850–viii. 1851	2,400	Captured by Shen Ti-hui
5 Huang Ta	x. 1850–iv. 1851	2,000	Killed by T'ao Yü-wen
6 Yen P'in-yao	viii–x. 1851	—	Killed in action
7 Wang Hsi-ts'ung	viii–x. 1851	—	Killed by Shen and T'ao
8 Su Ning-san	ix. 1851–vi. 1852	—	Captured in action
9 Li Shih-ch'ing	ix. 1851–vi. 1852	—	Captured in action

[a] 391.3.24–6, Memos from Hsü and Yeh, 25 Dec. 1850–10 March 1851. TK 13.1; 14.2; 17.2; 20.16; Imperial edicts, 8 Aug. 1850–11 Jan. 1851. HF 39.25–9; 40.14; 44.22–3; 61.12; 61.34; Imperial edicts, 10 Sept. 1851–30 June 1852. The dates (month and year) given in the table are only approximate, and the number of followers varied from time to time.

was drawing to a close, he wrote to Hsü remarking that if he did manage to eliminate this group of rebels, he would be more confident of being able to conduct future campaigns successfully.[11]

Lien-chou, July 1850 – June 1852

Indeed Yeh would soon realise that there was abundant opportunity for him to exercise his military talents, because incursions occurred not only in Ch'ing-Ying but in all regions bordering on Kwangsi. As early as July 1850, Lien-chou, in the extreme west of Kwangtung, was invaded by bands of rebels and for the next three years, continued to suffer similar disturbances (see Table 8). The situation posed many problems. Yeh was at this time busy with the rebels in Ch'ing-Ying, and Hsü had to remain at Canton to preside over the government. Thus neither of them was free to go to Lien-chou; besides, their separation made it difficult to co-ordinate their strategy. Moreover, the rebellion at Ch'ing-Ying had taken up a large portion of the government forces, leaving Lien-chou poorly defended. Finally, as in the case of Ch'ing-Ying, the invaders had local connections, who supplied them with provisions and intelligence. To overcome the shortage of soldiers, Hsü and Yeh had a militia organised for local self-defence; this limited the scope of manoeuvre by the rebels. These militia units were very active, and indeed one detected

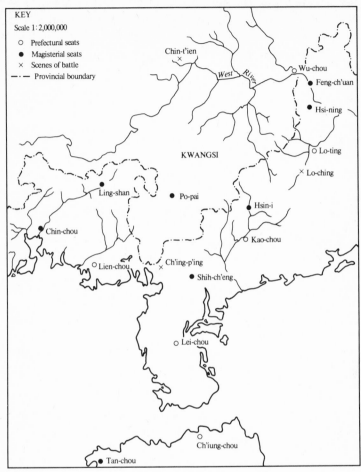

KEY

Scale 1:2,000,000

○   Prefectural seats
●   Magisterial seats
×   Scenes of battle
—·— Provincial boundary

Chin-t'ien
×

West River

○ Wu-chou
● Feng-ch'uan

● Hsi-ning

KWANGSI

○ Lo-ting

× Lo-ching

● Ling-shan

● Po-pai

● Hsin-i

● Chin-chou

○ Kao-chou

○ Lien-chou   × Ch'ing-p'ing

● Shih-ch'eng

○ Lei-chou

○
Ch'iung-chou

● Tan-chou

Map 6. The campaigns in Lien-chou, Tan-chou and Kao-chou

and captured a prominent rebel leader, Fang Wan. Some of the men
were even hired as mercenaries to supplement government troops: at
one time in the encampment at Ling-shan, for example, only 562 of the
5,269 men were regulars, the rest being mercenaries of this kind.[12]
Although the government forces were thus reinforced by mercenaries,
they were still far inferior in number to the rebels, who were sufficiently
strong to besiege many important cities. An intensive search for local
collaborators successfully deprived the expatriates of native support
and weakened their prospects of overrunning the cities. Then confident
that the militias were capable of local self-defence, Hsü and Yeh
concentrated their troops to deal with the various rebel groups one by
one; by June 1852, the area was cleared of invaders. All this time, Hsü

and Yeh planned their strategy by correspondence, and despite the shortcomings of this means of communication, they directed the campaign so well that even the emperor was impressed.[13] The cordiality and co-operation between the two colleagues were all the more remarkable when contrasted with the discord among the leaders in Kwangsi and the subsequent military reverses there. The insurrections there had become so serious by 1851 that the emperor sent an imperial commissioner, Chou T'ien-chüeh, to put them down. Chou failed to secure the co-operation of the other military leaders of the province, such as Commander-in-chief Hsiang Jung; worse still, he found that even the brigadiers would not obey his orders. As a result, his war efforts proved futile. In his annoyance the emperor remarked that Chou, despite his courage, was completely incompetent in handling his subordinates.[14] Chou was consequently replaced by Sai-shang-a.

Their success was also evidence of the ability of Hsü and Yeh to choose the right man as the field-commander. For example, the prefect of Lien-chou, whose cowardice prevented him from leading his troops against the first group of invaders, was immediately dismissed. He was replaced by Prefect-Designate Shen Ti-hui, whose outstanding military talent in suppressing the rebels in 1849 had already won him a peacock's feather. Once in Lien-chou, he was given every opportunity to prove that he was a capable commander. He captured the rebel leader Huang Ta,[15] and dispersed other groups of rebels. By the end of the campaign, he was already promoted to the post of circuit intendant of Kao-lien. He was ordered to lead his victorious troops from Lien-chou to Kao-chou,[16] where Yeh had arrived to suppress a powerful rebel group led by Ling Shih-pa. Before studying this new phase of the war, an incident that took place at Tan-chou concurrently with those at Kao-chou may be mentioned in passing.

Tan-chou, July 1851 – July 1852

At Tan-chou in Hainan Island (see Map 6) there was also a rebellion; as in the case of Lien-chou, Hsü and Yeh were concerned with putting the right person in command. The magistrate who failed to deal with the situation competently was dismissed and arrested. The brigadier of Ch'iung-chou, who led his troops to suppress the revolt, was equally inefficient and suffered the same fate. Subsequently, the circuit intendant of Lieh-ch'iung, Chiang Kuo-lin, was called in, and Colonel Wu Yüan-yu of the regiment at Lung-men was appointed acting brigadier of Ch'iung-chou. Both were able officers, and within a year the rebellion was put down.[17] They were to play an important role too during the *Arrow* War, with Chiang as provincial treasurer, and Wu as commander-in-chief of the marine forces.

Kao-chou, January 1851 – August 1852

Yeh rejoined Hsü at Canton shortly after his final victory in Ch'ing-Ying, in April 1851. However, the situation in Kao-chou, which had been infested by powerful rebel groups notably the one under Ling Shih-pa, soon became so serious that Hsü decided to conduct the campaign personally. On 24 July 1851, he set out for Kao-chou.[18]

Ling Shih-pa was a native of the prefecture of Kao-chou. He went to Kwangsi in 1847 and joined the Taipings, then known as the God-Worshippers, at Chin-t'ien. In 1849, he came back to Kao-chou, gathered about 3,000 followers, and after some skirmishes with government troops, left with his band for Chin-t'ien on 14 February 1850. On the way, a large number of God-Worshippers and bandits in the magistracy of Po-pai joined him, swelling his ranks to an estimated 10,000. He was, however, intercepted in Kwangsi and was unable to rejoin the Taipings. He sent an urgent appeal to Chin-t'ien for help. This brought a considerable relief force, which was also intercepted.[19] Thus, for a long time Ling Shih-pa and his group roamed Kwangsi, besieging several cities. Eventually he decided to return to his native land, Kao-chou, and set up his headquarters at a place called Lo-ching (see Map 6) in May 1851.[20] Of all rebel groups in Kwangtung at this time, his was to become the most formidable, as it had a political aim – to overthrow the Ch'ing dynasty – and it had a common religious fervour which bound its members so tightly together that even Yeh was very much surprised at their zeal.[21] Besides, the extremely mountainous terrain at Lo-ching afforded them an almost impregnable position. They built forts, mounted cannon and laid traps on the hillsides to strengthen the defence still further. The natural obstacles and the sophistication of Ling's defence were such that from July 1851 to June 1852, all of Hsü's offensives proved futile; nor were Hsü's attempts to lure Ling out of his base any more successful.[22] At the same time the situation in Kwangsi had further deteriorated. The rebels overran the prefectural city of Yung-an and from there proceeded to besiege the provincial capital, Kuei-lin. All four brigadiers of the province were killed in action. The emperor ordered Hsü to lead his *corps d'élite* into Kwangsi without delay, and Yeh subsequently took over command in Kao-chou.[23]

Confronted with a new and difficult situation, Yeh wanted first of all to make full inquiries into the causes of Hsü's lack of success. Hence he was determined to be as near the battlefield as possible. Whereas Hsü directed the campaign from Kao-chou and then from Hsin-i after 30 January 1852, Yeh set up his headquarters at Lo-ting, which was only half as far from Lo-ching as Hsin-i, being only a few miles from the scene of action. 'In this way', he wrote 'I hope to know the situation intimately, and be able to give the appropriate orders.'[24] His investigations showed that the defence radius of Lo-ching extended about six miles, within which area concentric rings of forts had been built. There were also hundreds of rebels manning cannon or bearing muskets, who had been stationed in the woods, in slit trenches, and even in ordinary houses equipped with loopholes. Entrance to Lo-ching could be obtained only by narrow and crooked paths, often bordered by great ponds, which rendered massive frontal attacks extremely difficult. Moreover, these paths were full of covered pits at the bottom of which were planted bamboo or iron spikes. The rebels declined to fight pitched battles but waited for the attackers to advance well within range of their hidden artillery before catching them in a crossfire. The losses inflicted on the government troops were, therefore, heavy: more than 300 killed and nearly 3,000 wounded in the twelve months during which Hsü conducted the campaign. Furthermore, most of them had fought in Ch'ing-Ying before, and after two years of war (one in Ch'ing-Ying and one in Kao-chou), they were beginning to show signs of fatigue. Indeed, the inheritance of a depleted and demoralised army was the greatest of the immediate difficulties confronting Yeh. He ralised the importance of boosting the morale of his army. Consequently he took the daring risk of transferring to Lo-ching the 2,160 troops guarding Feng-ch'uan, a strategic point between Kwangtung and Kwansi, on the calculation that since the two places were not too far apart, the troops could always withdraw rapidly to the frontier on any alarm. He also decided to give his troops a good rest, so that they might recover from the wounds they had sustained. Furthermore, he wanted to give himself time to collect detailed information about the enemy, on the basis of which he would plan his strategy. One way of doing this was to capture and closely examine rebel infiltrators. Within the first 20 days of his arrival at Lo-ting, more than 200 of these were arrested. Their depositions gave valuable information about the rebel camp and the details of its defence. Yeh promised them a full pardon if they would act as guides in the front line in the event of a major attack on the rebel camp.

The captives also testified that the rebels were running out of food. To dishearten them further, Yeh launched a vigorous detective campaign to arrest any person who secretly treated with the rebels and prevented further infiltration of supplies to Lo-ching. This made the rebels desperate enough to come out from hiding and gather the tares which grew in abundance around Lo-ching. Consequently, Yeh hired 300 labourers to cut the tares, and successfully foiled all attempts by the rebels to intervene. Thus Ling Shih-pa was like a cornered lion; Yeh had to consider the danger of a desperate sortie. Realising that the critical moment had come, Yeh mobilised all his troops and fixed the date of an all out attack for the night of 28 July. And from 16 July onwards, he started to worry his enemy day and night by fake attacks. The rebels were naturally concerned at the beginning, but relaxed their vigilance when the alarm became an everyday occurrence.

Yeh frequently summoned his officials and officers and advised them to share the hardships of the rank and file, and to show greater concern for their welfare, so that the latter would obey orders and be courageous in battle. He also recommended that they should be humble and always ready to discuss tactics with one another, and warned them that anyone harbouring jealousy against, or refusing to co-operate with his colleagues would be severely punished. He always notified them of whatever intelligence he had obtained, so that they too might know in detail the latest developments. The gentry were also mobilised; they were asked to organise militia to supplement the regulars. Maps of Lo-ching and its surroundings were drawn to help in the planning of the campaign.[25]

When everything was ready, Yeh gathered his officials and officers for a final briefing. He had decided that all the forts should be levelled before the full weight of his forces fell on Lo-ching itself, to prevent them being caught in a crossfire from the forts and the rebel headquarters. Therefore when the night of the attack came, the troops began by bombarding the forts at the signal given by Brigadier Fu-hsing, whom Yeh had appointed field commander. Yeh saw in Fu-hsing a capable military commander, and had always discussed with him the planning of the campaign. There was nothing more gratifying to Fu-hsing than to have his ability recognised; in return, he showed exceptional bravery in this battle. At the head of his troops, he made a dash right into the rebel headquarters. He fell from his horse, broke a rib, vomited blood, remounted, and continued his charge. His bravery was a source of great encouragement to his men. As a result of well conceived strategy and high morale, the government troops quickly destroyed all the forts and advanced into Lo-ching from three directions. Lo-ching fell at noon, and with it, more than 2,000 rebels. Among these was Ling Shih-pa, who was killed in action.[26]

The campaign at Lo-ching was a crucial one, because the rebel leader Ling Shih-pa was a member of the Taipings. Certainly the emperor took it very seriously, and remarked that Ling and Wei Cheng (who was then considered the leader of the Taipings in Kwangsi) led two very important, mutually supporting sections of the Taiping movement, and that so long as Ling was not eliminated, Wei would be as strong as ever, and the campaign of suppression in Kwangsi would remain extremely difficult.[27] Hence the emperor was greatly pleased to learn of the victory at Lo-ching, and conferred on Yeh the title of governor-general. Eleven days later, Yeh was appointed acting governor-general of Liang Kuang. It says much for Yeh's military ability that he was able to achieve in forty-two days what Hsü had failed to do in a year. However, this does not mean that Hsü was totally incompetent as a military commander; his success in at least containing Ling at Lo-ching was a merit for which he was awarded the honorific title of Senior Tutor of the Crown Prince.[28]

Shao-chou, October 1852 – January 1853

When Yeh was on the point of withdrawing his victorious troops from Lo-ching in July 1852, he received intelligence that the Taipings had invaded Hunan and were threatening the north of Kwangtung. Indeed, the Taipings had gone as far as Yung-chou on 10 June.[29] This city, like Ch'üan-chou which the Taipings had just captured and abandoned, was situated by a tributary of the Yangtze River called Hsiang Chiang. Instead of fighting downstream to Changsha, they turned south to occupy Tao-chou. For over three months they lingered in the cities north of the Kwangtung border, with their headquarters at Ch'en-chou (see Map 7). Hung Hsiu-ch'üan and other leaders remained at Ch'en-chou, while Hsiao Ch'ao-kuei (West King) led three to four thousand Taipings north to attack Changsha. If Hsiao had not been killed by a cannon ball at Changsha on 11 September, causing an overwhelming outcry among the Taipings for vengeance, it is doubtful whether Hung Hsiu-ch'üan would eventually have left Ch'en-chou, which he did, although two weeks later.[30]

Here, two important questions arise. First, why did the Taipings turn south towards Kwangtung after Yung-chou, if the general assumption is that they wanted to fight north?[31] The explanation given by Chien Yu-wen and Kuo Ting-i is that the Taipings had suffered a severe setback between Ch'üan-chou and Yung-chou. A close reading of Chien's *T'ai-p'ing t'ien-kuo ch'üan-shih*, however, shows that the Taipings were fired upon by imperial troops on the west bank of the river along which they had been sailing. They rallied on the east bank,[32] and could still have proceeded north if they had wanted to; as mentioned, some did go as far as Yung-chou before turning south to Tao-chou. When some of the Taipings did go north again, it was as late as 26 August, and the group consisted of only a small detachment estimated at three to four thousand men.[33] This leads to the second question: why did Hung Hsiu-ch'üan remain north of Kwangtung for over three months, and show no sign of moving north until his West King was killed at Changsha? Obviously, there must be reasons other than that given by Chien, namely, that the Taipings wanted a breathing space to regroup themselves.[34]

Kuo Ting-i comes nearer the main reason when he says that while the Taipings were thus hovering over north of Kwangtung, many of their leaders debated whether they should return to Kwangsi or fight their way into northern Hunan because many had become homesick. Only Yang Hsiu-ch'ing (East King) was in favour of going north, but it was he

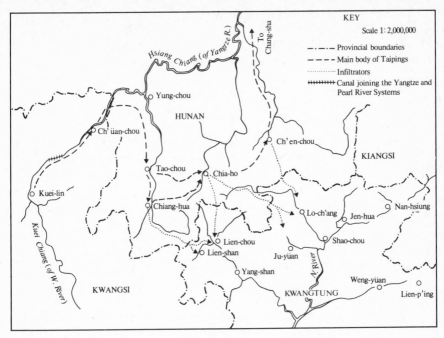

Map 7. The campaign in Shao-chou, Oct. 1852–Jan. 1853

who prevailed.[35] Unfortunately, Chien, while quoting Kuo about the debate, omits its cause rather than developing it further. The Canton Archive, however, confirms Kuo's view. It even indicates that Hung Hsiu-ch'üan had expressed to one of his confidants the desire to fight his way back to Kwangtung, his native land, to set up his eastern capital there, and to make his base in Kwangsi his western capital.[36] This, perhaps, helps to explain why the Taipings turned south towards Kwangtung after their military reverse near Yung-chou; and why they were hanging around for over a hundred days north of Kwangtung. For, during this period, many spies were sent back to Kwangtung by the Taiping leaders including Hung Hsiu-ch'üan himself.[37] These infiltrators stirred up the disaffected groups in north Kwangtung (Shao-chou prefecture), who subsequently responded by rising in revolt.

Yeh hurried to the scene. It is not clear when exactly he arrived at Shao-chou, but a draft communication from him to Bonham stated that he was going to Shao-chou on 30 October.[38] This hardly mattered, however, as he had strengthened the frontier defence considerably during the campaign in Ch'ing-Ying, which he personally conducted. On hearing the threat of the Taipings on north Kwangtung, he must have expected that spies would come first, and therefore issued specific instructions for their detection and arrest. Taiping infiltrators, whether they came individually or in groups, disguised as merchants or travellers, were consequently captured without much difficulty.[39] It remained for Yeh to deal with the local rebels on his arrival. With him came 3,000 troops from Lo-ching, but the courageous Brigadier Fu-hsing had unfortunately been ordered by an imperial edict to leave him and to engage the Taipings in Hunan. Hence Yeh asked the newly appointed commander-in-chief, former brigadier of Shao-chou, K'un-shou to remain there for the time being, instead of taking up his new office in distant Hui-chou.[40] As usual, Yeh had maps drawn of the various districts of the circuit[41] and studied them closely. He also sent agents to collect information about the intentions and movements of the rebels. Consequently he deduced that the areas bordering on Hunan and Kiangsi required the most attention. He, therefore, divided his troops into two sections, the division in the west dealing with Hunan region and the one in the east with Kiangsi. The native rebels he quickly overcame;[42] those who tried to retreat into either Kwangsi or Kiangsi were driven back: in the five major battles with the fleeing bands, 1,747 rebels were killed.[43] The governor of Kiangsi, Chang Fei, was so impressed by Yeh's rapid success that he wrote to him saying that even Kiangsi benefited immensely from his military genius.[44]

By the end of 1852 the Taipings had gone further north along the Yangtze River, having no doubt realised that they did not stand much chance of success against a governor-general who was so well prepared. Yeh subsequently returned to Canton, leaving K'un-shou in charge of the military situation in Shao-chou.

Conclusion

For anyone politically committed to overthrowing the imperial government, Kwangtung was an ideal place in which to operate. It was one of the richest provinces, and its foreign trade was one of the most important sources of revenue to the empire. Strategically, it was possible to establish friendly relations with foreigners and obtain from them, if not diplomatic recognition, at least supplies of arms and provisions. All these would be denied to the rebels if they continued to fight in the inland provinces such as Kwangsi and Hunan. Geographically, the north of Kwangsi was very mountainous, and to advance on Kuei-lin, as did the Taipings, meant fighting uphill, a task far more difficult than going down the West River into the fertile Canton delta. Finally, there were in Kwangtung many secret societies, disaffected peasants, unemployed porters, and bandits who were ready to join in a general insurrection against the government – a fact of which many of the Taiping leaders, being natives of the province, were aware, and which was demonstrated by the so-called Red Turban Revolt discussed in the next chapter.

Therefore the Taipings had every reason to occupy Kwangtung first. The events described in this section may help to explain why they could not do so. Their fellow rebels who invaded northwest Kwangtung were crushed by Yeh in Ch'ing-Ying. Those who tried their luck in the west of the province, in Lien-chou, were routed. An important section of their own people, Ling Shih-pa and his group, were utterly destroyed by Yeh at Lo-ching. When they had occupied the south of Hunan and were preparing to descend upon Kwangtung from the north, few, if any, of the scouts they sent across the border to spy out the land returned; and most of the secret societies who rose in revolt at their request were subdued. Eventually the Taipings gave up hope of taking over Kwangtung and instead fought their way down the Yangtze River to Nanking, another very rich city comparable to Canton, and set up their capital there.[45] Thus, Yeh played a decisive role in the development of the Taiping Rebellion in its early stages; but for him the history of mid-nineteenth-century China might have been very different.

The Taipings, however, never ignored the strategic importance of Kwangtung. Once they had established themselves in Nanking in 1853, they began despatching their secret agents back to Kwangtung to contact the secret societies there in the hope of stirring up a general uprising.[46] Furthermore, the success of the various campaigns described in this section did not ensure that those areas were free from disturbance thereafter. The most formidable bands of rebels of the time were suppressed, but they were succeeded by others. Bands of Kwangsi rebels continued to infiltrate Ch'ing-Ying.[47] Bands from the same province, led by Hsieh San and others, continued to infest the prefecture of Lien-chou. The situation in Kao-chou was even worse; several thousand Kwangsi rebels led by Sung Ch'i-ta, Ch'iu Ta, Tu Ta-chiang and many others raided the prefecture.[48] Finally, Commander-in-chief K'un-shou, whom Yeh ordered to remain at Shao-chou temporarily, was indeed unable to take up his new office at Hui-chou till 1855.

Worse still, the local disaffected elements, especially the secret societies, were very much excited by these disturbances which kept the local officials and officers very busy indeed. One of the secret society proclamations, which appears among British Foreign Office papers, reads, 'The ancient books tell us that once in five centuries some man of talent beyond his fellows will appear, on whom the hope of the nation will depend. That period has elapsed since the rise of the Ming dynasty, and it is full time that a hero should come forward and save the nation.'[49] The explicit political aim of the secret societies was to overthrow the Ch'ing dynasty; they were convinced that it was high time for them to take action, the whole of Kwangtung was like dry timber, which would burst into flames at the first spark.

6 The general insurrection, 1854–8

The year 1853 witnessed several significant events culminating in the general insurrection which began in 1854. To begin with, the summer of that year brought some of the worst thunderstorms and floods that the province had ever known.[1] The fact that the previous summer, that of 1852, had seen much flooding and the ruination of many crops[2] meant that even an ordinary peasant, let alone the poverty-stricken tenants, would have spent all his savings (if he had any) by the winter of 1853. It has been observed that Yeh's policy in these natural calamities was to spend money on repairing the dykes rather than on social relief. Starvation had caused a good many rebellions in the past, and it certainly played an important role in the widespread revolts in Kwangtung.

The peasants were further antagonised by the tax-collectors, who, under a vigorous administrator like Yeh and at a time when the imperial government was imperilled owing to financial difficulties, spared no efforts in collecting the full amount of tax and never failed to extort extra sums for their own pockets. Force and torture were by no means rare in the process of achieving these aims, and very often the peasants retaliated by killing their oppressors.[3] The interests of the gentry, who were the biggest landowners, were likewise affected by the floods, but their reaction pushed the farmers still further towards rebellion. They tried to guarantee full payment of rents by tortures and executions, and what happened in Po-lo, described in chap. 4, was a typical example. The peasants' incentive to rebel was increased by the gentry in yet another way. The latter sought to further their landed interests by lauching a large-scale campaign of refusal to pay taxes (k'ang-liang). They often drew attention to their supposed grievances by refusing to sit for prefectural or provincial examinations.[4] Although, as will be seen in the next chapter their unjustified protests were completely overruled by Hsü and Yeh, their challenge to authority, the reckless manner it assumed and the agitation it produced, served to embolden the disaffected peasants.

The discontented masses also received much encouragement from the examples of the Kwangsi rebels who infested Kwangtung at the beginning of the decade, and many disgruntled peasants and local bandits had already joined the invaders. Indeed, great excitement was aroused in the city of Canton by the news of the Taipings' capture in rapid succession of important cities such as Wuchang, Anking, and Nanking.[5] It only required a little leadership and guidance for there to be open rebellion: this was provided by the Taiping agents and the local secret societies. The agents sent by the Taipings at Nanking to Kwangtung were professional agitators who realised that their mission was not so much religious as political and strategic. They did not attempt to impose their own religious practices but identified themselves with those of the local secret societies, and posed as important figures of sister societies. They claimed to be heroes of the Taiping revolutionaries who had successfully captured the southern capital of the empire, Nanking. In this way they managed to infiltrate the secret societies and occupied positions in the largest rebel camps, such as those of Kan Hsien and Li Wen-mao.[6]

Agitators were sent into the countryside preaching their philosophy of the millennium, that in every five hundred years a messiah would be born to save the nation from peril; and that this time was at hand and a leader would come forth to deliver them from the tyrannical Manchus. By the beginning of 1854, Yeh's secret agents were already sending him urgent despatches informing him that every day in the suburbs of Canton, hundreds upon hundreds of people were secretly assembling and then as secretly dispersing.[7] These assemblies were in fact secret society gatherings in which were held the ceremonies of admitting new members, and they took place not only in the suburbs of Canton, but throughout the province. Yeh, jointly with Po-kuei, issued a notice forbidding illegal gatherings, which was printed and distributed widely.[8] But it was too late to stop the deluge that was about to burst upon the entire province. Kwangtung was thrown into an uproar, such as had seldom been seen before. It was sparked off in the Canton delta, and then almost overnight the whole of the Pearl River and Han River regions were in the hands of the rebels. This chapter discusses the general insurrection in these three major areas.

The Canton delta, June 1854–March 1855

Besides the disaffected peasants and rural tenants, Canton had another group of potential rebels in the persons of porters, coolies and compradors who lost their jobs in 1853 because of a very bad trade recession.[9] The discontented, both urban and rural, drifted into the secret societies. The fires of insurrection were lit on 17 June 1854 by Ho Liu, who led members of a secret society in an attack on the magisterial city of Tung-kuan (about 20 miles east of Canton) and sacked it.[10] On 4 July, Ch'en K'ai and his 7,000 followers captured the town of Fo-shan, about 15 miles south-west of the provincial capital; his army was rapidly swollen by tens of thousands, 3,000 of whom had come from as far as

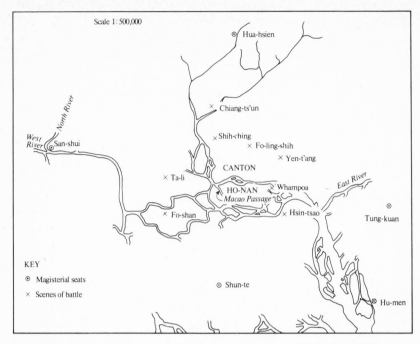

Map 8. The campaign of the Canton delta, June 1854–Mar. 1855

Kwangsi.[11] The magisterial city of Hua-hsien, 25 miles north of Canton, was overrun by Kan Hsien; that of San-shui, which was equally far to the west, was besieged by Ch'en Chin-kang.[12] In the south, Shun-te fell on 1 August to Ch'en Chi. Thus the delta was in conflagration, with Canton in the midst of it. More dangerous were the uprisings which erupted in the immediate vicinity of the city, such was those led by Li Wen-mao at Chiang-ts'un, by Ch'en Hsien-liang at Yen-t'ang, and by Lin Kuang-lung in Ho-nan (see Map 8). These latter groups were slowly joined by those who had sacked the various magisterial cities; now they converged with a common goal, Canton itself.

It is difficult to know exactly how many groups of rebels there were, but the total number of insurgents around Canton was estimated at no less than 200,000, possibly more. Every rebel wore a red turban, and red flags were used;[13] hence some historians have referred to the insurrection as the 'Red Turban Rebellion'.[14] They formed a loose alliance over which Li Wen-mao, as leader of the strongest group, exercised some control. Li made the following arrangements for the campaign: Ch'en Hsien-liang, with his army of about 30,000, should attack the city from the east; Kan Hsien from the north, Li himself from the west, and Lin Kuang-lung should take control of the river south of the city. It was also agreed that Ch'en K'ai should lead his army, upwards of 100,000, to join in the attack on Canton.[15] Li also asked Ho Liu, who had sacked the magisterial city of Tung-kuan and then that of Tseng-ch'eng, to bring his troops, 10,000 strong, to reinforce Ch'en Hsien-liang in attacking Canton from the east.[16]

Yeh was confronted with imminent disaster. There was little that the rest of the country could do to help him, although the emperor did despatch some reinforcements from the neighbouring provinces: a fleet of war junks from Kwangsi, 2,000 troops from Fukien, 1,000 from Hunan, and 4,000 from Kiangsi. These troops were busily occupied with the local rebels once they entered Kwangtung, and although they made important contributions towards suppressing the general insurrection of the province as a whole, they never managed to fight their way to Canton to help lift the siege.[17]

Nor was there much assistance forthcoming from other parts of the province, which were in complete turmoil. In fact, the prefects and magistrates were themselves constantly sending urgent despatches to Canton appealing desperately for help. Worse still, the Taipings had directly and indirectly tied up the majority of Yeh's best soldiers and generals. In the course of the campaign with Ling Shih-pa, for example, about 10,000 of the province's *corps d'élite* were mustered from different regiments. By the end of the campaign more than 3,000 were temporarily or permanently disabled; upwards of 3,000, including the formidable Brigadier Fu-hsing, were sent to fight the Taipings in Hunan, and the rest Yeh transferred to north Kwangtung[18] where, to forestall a Taiping invasion, they and Commander-in-chief K'un-shou were instructed to stay. Indeed the situation at Shao-chou continued to cause so much concern that the emperor, unaware that Canton itself was in imminent danger, ordered Yeh, after his return to Canton, to be always ready to go back there in the event of any emergency.[19] Furthermore, the demand on the military resources of Kwangtung after the fall of Nanking to the Taipings was insatiably great, as there was every likelihood that the Manchu dynasty would fall at any time. Yeh himself complained that most of his good generals and soldiers were transferred to fight in the province of Kiangsi and none of them were able to return to help him suppress the Red Turbans.[20]

Yeh had to face the situation alone. He would need all his intelligence and imagination to survive. He had to make the most of the little he had at his disposal to fight the rebels, and he had to win, because so much was at stake. He might be nervous at heart, but he could not allow his emotions to betray him; his entire demeanour implied that victory was certain so as to build up confidence among his subordinates. He conducted the campaign in person by setting up his war office in the Chen-hai Tower on the Yüeh-hsiu Hill, which was in a commanding position overlooking the city and the river.[21] From this tower he directed many decisive battles, and witnessed numerous other fierce engagements. This was to be the climax of his military career, to which he referred in one of his last poems.

The deployment of troops

Yeh's army compared most unfavourably in numbers with the combined forces of the rebels. According to one account Canton had at that time 5,000 Banner troops, 4,000 Green Standard troops, 2,000 mercenaries from Ch'ao-chou (half of whom arrived at Canton as late as 19 July) and 4,000 mercenaries from the delta.[22] Therefore it was 15,000 against tens of thousands. Furthermore, the composition of such an army presented many problems. Yeh had in fact summoned to Canton from all Green Standard units throughout the province, however small, any troops that could possibly be spared, whether they were regulars or auxiliary soldiers and mercenaries attached to the unit (see Table 9). Their differences in dialect and customs made it difficult for them to co-operate. Yeh's solution was to assign different positions of defence to different units and let the officer of each unit continue to be the commander, instead of amalgamating them all and putting new commanders in charge. Faithfully carrying out Yeh's instructions, commanding soldiers whom they knew very well, these officers were able to score victories which contributed towards beating off the besieging rebels after prolonged and bitter fighting.

The gentry too, were fully mobilised. Yeh asked them to hire their clansmen as mercenaries and allowed them to fight as individual units within a big army. The mercenaries from Ch'ao-chou were generally very good soldiers; among them, the unit led by Sub-magistrate Designate Cheng Hsi-ch'i was particularly famous. From the delta, Chu Kuo-hsiung (a military *chü-jen*) and his mercenaries from Tung-kuan, and the mercenaries from Hsiang-shan led by another member of the gentry called Lin Fu-sheng were among the most outstanding units.[23]

A field-commander had yet to be found. The commander-in-chief of the land forces had to stay at Shao-chou; all the land brigadiers were busily occupied with the suppression of local rebellions, and the marine commodores with the pirates and the Taipings in the Yangtze River whence they had been transferred.[24] Yeh realised that the circuit intendant of Kao-lien, Shen Ti-hui, who had proved his exceptional military talents during the campaigns at Lien-chou and Kao-chou, would serve his purpose.[25] It proved to be a piece of good judgement, because Shen emerged as one of the most formidable generals of his time. It is not clear why Yeh dropped the Tartar general, head of the Banners, as a candidate for this important post; perhaps there is some

Table 9
Green Standard troops summoned for the defence of Canton[a]

A. Land forces

	Place of origin	Officers	Regulars	Auxiliaries	Mercenaries
1	Governor-general's regiment	12	1,000	—	—
2	Governor's regiment	9	490	—	—
3	Commander-in-chief's regiment	5	200	—	—
4	Ch'ao-chou brigade	3	————300————		
5	Tseng-ch'eng battalion	5	200	—	—
6	Ch'ao-chou brigadier's regiment	5	————400————		
7	Hsin-hui battalion	9	350	—	350
8	Howqua's contribution	3	(Appointed from military hierarchy)		800
	Total	51			4,090

B. Marine forces

	Place of origin	War junks	Officers	Marines	Sailors	Mercenaries
1	Hsiang-shan regiment	9	9	240	120	30
2	Commander-in-chief's regiment	11	15	593	—	—
3	Yang-chiang brigade	3	4	145	—	—
4	Ch'iung-chou brigade	25	7	250	—	—
5	Governor-general's marine regiment	—	2	100	—	—
	Total	48	37	1,478		

[a] This table is adapted from 253A.3.88. Some of the numbers given here are totals of the same unit but coming at different times; some of them are the total of a mixture of different kinds of soldiers.

truth in the derogation of the man as 'only a type and specimen of the great imperial sham'.[26] In fact there was hardly any reference in Yeh's archive to the mobilisation of the Banners to suppress the local sporadic revolts of 1849–53. During the siege of Canton, the Banners were responsible for guarding the inner city (*lao-ch'eng*, old city),[27] while the task of defending the outer city (*hsin-ch'eng*, new city) and of beating off the rebels was left to the Green Standard and mercenaries.[28] It was only when the rebels were driven from the immediate vicinity to the east and north of Canton that 'Deputy Lieutenant-General Lai-ts'un also led his Banner troops to join in attacking the retreating rebels.'[29]

The establishment of a military government

Yeh decided that in time of emergency there was no room for delegation of power. Whereas there was normally a division of responsibility among offices of the provincial level, namely, those of the provincial treasurer, provincial judge, salt comptroller and grain intendant, Yeh amalgamated these different branches of the provincial government into a temporary body called the Military Supply Bureau, which was in effect a military government, exercising absolute control over every aspect of life in Canton and receiving orders from Yeh alone.[30] This bureau was divided into various departments, such as the department for strategic planning (*t'i-tiao-chü*), the war office (*ping-fang*), secretarial office (*sheng-se-k'o*), contribution department (*chüan-shu-chü*), the bursary (*chih-ying-so*), the ammunition department (*chün-chuang-chü*) and the registry (*kua-hao*).[31]

Within this central body, Yeh listened to opinions and sought suggestions of measures to be taken. The personnel of the bureau acted as a body of advisers. The first assignment was the planning of the defence of Canton. There followed an account of the suggestions arising from such a conference. They proposed that since the strength of the government fleet defending Canton was only equal to that of the rebel fleet, high rewards had to be offered. The gentry around Canton used to organise militia under the supervision of the governor-general's regiment, and Yeh was to interview them and encourage them either to lead their units in the active defence of the city or to be constantly ready for mobilisation if remaining in their villages. Security measures should include the assignment of responsible officials to fixed areas for house-to-house checks, and daily reports from local constables (*ti-pao*) about the inhabitants of the regions under their charge. Finally, it was suggested that the numerous unemployed young Bannermen should be recruited as mercenaries attached to their own Banners.[32]

Besides seeking advice from the bureau, Yeh sometimes delegated decisions to it as well. In January 1857, for example, the magistrate of Ch'ing-yüan, whose city had been besieged for nearly two months by the rebels, appealed to Yeh for more reinforcements and a sum of 5,000 taels as military finance. Yeh referred this to the bureau with a covering letter in which he wrote, 'I have granted his request for reinforcements and mobilised several troops. As regards the 5,000 taels, please promptly decide if we could afford it or not.'[33] On receiving Yeh's query, the secretarial office immediately arranged for the principal officials of the bureau, consisting of the four officials of the provincial level above mentioned, the intendant and acting intendant of Chao-lo circuit, the acting prefect of Kuang-chou and prefect of Lo-ting, to have a committee meeting. After careful deliberation, it was decided that only 2,000 taels should be allotted to Ch'ing-yüan. Yeh agreed, and the bureau proceeded to appoint a commissioner to escort the silver to the besieged city, and to notify all regiments who happened to be in places *en route* from Canton to Ch'ing-yüan to afford the treasure due protection.[34]

Security measures

Yeh had hitherto contained, besieged and defeated his enemies in his military operations; he had not fought any battle in which he was in the reverse situation, himself under siege. Humbly he requested information from the public and his subordinates about the way in which Kuei-lin, the provincial capital of Kwangsi, had survived the siege laid by the Taipings. As a result he received many reports about the reorganisation of the *pao-chia* system in that city, how the various militia units in the neighbourhood of Kuei-lin had taken turns to defend the city, and how the expatriates, mostly merchants, from other provinces, had organised themselves into jointly-responsible units to detect strangers who might be rebel spies.[35] Benefiting from the experience of others as well as from his own, when he had been responsible for the defence of Canton during the Entry Crisis of 1849, Yeh set out to devise measures to secure the safety of the city.

As in 1849, self-defence corps were organised on the basis of streets in the new city, and hence they came to be known as 'militia of the allied streets' (*lien-chieh t'uan-lien*). The 'officers', like the militiamen, were civilians, and consisted of captains (*tui-chang*), deputy captains (*ch'i-t'ou*), duty officers (*chih-shih*) and assistant duty officers (*hsieh-li chih-shih*). Yeh however would not leave a civilian force completely in the hands of civilians. Apart from keeping a register of the names and birthplaces of its leaders,[36] he placed the militia under the control of ward committees, which in turn were supervised by four general committees, one for each quarter of the city, composed of influential citizens and presided over by one of the four principal officials of the Military Supply Bureau.[37] The formation of this militia required the registration of the population of the city. 'Yesterday', wrote an English contemporary, 'the magistrates ordered that every house should suspend over the door a tablet to be furnished by the government, having inscribed on it the number and descriptions of the inmates, that thus means might be afforded of detecting evilly disposed characters.'[38] The chief duty of the militia units was to patrol their respective streets, detaining and interrogating any stranger they came across. In this respect they were preferable to the regulars, who might not necessarily know the inhabitants. When the Chinese New Year (17 February 1855) was approaching, Yeh ordered the street patrols to be intensified to cope with the traditional extra hustle and bustle of the city. Strategic check-points were set up in each street, and militiamen on duty were increased by forty in big streets, thirty in medium and twenty in small streets. Identical wooden seals were distributed to the duty officers, so that in case of alarm in one street, a messenger might be despatched with the seal to request help from neighbouring streets, whose militia might likewise take their seals to identify themselves.[39] The militia of the allied streets certainly made important contributions towards the security of Canton. Apart from maintaining rigid precautions within the city, they also released large bodies of regulars to defend the city walls and to fight the rebels. It was largely due to Yeh that this militia came into existence, and it was undoubtedly a considerable task to run it: financially, for example, although the militia of the allied streets were self supporting, Yeh had to examine their accounts to make sure that they were free from embezzlement, which might have injured the morale of the whole organisation.[40]

Yeh's intelligence network also spread into every corner of the city, carefully scrutinising anybody who might be connected with the rebels. In October 1854, a plot was discovered in which some *yamen* employees who were members of secret societies conspired to admit the rebels through the north gate of the city.[41] Various rebel spies who were working in the office of the provincial judge and of the grain intendant were likewise detected. Others who were in Canton with a similar mission were also exposed.[42] All these cases testify to the efficiency of Yeh's secret service. Much of the intelligence work was carried out by members of the gentry, whose greatest *coup* was the abduction and arrest of the leader of the secret societies, called Ch'en Sung, who commanded indisputable respect from the heads of major societies and who in fact directed many of the important uprisings led by Ho Liu, Li Wen-mao, Ch'en K'ai and Kan Hsien.[43] Historians have always attributed the ultimate failure of the Red Turbans to their apparent lack of co-ordination and central command. Had Ch'en Sung lived, the rebellion would indeed have taken a very different course. Yeh's efficiency and his shrewdness in winning the unswerving support of the gentry was impressive, for they went to great trouble to serve his cause.

The management of supplies

Logistic support to the army was another important matter which demanded Yeh's personal attention. There were different departments within the military organisation which dealt with munitions. Normally the Banners and certain regiments of the Green Standard were authorised to manufacture gunpowder.[44] Yeh realised that one way of making up for the deficiency of troops was to possess superior artillery fire. Hence he ordered new sets of machinery for producing gunpowder of the best possible quality.[45] The gunpowder thus produced was transferred to the central gunpowder store (*huo-yao-chü*) before being issued to the various units of the army. In times of extreme urgency all units of the army were empowered to make whatever quantity of gunpowder they could. Yeh also ordered that all small cannon be melted and recast into more up to date and powerful artillery.[46] A different department, the arsenal (*chün-chuang-so*), cast cannon balls, shot and other projectiles. These in turn were transported to the three government munition stores, Ta-yu Ts'ang, Yung-feng Ts'ang and Hai-chu Fort.[47] There was yet another department, called the *chün-ch'i-chü*, which stored war materials such as wickerwork shields, iron bars, gongs, ropes, net and the like. Yeh ordered this department to inspect all its materials in store and sell those which were no longer suitable for use in battle so as to make room for new weapons.[48] He also required all the above mentioned departments to send him monthly reports,[49] in order that he should be fully informed of the situation with regard to military supplies. Since the immediate threat to Canton in 1854 came from the land, especially in the north and east of the city, Yeh had many cannon removed from the war junks and placed on the walls north of Canton to strengthen the defence there.[50] He also bought large quantities of arms from Hong Kong and from the foreign merchants in Canton.[51]

The next question was the supply of food. The quantity of rice the Cantonese normally kept in stock would not enable them to survive a six-month siege. The rebels did not completely prevent any goods going to Canton from the countryside, allowing the passage of, for example, groundnut oil after levying a tax of 0.2 taels on each barrel, 0.1 taels on a pig and an equal amount on a cage of chickens or ducks; but no wood, vegetables or staple foodstuff of any kind were allowed to pass through their check-points along the routes to Canton.[52] In fact, even if there had been no interference by the rebels, very little rice would have found its way from the countryside to Canton because of the natural disasters of the previous years; nor was the crop of 1854 a particularly good one. Rice had to be imported, and it was no easy task to feed 15,000 troops in addition to the population of about one million Cantonese.[53] Yeh took no chances. He had a report prepared, possibly on the information provided by Chinese merchants who traded with southeast Asia, about the condition of rice production and recent harvests in various parts of Indochina, and the time it would take to ship rice to Canton.[54] His next step was to encourage these merchants to import rice from abroad. The latter in turn hired convoys of British vessels or other foreign steamships to tow the rice boats once they entered the Pearl River so as to avoid interference from the rebel fleets blockading Canton.[55] Many foreigners joined in this lucrative trade; ship after ship, fully loaded with rice and other goods, proceeded into the city.[56] For example, an American named Endacott was reported to have become a multi-millionaire by selling goods to the besieged city.[57] There were of course periods when rice was very scarce and expensive, but on the whole, Yeh managed to keep the situation under control by dealing harshly with hoarders and preventing the prices rising beyond a certain level.[58] Indeed his concern was that not only should his troops be properly fed, but that the citizens should have sufficient to eat, lest unrest should arise from starvation. He required the officials concerned to make a report to him every five days about the amount of rice imported during this period.[59]

The rebels wanted to starve Canton into submission; they, ironically enough, had to send their secret agents into Canton to buy the goods and ammunition they wanted, but these agents were quickly detected and severely dealt with.[60]

The campaign[61]

Strategically, it would have been fatal to allow the forces of Ch'en K'ai at Fo-shan, 100,000 strong, to join in the siege of Canton. Yeh was determined to prevent this happening at all costs. On 6 August he summoned to Canton prominent members of the gentry, notably Liu Ping-yüan, Ou-yang Ch'üan, and Ho Ying-ch'un, of the villages between Canton and Fo-shan such as Ta-li and Ssu-pao. These members of the gentry were interviewed by principal officials of the Military Supply Bureau, with whom they discussed and planned to intercept Ch'en K'ai, and from whom they received a supply of large cannon and ammunition. They went home just in time to face Ch'en's soldiers. On 19 August, Ch'en K'ai, anxious to join forces with Li Wen-mao, sent two regiments against Ssu-pao. The gentry of this area were well prepared: with the militia they had organised, the firm alliance they had formed among the Ninety-six Villages already mentioned, and the supplies they had received from Canton, they successfully beat off the attack. After this battle, the gentry were confident that they could remain masters of the land, but were worried about the river, and appealed to the Military Supply Bureau for a fleet of government war junks, suggesting several strategic points along the river which should be guarded and from which any rebel troops who tried to cross the river could be fired upon. On 30 August Ch'en K'ai led a force of about 100,000 in a full scale assault on the Ninety-six Villages. Again he was defeated.[62] This was one of the decisive battles of the campaign in the delta. It successfully prevented Ch'en K'ai joining forces with Li Wen-mao, thus increasing the chances of Canton's survival.

At Canton itself, severe fighting outside the city walls began on 30 July. The situation was so precarious that, in the words of a British consular report, 'The flight from Canton to all parts of the surrounding country as well as to Macao and Hong Kong continues. It began with the wealthy, but the poorer inhabitants now swell the stream of fugitives in great numbers.'[63] Yeh was unmoved. He ordered his troops to keep their positions of defence to repulse any attack directed against the city, but not to go in pursuit of the enemy for more than a short distance, 'lest they should become the victims of some stratagem'. 'The governor-general, governor and Tartar general, frequently survey the proceedings of the military from the tower on the city wall, or some other commanding position, and with their own hands dispense rewards to those who have distinguished themselves in combat, on their return.'[64] Although Yeh's troops were inferior in number to the rebels, they were far better trained and possessed in abundance powerful artillery of which their enemies were desperately short.[65] Therefore the rebels, after a month of profitless skirmishes, resolved to launch a full-scale attack on Canton both from the east and from the north. Both attacks were repulsed. Taking full advantage of the high morale thus raised among his soldiers, Yeh ordered a surprise counter-attack in the east. The victory was complete: Ch'en Hsien-liang's headquarters at Yen-t'ang was captured and he fled to Hsin-tsao (Blenheim Reach) where he was to operate henceforth as a force on the Pearl River only.[66] The victory in the east enabled the government troops to concentrate on the north. On 28 October, Niu-lan-kang, a major stronghold of the rebels in the north, was levelled by Lin Fu-sheng and his mercenaries. Colonel Wei Tso-pang led various regiments to pursue the rebels still further north, crushing two other strongholds and burning down upwards of 600 encampments. In the west, Shen Ti-hui sailed north with a fleet of war junks. He circled behind the headquarters of Li Wen-mao at Fo-ling-shih and mounted a surprise attack. The rebels were dispersed and fled still further north. Thus by about the end of December, the insurgents were driven from the immediate vicinity of Canton; and though the siege was not yet lifted entirely, the city was free from imminent danger.[67]

The rebels, however, were still lurking at some distance north of the provincial capital. According to the deposition of a rebel captured on 14 January 1855, the various rebel leaders were again planning another joint attack on Canton, this time mainly from the river. From the east Lin Kuang-lung was to sail up the Pearl River with 145 junks; Ho Liu and his fleet were to attack from the south, advancing up the Macao passage. The combined forces of Kan Hsien and Chou Ch'un including about 20 junks, were to attack from the west. Finally, Li Wen-mao was to attack once more from the north. But Yeh had in fact decided not to await any further attack but to follow up the recent victories by driving the rebels clear of Canton. On 7 January, the last strongholds of the rebels in the north were taken; Shih-ching was overrun by Tseng T'ing-hsiang,

Ta-kang by Lai-ts'un and Kuan-ch'iao by Wei Tso-pang.[68] Meanwhile
Shen Ti-hui, after his triumph at Fo-ling-shih northwest of Canton,
turned his attention to Fo-shan. With two outstanding commanders,
Magistrate Designate Hsieh Hsiao-chuang and Sub magistrate Chang
Chin-chien, and the help of militia from the Ninety-six Villages and from
Shun-te, he recovered the town on 17 January, after twenty-three days
of bitter fighting. Ch'en K'ai fled with remnants of his men to Shun-te,
and later joined forces with Li Wen-mao, who had been driven away
from the north of Canton, and they made their way up the West River to
Chao-ch'ing.[69]

The rebels on land had been dispersed. Attention could now be turned
to those on the river. Lin Kuang-lung, leader of the rebels south of
Canton, had been reinforced by Ch'en Hsien-liang and Ho Liu after
their defeat east of Canton, first on 8 September 1854 and again on 7
December.[70] The strength of these three rebel groups combined was
certainly very impressive, so much so that the British consul at Canton
wrote to Sir John Bowring 'to request that the admiral be moved to
detach to Canton such force as His Excellency deems requisite for the
safety of the British life and property, for at the present moment the city
is menaced by a large piratical fleet'. As a result, H.M.S. *Barracuda* was
despatched to Canton.[71] In fact Canton had been in a far more dangerous
position four months previously, when it was attacked on three sides by
an overwhelming number of rebels, but to the foreign communities who
lived on the waterfront in the southern part of the city, danger had
seemed distant; it was not until a rebel fleet was actually in sight on 2
December that they felt themselves endangered and fell into a panic. In
this situation Yeh made the unprecedented request that the British ships
of war which were 'also in the river for purposes of protection' should
join in the suppression of 'the thieves in this river', a request which led
Bowring to believe that 'great must be the alarm and extreme the
perplexities and perils' in the city; it was regarded by Bowring at the
time as 'an application' and by many Chinese historians since then as
'begging' 'for assistance from Her Majesty's forces'.[72] There are
several points which one may venture to clarify in respect of this
popular belief.

It was true that the strength of the government fleet compared most
unfavourably with that of Lin Kuang-lung alone. The government junks
guarding the Macao passage, 'which is the last barrier in advance of the
city, did not exceed 50, while the enemy counted 2000 sails large and
small',[73] and obviously were undisputable masters of the river. On the
other hand, it has been shown that the rebels were no match for Yeh's
troops on land. Some time later, Ho Liu's fleet attempted to advance on
Canton from the east, but found it impossible to go beyond Whampoa,
and was eventually driven back by powerful artillery from the forts

guarding the city.[74] Further evidence that Canton was not in such imminent peril as she had been was provided by the behaviour of the common people, who 'show no symptoms of the excitement they exhibited at the beginning of the disturbance'.[75] Therefore one has reservations about accepting the view that Yeh 'desperately asked for British naval intervention'.[76]

The course of events tends to reinforce these reservations. On receiving Yeh's letter, Bowring, besides making it clear that the policy of his government was one of absolute neutrality, added, 'As the circumstances appear so urgent, I shall, accompanied by the Admiral and several ships of war, proceed to Canton on Wednesday next'.[77] However, Bowring's trip to Canton proved completely fruitless, because the Chinese authorities refused to see him 'to discuss matters which interest them so deeply'.[78] Why then was British favour sought? One contemporary Chinese official at Canton described it as the result of Shen Ti-hui's urging Yeh to do so.[79] It is difficult to imagine how the field-commander, himself described as a 'fiery man',[80] could have possibly humbled himself to supplicate for foreign aid if it was not a matter of utter necessity. Again, one wonders how much weight the views of a circuit intendant made field-commander to fight the rebels, carried with a strong character such as Imperial Commissioner Yeh when it involved foreign affairs. Perhaps a study of the original communication between the two parties might throw some light on the situation.

The episode began with a letter addressed to Sir John Bowring, without date or seal, but self-styled as a communication from the gentry and merchants of Canton. It requested Bowring to send his fleet to join their expedition to suppress piracy, which was causing great damage to merchants, English and Chinese alike.[81] Bowring's reaction was that, had the communication been sent through Yeh, he would have given it his 'careful attention and early reply'.[82] Then Yeh sent, on 7 December, the following letter to Bowring, which was subsequently translated:

From Yeh, Imperial Commissioner &c.
Previously, when Mr. Consul Robertson informed me of the disturbances made by the Ko-lahn pirates, and requested me to join in destroying them, I despatched men of war for this purpose, and many of the robbers were seized and confessed. This was proof of our mutual hatred of these people, was deserving of great praise, and a source of comfort. And now that the thieves in this river have become so strong and troublesome, and are in the vicinity of the foreign dwellings, although I have already sent my soldiers and volunteers to arrest their progress and destroy them, yet as I hear that the ships of war of your honourable nation are also in the river for purposes of protection, it is proper that we should act in concert in the important design of destroying and seizing these offenders.
I take this opportunity of wishing you happiness, &c.[83]

By going through this communication, one will observe that the paramount interest of the Chinese was the suppression of *piracy*, which was so dangerous to the merchants. Hence one suspects that the rich merchants of Canton, who almost single-handedly financed the campaign by donations when all government resources had dried up,[84] might have formed a kind of pressure group, inducing Yeh to seek British co-operation in restoring trade to normal as soon as possible.[85] From Yeh's point of view, it was also in the interest of his government to restore trade and hence the proceeds from import and export duties; and of course he saw no reason why foreigners should not be favourably disposed towards such a project since their commerce also suffered drastically from the disturbances, especially from the 'river pirates'. Just a month before, the British navy had sought the co-operation of Chinese marines to stamp out pirates based at Kao-lan (Ko-lahn) in the mouth of the Pearl River,[86] and Yeh saw no reason why this aid should not be reciprocated. Furthermore, it did not occur for a moment to Yeh that there was a civil war as such going on in Kwangtung; it was the imperial government suppressing 'robbers' and 'thieves in this river', and after all, British warships had come to Canton to protect their subjects and property. Therefore, if the merchants did suggest seeking British co-operation, Yeh could see no objection to following such a course. This was possibly why he allowed the merchants to write to Bowring at all about a matter of international co-operation. When he found that Bowring's reaction was that if only the communication had been forwarded by him, it would have met the latter's 'careful attention and early reply', he thought he sensed a favourable response and consequently had no compunction about addressing Bowring directly. Naturally the flat refusal from Bowring took him completely by suprise. He must have felt that he had been tricked,[87] and was consequently all the more convinced that foreigners were unpredictable and treacherous. Equally, the ultimate disappointment of Bowring at Canton served to strengthen his belief that the mandarins were 'obstinately proud and unteachably ignorant'.[88]

To return to the campaign on the river, desultory fighting continued after the severe engagement on 7 December. Fifteen days later, Lin Kuang-lung was killed in action in Ho-nan,[89] and when Ch'en Hsien-liang arrived from Hsin-tsao the next day, he ordered a full-scale offensive against Ho-nan to avenge the death of his ally. The attack was repulsed. In January 1855, victorious troops returned from the campaign north of Canton and inflicted a crushing defeat on the rebels on the river. Ch'en fell back to Hsin-tsao. In February, Shen Ti-hui also returned triumphantly from Fo-shan. The government troops reorganised themselves and set out on 5 March under their field-commanders on land and on water to deal with the last group of rebels threatening

Canton, those in the south.[90] One after another the rebel strongholds in Ho-nan fell before them. Three days later, there was a 'total defeat of the rebel force in Blenheim Reach...with the loss of all their heavy vessels of war, the capture of their depot, the village of Sanchow [Hsin-tsao], with all their provisions, materials &c., and their flight'.[91]

At long last, Canton was safe. Yeh breathed a sigh of relief, and so did the foreign community, among whom Consul Robertson wrote to Bowring, 'I am in great hopes this affair will crush the local disturbance, which has so seriously affected the city for months, and that we may hope for a quiet future, and release from the anxieties it has entailed upon Your Excellency and, I may add, myself.'[92] Perhaps Yeh's relief was greater, and more deserved for having been laboriously gained. For practically every battle fought, he had maps drawn, showing not only the topography and human dwellings of the area, but also the positions and strength of the troops of both sides; in the case of those about the river, comments about the direction of the wind which was likely to affect either the advance or retreat of the war junks were also included.[93] These maps gave him an intimate knowledge of the situation and enabled him to conduct the campaign wisely. Many of the engagements near Canton he watched with his own eyes, and for those out of sight of the city, he despatched his secret agents, mostly members of his bodyguard, to the scene under instructions to report directly to him.[94] In this way he had a vivid picture of the behaviour and morale of both sides, and hence was able to calculate realistically the factors which might affect the outcome of each individual engagement. Yeh was undoubtedly a painstaking and capable military organiser, and his success was by no means just a piece of good luck.

Conclusion

Canton survived, alone, while city after city in the Yangtze area fell in spite of the help of troops from all over the empire, and with them fell their governors-general and governors, Tartar generals and Green Standard commanders. It is instructive to compare Yeh with the imperial commissioners sent to suppress the Taipings. Of these, the first, Chou T'ien-chüeh, was appointed in 1851 but recalled after a few months because of his failure to manage his subordinates.[95] His successor Sai-shang-a soon had to confess that he was unequal to the task and begged Peking to replace him with a more capable commander.[96] Then Hsü Kuang-chin took over; yet the very person whose 'calm, perseverance and competence I know very well' (said the emperor),[97] was also dismissed in 1853. Hsiang Jung was in turn entrusted with this task, but the burden crushed his health and he died.[98] Therefore by the beginning of 1855, nearly all of Yeh's peers had gone,

5

and the prominent figures of the next generation, men like Tseng Kuo-fan and Li Hung-chang, were only beginning to emerge. That was possibly why an English observer of the time described Yeh as '*the* great Chinaman of the present day...the second man of the empire.'[99] Had Canton fallen to the rebels, the effect would have been disastrous for the morale, strategy and military supplies of the whole imperial army, and the survival of the Manchu dynasty would have been very much an open question.

There are many reasons which may have accounted for the survival of Canton. Yeh's ability as military organiser, as reviewed in this section, in his deployment of troops, the military government he organised, the security measures he adopted, the management of supplies, and his actual direction of the campaign, were certainly major factors. The remarkable performance of his officers, especially his field-commander, was equally important, as were the financial contributions of the merchants and the support of the gentry, the interests of both being in this case identical with those of the government. However, the commanders were selected by Yeh and it was due to his policies that the merchants and gentry rallied so effectively to his side, so that these factors also may be set to his credit.

On the other hand, the weakness of the rebels must not be overlooked. Their numerical superiority was considerably compromised by their lack of training, discipline and modern weapons. They had immense difficulties in obtaining provisions; their initial moderate policy of levying tolls in the territories they occupied was not particularly welcomed by the inhabitants, and their later desperate resort to plunder antagonised the general populace. Consequently, the villages not yet affected by the rebellion fervently responded to the government's call to organise militia for self defence and to intercept the advance or retreat of the rebels. Another result arising from the scarcity of provisions was the dissension among the various rebel leaders over the division of booty. Foreigners observed that 'there seems no unity of purpose nor combined action among the different bands of rebels.'[100] This was to a large extent true, because their alliance was a very loose one; Li Wen-mao had trouble even within his own camp, let alone giving orders to others – in fact he 'invited' rather than commanded the others to perform one function or another.[101] Had Ch'en Sung lived, his undisputed prestige might have furnished the leadership the rebels wanted and events might have taken a different course; but he was arrested by Yeh when he was still organising the rebellion.

The part played by foreigners was also very important. The ammunition and food with which they supplied or helped to supply Canton were essential for the survival of the city. Furthermore, the mere presence of foreign vessels was alone sufficient to limit the rebels' freedom of manoeuvre on the river. M. C. Morrison, the interpreter at the British Consulate in Canton, commenting on an engagement on 7 December, wrote, 'It is difficult to account for the neglect of the rebels to press their advantage except in supposing that they may have been deterred from advancing by the presence of foreign ships of war, of whose intentions they are suspicious.'[102] Ch'en Hsien-liang complained to Bowring about this; he was rebuffed.[103] Eventually he took the drastic decision to make the blockade absolute by the end of February, 'notifying to British subjects to remove their property from Canton within a given period, and thereafter that the River will be closed to the passage of foreign vessels and steamers'.[104] Bowring refused to recognise Ch'en's right to do so; and when it happened that 'scarcely a day passes in which the so called rebels do not stop ships and boats bearing the British flag, many of which they pillage', he considered 'that a collision can hardly be avoided, if our trade is to receive protection'.[105] Collision was avoided only by the complete victory of Yeh's troops at Hsin-tsao eight days later.

The Pearl River

Once Canton was safe, Yeh was able to turn his attention to the rest of the province and in particular, the Pearl River region, where numerous magisterial seats had already fallen, and many more were yet to fall. The most serious was the loss of the prefectural city of Chao-ch'ing. Since the North, East and West Rivers all converge on the delta, it is very easy to descend on Canton by these three rivers. Hence the prefectural cities of Shao-chou on the North River, Hui-chou on the East River, and Chao-ch'ing on the West River are strategically vital for the safety of Canton, because they form a triangle around it, serving as outposts for its defence (see Map 9). Had all these cities fallen, then most of the rebels of the province could have descended on Canton, and its chances of survival would have been very small indeed. As mentioned, Chao-ch'ing was overrun, and the rebels along the West River, including those from as far as Kwangsi, sailed downstream to join Ch'en K'ai, whose troops were thus swollen by tens of thousands. It was fortunate that Ch'en K'ai's troops were repulsed by the Ninety-six Villages and were thus unable to join in the attack on Canton, and that both Shao-chou and Hui-chou successfully beat off repeated attacks and sieges by the rebels. Consequently, it was only with the rebels in the delta that Yeh had to deal at Canton.

To Yeh therefore, the end of the hostilities in the delta only meant the beginning of another campaign in the whole Pearl River region. Knowing that this would involve mobile instead of static warfare, and

Table 10

Prefectural and magisterial seats in the Pearl River (including the delta) and the Han River Regions fallen to the Red Turbans, 1854–5[a]

Cities	Date lost	Date recovered	Chief official	Chief officer
		A. Pearl River		
(1) *Kuang-chou*:				
1 Tung-kuan	17.6.54	30.6.54	Dismissed	Killed
2 Tseng-ch'eng	10.8.54	21.9.54	Wounded	Pardoned
3 Hua-hsien	13.7.54	16.10.54	Died previously	—
4 Lung-men	20.9.54	27.10.54	Killed	—
5 Ch'ing-yüan	4.8.54	18.4.54	Pardoned	Killed
6 Shun-te	1.8.54	4.5.55	Killed	Killed
7 Ts'ung-hua	17.11.54	18.1.55	Burnt	—
8 Fo-kang	9.8.54	21.5.55	Killed	—
(2) *Hui-chou*:				
1 Ho-yüan	8.10.54	27.12.54	Died previously	Killed
2 Po-lo	20.12.54	11.2.55	Pardoned	—
3 Ch'ang-ning	12.10.54	12.10.54	Pardoned	Pardoned
4 Hai-feng	2.9.54	18.9.54	Killed	Killed
(3) *Shao-chou*:				
1 Ying-te	3.8.54	12.6.55	Dismissed	Pardoned
2 Lo-ch'ang	8.9.54	25.9.54	Dismissed	Dismissed
3 Jen-hua	26.2.55	26.2.55	Dismissed	Dismissed
4 Ju-yüan	15.10.54	17.10.54	Dismissed	Dismissed
(4) *Nan-hsiung*:				
1 Shih-hsing	25.9.54	18.10.54	Dismissed	Pardoned
(5) *Chao-ch'ing*:				
1 Chao-ching (city)	5.8.54	21.5.55	Killed	Retained
2 Te-ch'ing	3.4.55	3.4.55	Pardoned	Pardoned
3 Ho-shan	6.8.54	10.9.54	Killed	—
4 Feng-ch'uan	29.8.54	21.5.55	Killed	Dismissed
5 Ssu-hui	13.8.54	27.4.55	Pardoned	Pardoned
6 Kuang-ning	15.8.54	15.8.54	Pardoned	Pardoned
7 Kao-ming	22.7.54	25.7.54	Pardoned	Pardoned
8 K'ai-p'ing	12.8.54	27.10.54	Killed	Killed
9 Hsin-hsing	1.8.54	2.8.54	Pardoned	Pardoned
(6) *Lo-ting*:				
1 Tung-an	5.8.54	5.8.54	Wounded	Killed
(7) *Lien-chou*:				
1 Lien-chou (city)	22.9.54	2.4.55	Pardoned	—
2 Yang-shan	25.9.54	25.1.55	Pardoned	Killed
3 Lien-shan	25.9.54	25.1.55	—	—

[a] This table is adapted from 279A.3.35. 'Killed' means killed in action; 'retained' means dismissed from the ranks but allowed to keep the post. The dates come in the order of day, month and year.

Table 10 (*cont.*)

Cities	Date lost	Date recovered	Chief official	Chief officer
		B. Han River		
(8) *Ch'ao-chou*:				
1 Hui-lai	7.6.54	6.10.54	Killed	Killed
(9) *Chia-ying*:				
1 Ch'ang-lo	26.7.54	17.10.54	Killed	—

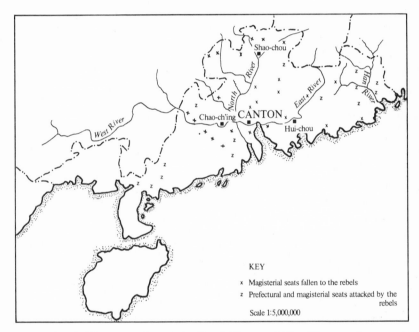

Map 9. The campaign of the Pearl River and Han River regions.

that his troops would be fighting upstream most of the time, Yeh ordered
the construction of large numbers of boats for use in shallow water.[106]
Then instead of spreading his troops to cover all three tributaries, he
instructed Shen Ti-hui to concentrate on one before going on to the
others. The first task lay in the west, to recapture the city of
Chao-ch'ing. As for Yeh himself, he decided to remain at Canton; he felt
sure that his officers, who had proved their true worth in more than six
years of warfare, were capable of good judgement and wise decisions.
Furthermore, he had complete confidence in the ability and resourceful-

ness of his field commander. Indeed, he regarded it a good policy that he, as governor-general and head of both the civil and military hierarchies, should remain at the provincial capital in order to have a balanced picture of what was happening in the whole province so that, if necessary, he could give general directives to his officers. Moreover, he had to look after the problem of provisions. Rice, according to a British consular report of the time, 'has risen to double its ordinary price and serious apprehensions of a famine are entertained'.[107] To ensure a continuous supply of provisions to his army who were about to embark upon the task of rural pacification, Yeh sent some government agents, who could now be spared because Canton was no longer in immediate danger, 'to the Straits and Manila to purchase rice, and a fleet of cruisers has been despatched to convey a number of junks laden with the grain from the west coast [of Kwangtung, less affected by the rebellions] which are blockaded by pirates in ports on the route'.[108] This operation was a success: 'Large importations of rice from abroad have made food again abundant, and the seasonable rains which have terminated a long continued drought have contributed to the diminution of the previous high prices'.[109] Meanwhile, foreign vessels made idle because of the failure of tea to arrive at Canton continued to engage in the rice trade, and now that they had to compete with the government of Canton, the foreign merchants found that by July 1855, 'the rice market is still very dull and prices are again a shade lower...the dealers are now engaged working off their large purchases'.[110]

Yeh's remaining at Canton and taking care of provisions did not, however, mean that he was out of touch with the development of the campaign. He required his officers in different areas to send him reports about each engagement and to draw him maps of the places involved. He also sent his bodyguards secretly to important scenes of action to report to him directly about the conduct of the battle and the behaviour of the government troops as well as that of the enemy.[111]

The West River

As mentioned, Yeh's first object in the campaign of the Pearl River region was the recovery of Chao-ch'ing. Meanwhile, Ch'en K'ai, after his defeat at Fo-shan, retreated westwards with his troops. On the way he was joined by Li Wen-mao and his followers after their failure to take Canton. When they arrived at Chao-ch'ing, they were welcomed by the rebels who had occupied the city, and Ch'en K'ai was elected leader of this combined force. However, before the rebels had regrouped themselves properly, Shen Ti-hui, with the new and well-equipped light boats, was already in hot pursuit, levelling their strongholds in rapid succession as he went. Ch'en K'ai's fleet of about 700 boats, which sailed down the river in an attempt to halt Shen's advance, was dispersed on 20 April 1855. The next day, the area was covered with heavy fog. Taking advantage of the weather, Shen, while staging a fake attack on the rebel fleet guarding the last barrier to the city, sent his *corps d'élite* ashore to surprise the defenders in the forts. Suddenly the rebel fleet found itself fired upon not only from the government junks but from its own forts on both sides of the river; it fled in confusion back to the city and helped to take away whatever supplies it could before deserting Chao-ch'ing with the rest of the troops and sailing further up the West River into Kwangsi.[112]

The North River

The North River was Yeh's next target, for both strategic and commercial reasons. Shao-chou had been besieged three times, from 25 July to 15 October 1854, during the last ten days of October, and from 29 November 1854 to 22 May 1855. These sieges involved not only the effective isolation of the city from outside but also violent attacks on it. The third siege was especially dangerous because the local rebels were reinforced by the troops of Ho Liu, Kan Hsien, Ch'en Chin-kang and others who had been defeated in the campaign in the Canton delta. Fortunately the 5,000 mercenaries from Kiangsi (4,000 were recruited in Kiangsi and 1,000 at Shih-hsing in Kwangtung), 2,000 troops from Hunan and various regiments from within the local circuit of Nan-shao-lien arrived in time to help lift the siege; otherwise the city might well have fallen. Having failed to take Shao-chou, the rebels divided into two groups, one marching north into Hunan to join the Taipings, the other south to Ying-te.[113] Thereafter, there was the danger of the northern group descending on Kwangtung with the Taipings, and of the southern one attacking Canton again. All strategic points along the North River had to be recaptured as quickly as possible. Commercially, the North River was the main route by which tea for export came down to Canton. The rebels, as M. C. Morrison put it, 'obstruct the main roads from hence to the North and West, and so prevent mercantile traffic. A large proportion of last year's crops of tea is thus detained at Shao-chow-foo. A small quantity only having arrived here after paying heavy blackmail, and some having been plundered by the rebels'.[114] As a result, foreign merchants complained that 'teas are difficult to obtain at anything like reasonable terms'.[115]

After the recapture of Chao-ch'ing, therefore, Yeh ordered that Shen Ti-hui, instead of pursuing the rebels further west, should immediately turn his attention to the North River. With his light boats and victorious troops, Shen swept north, crushing all rebel fleets and forts on the way. Confronted with such a formidable force, the rebels occupying Ying-te retreated once more in the direction of Shao-chou; by the middle of June, most of the prominent Red Turban leaders such as Kan Hsien, Chou Ch'un and Ch'en Chin-kang had fled to Hunan one after the other. By this time Yeh felt that the situation in northern Kwangtung was under control and instructed Commander-in-chief K'un-shou, who had been obliged to remain at Shao-chou by the critical situation there since 1853, to withdraw and return to his headquarters at Hui-chou, on the East River, where again his immediate task was the suppression of the rebellion.[116]

The East River

The rebellion here began as early as 26 June 1854. It was as devastating as those in the other regions; many magisterial seats were lost and Hui-chou was attacked several times. The local authorities were quite helpless against the marauding rebels, and it was not until reinforcements began arriving in the following year that they felt they could launch a counter-attack. In March 1855, a small flotilla of boats came from Canton. On 5 May reinforcements from the province of Fukien also arrived. But it was not till the appearance of K'un-shou on 29 August that a major offensive was planned.

K'un-shou was a very capable commander, whose merits during the campaign in the North River region had won him the title of Junior Tutor of the Crown Prince. Still, he found his new task laborious and lengthy. It was not until 7 June 1856, when the major rebel group led by Ti Huo-ku retreated into Kiangsi to join the Taipings, that the area could be described as pacified,[117] and K'un-shou was immediately transferred by Yeh to fight in the West River region, which Shen Ti-hui had had to leave prematurely.

Conclusion

The campaign of the Pearl River may be described as successful. Before it began, Yeh consulted his advisers on strategy. One of them cited a debate on strategy during the widespread rebellion in Liang Kuang in the late fifteenth century, as to whether the rebels should be dispersed or expelled from Kwangtung en masse.[118] The adviser went on to say that both opinions were sound in their own way, and we have seen that Yeh's troops had succeeded in doing both. They had crushed the rebels besieging Canton and had driven the rebel groups led by Ch'en K'ai and Li Wen-mao away from Kwangtung up the West River into Kwangsi, those led by Kan Hsien and Ch'en Chin-kang along the North River into Hunan, and those led by Ti Huo-ku away from the East River into Kiangsi; they had also recaptured the lost cities and dispersed the rebels into the countryside.

However, the success was not complete. In the West River region, for example. Ch'en K'ai and others overran the city of Hsün-chou in Kwangsi and continued to expand their territory by taking the neighbouring cities such as Wu-chou, Kuei-hsien, P'ing-nan and others. In the battle at P'ing-nan, Hsieh Hsiao-chuang, who had been sent by Yeh with 1,000 mercenaries to assist the city in its defence, was killed.[119] This was a serious loss, as he had been the right-hand man of Shen Ti-hui during the fighting at Fo-shan. The fleets Yeh despatched into Kwangsi to deal with these rebels also suffered severe reverses.[120] The whole of 1856 was marked by continuous fighting, with the government forces losing more and more ground. At one stage Yeh was so apprehensive that the rebels would descend on Kwangtung again that he deployed squadrons of war junks to defend Feng-ch'uan and built numerous forts on both banks of the river.[121] Fortunately for him, the victorious rebels decided not to press their advantage but to try their luck in the north of Kwangsi, and by the end of 1857, were planning to attack the provincial capital, Kuei-lin. The attack eventually came at the beginning of 1858,[122] at the same time as Canton fell to the British and French allied forces.

Nor was the North River region entirely free from disturbance. In late 1856, for example, Ch'en Chin-kang and his group returned from Hunan and joined some local rebels in an attempt to retake Ch'ing-yüan. The defence of the city was very poor indeed, and in despair, the magistrate committed suicide. Yeh had to transfer the brigadier of Nan-shao-lien from Shao-chou down to Ch'ing-yüan to defend it. Early next year, Chu Kuo-hsiung also led his mercenaries to reinforce the city which, after much hardship, survived a two month siege. Since then, rebel groups continued to menace the countryside well after Yeh was captured by the British.[123]

The Han River

This region was also badly flooded in the summers of 1852 and 1853 and in the spring of 1854, and before long, the whole area – the prefectures of Ch'ao-chou and Chia-ying – was infested by rebels who troubled the region for nearly three years. Prominent rebel leaders included Ch'en Niang-k'ang, Wu Chung-shu and Hsü A-mei. Little assistance came from Canton, and the local officials under the leadership of Circuit Intendant Ts'ao Li-t'ai and Prefect Wu Chün had to rely on their own forces to suppress the rebellion. It was mentioned (in chap. 3) that Wu was a demanding superior and took pains to train his magistrates to be resilient and efficient administrators. In the end his efforts paid dividends; a study of Map 12 and Table 9 will show that although many magisterial seats were attacked by the rebels in the Han River area, only two fell.

There is little evidence that Yeh ever played an active role in the campaign of the Han River region. One exception was perhaps his instruction in May 1857 to the troops of Ch'ao-chou to march up the river into Fukien to fight the Taipings, who were threatening to invade Kwangtung. The result was the complete defeat of the Taipings, and within five days no less than 3,000 dead bodies floated down the Han River into the South China Sea.[124]

Conclusion

Apart from his family background, Yeh's knowledge of military affairs was obtained chiefly from the battlefield. He began his military career as a field-commander in the campaign in Ch'ing-Ying, and we have seen the ability that he demonstrated in this capacity. This experience enabled him to calculate realistically the behaviour of both his own rank and file and that of his enemies, and to recognise the factors that decide the outcome of a campaign. Later, as an organiser assembling his own forces, he was thus able to draw on first-hand knowledge of the ability of individual officers and of the fighting capacity of the various regiments, which he had gained during his early service. With these forces he secured complete victory at Kao-chou and maintained the defence of Canton in apparently hopeless circumstances.

On examination, his tactic on the outbreak of the general insurrection appears to be one of grouping his troops to protect certain strategic cities in which most of the wealth of the province was concentrated, such as Canton, Shao-chou, Hui-chou, Ch'ao-chou, Kao-chou and Chao-ch'ing. If these cities managed to hold out against attacks until the rebels should disintegrate internally, either through dissatisfaction with lack of success or through the strain created by lack of supplies, his troops could launch counter-attacks from their bases in the cities. This strategy proved successful, and all the cities except Chao-ch'ing survived repeated and violent attacks; then when the rebels around Canton were beaten off, he sent his troops to help the other cities. As for the countryside, it was left entirely to the mercy of the rebels for the time being. It was here that the gentry played a dominant role. Supported by the militia that they had organised and financed out of their own resources, they led their clansmen to the assistance of the prefectural and magisterial seats and helped to lift the siege or recapture these administrative centres when they had fallen to the rebels. However, regaining control of urban areas did not mean the end of the rebellion; countless marauding bands were still at large, plaguing the countryside. Yeh was still engaged in a vigorous campaign of rural recovery as late as the end of 1857, on the eve of the capture of Canton by the British and French forces; he was not given time to finish his task.

Nevertheless, his achievements were sufficient to shape the history of his time. He not only suppressed the sporadic revolts of 1850–3 and kept the general insurrection in Kwangtung under control, but foiled the attempts of the Taipings to take Kwangtung by invasion from the west, north and east. Had the Taipings succeeded in their initial intention to occupy the province in the early 1850s, the Red Turbans would certainly have rallied to their support and with the wealth of the province, the foreign trade at Canton, and recruitment from its war-like inhabitants, they would have had a far better prospect of ultimate victory. To this extent Yeh may be ranked with Seng-ko-lin-ch'in and Tseng Kuo-fan as saviours of the empire. His tragedy was that because of his defeat in the *Arrow* War, all his merits were blotted out by reproach and disgrace.

In fact his failure in the *Arrow* War was a direct result of the disturbances in Kwangtung and in China as a whole. The sporadic revolts which began in 1849 in various parts of the province had tied down a large number of his soldiers in the countryside. The outbreak of the Taiping Rebellion and subsequently the fall of Nanking in 1853 created a heavy strain on Kwangtung (see next chapter). When the Red Turban Rebellion erupted and Canton was besieged in July 1854, Yeh was deprived of most of his regular troops and he broke out from the city only with great difficulty. However, the situation in the countryside remained so serious that he had to risk the safety of Canton by despatching all the troops who had been gathered for its defence into the rural areas. Thus, when Admiral Seymour attacked Canton in late October 1856, he encountered very little resistance, and withdrew only because he did not have sufficient troops to occupy the city and because he was constantly harassed by his enemy's irregular military man-oeuvres. Yeh could not recall his troops from the interior just to forestall the possible renewal of British assaults, because such an action would mean the abandonment of the rural areas or even the collapse of his government. The threat of the Taipings on the Han River region in east Kwangtung in May 1857 must have convinced him still further that his soldiers had to remain where they were. Hence he attempted to settle the foreign dispute by every means other than pitched battles. When the British suddenly turned up with powerful reinforcements and French allies in late 1857, he was doomed to become a prisoner of war.

Part four

The paymaster general[1]

Pas d'argent, pas de Suisse. If Yeh were to engage sufficient troops to cope with the unrest, vast quantities of extra revenue had to be found. He could not expect any fiscal support from either Peking or the other provinces; on the contrary, he was constantly called upon to help them to meet the astronomical cost of the campaign against the Taipings. This part examines Yeh's role as paymaster general, trying to arm and victual nearly half the troops of the empire.

---

7 Conventional management of finances

Local expenditure, 1849–53

By statute, financial matters were no concern of a governor-general. It was the governor who was responsible for them. But as we have seen, because of the unusual circumstances of the time and his outstanding ability, Yeh took over control of public finance. However, this does not mean that he had more freedom than a governor in handling public money. The uses to which revenue must be put, both national and local, were specified by the central government. Hence in the case of a mishap which demanded extra money, little if any could be expected to be forthcoming from the regular provincial budget. Indeed, various mishaps did occur even before the period of sporadic revolts. They are listed in Table 11, for the year 1849 alone. These urgent expenses were met by transferring funds already earmarked for other purposes, and the Liang Yüan had no other means of replacing these funds than requesting permission from the emperor to invite contributions from the gentry and merchants of the province.[1] This was a signal of grave danger to the government; it gave the warning that the provincial budget would be thrown into a state of confusion, with far-reaching effects, should it continue to be tampered with in this manner in the years to come. However, 1849 was only the beginning; it was followed immediately by the period of what has been referred to as Sporadic Revolts of 1850–3.

Table 11
Unexpected expenditure in 1849[a]

Event	Expenditure (taels)
1 Commander-in-Chief Hsiang-lin's expedition to Ch'ing-ying	47,000
2 Preparation for defence during the Entry crisis	32,000
3 Suppression of pirates	46,000
4 Defence preparations during the Amaral Crisis	17,000
5 Defence of the prefectures of Kao-chou and Lien-chou against bandits from Heng-chou in Kwangsi	30,000
Total	172,000

[a] 391.3.34 Hsü and Yeh to emperor (1850). The figures in this document were round numbers, with digits below 1,000 omitted, presumably to make easy reading for the emperor. João Maria Ferreira do Amaral, governor of Macao, was assassinated near the Barrier in Macao and caused a diplomatic incident (Morse, *International Relations*, 1,340).

The five campaigns discussed under this heading in chap. 5 referred only to the major revolts; there were disturbances in other areas as well, such as Ts'ung-hua and Nan-hsiung in the north, Hui-chou and Tung-kuan in the east, and Chao-ch'ing and Feng-ch'uan in the west. Table 12 is a list of all the expenditures thus incurred.

The actual amount of money spent on each campaign was in fact more than that listed in this table. Let us take Ch'ing-ying as an example. The silver drawn from the provincial treasuries, according to the report from which this table is made, was 507,255.588 taels. In addition, a total of 244,152.088 taels was spent independently by the various prefectures and magistracies on the war effort, of which only 85,496.729 taels were later repaid out of the sum (of 507,255.588 taels, as mentioned) drawn from the treasuries at Canton, so that in fact 158,655.395 taels more were spent. On top of this, four magistracies had still not made statements of the amount of money they had similarly expended when the report was made. This means that the total expenditure exceeded 665,910.947 taels, and that over a hundred thousand taels were extracted from the local units of government in one particular campaign alone. The local units in turn shifted this extra burden on to the shoulders of the populace.[2]

The treasuries of the province were unable to meet these war expenses because they were already empty by the time of the very first

Table 12
*Sums drawn from the provincial treasuries to meet the expenses
of suppressing the Sporadic Revolts, 1850–3*[a]

Events	Expenditure (silver in taels)
1 Ch'ing-Ying	506,255.588
2 Lien-chou	227,557.249
3 Tan-chou	71,399.168
4 Kao-chou: under Hsü	994,673.506
under Yeh	374,091.604
5 Shao-chou	40,000.000
6 Ts'ung-hua	6,000.000
7 Nan-hsiung (defence)	4,000.000
8 Hui-chou	33,178.190
9 Tung-kuan (Ssu-ma village)	26,857.700
10 Chao-ch'ing	44,000.000
11 Feng-ch'uan (defence)	226,234.950
12 Mercenaries sent into Kwangsi	18,785.014
Total	2,573,032.969

[a] This table is adapted from 253A.3.85. The figures in this document are sometimes contradictory but the table has taken its figures from those marked 'drawn from the treasury' rather than the 'totals' given in the document.

campaign, in Ch'ing-Ying (1850–1). In his reply to Grand Councillor Ch'i Chün-tsao's inquiries, Yeh wrote,

The treasuries of Kwangtung are now empty and all our reserves are gone, because no less than 2,700,000 taels had been given to Kwangsi as military finance since the rise of the Taipings. Our campaigns are financed by whatever is left in the customs treasury, by contributions, and forced loans from the prefectures and magistracies which are as a result entirely exhausted too.[3]

If the treasuries in Kwangtung were empty, and the province as a whole exhausted, in 1851, the interesting question, and one which is certainly worthwhile studying, is how did Yeh manage to survive the sporadic revolts in 1850–3 and then the devastating general insurrection from 1854 onwards. Indeed, he was able to find the means to finance not only the suppression of the widespread local uprisings, but to meet the astronomical demands made on him by the imperial army fighting in central China. In fact it might prove illuminating, before going into details of his financial policies, to see how much financial assistance he was making to other provinces to pay the imperial troops fighting the Taipings during the years 1850–3 alone.

Table 13

Financial assistance to the other provinces from the Kwangtung provincial treasury, 1850–3[a]

Date	Source of fund	Sum (in taels) of silver)
	A. To Kwangsi	
1 16.11.50	Autumn land tax	50,000
17.11.50	Autumn land tax	50,000
2 28.2.51	Spring land tax	75,000
1.3.51	Spring land tax	75,000
3 14.3.51	Miscellaneous	65,000
15.3.51	Miscellaneous	65,000
4 23.4.51	Autumn land tax	43,000
5 20.8.51	National allotment, 1851	59,936.765
8.11.51	National allotment, 1851	40,000
6 11.11.51	Miscellaneous	70,000
12.11.51	Miscellaneous	70,000
13.11.51	Miscellaneous	70,000
14.11.51	Miscellaneous	70,000
7 23.12.51	Miscellaneous	75,000
30.12.51	Miscellaneous	75,816.897
8 14.4.52	National allotment, 1852	50,000
9 13.5.52	Contributions for military finance	62,316.30558
14.5.52	Contributions for military finance	60,000
13.6.52	Contributions for military finance	20,000
26.8.52	Contributions for military finance	53,000
27.8.52	Contributions for military finance	53,000
23.12.52	Contributions for military finance	15,000
10 23.7.53	Contribution for militia	11,000
24.7.53	Autumn land tax	129,000
11 28.7.53	Funds for gunpowder	26,000
	Salt revenue	30,000
	B. To Kweichow	
1 16.4.50	National allotment, 1850	40,000
2 1851 and 1852	National allotment, 1851–2	Intercepted by Kwangsi[b]
3 8.5.53	National allotment, 1853	27,000
	C. To Hunan	
1 27.1.53	Salt revenue[c]	25,700
	D. To Hupeh	
1 20.2.53	Land tax, etc.	70,000
2 22.2.53	Land tax, etc.	70,000
3 24.1.53	Land tax, etc.	68,450.3

Table 13

Date		Source of fund	Sum (in taels) of silver)
		E. To Kiangsi	
1	3.6.53	Contributions	7,000
2	7.7.53	Contributions	10,000
	30.7.53	Miscellaneous	16,261
	31.7.53	Contributions	10,000
		F. To Fukien	
1	Post 4.8.53	Miscellaneous	43,000
2	15.9.53	Contributions	43,100
	Total		1,863,581.26758

[a] 68.4.23; 279A.3.3; 279A.6.25; 121B.7.1,7,8,12,13; 327.3.45. The dates refer to those when the actual journey of conveyance of silver to the various destinations began at Canton. All the sums listed, except those entitled 'National Allotment' which was an arrangement for the richer provinces to help pay the troops stationed in the poor provinces, were extra demands on the resources of Kwangtung.
[b] The total was 130,000 taels.
[c] The provincial treasury which housed land tax had an arrangement with the salt treasury to receive an annual sum from the latter to defray certain expenses. The customs treasury, however, was not in any way related to these two; see Table 14.

Financial assistance to other provinces, 1850–3

Before the general insurrection in Kwangtung, thousands of taels of silver continued to pour out of the treasuries of the province to pay the imperial troops who were engaged with the Taipings, first in Kwangsi, then in Hunan, Hupeh, Kiangsi and Fukien. To simplify lengthy descriptions, the necessary details are summarised in Tables 13 and 14. It will be seen from Table 13 that a great portion of the funds from the provincial treasury came from contributions; the income from the land-tax in Kwangtung, however great, was simply incapable of meeting the never-ending demands of the time. There was also a continuous flow of silver from the customs treasury to Kwangsi, but there was a limit to what this source too could provide. As Table 14 shows, for six months in 1853, from 22 January to July, there were no deliveries, partly because the Taipings had moved from Kwangsi to Hunan and partly because there was a severe recession of trade. This was to worsen in the years to come (see Fig. 5), with the breakdown of order in the province. To repeat Yeh's statement to Grand Councillor Ch'i Chün-tsao in 1852, 'In the words of Your Lordship, Kwangtung is in imminent danger of complete impoverishment'.[4] The following pages attempt to analyse

Table 14
*Financial assistance to Kwangsi from the Kwangtung
customs treasury, 1850–3*[a]

Date	Sum (in taels of silver)
1 18 and 19.11.50	100,000
2 6 and 8.10.50	100,000
3 19 and 20.2.51	100,000
4 13 and 16.6.51	200,000
5 28.8.51	110,000
6 3.9 and 2.10.51	200,000
7 14 and 21.10.51	490,000
8 7 and 8.12.51	149,183.103
9 20.12.51 and 15.2.52	280,000
10 17.5.52	70,000
11 13.6.52	50,000
12 16.6.52	80,000
13 6.8.52	60,000
14 3.9.52	60,000
15 1.10.52	50,000
16 3.10.52	70,000
17 23.12.52	50,000
18 1.1.53	50,000
19 17.1.53	50,000
20 30.1.53	50,000
Total	2,369,183.103

[a]   279A.6.14,15; 121B.7.13. The title of 279A.6.14 is 'Financial assistance to Kwangsi from the Kwangtung customs treasury, Nov. 1850–July 1853'; obviously there was no assistance to Kwangsi from 22 Jan. to July 1853, the reason being that by the end of 1852, the Taipings had fought their way into Hunan and government funds were hence directed hither instead of Kwangsi, the first sum from the Kwangtung customs treasury being 200,000 taels (see 253A.3.10).

Yeh's financial policy in this apparently hopeless situation in terms of the management of existing sources of revenue, the exploitation of extraordinary sources, and the management of expenditure.

The management of existing resources

There were three main sources of revenue in Kwangtung, taxation on land, salt and trade. This section examines Yeh's policies towards each of them.

The land tax

In the early Ch'ing period the poll tax was abolished, and the land tax increased to make up for the lost revenue. The gentry, who constituted a great portion of the landowners, were thus compelled to pay more tax on the land they possessed and the tenants were allowed to go tax-free. This was meant to help the poor; and in Kwangtung, where land ownership was concentrated in a few hands (see chap. 2), the tenants ought to have benefited. They did, for some time, when the government was efficient and well-organised. By the nineteenth century, however, the increasing financial difficulties of the government had obliged it to impose non-statutory surcharges. Of the four surcharges attributed to 1908,[5] three were already extant in the 1850s.[6] The one that was not, was created after the Boxer Uprising of 1900, for paying the indemnity. Needless to say, the gentry in Kwangtung were particularly unhappy about the extra burden, as they owned most of the land. Slowly, they developed their own means of extracting compensation. First they raised the rents and went to the extent of using torture and execution to enforce the payment of full rents, against which, as described in chap. 3, there was nothing Yeh could do. Secondly, they tried to avoid paying the land tax by various attempts to discredit the local officials. We have seen how Yeh harnessed the energies of the gentry to serve his cause, and how indispensable was the role played by this class in this period of confusion; however, this does not mean that there was no potential conflict between the government and the gentry. Indeed, it was not until Hsü and Yeh had forced the more unruly section of the gentry to recognise that they were dealing with determined administrators, that they took orders from Canton. This happened in 1851, officially the first year of Emperor Hsien-feng's reign. It has been suggested that Hsien-feng remitted the land tax of 1851 in order to secure popular support.[7] However, it was customary for an emperor to cancel arrears of the land tax in the first official year of his reign, and Hsien-feng was no exception. Late in 1850, the year in which his father died and in which he assumed power, he issued a decree to this effect to apply to the following year, officially the first year of his reign. Hence the Ministry of Revenue ordered that collection of the tax should continue in 1850 until the deadline for that year was reached. Both the imperial edict and the order of the ministry were published; but the gentry, in an attempt to avoid paying the rest of the land tax of 1850, asserted that the official notice transmitting the order of the ministry was a forgery by the local officials for their own profit. The gentry of Tung-kuan tore down this notice and declared that any tax collector who dared to go down to the villages would be tied up and beaten. They also put up red placards calling for a mass refusal to attend the magisterial examination and condemning the magistrate for ill-treating the local gentry by prosecuting them on false charges of sedition and refusal to pay land tax. At the same time, the students of Hsi-hu Academy in Nan-hai protested against a cut in the funds allotted to them,[8] but were firmly rebuffed by the prefect of Kuang-chou. In retaliation they sent an unsigned letter to Hsü accusing the prefect of irregularities and threatening a mass refusal to take the public examination. However, when Hsü asked for the students who staged such accusations to step forward as witnesses, the answer was again the posting of red placards proclaiming that there was no need to be afraid of the Liang Yüan, whose bark was worse than their bite. The gentry in the various magistracies in the Canton delta followed suit and also used mass refusal to take public examinations as a means to protest against the paying of the land tax.

Hsü and Yeh stood firm. They decided to make an example of the gentry of Tung-kuan and Nan-hai by sending a memorandum to Peking in which they recommended a cancellation of the public examination in Tung-kuan and prohibition of the students of Hsi-hu Academy from taking part in any examinations, pending investigation and punishment of the ring-leaders. The gentry of Kwangtung had not seen such resolute administrators for a long time; they became scared, and the uproar died down.[9] Although the candidates from Tung-kuan who came to Canton for the provincial military examination in October of the following year staged a further protest to Acting Governor Po-kuei, the issue was no longer one of refusal to pay land tax, but of compensation for the death of their fellow student, Li Tzu-hua, who was arrested during the protest movement and committed suicide while he was in custody.[10] It is significant to note that when Yeh returned from the campaign in Ch'ing-Ying to supervise the civil provincial examination in 1851,[11] the gentry tamely sat for the test; it was only when he was away from Canton fighting another campaign that some of them dared to stir again. One may therefore safely conclude that Yeh's firm policy during the incident of 1851 curbed the gentry and safeguarded the land revenue of the province from one of its many enemies.

The corruption of officials posed another problem, but as described in chap. 4, Yeh was to a large extent successful in checking it. Far more serious, however, was the extortion by the very junior tax-collectors. The surcharges imposed on the land tax mentioned above were channelled to pay the local *yamen* staff: secretaries, clerks and runners, who were often appointed tax-collectors and who, therefore, had a vested interest in collecting as much surcharge as they could. Worse still, the number and amount of these surcharges varied from place to place; this gave the tax collectors an opportunity to invent new charges or even exact money from the landless as well. Therefore, tax-collectors continued to be assaulted in the countryside (see chap. 4). Given time,

Yeh might have been able to put his house in order; but time was not forthcoming as the region under his rule was soon thrown into political turmoil, against which he had to mount a military solution. However, he did urge his subordinates and the gentry to resettle those uprooted by the rebellions,[12] in order to benefit from a revived agriculture, and while the disturbances lasted, to collect as much tax as possible. Inevitably, the income from land dwindled considerably in the 1850s. Even during the period of sporadic revolts, the situation was already very serious. What happened in the magistracy of Ssu-hui in the West River region may serve as an example.

As mentioned, all land-tax payments in arrears at the end of 1850 were written off by the new emperor, Hsien-feng. Still, even though the burden of taxation on the people was thus eased, the magistrate of Ssu-hui found it difficult to collect sufficient tax to meet the annual quotas of 1851, and as late as 7 July 1852, there was still a shortage of 1,630 taels of silver and more than 200 *shih* of rice. It must have been commonplace throughout that region for Yeh to have requested from Peking a postponement of the deadline for delivery of the tax. However, news of the edict granting the request came too late for the said magistrate to do anything but make up the deficiency with part of the tax collected for the year 1852, and he was left with far less than normal time to collect tax to meet the quotas for 1852. Worse still, the next month saw his territory troubled by two bands of rebels from a neighbouring magistracy. The villages were thus sacked and he had to spend much money organising militia for self-defence, and more than 6,000 taels were taken from the magisterial treasury – out of the tax collected for the year 1852 – to finance the suppression of the rebellion. Helpless, the magistrate resorted to requesting a grant of several thousand taels from the provincial government to meet the tax requirement before the deadline for delivery, on the grounds that he had received no military finance from Canton during the disturbance;[13] but the provincial treasury had already spent all its reserves. Indeed it was unheard of that a magistracy, instead of delivering silver to the provincial treasury, should ask the latter for a grant to meet its tax quota. Consequently, when the deadline for the delivery of land tax came, Kwangtung was 264,846.9210 taels short of the provincial quotas of 926,055.8780 taels, a deficit of nearly thirty per cent.[14]

If the sporadic revolts were financially ruinous, the general insurrection was disastrous. In 1854, when the general insurrection began, an account was made to Yeh stating that the military finance of the year was 1,322,487.3290 taels, but the provincial treasury was able to pay only 261,642.6680 taels from the land tax collected in both 1853 and 1854, the deficit being 1,060,844.6610 taels (80%), of which, 530,000 taels, should have come from the salt treasury and and the rest from the

Table 15[a]
Land-tax deliveries

Year	Deliveries (taels)		Deficits (taels)		% de-
	Tax	Surcharges	Tax	Surcharges	livered
A. By 20 January 1856[b]					
1854	451,986.1260	68,328.4515	486,236.5280	113,480.1795	46.455
1855	135,812.0110	14,080.0820	787,674.2880	163,416.8910	13.614
B. By 29 November 1857[c]					
1854	657,718.3663	133,642.8674	273,625.5403	48,165.7636	80.126
1855	731,176.1180	137,667.4590	192,390.3920	39,829.5140	78.327
1856	704,078.8440	132,516.5050	219,411.8500	44,981.1800	75.985
1857	Not listed				

[a] One will find that the land tax and surcharges levied varied slightly from year to year, which might have been caused by clerical errors. Nevertheless, the quotas for the land tax of all three years (1854–7) were below 940,000 taels, which was considerably lower than the 1,223,000 taels of 1908 given by Wang, *Land – Tax, 1753 and 1908*, p. 16. Equally the surcharges amounted to less than 8% of the land tax, as contrasted with the 10% of 1908 given by Wang (p. 17).
[b] 327.3.14 Report on provincial treasury for the period 7–20 Jan. 1856.
[c] 44.8 Statement of balance of provincial treasury for 1854–7.

land tax of the year. Meanwhile, a total of 195,899.6590 taels of miscellaneous surcharges was collected in 1854, but the sum demanded of this source in the same year was 323,905.0634 taels, the deficit being 128,005.4044 taels (40%).[15] As the rebellion wore on, both deficit and tax arrears accumulated. To cope with the deficit, Yeh attempted to tap new resources, as will be discussed later. With regard to the arrears of land tax, the only way open to him was to keep his troops in the countryside to back up his subordinates, whom he pressed extremely hard, collecting tax of the current year and of previous years. A study of Table 15 indicates that Yeh's policy could be described as successful, considering the disturbed state of the province.

Salt revenue

The salt industry was a government monopoly so far as production and distribution were concerned. Salt was produced along the coast of the province of Kwangtung, but distribution was centred on two points, Canton for the Pearl River region, and Ch'ao-chou for the Han River region. Thus the area of distribution included the whole of Kwangtung and Kwangsi, the southern parts of Kweichow, Hunan, Kiangsi and the eastern districts of Fukien. It formed what was known as the Kwangtung salt market (*Yüeh-yen hsiao-ti*), and salt produced in places

Table 16
Allocations (taels) from the salt revenue to the army, 1851–3[a]

Year	Allocation	Sum paid	Sum in arrears	Arrears (%)
1851	560,000	446,335.93	113,664.07	20.297
1852	520,000	120,000.00	400,000.00	76.923
1853	480,000	Nil	480,000.00	100

[a] 253A.6.1 Allocations from salt revenue to the army, 1851–3.

other than Kwangtung could not be sold in it.[16] Merchants licensed to engage in salt trade purchased salt at its cost of production, and were charged a fee for the licence, from which the salt revenue was in the main derived. Miscellaneous surcharges also contributed to this revenue. Like the land tax, government income from salt had an annual quota (661,534.0480 taels) to meet. Unlike the land tax, there was no cancellation of the standing arrears in 1851. Fortunately, the salt treasury had been able to meet the annual quota (*o-cheng*) till 1850, when it, too, was affected by the rural disturbances, leading to a deficiency of 35,450.820 taels (5%). However, 1850 was only a beginning, for the deficiency of 1851 was 140,029.133 taels (21%), and that of 1852 was 154,387.384 taels (22%).[17]

The annual quota from the salt revenue was largely allotted to victual the regular troops, both local and national. A study of Table 16 gives a clear picture of the considerable decrease in this source of income even in the period of sporadic revolts. As shown in this table, although there were drastic cuts each year in the allocation to the army, the sums actually paid were still hopelessly below the mark, and the arrears mounted. There are no independent reports, such as the one from which this table draws its information, after 1853, obviously because all resources of the province were brought under the centralised control of the Military Supply Bureau; but if the state of the salt revenue in the period of local revolts was such as has been described above, it must have been far worse during the years of the general insurrection.

Besides meeting the annual quota, the sale of salt licences was expected to yield more to meet other expenses. Part of this surplus (*ying-yü*) was allotted to victual the marines of Kwangtung. Table 17 below shows the standing arrears in 1853. The prefectures of Shao-chou, Chao-ch'ing and Ch'ao-chou were the most important areas in the North River, West River and Han River regions respectively. The fact that profits from the salt monopoly should decline when the population and hence the consumption continued to increase, and that payment in arrears from the salt treasury should date back to 1826, suggests that

Table 17

Payment in arrears from salt surplus to victual the marines, 1853[a]

Source	Annual allotment (taels)	Arrears From	To	Sum (taels)
1 Salt treasury	30,000	1826	1853	394,700
2 Nan-shao-lien circuit	60,000	1852	1853	75,000
3 Chao-ch'ing prefecture	20,000	1849	1853	96,000
4 Ch'ao-chou prefecture	20,000	1850	1853	66,000

[a] 279A.6.18 Payment in arrears from salt surplus to marines, 1853.

something must have been wrong with the salt administration. The surplus dwindled to almost nil in 1852, but the marines had to be paid. There was a report to Yeh in this year that since no money at all was forthcoming from this source, the two squadrons of marines on the west coast were paid by funds transferred from ten miscellaneous sources.[18]

According to a regulation laid down by Emperor Yung-cheng (*reg.* 1723–35), 'every grain of salt produced belongs to the government; no private dealings in salt will be tolerated. The monopoly of the sale of salt in defined areas [*pu*] shall be sold to merchants at a fixed annual sum'.[19] The Kwangtung salt market was divided into 188 *pu*, of which 159 were in the Pearl River region (75 in Kwangtung, 8 in Hunan, 1 in Kweichow, 66 in Kwangsi and 9 in Kiangsi) and 29 in the Han River region (14 in Kwangtung, 7 in Kiangsi and 8 in Fukien).[20] The first areas to suffer were those in Kwangsi, which was infested by rebels from the late 1840s onwards. Indeed, of the 35,450.820 taels in arrears in 1850, upwards of 17,775 taels (50%) should have been paid by merchants who had either deserted the areas or refused to continue the contract when it came to an end.[21] The hopeless arrears in the 1850s can partly be explained by similar situations in Hunan, Kiangsi and Fukien, and above all, the sporadic revolts and the general insurrection in Kwangtung itself.

In the absence of licensed merchants, smuggling flourished. Armed bands of outlaws took over a large part of the salt trade in Kwangsi.[22] In Kwangtung itself, even the government troops, mainly mercenaries, wanted a share in this illicit, but lucrative business.[23] Meanwhile, Hong Kong had become a centre for hoarding salt and smuggling it inland.[24] British nationals availed themselves of their right to fly the British flag, although it was for 'purposes so nefarious'.[25] Even the Chinese merchants, and not necessarily those resident in the colony, employed foreigners on board their lorchas, which could then pretend to enjoy extra-territorial rights.[26]

In response to this breakdown in the government monopoly, Yeh's advisers suggested two lines of action: measures to prevent smuggling and measures to lessen the expenses of the authorised merchants. It was hoped by intensive patrols and surprise checks to cut back the illegal sources of supply; and by relieving merchants of the burden of transport costs, by lowering licence fees and surcharges, and remitting licence fees in arrears, to reduce the price of government salt.[27] There is no evidence in Yeh's archive of his adopting the suggestions about licence fees and surcharges – perhaps it was beyond his power to do so; but he did take up the other suggestions. In Ch'ao-chou (Han River region), there was a vigorous campaign to raise funds for financing the transport of salt from the centres of manufacture to the centes of distribution.[28] At Canton new regulations were drafted in an attempt to discourage smuggling:

Draft regulations for salt administration at Canton

1. Every grain of salt conveyed to Canton belongs to the government and must not be allowed to trickle away. Even the salt swept out of the cracks in the junks by the dustman should be collected for distribution.

2. Officers at the distribution points used to take a portion of salt as subsidies. From now on, sums of money equivalent to the sale price of portions of salt taken as subsidies should be paid to them instead.

3. Labourers at the distribution points used to take one out of every 500 bags of salt as a subsidy. From now on, a sum equal to the sale price of such a bag of salt should be paid instead.

4. Sailors in the salt boats should be paid only their wages and should under no circumstances be allowed to demand any salt as subsidies.

5. Labourers employed by the salt merchants are paid a substantial sum of 0.0035 taels for each bag of salt handled; under pain of arrest and trial, let no one take any salt for himself.

6. Employees of the Southern Store used to take 3 out of every 100 bags of salt destined for Yünnan as subsidies. This practice should be allowed to continue but no more than three bags should be taken.

7. Intensive river patrols should be maintained, day and night. The officials keeping watch over the weighing and distribution of salt will be held responsible for any abuse arising from these procedures.

8. Once loaded with salt, the boats should immediately leave Canton for their respective areas of the salt market.

9. The salt comptroller should be ordered to issue these regulations to the various departments of his hierarchy, to be strictly obeyed under pain of immediate arrest.[29]

As for the foreign merchants engaged in salt smuggling, and the Chinese merchants who employed foreigners as captains to 'protect' their illicit traffic in salt, Yeh took the drastic action of seizing and detaining their lorchas whenever and wherever he could, so long as he had sufficient evidence to justify his action.[30] The greatest impediment to the salt administration, however, had been the general breakdown of law and order. Once the rebellion was under control, Yeh immediately despatched commissioners to the various areas of the salt market to reorganise salt administration. In 1855, for example, northern Kwangtung was still in great confusion although the siege of Canton had been lifted, but without delay Yeh sent commissioners to this area to revive the salt trade in conjunction with the merchants. As a result, 160,000 bags of government salt were sold by the end of the year, thus fulfilling the licence-fee quota of 1853.[31]

Fresh difficulties arose in 1856. The province of Hunan was devastated by the Taipings, and the authorities decided, as a means of raising some money, to levy a tax called *likin*[32] on Kwangtung salt once it had crossed the border. Whereas the licence fee of a bag of salt was 0.6 taels, the *likin* was 0.4 taels, which meant an increase of two-thirds in the price of salt in the areas in Hunan. Yeh feared that the large increase in the price of government salt would greatly encourage smuggling. Hence he sent the deputy salt intendant, Ku Ping-chang, to Hunan, where he successfully negotiated an end to this practice. However, a few months later, Hunan again had to resort to the same arbitrary action. Although Yeh's advisers could furnish him with perfectly valid legal arguments against the *likin* on salt, Peking reluctantly refused to intervene, because the government of Hunan had to be financed somehow. An even greater problem arose with a proposal by the authorities in Kwangsi for a change in the control of the salt trade. They suggested that, since many of the licensed merchants had fled, been killed or gone bankrupt during the insurrection, a licence should not be necessary to purchase salt from the government factories provided that the purchaser undertook to sell the salt only in Kwangsi. This would revive the salt trade in the open rather than the black market, and the government of Kwangsi would derive fresh income from taxing this trade. However, the government factories were situated in Kwangtung and the salt had to be transported through that province along the West River before reaching Kwangsi. It would be impossible to ensure that this salt was not sold *en route* in competition with the licenced merchants of Kwangtung. Yeh was strongly advised to reject this proposal.[33] What steps he actually took we do not know. As governor-general of both Kwangtung and Kwangsi, he had power over the latter which he did not have over Hunan, and he might have succeeded in rejecting a proposal which could prove detrimental to the whole system of salt administration in the Kwangtung salt market.

In brief, the salt administration was confronted with serious difficulties. First, the breakdown of law and order not only interrupted the salt trade but badly damaged the machinery of distribution and sale. It also brought its familiar concomitant, smuggling. Yeh's achievement in reviving the salt monopoly as soon as he managed to keep the disturbances under control was a substantial one. The intensification of patrols along the water routes (along which salt was largely and economically transported), produced the desired results. His seizure of foreign lorchas where he believed himself to be right was evidence of his courage and sense of justice. His firmness must have to some extent curbed the recklessness of foreign adventurers. Sir John Bowring, British Plenipotentiary at Hong Kong, was in no position to question Yeh's line of action. In his application to Yeh for the release of two British lorchas seized for smuggling salt, he had to admit that

It is provided by Article 12 of the Supplementary Treaty, that if any British vessel be detected smuggling, the Chinese authorities shall be at liberty to ' seize and confiscate all goods, whatever their nature or value, that may have been so smuggled; and may also prohibit the ship from trading further, and may send her away as soon as her accounts are adjusted and paid.'[34]

Where Yeh seemed to be least successful was in his attempts to prevent Hunan adopting a policy which could prove detrimental to the entire system of salt administration. This was a reflection, however, not on his lack of resourcefulness, but rather on the problems caused by the breakdown of central control at a time when the very existence of the dynasty was questioned by the Taiping Rebellion.[35]

Customs revenue

Yeh's concern with foreign trade dated back to as early as 1848. In that year, there was a severe trade depression, and Yeh, as provincial treasurer, directed an investigation into the cause of this fall in exports.[36] Since the Entry Crisis of 1849, he had always shared with Hsü the task of conducting foreign policy, and during the twelve months when Hsü was fighting in Kao-chou, Yeh assumed sole responsibility as acting imperial commissioner for foreign affairs. As the diplomatic transactions of this time were largely connected with trade, Yeh was given the opportunity to acquire knowledge of the working of the customs house. In 1854, when the widespread rebellion made it necessary to centralise control over all resources, the customs, more than ever before, came under the direct influence of the governor-general. He first ordered an investigation into the annual yield of the customs duties on imports and exports since 1848.[37] The result shows that whereas there was a gradual increase between 1848 and 1852, there was a sharp decline from 1853 onwards (see Fig. 5). The chief reason was of course the impact of the rebellion. 'At the north', wrote Interpreter Morrison, 'the districts of Ying-te Hsien in the department of Shao-chow Foo and Nan-hsiung Chow being held by the rebels, the line of traffic through the defile in the Meiling range is impassable.'[38] Yeh diverted the main body of his troops from the West River region to that of the North River as soon as Chao-ch'ing was recaptured, in an attempt

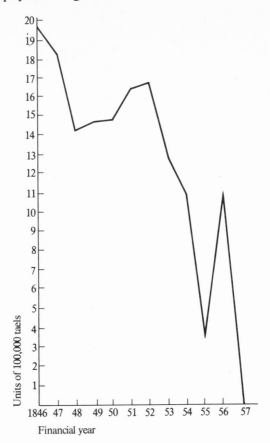

Fig. 5. Customs revenue, 1846–57

Note: 112.3.16, 137.1.23, 138.5.17 and *Tao-kuang Hsien-feng liang-ch'ao chou-pan i-wu shih-mo pu-i*(Nan-kang, 1966), nos. 173, 206, 229, 241, 159, 184, 303, 333, 360, 380 and 410. Each financial year consisted of 12 lunar months in disregard of the fact that once every four years there was one intercalary month. Furthermore, the revenue of 1854–6 as shown here represents that at Canton alone. Foreign trade was stopped throughout 1857.

to re-open trade. His strategy bore fruit. 'By the recapture of the town of Ying-te Hsien, on the 21 ultimo [June], the passage into Kiangse was opened, and some of the long detained teas of last year [1854] have since reached Canton.'[39] At the same time Yeh tried to ensure that transit duties on the trade which could take place were collected with the greatest possible efficiency. The whole system, its personnel, and its regulations about the terms of office and the delivery of taxes collected, was overhauled.[40]

A general survey of foreign trade was also carried out, and, despite

Bowring's remark that at Canton 'the frauds and evasions have always been fewer than at Shanghae',[41] some Chinese merchants had been discovered trying, in collaboration with foreigners, to avoid paying export duties, by pretending that their exports were foreign products which had come to Canton but were being transferred to the other ports and hence were entitled to apply for duty-free certificates for re-export. Consequently, the Hoppo issued a proclamation prohibiting such fraud and threatening heavy punishment.[42] After this, the Hoppo was required by Yeh to furnish him with a report every five days about the amount of taxes collected in the period, the total amount of taxes collected since the first day of the financial year, whether this total was more or less than that collected over the same span of time in the previous financial year, and by how much.[43]

Although the proceeds from customs of 1855 were miserably small, the sum collected, upwards of 342,000 taels, was evidence of Yeh's hard work and progress; but not satisfied with his achievement, he turned his attention next year to the foreigners and the suppression of smuggling between Hong Kong and the coastal areas. From Canton, Consul Alcock wrote,

The close vicinity of a free port where Chinese may both bring produce from the Coast, where it is least guarded, and purchase foreign goods for the different places not opened by treaty to foreign trade, free from surveillance, customs house levy or exactions under their own authorities at the place where the exchange takes place; and with many chances of escaping when they return are facts too obvious to escape the notice of more obtuse authorities than the Chinese. Various official acts of the Hoppo here show that he regards the trade of Hong Kong as entirely at the expense of the Chinese revenue, and would gladly prevent its extension or continuance, if he saw the means.[44]

This document is a vivid explanation of how and why 'the whole, or at least a great part of the coasting trade carried on in small craft is smuggling trade.'[45] The same document, unfortunately, did not elaborate on what the various official acts of the Chinese were, but we do have some idea of what measures the colony took to facilitate the extension and continuance of its trade with the coast. In March 1855, it passed an ordinance requiring the registration of 'vessels employed solely in trading with the mainland of China'.[46] Thus registered, a vessel, whether it was owned by a Briton or a Chinese,[47] could fly the British flag and claim British protection. Needless to say, smuggling was 'promoted and facilitated by this ordinance', and Lord Derby had 'the unexpected testimony of the Colonial Treasurer to that effect'.[48] Apart from the fact that the ordinance, as pointed out by Lord Carnarvon, was in no way warranted by the ordinary course of international law, it certainly never received the sanction of the Chinese.[49] Yeh was uncompromising. He resolutely seized and confiscated any lorcha carrying licences granted to it under this ordinance so long as he had sufficient proof that it was engaged in smuggling. Bowring, of course, could not raise very serious objections.[50]

Swatow was another focal point. It was an excellent port at the mouth of the Han River, where illegal trade had developed rapidly in 1855–6 because the ordinary channels of access to Canton had been closed by the rebels for a considerable length of time. Consequently, it was regarded by J. Jardine as the station of incomparably the greatest importance which was not recognised by treaty,[51] where a foreign trade amounting annually to several millions of dollars was carried on openly.[52] Yeh, jointly with Po-kuei, issued a proclamation prohibiting the smuggling of goods from the interior to Swatow, where they were 'sent by foreign lorchas to Hong Kong and Macao [and where] cotton, rice, goods, woollens and tin imported by foreign ships [were] smuggled ashore without paying duty'. He further declared that he had directed the local officials of the Han River region to concert with the military to seize and punish all offenders, to confiscate their vessels and cargoes, and to forbid the construction of any more of the fast boats used for smuggling.[53] It is interesting to note that this proclamation shows more of Yeh's desire to collect duties than of his concern over the breach of treaty by foreigners, who traded with a port 'which is not recognized by treaty'. Indeed, the proclamation could be read to imply that so long as duties were paid, he was quite prepared to let this technically illegal trade go unnoticed, at least unofficially. To this extent, Yeh may be regarded as a shrewd minister of finance, as well as a practical politician: the political and financial problems of his government were such that he was wise to let sleeping dogs lie, on condition that the customs treasury received the appropriate amount of revenue. If he were asked officially by foreign diplomats to open Swatow for trade, his answer would no doubt be negative. He would plead, as he always did, that only the emperor had power to grant such a request. But the fact that he appeared willing enough to turn a blind eye, at least for the time being, to this unofficial opening of the port, contrary though it might be to the prescription of Peking, is, like the suggestion to hire the unemployed Bannermen as mercenaries, evidence of his courage and his predicament.

As a result of his policy regarding trade at Canton and along the coast of Kwangtung, the customs revenue of 1856 was considerably revived. That collected at Canton alone returned to the one million mark (1,080,240.057 taels), which was almost three times as much as that of the previous year.[54]

Interest from loans to money-lenders

This was also an important source of income to the province. When the Ch'ing empire had been stronger and more powerful, there was a surplus of revenue over expenditure, and the surplus was invested with the money-lenders. In 1796, for example, 230,000 taels were thus invested, and in 1825, yet another sum of 100,000 taels. During the reigns of Emperor Chia-ch'ing (*reg.* 1796–1820) and Tao-kuang (*reg.* 1821–50), the one million taels of reserve capital for the production of salt were also invested. The interest from these loans was allotted to meet expenses such as financing homes for infants, academies, purchase of military equipment, Bannermen's pensions, capture of law-breakers, and even the pay of troops.[55] The total annual pay of the soldiers of the governor-general's regiment manning the fourteen forts along the Pearl River, for instance, amounted to 7,680 taels, of which 3,280 taels (43%) was met from this source.[56]

A great many of the money-lenders invested in foreign trade, which before the Opium War was both safe and lucrative. However, after the conclusion of the war, the trade monopoly which had afforded them protection was abolished at the behest of the British. The Chinese merchants were thus less able to withstand the commercial crisis in 1847–8 and there was a wave of bankruptcies among those who had invested in foreign trade,[57] including money-lenders to whom government funds had been entrusted. Therefore by the end of the 1840s, organisations which relied on the interest partly or wholly as a source of income had already begun to suffer. Worse was yet to come in the following decade, which was marked by endless rebellions.

Unrest disrupted trade; this was bad enough for the money-lenders. But besides this, a great part of their resources was also invested in land, in the form of loans to the peasantry. This in itself and the sometimes extortionate rates of interest charged contributed to social unrest in the province and, not unnaturally, pawn-shops and the houses of money-lenders were obvious targets for the heavily indebted peasantry during the uprisings. The general insurrection of the 1850s therefore damaged this source of government revenue at least as badly as the land tax, salt monopoly and customs duties. In some ways it was even worse hit, because the damage could be permanent – once a money-lender was plundered, he lost at best a part of his capital, or at worst the whole of it.

Yeh was not in a position to help these money-lenders (and, in the last analysis, his government). He could not forestall an economic depression, nor was he able to do much about it when it did happen. As for the general breakdown of law and order, he could settle it by military means. But even when peace was restored, the pawn-shops that had been plundered were in all probability destined to remain closed for good, except in the rare cases in which the personal fortunes of the individual owners were revived. This is of course not to say that Yeh showed no interest in the money-lenders, whose fortunes were so closely connected with the income of his government. When the outlaws took advantage of the confused situation to rob a pawn-shop, for example, he would immediately send his special agents to the scene to conduct an inquiry and inspect the damage done.[58] He would even take the trouble of personally examining a thief if the latter were captured, in the hope that at least part of the lost property might be recovered.[59]

8 Yeh's innovations

The management of expenditure

We have seen the marked contrast between soaring expenditure and a rapid decline of resources, despite Yeh's remedial measures. As mentioned, since the taxes had to be remitted to Peking *in toto*, Yeh was free to manipulate only the surcharges, which were originally meant for financing the local government. Consequently, he resorted to managing expenditure in a manner as ruthless as the way he dealt with the rebels. Let us take item 5 in Table 11 ('Unexpected Expenditure in 1849', p. 122) as an example. Here the expenditure quoted is 30,000 taels; the actual expenses were in fact 29,921.94 taels. However, Yeh sanctioned an expenditure of only 21,870.00 taels (70%). The local officials had to find the remainder.[1]

Again, when Yeh conducted the campaign in Ch'ing-Ying a year later, the quartermaster of his army had to make a list of each item of expenditure, however small, including uniforms, weapons, ropes, lanterns, paper, sandals, or even pots, pans and cooking oil.[2] As for the money expended by the various local officials who led individual expeditions against the rebels, he applied the same drastic cuts and sanctioned only what he regarded as 'justified' expenses.[3] After the campaign of Ch'ing-Ying was over, the task remained of detecting and arresting individual rebels who went into hiding. Yeh appointed commissioners to perform this function. These commissioners were required to list the daily expenses incurred, specifying on each occasion whether they were staying in a particular place (name given) to carry out their duties, or whether they were travelling from one place to another (again, names given), the number of soldiers that accompanied them and the number of porters employed.[4]

During the campaign against Ling Shih-pa in 1851–2, Hsü had promised that anybody who managed to capture the rebel leader alive would be rewarded with 10,000 taels. However, when Yeh took over the direction of the campaign and Ling was subsequently killed by one of the officers, he was prepared to give that particular soldier 1,000 taels only, by way of reward. This was unusual enough to cause much comment among his junior officers.[5] But he took the line that the complete victory at Lo-ching was an achievement which belonged to the entire army, and to reward the one single officer, who happened to have killed the rebel leader, with a huge sum of 10,000 taels, would be bad for morale.

When the campaign was over, his task became one of checking the expenses incurred. His officials were required to give the fullest possible details of expenditure, chiefly on the payment of the troops and of the porters, on rewards and on compensation for wounds and deaths, on transport of troops and on the manufacture of munitions. Such was his demand for clarity of accounts and strict control of expenditure that the report prepared by Prefect Li of Kao-chou, for instance, was twice rejected for insufficient details.[6] However, his subordinates who were not trained as, or endowed with the natural gift of being, good accountants, suffered because they had to cover the deficit themselves. Yeh's policy was a necessity for survival. It might be harsh, but perhaps not unfair. Nevertheless, it was the cause of much complaint among some of his junior officers.

As the disturbances became widespread, more and more local officials were affected by this harsh policy. Let us take the magistrates as a case study. When a magistrate completed his usual three-year term of office, he had to send a balance sheet to the provincial government to be audited. One extra item now appeared on these accounts – the hiring of mercenaries to fight the rebels, and all its familiar concomitants: rewards, compensation for the wounded and the dead, military equipment, travelling expenses and so on. The magistrate had to spend the money first and then reclaim it from the provincial government. Whether he would recover the full amount depended on the audit at Canton. For purposes of analysis, Table 18 lists the verdicts in a number of such cases. The table shows that the expenditure was sanctioned in only two cases out of fifteen. Abuses or incompetence on the part of the magistrates concerned might have been the cause of the other verdicts, but to Yeh ignorance or incompetence in finance was no excuse for mismanagement of public funds. The resentment of some of the officials was finally expressed in a petition to Yeh, the conclusion of which reads:

Capable personnel is essential for a sound economy; tight control of expenditure is of little importance, and to regard the aim of good management of public finance as being to economise on expenses is very shallow indeed – it is very ungenerous and unkind, and will inevitably invite dishonest practices which will have even more serious consequences. The savings we try to make now may be the cause of expenditure of thousands in the future.[7]

This document cannot have failed to bring home to Yeh the fact that some of his subordinates must have been harbouring grievances against him after being found guilty of mismanagement of expenditure perhaps through no fault of theirs. Hence, to make things simpler and easier for his subordinates as well as to ensure good management of government funds, he commanded the Military Supply Bureau to draft some regulations which might serve as guidelines for his juniors. These regulations are briefly listed in Table 19.

Table 18
Magistrates with back debts[a]

Magistracies	Magistrates	Sum (in taels) spent in advance on paying mercenaries	Verdict
1 Ts'ung-hua	Chou	2,261	Cut
2 Ch'ü-chiang	Fu	2,728	Not Sanctioned
3 Weng-yüan	Ch'e	4,647	Cut
4 Lo-ch'ang	Wan	2,800	Not Sanctioned
5 Ying-te	Sun	11,700	Cut
6 Ch'ang-ning	Li	15,000	Not Sanctioned
7 Kuang-ning	Ch'eng	32,500	Auditing by MSB
8 Te-ch'ing	Hu	24,300	Auditing by MSB
9 Lien-p'ing	Wu	5,600	Auditing by MSB
10 Hsin-i	Hsia	1,260	Sanctioned
11 Hua-chou	Wang	7,640	Sanctioned
12 Ling-shan	Yang	5,530	Waiting Sanction
13 Shih-hsing	Mo	6,600	Cut
14 Lo-ting	P'eng	18,390	Cut
15 Hsi-ning	Wang	16,540	Cut

[a] 279A.6.7. MSB means Military Supply Bureau. Most of the magistrates mentioned completed their terms of office by the end of 1851.

The exploitation of extraordinary sources of revenue

The drying-up of the normal sources of revenue rendered it imperative to find new ones; but these were not forthcoming. To finance his campaigns and those of the empire, Yeh resorted to levying certain additional and extraordinary impositions on the wealth of the people. These were mainly three: contributions, increased taxation and confiscation of rebel property.

Contributions

The national income of the Ch'ing empire was barely sufficient, with some surplus at the beginning of the dynasty, to meet the ordinary national expenditure. However, there were four constant items of extraordinary expenditure: military campaigns (mainly the suppression of rebellions), water-works (especially along the Yellow and the Huai Rivers, whose floods were the source of chronic suffering to the Chinese), relief work (during natural calamities) and colonisation of virgin land within the empire.[8] To meet these extra expenses, contributions were invited from the people, who would then be

Table 19
*Regulations as regards expenses involved in the
suppression of rebellions*[a]

| | | A. Military personnel | | |
	Rank	Daily pay (taels)	Accompanying porters[b]
1	Colonel	2b	0.35	10
2	Lieutenant-Colonel	3a	0.35	8
3	Major	3b	0.25	6
4	First Captain	4a	0.20	4
5	Second Captain	5b	0.15	4
6	Lieutenant	6a	0.12	2
7	Sub-Lieutenant	7a	0.12	2
8	Ensign	8a	0.08	1
9	Colour Sergeant	9a	0.08	1
10	Sergeant	9b	0.08	1
11	Soldier, clerk	—	0.07	30 (For 100 soldiers)[c]

B. Civil officials commanding mercenaries

	Rank	Monthly pay (taels)	Accompanying porters[d]
1	Prefect (1st class)	4b	28.00	12
2	Prefect (2nd class)	5a	19.14	12
3	Magistrate	7a	19.14	12
4	Assistants[e]	—	12.00	6

C. Mercenaries

Different units are paid differently, according to the contract signed at the time of their recruitment. They should be paid according to these contracts, but no demands of subsidies in the form of rice or miscellaneous expenses will be entertained.

[a] This table summarises the information given in 112.4.6.
[b] Each porter was paid (0.08 taels daily) only during mobilisation, and only by his officer (to prevent extra demands on local officials).
[c] Their job was to transport cannon and ammunition.
[d] 20 porters were alloted to every 100 mercenaries.
[e] They were vice-prefects, vice-magistrates and other similar officials.

rewarded with official posts and titles according to the amount of money donated. However, to invite contributions was considered undignified by the emperor, because what it amounted to was in fact a sale of government posts. It also had a deleterious effect on administration, as certain courtiers pointed out.[9] Hence the emperor was often caught between the requirements of dignity and his need for money. Fortunately, such contributions were only temporary measures, and there were fixed periods in which they could be made; but with the gradual decay of the Ch'ing dynasty and the rapid increase in population without a parallel increase in production, the ordinary sources of revenue of the government dwindled. When Emperor Hsien-feng came to the throne in 1850, he was confronted with two almost insurmountable difficulties, the widespread unrest in China, especially in Kwangsi, and the paucity of resources to cope with it. Therefore an invitation for contributions was proposed, but he dismissed the suggestion.[10] However, he had cancelled the land tax arrears of the empire up to the end of 1850 as a sign of benevolence to his people before he officially started his reign the next year.[11] As a result, the Ministry of Revenue reported that only 640,000 taels of land tax collected in the first half, and 2,000,000 taels in the second half of 1851 were delivered to its treasury.[12] These two sums could hardly be regarded as the normal national income.[13] Hence when he ordered the Ministry and Kwangtung to send financial assistance to Kwangsi for the suppression of rebellions there, Grand Councillor Ch'i Chün-tsao, as supervising minister[14] of revenue, replied that there was little his treasury could spare, and that he had received a report from Kwangtung to the effect that every tael had to be spent on strengthening the defence of the hundreds of miles of border with Kwangsi to prevent the intrusion of rebels from that province. In fact Ch'i had written privately to Yeh to inquire about the financial situation in Kwangtung, and Yeh replied that the treasuries of the province were empty. Subsequently Ch'i, as head of the Grand Council, after consultation with his colleagues, suggested to the emperor on 28 November 1851 that contributions to help the military finance of both Kwangtung and Kwangsi should be invited from the merchants and people of Kwangtung.[15] Reluctantly, the emperor agreed. The period for contributions was to be twelve lunar months, from 22 December 1851 to 26 January 1853. By the end of January 1853, it became apparent that even more money was needed. The period for contributions was extended for another nine months, from 13 April 1853 to 6 January 1854, at the end of which it was extended for yet another nine months. After this, a request for extension was made and granted every year, and contributions became almost a permanent feature.[16]

Contributions managed by Yeh may be classified under the following headings: contributions from the merchants, from the officials, and from the gentry.

Contributions from the merchants. Since the T'ang period Canton had been a prosperous seaport. Even when the coast of China was closed to foreign trade in the early Ch'ing period, Canton remained the exception. Thus the merchants of this city were among the wealthiest in the empire, and one might always predict good results in a campaign to invite donations from them. In this sense, Yeh was very fortunate. The emperor, as mentioned however, considered it undignified to ask his subjects to make donations to meet government expenses. It was only after much pressure from his ministers that he finally agreed to the proposal that Cantonese merchants should be asked to contribute towards military finance in Kwangsi. He was unhappy about the project for yet another reason. Contributions had always in the past been managed directly by the central government. Ch'i's request was that, since the rebellions were in far-away Kwangsi, it was expedient and far simpler to let the local authorities of Kwangtung undertake the task. Having reluctantly granted Ch'i's request to embark on a new campaign for donations, he possibly regarded it as a further loss of face for Peking if the central government did not have a hand in its management. Hence the Ministry of Revenue was commanded to issue an amendment to the effect that funds derived from the contributions in Kwangtung should be delivered entirely to Kwangsi, and that the authorities in Kwangsi should report to the Ministry the names of the donors only on receiving the funds; and only then would the Ministry proceed with arranging the appropriate rewards.

After Yeh had received the imperial edict to re-institute contributions, he transmitted it to his subordinates throughout the province for publication. He had also appointed for this purpose members of the gentry who volunteered to finance the project out of their own resources and to set up contribution bureaus in various parts of the city of Canton. His prefects and magistrates were ordered to induce the local gentry to do the same. Representatives from these contribution bureaus approached the rich merchants. They induced them to make donations on the ground that, although in theory they would be contributing to help the military finance of Kwangsi, in actual fact they would be helping to strengthen the security of Kwangtung itself. Out of vanity – by purchasing the title they became members of the gentry – and the fear that their trade would be disrupted by rural disturbances, the merchants responded actively to the call and within a short period more than 30,000 taels were collected in Canton alone. However, the amendment from the Ministry of Revenue immediately halted this promising progress, for various reasons. The expenses involved in the new and clumsy procedure were 37.5 per cent higher than the actual 'cost' of, for example, the title of a 9b rank official. The time it would take for the donor to receive the title would, at the earliest, be five or six years. This was of course far too long for anybody to wait. Moreover, the contributors desired that at least part of their donations should be used to strengthen the defence of their native province rather than being transferred wholesale to Kwangsi.

Instead of addressing the emperor or Ch'i himself, Yeh asked Wang

Han-ch'iao, who was a former student of Ch'i and who was appointed by Yeh as one of the commissioners responsible for the project, to write a private letter to Ch'i explaining the situation. Ch'i took up the matter with the emperor, who, under the pressing demand for funds, once more swallowed his pride and cancelled the amendment. This was not the end of his loss of face. He had to concede even further in the years to come. In 1853, the empire was confronted with a major financial and political crisis. Financially, the sum of more than twenty-seven million taels spent on resisting the Taipings had exhausted the imperial treasury in Peking and impoverished most provinces. It will be useful to repeat here that the national income from the land tax of 1851 was only about two and a half million taels (which was less than 9 per cent of the national quota). Politically, the capture of Nanking by the Taipings and the establishment of their capital there was a severe blow to the Manchu dynasty. More dangerous still, the rebels soon began sending divisions to attack Peking itself. In desperate need of military funds, the emperor offered a discount of 20 per cent on the sale of government posts, and 36 per cent on the sale of titles. It had indeed become a matter of survival, and all other considerations had to be put in the background.

Thanks to the tireless efforts of Yeh and his colleagues, a total of 2,431,079.2 taels were obtained by 1857 through the sale of titles alone.[17]

Contributions from officials. In May 1852, Hsü and Yeh tried to encourage contributions by each donating 10,000 taels from his own income.[18] Their subordinates, civil and military, were thus obliged to follow their example. Gradually Yeh institutionalised the practice. From the first day of the third year of Emperor Hsien-feng's reign, his accountants were required to send him a report every ten days about the officials who had made donations, their names and the sums donated. Each report was divided into two sections, the first dealing with officials of the fifth rank (intendant level) and above, and the second with those below the fifth rank. Then Yeh sent a quarterly report to Peking about the contributions made by himself and his subordinates, who were thus either accorded merits or promoted to the posts appropriate to the sums donated. From the initiation of contributions in Kwangtung in 1852 to the end of 1853, a total of 23,520 taels had been donated by the civil officials and military officers of the province.[19]

However, long before this date, Yeh had found the system of voluntary contributions from his subordinates unsatisfactory in view of the immense fiscal demands of the military campaigns of his time. He wanted to make it a constant and stable source of revenue. From the second half of the third year of Emperor Hsien-feng's reign (4 August 1853) onwards (i.e., merely six months after Yeh had institutionalised the system of contributions by officials), Yeh ordered that all the officials in Kwangtung who were above the seventh rank were to be paid only 60 per cent of their subsidies, 40 per cent being retained for military finance until the rebellion was over. It will be remembered that subsidies to Ch'ing officials were the main source of income to them, their salaries being only nominal sums. Forty per cent of the subsidies of all officials in Kwangtung above the seventh rank must have constituted a handsome sum of money. Not surprisingly, the emperor and the Ministry of Revenue readily approved of Yeh's action.[20] On the other hand it is to be expected that after 1853, voluntary contributions by officials would have ceased.

Contributions from the gentry. One of the reasons why Yeh found the financial contributions of the officials unsatisfactory was that the officials already had posts in the government. To make generous donations would certainly increase their merits recorded in the Ministry of Personnel, but would not actually gain them immediate promotion. It was different with scholars who had successfully passed the various levels of public examination (civil service examination) and who had not yet received an official appointment. As mentioned, the number of vacancies was far fewer than the number of deserving candidates. Therefore fiscal contributions had become an important means whereby wealthy members of this scholar-gentry class could acquire official posts. Accordingly, Yeh also institutionalised this practice from the very beginning, setting up contribution bureaus not only in Canton but throughout the province, and had reports made to him every ten days about the income from this source.[21]

It is not clear how much money was thus collected. Since the gentry had been asked by Yeh to use their own resources to organise and finance the local militia, it is doubtful whether they were able to spare large sums of money for the central government, where most of the donations went. Naturally, they attached a high priority to local interest and personal safety. Even those who did not respond to Yeh's call to organise militia for self-defence would have fallen an easy prey to the plundering rebels and would thus be unable to make substantial contributions anyway. Moreover, wealthy members of the gentry were only a minority, and it is unlikely that a movement of this kind could have been very fruitful without mass support.

Increased taxation

Just as Yeh was dissatisfied with the fluctuating, uncertain, and short-term nature of voluntary contributions from the officials, so was he unhappy about those from the gentry and the merchants for the same reason. He wanted an assured and steady income so that he could plan accordingly. Furthermore, he wanted contributions to be on a broad basis rather than be dependent on a handful of wealthy merchants or members of the gentry. His subsequent policies were in effect a forced increase of taxation. It began in Canton during the siege, and was extended to other parts of the province as his troops slowly began to recapture the lost cities.

During the siege of Canton, large sums of money had been collected from the shops in the city in the form of donations; sums equivalent to one month's rent had also been contributed by the shopkeepers. As the campaign wore on, Yeh thought it desirable to systematise and perpetuate this occasional income from shops. It was suggested to him that a sum equivalent to two per cent of the sale price should be levied on goods for export. This levy was to be made monthly on the total amount of export goods that passed through the hands of the Chinese merchants at Canton. In order to avoid complaints from foreign merchants, this measure, which was *de facto* a new tax, was to be represented as a kind of voluntary contribution on the part of the Chinese merchants and therefore ought not to lead to a rise in the price of exports. It was further suggested that this practice should be abolished once peace was restored and the usual sources of revenue returned to normal.[22] It is not clear whether Yeh adopted this policy or not. Very likely he did. Although such a step would inevitably put up the price of export goods, an increase of two per cent or so should be moderate enough not to have brought forth a violent protest from foreign merchants. The businessmen engaged in domestic trade were less fortunate. Yeh sent his agents to set up contribution bureaus in the various centres of domestic commerce in the rich Canton delta (see Map 10), to estimate the annual gross income of the shops and to demand (*p'ai-chüan*) an annual contribution of twenty per cent of the gross income. Their main targets were merchants dealing in daily necessities such as cloth, cotton, and cooking oil (see Table 20). The so-called contribution had indeed become taxation. Yeh's agents had to go, together with the magistrate of the area, from shop to shop urging the payment of 'contribution' in much the same way that tax-collectors had to go from village to village urging the delivery of land tax.[23] Most merchants, however reluctantly, complied with these new demands of the government; but a few decided to go into hiding, and they were hunted as outlaws by Yeh's agents.[24] The rich families who had taken refuge in Canton or elsewhere before their home towns were sacked by the rebels were also targets for Yeh's officers.[25]

The same fate befell the merchants of the Han River region,[26] where, as mentioned before, 'a foreign trade amounting annually to several millions of dollars was carried on openly at Swatow'. We have seen Yeh's measures for suppressing this illegal foreign trade. Even if the

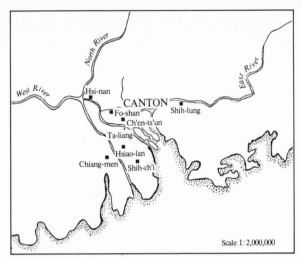

Map 10. The commercial centres of the Canton delta

steps he took were not entirely effective, he was at least able to make up for part of the customs revenue lost through smuggling by squeezing the merchants fattened by it.

Increased taxes were exacted from the gentry as well. In an attempt to make donations from the gentry a regular source of income, it was suggested to Yeh that in the past the gentry had had to pay *corvée* to the state, but as a result of the benevolent rule of the present regime, the *corvée* had been abolished. Out of gratitude therefore, the gentry should have no objection to its revival to help the government, which was now in extreme financial difficulties.[27] The common people were also affected by this general tendency to increase taxation. For example, it was suggested to Yeh when the defeated rebels took to the sea, that 0.3 taels should be levied on each *mou* of land in the coastal areas in order to finance the suppression of the pirates.[28] Again it is not clear whether Yeh took up these two proposals or not. It is highly probable that he did. There was yet another policy, which we know for sure that he did adopt. This was to ask individual villages to contribute collectively to local defence.[29]

Finally, a source worth mentioning from which Yeh drew fresh income was the seizure of property belonging to the rebels. When the native land of the rebels was recaptured by government troops, Yeh very often solicited the help of the local gentry in making a list of property belonging to rebels in order to confiscate it.[30]

The various forms of increased taxation and the seizure of rebel property were regional matters, and the income thus derived were

Table 20
*Forced contributions from merchants dealing in cloth, cotton
and oil at the commercial centres in the Canton delta*[a]

Town	A. Cloth Estimated gross annual income (taels)	Contributions[b] demanded (taels)
1 Shih-lung (Tung-kuan)	120,000	24,000
2 Ta-liang (Shun-te)	40,000	8,000
3 Ch'en-ts'un (Shun-te)	10,000	2,000
4 Shih-ch'i (Hsiang-shan)[c]	20,000	4,000
5 Hsiao-lan (Hsiang-shan)	20,000	4,000
6 Chiang-men (Hsin-hui)	50,000	10,000
7 Hsi-nan (San-shui)	40,000	8,000
Total		60,000

	B. Cotton	
1 Fo-shan (Nan-hai)		7,000
2 Shih-lung (Tung-kuan)		15,000
3 Ch'en-ts'un (Shun-te)		5,000
4 Chiang-men (Hsin-hui)		6,000
5 Hsi-nan (San-shui)		

	C. Cooking oil Estimated monthly oil con- sumption (barrels)	Contributions[d] demanded (taels)
1 Shih-lung (Tung-kuan)	50,000	3,500
2 Hsi-nan (San-shui)	10,000	700
3 Chiang-men (Hsin-hui)	30,000	2,100
4 Ch'en-ts'un (Shun-te)	10,000	700
5 Fo-shan (Nan-hai)	20,000	1,400

[a] This table summarises information given in 112.5.5 and 279A.6.30.
[b] They constituted 20% of the estimated gross annual income of the shops.
[c] Shih-ch'i was the magisterial seat of Hsiang-shan.
[d] A sum of 0.07 taels was levied on each barrel of oil.

channeled to meet local expenses. We have seen the unfavourable reaction of the Cantonese merchants towards the policy to transfer their donations wholesale out of Kwangtung. Given such feelings of regional attachment, it is perhaps not unduly speculative to say that, in general, measures to increase taxation were more successful than the campaign for donations. Furthermore, details regarding the procedure of donation, whether by the merchants, the officials or the gentry, had to be reported to Peking. From the administrative point of view therefore, a regional policy such as an increase in local taxation should be simpler and consequently have a better chance of success than the campaign for donations, which was closely connected with the bureaucracy of the central government.

Conclusion

The imperial tax structure was fundamentally weak. The personal inadequacies of officials or the intervention of natural disaster could jeopardise receipts. The customary cancellation of arrears of land tax in the first year of a new reign, as in 1851, meant a considerable loss of revenue. Receipts from the conventional taxes (land, salt and customs) declined in times of political crisis or economic depression, as in 1853. The sale of offices, resorted to in such circumstances to make good the deficit and to meet the extra expenses, was a most unreliable source of revenue once it became a permanent feature. Thus in time of war an intolerable strain was put on the tax structure. It has been seen that astronomical sums had been spent on military affairs in Kwangtung between 1849 and 1853. During the same period, the financial demand in Kwangtung to arm and victual the imperial troops fighting the Taipings first in Kwangsi, then in Hunan, Hupeh, Kiangsi and Kiangsu, had been enormous and never-ending. It was due to Yeh's able management of public money that these unusual demands, local and national, were partially met. Nevertheless, the resources of Kwangtung were seriously strained, and the repercussions of the disturbances in south China as a whole on the economy of the province became apparent in 1853, when revenue from the normal sources, namely land tax, salt monopoly, customs duties and investments, dropped sharply. Financially, therefore, Kwangtung was crippled in 1853, and any government would have had great difficulty in coping with the situation even in the relatively peaceful period of the sporadic revolts of 1850–3. However, what came after 1853 was no longer sporadic revolts but a general insurrection. It was almost inconceivable that Yeh, with so few funds at his disposal, could have survived this major political storm.

The fact that Yeh did survive was ample testimony that his financial measures, his management of expenditure and his exploitation of extraordinary sources of revenue, were successful, indeed so successful that not only was he able to finance the campaigns in Kwangtung itself but he was soon in a position to resume his role as paymaster general to the imperial troops fighting in central China. From 1853 to 1854, Yeh had been sending fleets, regiments, cannon, ammunition, rice and funds to Kiangsu,[31] Anhui, Hunan, Hupeh, Fukien and Peking.[32] These supplies of manpower, war materials and funds were temporarily halted by the siege of Canton during the latter half of 1854 and the beginning of 1855, but were quickly resumed once the siege was lifted.[33]

It will be useful to compare Yeh's ability as public financier with that of his colleagues in other provinces. The Imperial Commissioner of Kiangsu, Hsiang Jung, repeatedly requested Peking for financial assistance from Kwangtung and eventually succeeded in irritating the emperor, who, accordingly, issued the following decree on 17 May 1854.

Kwangtung is giving financial assistance to large areas suffering from the rebellions, not to Kiangsu alone. The burden on that province is already unbearably great, and the distance between Kwangtung and Kiangsu is such that funds from the former will never be able to reach the latter on time. The said imperial commissioner [i.e. Hsiang Jung] does not try to derive funds from the land tax, salt trade, customs duties or contributions in Kiangsu itself, but just sits there and waits for assistance to come from other provinces.[34]

Kiangsu was one of the richest provinces of China, perhaps richer than Kwangtung. The fact that Imperial Commissioner Hsiang Jung in Kiangsu should be dependent on Imperial Commissioner Yeh Ming-ch'en of Kwangtung for financial assistance is eloquent proof of the difference in the ability and attitude of the two in dealing with economic affairs and public finance. From Kiangsu we move to Kiangsi. In 1855, the governor of Kiangsi, Chang Fei, wrote to Yeh and complained that his province had been badly devastated by the rebels, and that both the salt comptroller and the grain intendant were at a complete loss as to what to do. Such a letter was not without its familiar concomitant: request for money.[35] Kwangtung had been devastated at least as badly by the Red Turbans; but Yeh, as we have seen, was not short of ideas, within the traditional framework of course, as to how the problem should be tackled. Quietly and steadily he revived the normal sources of revenue after the worst disturbances were over, and with the funds derived from the extraordinary sources that he exploited he was soon able to assist Kiangsi with fifty thousand taels of silver.[36] Let us now turn our attention to Chekiang, which also had been one of the richest provinces of China. Here, the provincial treasurer committed suicide because he found it impossible to cope with the financial difficulties of his time. He also found it quite beyond his ability to deal with the complicated administrative problems of grain transport along the Grand Canal, which had been greatly aggravated by the disturbances in the area.[37] Finally, we may conclude this comparative study of Yeh and his contemporaries with a private letter from one of the military commanders who had received a subvention from him. He expressed his gratitude in the following words: 'When the smoke of our cooking-stoves was about to fail, your news has suddenly made us feel satisfied before we have even tasted your bounty.'[38] It is therfore, perhaps not an exaggeration to entitle Yeh the paymaster general of the imperial troops both in Kwangtung and in other provinces in the 1850s.

However, there was at least one section of the official hierarchy that he failed to satisfy, and this was the Imperial Household. An annual sum of 300,000 taels from the customs revenue had been allotted to it to meet its sundry expenses. In 1853, the Ministry of Revenue reported to the throne that the financial situation was critical. Sensing that its income might be affected, the Imperial Household obtained a firm promise from the emperor that the Ministry of Revenue would not divert funds allotted to it to meet other expenses. Later, Yeh and the Hoppo informed the emperor that it would be difficult to send a lump sum of 300,000 taels to Peking at the end of each financial year, and proposed to send quarterly a sum of 75,000 taels. This proposal was accepted. However, after the first delivery in 1854, there was no further remittance until 25 April 1856, when, after much pressure, the Hoppo sent a memorandum to Peking, saying that a sum of 10,000 taels was forthcoming, and that the total of 576,200 taels (the official allotment of 525,000 taels in addition to surcharges of 51,200 taels) had been diverted to pay the troops of the empire. Despite repeated threats of impeachment by the department of the privy purse, Yeh had stood firm, not arguing, but quietly continuing his policy.[39] Thereby he risked his career through the possibility of losing court favour. Fortunately for him, the emperor appreciated his patriotism in ruthlessly putting the survival of the dynasty before the personal comfort of the imperial family and its immediate dependents. Otherwise, he might have suffered the same fate as Calonne, who tried to cut court patronage in *ancien régime* France, and as Lord Shelburne in Georgian England, who attempted to enact a similar policy in his short-lived ministry of 1782–3.[40]

In Kwangtung itself, there were also sections of the population who positively resented Yeh's financial measures. We have seen that much suffering had been occasioned among some junior officials, as a result of his stringent rules on expenditure. The senior officials, too, had little reason to love him. His move to legislate a cut in their main source of income – their subsidies – by forty per cent could not be expected to have their sympathy, although his own income was affected by the same legislation. The gentry of Kwangtung had been notorious for their lawlessness. They naturally felt very humbled when their move to refuse the payment of land tax in 1850 was crushed. Nor were they pleased with the subsequent step to revive *corvée*. The merchants engaged in either foreign or domestic trade had been badly squeezed by the government. They were first requested then forced to make donations; and finally, the campaign for 'voluntary donations' hardened into a new tax of two per cent on export goods and twenty per cent on domestic commodities. Yeh's decision to stop foreign trade altogether at the end of 1856 was the last straw to the merchants. The ordinary people had suffered immensely during the rebellion. Yeh's subsequent steps to increase the land tax and to 'tax' their villages collectively in the form of donations would never have been popular. Thus Yeh found himself in a most peculiar position. He was often resented as much as he was feared,[41] and there must have been many in Kwangtung who would have gladly seen him go. It is not surprising, therefore, that defamatory ballads such as the one that begins part 5, should have been written after all, and should have quickly become very popular among the Cantonese.

Part five

The imperial commissioner for foreign affairs[1]

He did not treat, nor made defence,
Nor yielded, nor showed fight;
He did not die a soldier's death,
And did not take to flight.[2]

This was the verdict passed by a Cantonese ballad-maker on Yeh's conduct during the Second Opium War. Although these six points referred specifically to the war, the first has some relevance also to his entire career as imperial commissioner, and will be covered by chap. 9 in this section. Chap. 10 examines in detail Yeh's offensive and defensive measures.

---

9 A survey of Yeh's activities as imperial commissioner for foreign affairs

'He did not treat... Nor yielded'

Yeh, as described in the chapter on his early career, had no experience in dealing with foreign affairs until he came to Canton late in 1846. It was there that his concepts of diplomacy were gradually formed, especially during his first year of office, when two important diplomatic incidents occurred: the Entry episode of April 1847 and the Huang-chu-ch'i affair at the end of the same year. Referring to the former, David Jardine wrote:

Between 1 and 2 o'clock of the night I was roused out of bed by Mr. Macgregor who called to communicate the news of the fleet of steamers having arrived at Whampoa – having on their passage disabled all the guns (about 500) of the forts at the Bogue.[1]

The mob has made one or two attempts at riot but has been quickly dispersed by the soldiers [English]...[2]

The only difficulty appears to be entry to the city. Keying is most awkwardly situated, he has no objections to their going in, but his views on this head are opposed to all the other officials and the people.[3]

Contrary to popular opinion, Ch'i-ying yielded to the show of force and promised the British that they should enter the city two years hence, on 6 April 1849. This incident, Jardine wrote on, 'will I think have the effect of causing his recall and probably disgrace, opposed as he is by all the other authorities and literati here.'[4]

The Huang-chu-ch'i incident, in which six Englishmen were killed and two Chinese villagers shot dead in an armed conflict,[5] confirmed Yeh further in whatever opinion he may have formed about foreign affairs. The British Plenipotentiary, Sir John Davis threatened to withdraw the entire British community from Canton as a prelude to war if sufficient redress was not effected promptly.[6] Ch'i-ying again capitulated, but the villagers were in open defiance to his orders to surrender the ringleaders. They barricaded themselves inside the village and circulated fiery placards calling upon all able-bodied men in the neighbourhood to assemble for the defence of their homes.[7] A large body of Chinese soldiers was sent against the village, and subsequent reports about the outcome of the expedition were varied. Ch'i-ying claimed that his men arrested and beheaded on the spot four ringleaders.[8] British merchants in Canton, however, were convinced that since Ch'i-ying was powerless against the rebel villagers short of an armed confrontation, which he would not dare contemplate as the weight of public opinion was with the villagers, the four victims were in fact culprits in jail for other offences, not the real ringleaders.[9]

Yeh, as provincial treasurer, was not directly involved in any of these diplomatic encounters, but he watched with great interest what was happening. He saw the way Ch'i-ying was browbeaten by Davis. He also saw the violent reaction of the people to their imperial commissioner's appeasement policy, to the point of open revolt. In short, he saw two forces at work, a high-handed foreign pressure and a violent domestic reaction. His own inclination was to steer a middle course between the two hazards, endeavouring to win the support of the people by respecting their wishes, while at the same time avoiding needless provocation of the foreigners and treating them with a combination of consideration and firmness. Probably at this time he formulated his approach in the following memorandum to Peking:

The sole object of the foreigners is to trade, and hence they take care not to offend the people, with whom they do business. . . Therefore, we should aim at uniting the people of Kwangtung, who incidentally are highly inflammable, in a common effort to cherish the foreigners in peacetime and defend our territory in case of crises.

As regards their minor demands, there is no harm in granting them, as a sign of our generosity and goodwill, so that conflicts may be avoided. On the other hand, we must not yield to every one of their demands, and thereby damage the reputation of the empire.[10]

Apparently he was opposed to Ch'i-ying's appeasement policy because it impaired the prestige of the empire. However, there is no evidence of his being an anti-foreign fanatic, as so many historians have been fond of painting him; his view of diplomacy was basically a defensive one, not aggressive and certainly never provocative.

As already mentioned, Ch'i-ying had given the British a firm promise that they would be allowed to enter the city of Canton on 6 April 1849. In 1848, however, Hsü Kuang-chin had replaced Ch'i-ying and Yeh was appointed governor of Kwangtung; therefore, when this date was drawing near, the task of giving effect to Ch'i-ying's promise rested on the shoulders of these two men. Now that Yeh had the opportunity of being directly involved in foreign affairs, the views he had formed in 1847 began to influence his approach. His attitude was simple and clear-cut: 'The object of having good relations with the foreigners is to protect the people, and only by making the people contented can we keep the foreigners in check.'[11] He was convinced that permission for the foreigners to enter the city would only do harm. He saw himself and his colleagues caught, as Ch'i-ying had been, between foreign and domestic pressures. To give in to the foreigners would be to invite rebellion, which would leave the autorities helpless before further demands. Siding with the people, on the other hand, would win their support, and this would increase the chances of successful resistance to foreign aggression. In the end his views prevailed.

Once the policy of resistance was decided on, there was a division of responsibilities among the principal officials of the province. Hsü, accompanied by Grain Intendant Po-kuei, Colonel K'un-shou (head of the governor-general's regiment)[12] and the famous Chinese merchant Howqua,[13] went to Hu-men to negotiate with Bonham, the successor of Davis. In Hsü's absence, the provincial treasurer, Li Chang-yü, acted in his place so far as civil affairs were concerned.[14] Yeh, assisted by the Tartar general and brigade generals of the Banners and the commanders-in-chief of the land and marine forces of the Green Standard, was vigorously engaged in preparations for the defence of Canton.[15] The militia units were also mobilised. Admiral Collier reported that large bodies of armed villagers had come into the city and were parading near the factories. S. Wells Williams, the editor of *The Chinese Repository*, who was at Canton at the time, wrote on 26 March that 'The people have begun to parade the streets at night in uniform and armed with spears, matchlocks and muskets. Perhaps 10,000 have been enlisted.'[16] A placard written a few weeks later recalled that 'Each man was ready to defend the country, each family prepared to fight, the streets shone with the gleam of weapons, and the sound of gongs and drums filled the heavens.'[17] Ch'i-ying's appeasement policy had long been a source of constant humiliation and frustration to the Cantonese. When Yeh's call to arms reached the villagers the news was almost too good to be true. Their desire to defend their homeland was no longer suppressed by the officials but was actually encouraged. Thousands of robust peasants rallied to Yeh's support, and paraded through the streets of Canton (especially near the foreign community) with an air of self-importance and pride. After prolonged and desultory negotiations, the episode concluded with Bonham's communication to Hsü, in which he said: 'The question at issue rests where it was and must remain in abeyance. The discussion of it cannot, at present, be further pursued between Your Excellency and myself.'[18]

The Cantonese thought they had scored a great diplomatic victory.[19] They were so overjoyed that they erected six grand triumphal arches to commemorate the merits of Hsü and Yeh.[20] The emperor, too, was deeply moved.

For nearly ten years, I have had to suffer foreign humiliation quietly ... Thanks to the outstanding ability of the said Liang Yüan to satisfy the people and cherish the foreigners, the entry question is settled for ever without firing a shot; my joy is beyond description. Let Hsü be made a viscount ... and Yeh a baron.[21]

Many high-ranking officials also wrote to Yeh congratulating him on his brilliant success. Here are two selections.

> Your Lordship and Lord Hsü
> With one stout heart and true
> The crisis did repel,
> And all men wished you well;
> As a great feat, sir earl,
> To gain the dragon's pearl.
> Deeply my heart admires,
> And quenched are conflict's fires.
> To vanquish without fight
> Requires a hero's might.[22]

> My Lord, and Viceroy Hsü,
> In concert guide their crew,
> Thwart foreign chief's foul game,
> Diffuse the empire's fame.
> Ten years show no such trump.
> This generation's laud
> The annals should record.
> For pleasure I must jump.[23]

Yeh's policy ended in great triumph, and triumph consolidated his views into a formula: respect the wishes of the people and unite with them in a common effort to resist fresh foreign demands.

Six months later, in September 1849, Bonham made another attempt at persuading Hsü to give effect to the 1847 agreement. This greatly puzzled Hsü, who had understood Bonham to have given up for good the right to enter the city, and he, therefore, refused even to transmit Bonham's petition to Peking.[24] Accordingly, on 27 April 1850, Bonham set out for Shanghai. Before his departure, he sent a note to Hsü professing the object of his trip to be one of inspecting the conditions of trade in the five treaty ports. Consequently the news from Peking that Bonham had tried to communicate with Ch'i-ying and Mu-chang-a in the north confirmed Hsü's and Yeh's suspicion that Bonham's trip had dubious designs, and their belief that foreigners were untrustworthy.[25] When Bonham returned to Hong Kong on 18 June 1850, his communication to Hsü three days later made no reference to his attempt to contact Ch'i-ying and Mu-chang-a, and was unfortunately interpreted by Hsü and Yeh as yet more evidence of the treachery of aliens.[26] Another result arising out of Bonham's trip was his intention to excavate coal in Taiwan and to exchange the ports in Fukien for those in Taiwan. This was also taken as evidence of British territorial ambitions. In response to these new demands, Hsü's and Yeh's approach was strict observance of treaty provisions,[27] to which Yeh stuck to the last word during the negotiations for the so-called treaty revision in 1854. Since Yeh and Sir John Bowring (Bonham's successor) were the two men responsible for this episode, it will be useful first to compare their respective attitudes.

Bowring was British Consul at Canton from 1849 to 1853, and was promoted to the post of plenipotentiary at the end of 1853.[28] He took up his new appointment in 1854, and immediately requested an interview with Yeh, who had become imperial commissioner for foreign affairs in 1852. Yeh was perfectly willing to see him; but bearing in mind the serious consequences should Bowring be allowed to go into the city, Yeh proposed to see him in Howqua's package house or at the Bogue.[29] However, Bowring insisted that Yeh should see him within the walls of Canton, convinced as he was that 'until the city question at Canton is settled, there is little hope of our relations being placed on anything like a satisfactory foundation'.[30] Neither side would give way; the meeting never materialised. There was perhaps only one thing they held in common: distrust of the other party. We have seen how Yeh came to such a conclusion. As for Bowring, he declared that the foundation of his policy in China was his conviction that 'the purposes of the Chinese officials are distinctly and decidedly opposed to our own; so that distrust and not confidence is the only safe ground to occupy in relations with them.'[31] Bowring's main object for an interview with Yeh was to effect a revision of the Treaty of Nanking signed by Great Britain and China in 1842. This treaty contained no stipulation for revision, but Bowring claimed it on the most-favoured-nation principle, since there was such a provision in the American Treaty of Wang-hsia of 1843. Even so, Yeh was prepared to see him about this question. But as we have seen, Bowring's insistence that Yeh should do so within the city walls thwarted his own mission. Persistent in his purpose, Bowring went north in an attempt to obtain an imperial hearing, but was told that the imperial will was to refer him to the viceroy at Canton for all negotiations.[32] He went back to Hong Kong and sent Medhurst to Canton for preliminary discussions. Again, Yeh was perfectly willing to treat, and responded by despatching two 'respectable and suitable men, both being magistrates of important districts' to meet Medhurst.[33] However, Bowring's first and foremost instruction to Medhurst was to request an interview with Yeh within the city walls of Canton or in Hong Kong. The question of treaty revision was given only secondary consideration.[34] Yeh's reaction was to authorise the magistrates to arrange a meeting between himself and 'the British, French and American envoys, for the purpose of considering the question of treaty revision, either in the Dutch Folly Fort, or on board a British man-of-war anchored opposite the city gate, whichever might be thought most agreeable.'[35] Consequently, Medhurst complied with his third instruction, and returned to the colony without even entering into any negotiations. Had Bowring been more patient, or less obsessed with entering the city of Canton, he could have at least started the negotiations there and then. As for Yeh going to Hong Kong to see him, it was virtually impossible because the rebels besieging Canton had already begun attacking the city, and the effect of his departure on the whole campaign could have been disastrous. However, Bowring either failed or refused to recognise these facts and went north again to demand another important commissioner from Peking to treat with him, on the grounds that Yeh had refused to do so,[36] which, as we have seen, was untrue.

Bowring's second trip to the north proved equally fruitless. Frustrated, he returned to Hong Kong in time to receive the so-called application for assistance from Yeh as described in chap. 6. As mentioned, the net result of this episode was the reinforcement of Yeh's conviction that foreigners were unpredictable and perfidious, and of Bowring's belief that the mandarins were obstinately proud and unteachably ignorant. The issue was that Consul Robertson, acting in Bowring's place during the absence of the latter in Shanghai, had requested the co-operation of Yeh's fleet to suppress the pirates a month or so before Yeh asked a similar favour in return. Yeh was rebuffed, on grounds of neutrality which he could not understand. Worse still, Bowring thought that under the circumstances he could force Yeh's hand, and went up to Canton accompanied by the admiral and several ships of war, demanding an official interview.[37] Still, Yeh remained courteous but firm. Immediately on Bowring's arrival at Canton, he sent two magistrates to inquire after his health;[38] but of course Bowring's insistence once more on being received at Yeh's official residence within the city made it impossible for Yeh to give him a favourable answer. Worst of all, after Yeh had finally succeeded in defeating the rebel fleets at Whampoa and had driven them from the immediate vicinity of Canton, Bowring once again addressed him concerning the 'suppression of piracy by united action of British and Chinese naval forces'.[39] If Yeh had eventually managed to comprehend what neutrality meant in international law, he must have been exceedingly confused, wondering what his opposite number was actually trying to say or trying to do. In any case, he dismissed Bowring's communication as yet another example of the unpredictability of aliens; but observing his principle of courtesy, replied that he had already despatched fleets of war junks to exterminate the pirates and that he was pleased to find the British desirous of joint action, which was a sign of friendship between the two nations and worthy of praise.[40]

Naturally Bowring would not find much comfort in such a pointed compliment. Nor were his compatriots about to give him any. The British merchants soon lost their patience with him, accusing him of possessing 'neither the sound judgment nor the ability indispensable to the satisfactory negotiation of the approaching new treaty'.[41] His dismal failure in China persuaded him to look round for fresh fields of action in which he might regain his shattered reputation. Consequently he went to Siam, from whom he extracted a commercial treaty.[42] His success there did much to confirm his attitude that 'negotiations unsupported by a considerable fleet will terminate in disappointment and discomfiture.'[43] Indeed, it was while Bowring was busily preparing for his third expedition to north China, to be accompanied by a becoming naval force consisting of steamers of light draft and sufficiently armed – which he considered was of the highest importance for the successful result of the mission[44] – that the so-called *Arrow* incident occurred. Bowring's disappointment in China and his success in Siam may have made him the readier at this juncture to resort to coercive measures.

The *Arrow* incident is of such a complicated nature that it merits a separate study.[45] It suffices here to say simply that the dispute arose out of the arrest in Canton of the crew of a Chinese-owned and Chinese-manned vessel called *Arrow*, which had been registered in Hong Kong and had thus obtained the right to fly the British flag. During this incident, it was alleged that the Union Jack was insulted. As in all international disputes, it is difficult to ascertain the truth of this allegation. But it was the attitude of the parties concerned that made the incident such an important issue. It so happened that at this time the British Consulship at Canton was temporarily vacant and an aggressive young man called Harry Parkes was appointed acting consul. He was quick to exploit the affair to further British interests in China. He did not seem ever to have paused for a moment to examine the story he was told about the insult to the British Ensign, otherwise he would no doubt have noticed some important loose ends in it.[46] Even if he had done so, it is in any case doubtful whether he would have easily let go such an opportunity for action, totally devoted as he was to the course of imperial expansion.[47] Thus he busied himself with pestering the imperial commissioner with one demand after another.[48] Bowring also welcomed the incident, as he wanted to satisfy, among other things, his obsession to enter the city of Canton. 'Out of these troubled waters', he told his son, 'I expect to extract some healing food.'[49] Hence he fully backed up Parkes' aggressive proceedings, to the extent of employing gunboat diplomacy, until the relationship between the two countries was plunged into one of armed confrontation.

Yeh, on the other hand, took the view that the arrest of the crew was purely a domestic matter, and that he had sufficient evidence to prove that the Union Jack had never been insulted. Therefore he regarded British demands as totally unreasonable, especially Bowring's irrelevant and thinly veiled demand to enter the city of Canton. Thus he resolutely resisted British coercion, and Bowring was reduced to the state of making endless complaints about Yeh's obstinacy. 'Though we continue our pressure upon the Viceroy at Canton he has not hitherto been *pressable*, and it is indeed difficult to say what *is* to be done with such unmanageable material.'[50] In another private letter, Bowring unmistakably betrayed his feeling of helplessness or even despair. 'It is impossible to say what amount of pressure will move the Imperial Commissioner. Perhaps not even the destruction of the city, for he seems determined *not* to give way and we cannot *compel* him to hold intercourse with us.'[51]

It is evident that Anglo-Chinese relations in this period were bedevilled by distrust on both sides. From the outset, Bowring had no belief in the sincerity of the Chinese officials. He regarded Yeh in particular as obstinacy and bad faith incarnate.[52] His constant demands and complaints were a source of irritation to the Chinese and convinced them of the insatiable greed of foreigners. Their response, exemplified by Yeh, was to be courteous but unyielding. This in turn caused frustration and eventually resentment in Bowring. His attempts at negotiation with Yeh defeated themselves, because his demand that the talks should be held in the city was tantamount to insisting that the Entry question should be settled beforehand. His failure made him conclude that only the use of force could be efficacious.

For his part, Yeh had imbibed a thorough distrust of foreigners from his initial contacts with them in 1847, 1849 and 1850. He saw his suspicions confirmed when their demands were backed by the threat of force. None the less, it is not true that he was unwilling to see foreign envoys or to negotiate in person with them. He was always ready to meet them, but all of them followed Bowring's example, insisting on every occasion on what was something completely unthinkable in the circumstances in Ch'ing politics of the time.[53] He was willing to treat, and although personal interviews were made impossible by Bowring's stipulation, his voluminous correspondence shows that he was prepared to communicate by other means.[54] Even after the outbreak of hostilities, he did not lose hope of a peaceful settlement by negotiation. He first sent the famous Chinese merchant Howqua to approach Bowring through the businessman Sturgis.[55] Then he requested his naval commander-in-chief to ask Bowring what conditions would satisfy him.[56] Both overtures were, unfortunately, arrogantly dismissed by the British Plenipotentiary, who had determined to close all negotiations with him.[57] But Yeh was so persistent that in July 1857 he sent two mandarins to Hong Kong for deliberations on the means of putting an end to existing difficulties.[58] However, because of the appointment of Lord Elgin as Plenipotentiary Extraordinary, Bowring had, by this time, been forbidden by the Foreign Office to conclude any settlement, or even to correspond with the Chinese authorities at all.[59] Finally, when Lord Elgin was available, Yeh made the same proposals.[60] But it was in any case doubtful whether negotiations could have been successful because a treaty, according to the Chinese interpretation, meant a permanent settlement, and a revision might embody only minor changes (should they prove necessary after a period of time) within existing provisions.[61] What the British demanded, however, went far beyond what Yeh could give – the emperor would never allow any further major concessions to be made.[62] Moreover, it was against Yeh's own maxims of policy to yield to the excessive demands of foreigners and to suffer a diminution of imperial dignity. Finally, another dishonourable treaty would rouse public opinion in Canton and the whole empire against him. For these reasons, although Yeh was a flexible administrator, a resilient military organiser and a resourceful paymaster general, he was an intransigent imperial commissioner. Despite the fact that hostilities dragged on for over a year, bringing great difficulties and hardships to his government and his people, he still refused to yield any ground, because the demands, such as the legalisation of the opium trade, the opening of more treaty ports along the coast and the great Yangtze River, and the establishment of foreign legations at Peking, in fact constituted a new treaty that he was neither empowered nor disposed to sign. The accusation, therefore, that Yeh did not treat is a complete fallacy. The mockery, 'nor yielded', makes one wonder whether the author was Chinese at all, if he had wished to see Yeh yielding to the successive demands and ultimata of the British. The difficulties that confronted Yeh and the impossible position he was in never seem to have been recognised by historians who repeat the accusations. His unflagging efforts to maintain peace by negotiation, and to restore it when it was lost, has up to now been kept, to say the least, in a state of oblivion.

'Did not take to flight'

This statement may also be seen as a mockery and equally uncalled for. Obviously Yeh knew very well that a frontier official who surrendered to the enemy would put his family and relatives in peril and bring upon himself the perpetual curse of his contemporaries as well as posterity. Moreover, we have seen from Yeh's background and education that he was deeply influenced by the teachings of the sages and would not easily surrender and thereby disavow his loyalty to the emperor. Of course a good many scholar-officials in the past had capitulated, and a good many contemporaries had deserted their cities before the Taiping advance. It needs a strong character and will to remain calm and composed in circumstances that would throw most people into a panic. As it was, Yeh was smiling when the first report of British cannon in Ho-nan shook the parade-ground and the ears of his subordinates.[63] He was sitting sedately in his audience hall when his residence was bombarded and all his retainers frightened away.[64] This is not surprising if we recall his behaviour during the siege of Canton, when he and his government were confronted with imminent disaster. It is unfortunate that these exceptional qualities were not allowed by the political system of the time to be put to better use, such as his personal direction of a guerrilla war, because such action would anyway have been regarded as desertion of his city. Instead, these qualities became a cause of ridicule, failings held against a distinguished man.

Indeed, had Yeh been thinking only of his personal safety and career, he could certainly have left the city, and on justifiable grounds. Sir John Bowring wrote in August 1857: 'It is much to be feared that Yeh will escape from Canton on some plea or other – either to visit Peking, to look into the state of his provinces, or to march against rebels.'[65] Any one of these could have been a perfectly good reason for Yeh to leave. For ten years he had had no audience with the emperor, which was most unusual in Ch'ing history. A savage campaign between his own troops and the rebels in Kwangsi had been raging for over a year, and his presence there might have a decisive effect on the outcome. After all, he had never visited Kwangsi although it constituted half of his viceroyalty. However, he decided to stay in Canton. He was aware of the danger he was in, as is apparent from the fact that he sent away his family shortly before the fateful battle. He was too honest and responsible an official to desert his post when it needed his attention most. The eventual outcome of his determination to live or perish with the city under his jurisdiction, however, only earned him the most severe condemnation from his countrymen.

' He did not die a soldier's death '

This accusation provokes a very interesting question: What kind of person really was Yeh? The foregoing pages should not have failed to give the picture of a quiet, steady and determined man, who never lost his composure, and who always thought very carefully before he made a decision. Of all the records available, whether they are English or Chinese, official or private, journalistic or scholarly, there is only one instance based on a single account, when Yeh lost control of himself. That is the description, of *The Times* reporter W. Cooke, of the few seconds when the actual capture of Yeh took place:

When Captain Key seized him, his vast carcase shook with terror, and he completely lost all presence of mind. Perhaps this is not to be much wondered at. Fifty blue-jackets, with drawn swords and revolvers, were dancing round him like madmen, flourishing their cutlasses, throwing up their hats, and cheering at the top of their voices. He might well believe that his last moment was come.[66]

Dramatic though this story may have been, it must be true, because few, if any, do not panic when suddenly confronted with death. But all records agree that Yeh recovered remarkably quickly, though there were different ways of describing it. Cooke observed that 'during all these early scenes, however much he suffered from the infirmity of bodily fear, his arrogance never, after the first moment, forsook him'.[67] An attaché to Major-General van Straubenzee's staff reported to Lord Elgin that Yeh exhibited great self-possession and remained perfectly quiet while his boxes, of which the room was full, were opened and examined for papers.[68] Alabaster, who was the interpreter appointed to attend Yeh and who was alleged by Cooke to have been treated by Yeh with infinite rudeness and contempt,[69] described Yeh as being in excellent spirits when he was captured,[70] and said that he bore his detention with great tranquility and cheerfulness.[71] Rear-Admiral Seymour remarked that Yeh continued in his stolid composure.[72] Bowring, too, was surprised at Yeh's ability to bear himself up with the most extraordinary indifference.[73]

After the first moment of terror, Yeh must have pondered what his next move would be. Many of his colleagues in the Yangtze area committed suicide when their cities were besieged by the Taipings. Yeh did not. Throughout his career, he demonstrated beyond doubt that he took a positive view of life, that he had the courage and determination to challenge and surmount the most monumental difficulties. Personal considerations had always been of secondary importance to him; public duties were first. When he quietly watched his state papers searched and scattered all round him, he must have been thinking of what he could still do, in his capacity as imperial commissioner for foreign affairs, which would be of service to his country. To continue this role, he must preserve his dignity and must not let the thoughts of suicide or captivity influence his behaviour. Not surprisingly, when Consul Parkes told the Chinese Plenipotentiary that he was to go with the guard to the allied headquarters, the response was 'Who are you that address me in my own language?'[74] At the allied headquarters, he wore his mandarin cap, his red button and his peacock's feather. He seated himself in an armchair, with the other officials who poured into the room after him standing round and forming for him a little court.[75] Far from acting with diffidence, Yeh confronted his captors as though he were the host of a diplomatic reception. When he was taken on board the *Inflexible*, he quickly composed himself and indicated that 'he had come on to the ship solely to see Lord Elgin, and wondered why he had not kept his appointment. He had determined not to wait much longer.'[76] This gesture is certainly not unique to Yeh. When Napoleon was a prisoner of war under similar circumstances on board the *Bellérophon*, he made a similar gesture of protestation.[77] While the *Inflexible* was anchored in the harbour of Hong Kong, Bowring went to see him and asked for his autograph. He refused it on the grounds that it was impossible to write a neutral sentence in Chinese – every word could be distorted to mean something quite different. These manoeuvres on Yeh's part led Cooke to conclude, quite rightly, that: 'The Chinese minister evidently believed that we considered him still as a person from whom a treaty might be obtained, and he was prepared to make a good diplomatic fight.'[78] His expectations were never fulfilled. Lord Elgin had no intention of making a treaty with him. He waited day after day on board the *Inflexible* but nothing happened. It was reported that, at some point, one of his retinue pointed to the river and winked at him, suggesting that he should take advantage of the waters to end his life honourably.[79] He was unmoved.

> Then why not end? Truly as ready I
> To sacrifice my life as was Hsiang Shu,[80]
> Yet live I, when 'twere easier to die,
> And keep my wand of office whole, like Su.[81]

The fact that Yeh was detained on board a British steam-boat instead of being kept in the enemy barracks in Ho-nan must have led him to believe that he was going to be taken to England. Therefore he decided to live on so that he, like Su Wu, would be more useful to his country alive than dead.

10 A reappraisal of Yeh's 'do-nothing' policy during the *Arrow* War

This chapter examines Yeh's offensive and defensive measures during the *Arrow* War. The two, of course, were carried out concurrently. To avoid confusion, a chronology of major events is listed in Table 21.

'Nor made defence'

As already mentioned, the British resorted to gunboat diplomacy over the *Arrow* incident. On receiving Parkes' 24 hours ultimatum on 21 October 1856[1] Yeh prepared for the worst. The Military Supply Bureau was entrusted with the additional responsibility of meeting the foreign threat. He also set up a special Foreign Affairs Office (*tsung-pan i-wu*) to cope with the new situation. The office was headed by the circuit intendant of Chao-lo, Chang Pai-k'uei, and the former provincial judge of Kwangsi, Chang Ching-hsiu. Moreover, he immediately sent reinforcements of regulars and mercenaries, under the leadership of three second-captains, to strengthen the defence of the forts along the Pearl River from the Bogue to Canton.[2] Once more his city was threatened, but this time by a foreign power. There was little force at his disposal, far less than there was two years before, at the time of the siege by the rebels. The troops he had once mustered for the defence of the city he had now despatched to fight in the campaign of the Pearl River. The foreign invasion came altogether too suddenly and too soon for him to recall them even if he had so wished. When the ultimatum expired on the following day, Admiral Seymour and his fleet began to advance on Canton. The Chinese marines manning the forts, in obedience to Yeh's strict order to resist this foreign aggression, fired in defence when the British fleet tried to capture the forts, but were outgunned. By 2 o'clock in the afternoon, Seymour had fought his way successfully to Canton and gave Parkes the opportunity of sending another threatening letter to Yeh.

For his own experience during the siege of Canton by the rebels, Yeh realised that it was of vital importance that he, as head of both the civil and military hierarchies, should never betray any of his emotions or secret fears to his men. His entire demeanour throughout the foreign war was therefore once more calculated to indicate to his subordinates that there was no question about the safety of Canton, so as to build up their confidence and preserve morale. When Parkes' letter arrived, Yeh

Table 21

A brief summary of Yeh's activities during the Arrow *War*

8.10.1856	The so-called *Arrow* Incident occurred. Yeh regarded the seizure of the Chinese sailors as a purely domestic matter and believed that the British flag had never been insulted when the arrests were made.
14.10.1856	Parkes and Commodore Elliot seized what they believed to be an imperial war junk in order to force Yeh's hand. Yeh refused to succumb to this pressure.
16.10.1856	Nevertheless Yeh sent Howqua to see Parkes with a view to coming to an understanding about the *Arrow* affair. But Bowring instructed Parkes not to negotiate with him. Instead, further coercive measures were decided upon.
21.10.1856	Yeh reinforced the river forts from the Bogue to Canton. The forts nevertheless fell before Seymour's advancing fleet.
26.10.1856	Yeh closed the Customs Office (stopped foreign trade).
27.10.1856	Seymour started to shell the city of Canton. Yeh exhorted the Cantonese to respond actively to the foreign aggression by offering a reward of $30 for any Briton killed.
29.10.1856	Through Howqua, Yeh sent Mr Sturgis to approach Bowring for an end to the hostilities. Bowring dismissed this overture.
22.11.1856	Yeh ordered a counter-attack to recover the river forts.
1.12.1856	First Chinese naval victory near the Barrier Forts, giving Yeh an upper hand in the struggle for the control of the inner parts of the Pearl River.
14.12.1856	The foreign settlement at Canton was burnt down. Seymour had to have a trench dug round the site for protection against further Chinese attacks.
19.12.1856	Resolution passed in a public meeting in Hsin-an that Hong Kong should be made a battle ground as well.
14.1.1857	Seymour abandoned his stronghold at the site of the original factories.
15.1.1857	The British had to evacuate Whampoa. Attempt to poison the foreign community of Hong Kong.
15.2.1857	Seymour was compelled to withdraw from Canton altogether, but was unable to do so peacefully because Yeh sent his fleet after him.
21.5.1857	Yeh requested his naval commander-in-chief to sound out Bowring's disposition towards a peaceful settlement. Bowring, however, was determined to close all negotiations with Yeh.
24.7.1857	Yeh despatched two officials to Hong Kong in yet another attempt to start negotiations. But Bowring had (much to his regret) been forbidden by the Foreign Office even to communicate with the Chinese authorities.
21.10.1857	Yeh exhorted Lord Elgin to stop hostilities and to settle the dispute by peaceful means, but to no avail. An uneventful period ensued.
12.12.1857	Elgin sent an ultimatum to Yeh demanding the virtual surrender of Canton. Yeh hastily prepared his defence by hiring mercenaries and piling up stones and bags of quicklime on the city walls.
24.12.1857	Allied ultimatum to Yeh to surrender within 48 hours.
28.12.1857	Bombardment of Canton began.
5.1.1858	Canton fell. Yeh was taken prisoner.

was, in the absence of Governor Po-kuei who was visiting Peking, supervising the provincial military examination on the parade-ground. Seeing that Yeh was unmoved, one of his subordinates warned him that the consequences might be serious. Smiling, Yeh replied, 'Don't worry; they [the British] will leave after dusk. Please pass on my order that all war junks should retire and not fire on the enemy.'[3] The next day Yeh still went to watch the examination. At noon, the report of cannon shook the parade-ground – the British had begun to attack the forts on the waterfront in Ho-nan. Observing Yeh's orders, the marines guarding the forts left without putting up any resistance. Yeh still appeared indifferent to this new development, but not his subordinates, who, with the excuse that shooting on horseback was difficult because of the strong wind, begged him to adjourn the test. Yeh agreed, and requested all his subordinates to go to his office for a conference about the situation.[4]

Yeh's attitude was simple. He wanted to avoid foreign war, but when it was forced upon him, he did not want to fire the first shot and hence be accused of provocation. When the British fought their way up to Canton, Yeh could excuse himself to Peking on the grounds of pure foreign aggression. Once the enemy had actually intruded into the city bounds, his belief that the foreigners dared not antagonise the Chinese people, but always sought to bully the government, began to influence his policy. He restrained his troops from even firing on the enemy in defence when the latter tried to capture forts on the outskirts of the city, so as to let the Cantonese see with their own eyes that the British were the aggressors. By so doing, he hoped to achieve two aims: first, that the people of Canton would be provoked and would stand up to the enemy, who, he thought, would realise that they had by mistake antagonised the people and would retreat; second, if the British nevertheless insisted on a military solution, the alienated people of Canton would fully back up their government in the war effort. Only the latter expectation was fulfilled. 'Huge red placards mushroomed both inside and outside the city, calling on everybody to join in the battle against the invad-ers . . . several thousand militiamen paraded through the streets of the foreign factories.'[5] Yeh remained inactive; he was still waiting for the situation to develop. The British then decided to increase their pressure by bombarding his *yamen* every five to ten minutes from Monday 27 October. All his servants and bodyguards fled, but he remained seated in his hall, composed and undisturbed,[6] still trying to impress upon his subordinates that there was no need to panic. Meanwhile, he realised that it was time to adopt a positive policy, and issued this order:

The British have attacked our city, killing our soldiers and people; their crimes are extreme. I now command you, inhabitants of the whole province, to unite and spare no efforts in assisting the troops to fight any Briton, on land or water. $30 will be rewarded to anyone who succeeds in killing one Briton and brings his head to my office.[7]

From then on, he responded actively to the foreign threat. How he fought the war will be discussed under the section entitled 'Nor showed fight'. The present section examines his unrelenting attempts to build up his defence. The picture that emerges, however, is one of heart-breaking helplessness.

The revival of militia units

The first step he took to strengthen the defence of Canton was to revive the militia units. These units were organised during the seige of Canton and had made important contributions toward its eventual survival in 1854–5. Those of the so-called Allied Streets in the western quarter of the city, the centre of foreign trade, were especially well-organised because they were financed by the wealthy merchants, and the militiamen were employees in their shops. When the siege was lifted, they returned to normal life; but, once trained, it was easy for them to take up arms again and to regroup into units in an emergency. Hence, when the British fleet attacked the Hai-chu Fort on 25 October 1856, the militiamen of the Allied Streets unanimously formed themselves into columns and paraded through the streets of the factories. Shortly afterwards, a gentry proclamation echoed Yeh's call to take up arms: 'We, the Allied Streets, have been commanded by our government to revive the militia system for the defence of our homes. Should the British launch an attack, or bandits try to fish in troubled water, we should beat gongs in a united effort to annihilate all of them.'[8] Thus, it was not only against the Chinese troops, but against virtually all the inhabitants of Canton and the surrounding villages that Sir Michael Seymour was fighting. Understandably, the British admiral thought it expedient to withdraw from such hostile territory, and he did so on 15 February 1857.[9]

However, this peculiar form of militia movement was not meant to be a permanent feature. It came into being only in emergencies. By the end of 1855, when it became apparent that Canton was safe from any further rebel attack, mercenaries were hired by the Allied Streets to take over patrol duties from the militiamen, who returned to normal life. Similarly, when the British retreated from Canton at the beginning of 1857, the militiamen once more laid down their arms; and an additional number of mercenaries were hired instead.[10] The question of funds was a serious one. Since the second half of 1854, the wealthy merchants had made substantial donations to the government in an effort to lift the siege of Canton, and for more than twelve months, from 1854–5, they had financed the militia of the Allied Streets. During the same period, very little foreign trade was conducted because of the disturbances. The merchants were thus drawing on their reserves all the time. Not long after the rebels were beaten off, and inland mercantile traffic restored, foreign war broke out and Yeh closed the customs office on 26 October 1856. This proved the last straw because the stoppage of trade continued to the end of foreign hostilities, which lasted for fourteen months. Moreover, Sir Michael Seymour set fire to the western quarters of Canton on 12 January 1857, destroying large numbers of Chinese warehouses and the goods in them.[11] Therefore it must have been impossible for the merchants to keep up the militia movement in the prolonged war period purely from their savings, which had already been heavily drained. It is even doubtful whether they continued to keep their employees – the source of militia recruits – in their idle shops. The fact that no reference was made in Yeh's archive to an important organisation such as the militia of the Allied Streets when the fateful assault came in December 1857 may suggest that it had either disintegrated or ceased to exist. Indeed one wonders if the Allied Streets were able or willing to maintain for long even the system of patrols by mercenaries, whom they paid with funds gathered from donations, because the report about their payments stopped on 23 April 1857.[12] Regarding the militia units in the Canton delta, it was proposed to Yeh that he should send capable commissioners to the various magistracies to revive them.[13] He may have done so, but his success is doubtful, because the countryside had been devastated by the rebels, and the gentry had exhausted their means in fighting them. The militia movement had made important contributions during the Entry Crisis of 1849, the siege of Canton in 1854, the campaign of the Canton delta in 1855–6, and the British attack in 1856. The fact that it should ultimately have been crippled by these major events, made it extremely difficult to defend the city against the long-awaited final assault in 1857.

The recovery of the forts

The other major project Yeh undertook to defend Canton was to recover the forts occupied by the English. He reorganised the soldiers who had been responsible for their defence. He gave them medical treatment and compensation for wounds sustained in the battle to stop the British admiral intruding into the waters of Canton, and above all, time to regain their strength and morale. Owing to the financial difficulties of the time, he had been planning various cuts in the budgets of the province, among them the pay of the soldiers. Now that foreign war had broken out, he took the unusual step of increasing the wages of the marines responsible for manning the forts to boost their morale.[14] On 22 November, it was reported to Yeh that these marines were all ready for a counter-attack.[15] Because the Chinese troops fought bravely, and because Seymour was reluctant to remain in such a hostile land for long,

Table 22

The condition of cannon in some of the forts east of Canton
before and after the British assault at the end of 1856[a]

Fort	Before the assault		After the assault	
	No. of cannon	Weight (catties)	No. of cannon	Weight (catties)
1 Tung-ching	6	8,000	Nil	Nil
	6	5,000	Nil	Nil
	1	4,000	Nil	Nil
	4	3,000	Nil	Nil
	12	2,000	Nil	Nil
	1	1,500	Nil	Nil
	2	1,000	Nil	Nil
	39	Under 1,000	30	Under 1,000
2 Tung-an	6	8,000	Nil	Nil
	23	5,000	4	5,000
	5	3,000	Nil	Nil
	2	2,000	Nil	Nil
	4	1,000	Nil	Nil
3 Tung-ku	7	8,000	Nil	Nil
	7	5,000	Nil	Nil
	10	3,000	Nil	Nil
	3	2,000	Nil	Nil
	4	1,000	Nil	Nil
	—	—	10	Under 1,000
4 Chung-liu-chih-chu	1	34,000	Nil	Nil
	7	8,000	Nil	Nil
	6	5,000	Nil	Nil
	10	3,000	Nil	Nil
	8	2,000	4	2,000
	2	1,200	—	—
	13	Under 1,000	8	Under 1,000

[a] 253A.4.19 and 21. A catty-weight is equal to one and one-third pounds. The weights of Chinese cannon were always expressed in terms of a large and even number of catties. Catties are thus retained here to avoid awkward conversions to the perplexingly odd-numbered pound equivalents.

the forts were gradually recovered. But most of the big cannon in the forts had been either destroyed by the blue-jackets before they left, or carried away. Table 22 is a study of the condition of some of the forts before and after the British assault in 1856. It shows that nearly all the cannon heavier than 1,000 catties were either removed or destroyed. The forts were almost entirely disarmed. In Yeh's archive, there are no reports concerning the casting of new heavy cannon to replace those lost, obviously because of the abject poverty to which the province had been reduced. Instead, seven cannon (weighing between 700 to 1,000 catties) dumped in the east gate of the city after the siege of Canton was over, were recovered and put to use again.[16]

If the original forts, armed with cannon of thousands of catties, nonetheless fell in 1856, it was of course impossible for the marines to defend them, let alone use them to defend Canton, with a small number of little cannon when the British, reinforced by a large number of gunboats and French allies, returned to the attack a year later. The cannon fire from the fort at Hsiao-heng-tang in the Hu-men area proved too weak, and its range too short to prevent the enemies from landing; the marines fled. At Ta-heng-tang, therefore, the marines ran away immediately the British came into sight, without firing a shot. The third target was the San-yüan, which was the headquarters of the marines. The commander-in-chief, Wu Yüan-yu, left his post on a flimsy excuse, and his rank and file fled after him, including the mercenaries hired to strengthen the defence of the fort. The allies landed, set fire to the munition store and then deserted the place, which they did not think worthwhile leaving any soldiers to guard. Nor did the Chinese marines think it would serve any purpose to return there. At Sha-chiao, which was also near Hu-men, the officers buried the cannon to prevent them falling into the hands of the enemy. The thirty marines, who were ordered to stay and guard the fort, fled when they saw the enemy disembarking from their warships. 'It is shocking that the officers should be so cowardly, and the troops so disloyal.'[17] This was the conclusion of the commissioner who reported the above incidents to Yeh. Wu Yüan-yu was impeached in 1858 for failure to perform his duty.[18] However, he did have a record of bravery throughout his career, and he did fight courageously in 1856 to prevent the British forcing their way into the waters of Canton. In 1857, he was deprived of the means of doing anything effective at all.

Counter-espionage

Yeh's defence measures also included a vigorous counter-espionage campaign. During the British attack in 1856, the whole of his intelligence network was mobilised to detect any traitor who dared spy for the enemy or supply them with provisions. About seventy were arrested. Their crimes ranged from buying food for the British or selling it to them, and spying on the movement of Chinese troops, to actually serving on British warships, firing cannon on the city and trying to set fire to the city or to blow up Chinese fortifications.[19] After the British had withdrawn from Canton, Yeh ordered a certificate of identity to be issued to every citizen, and no one was allowed either to enter or to leave the city without it. Consequently, very little intelligence found its way to

Hong Kong.[20] However, it was not so easy to prevent the loss of important information outside Canton. On 4 April and again on 1 June 1857, some war junks were surprised by the British fleet, and numerous papers of strategic importance were thus seized.[21] These documents revealed all of Yeh's weaknesses in terms of finance and military strength,[22] and convinced Bowring that Canton could not hold out a day[23] when reinforcements arrived. Therefore Bowring tried persistently to persuade Lord Elgin to take Canton before approaching Peking, as a security for concessions.[24] His suggestion was eventually adopted,[25] and Canton fell as he had predicted.

Espionage

Finally, it should be mentioned that large-scale espionage was also carried out as part of Yeh's defence system. 'Spying must be constant, so that we may have up-to-date information about the enemy, on which we may appropriately formulate our conduct of foreign relations.'[26] This was one of the guidelines of Yeh's foreign policy. Even in peacetime, his agents used to send him regular reports about conditions in Hong Kong: the commercial situation, the arrival and departure of foreign shipping, and the movement of troops, or just a few words saying that all was well. There was, for example, a man called Hsiao Ting-an who sent him regular reports.[27] Important news printed in the English newspapers in Hong Kong was also laboriously translated, copied and smuggled to Canton for his persual.[28] When foreign hostilities broke out, his bodyguards, who had been supplying him with intelligence about the campaign in the Pearl River region, were given the additional task of spying on the movements of the British vessels in the Pearl River. For this purpose, one particular squad was chosen and interviewed by Yeh, who instructed them to send him immediately news of any fresh development; otherwise they should communicate with him once every five days.[29] Members of the gentry who served in the Foreign Affairs Office also sent their servants in hired boats to Hong Kong and Macao to collect information.[30] This office also had power to delegate military personnel to disguise themselves and go to the two colonies for the same purpose.[31] However, much of the intelligence was supplied by Chinese merchants in Hong Kong, who were engaged in foreign trade and hence were in daily contact with foreigners.[32] Yeh's sources of information ranged indeed very widely. He himself said, rather complacently, 'In the past, His Excellency Lin Tse-hsü was very fond of exploiting espionage; but he was misled by the intelligence he received because his sources were limited. As for me, I verify my information according to scores of different sources.'[33] Oddly enough, Yeh drew two chief conclusions from the masses of reports. First, that the British had been crushingly defeated by the Russians in the Crimean war; as a result, they had had to sue for peace, become a tributary state of the victor and pay an idemnity of 78,000,000 taels. It was in order to obtain money for the indemnity that the British insisted on entering the city of Canton, because once they had been in the city, they could levy a daily toll of 10,000 taels on the city, 10,000 taels on its suburbs, and 10,000 taels on the business transacted.[34] Second, that the Indian mutiny had been so costly in terms of life and resources, that the British were considerably weakened and were in no position to fight a third war.[35]

It is not difficult to account for the fantastic nature of these conclusions. Yeh's spies were not trained agents in the modern sense, but informants who reported rumours and whatever information they could glean from newspapers and conversations. Given their ignorance of the outside world and their poor English, it is not surprising that their reports could be wildly misleading. The British at Hong Kong, belatedly informed of the course of events in the Crimea and in India, reacted with near-panic to the reverses of their countrymen;[36] this reaction must have influenced the tenor of the espionage reports. Even if Yeh had had any reservations about these reports, their repetition and their uniformity must have convinced him of their truth.[37] Throughout his career, his agents had given him accurate and valuable intelligence. But whereas reports on matters within China had been based on genuine observation, reports about the foreigners were founded on hearsay and second-hand information, which he was not in a position to evaluate. Finally, Yeh, knowing the weakness of his position, and the possibility of a renewed British attack, may have accepted these reports as true because he wanted to believe that the British too had their weaknesses.

Conclusion

Despite Yeh's mistakes and eventual failure, it is inconceivable that he should have been accused of having made no defence. To begin with, he did reinforce the forts along the Pearl River to prevent the British Navy intruding into the waters of Canton in 1856; but after severe fighting these forts nevertheless fell, because of inferior fire-power. When the British had succeeded in fighting their way to Canton, Yeh, after three days of inaction with the intention of securing popular support, directed a resistance campaign both on land and on water so harassing to the enemy that Seymour found it necessary to evacuate Canton. Elgin also admitted that 'since this quarrel commenced we have been led into many serious mistakes by underrating the power of resistance possessed by the enemy.'[38] Moreover, hostilities continued for another fourteen months, during which period Yeh's defence measures included the recapture of the forts, the revival of the militia movement, the espionage and counter-espionage campaigns. It is true that these measures, though painstaking, were ineffectual; but it would be malicious to suggest that Yeh did not make preparations at all to defend Canton.

'Nor showed fight'

When the British began bombarding the city of Canton on 27 October 1856, Yeh actively prepared for a counter-attack. Foreign war had started; it may be divided into six phases for discussion: the campaign at Canton, the war on the Pearl River, the campaign at Hong Kong, and propaganda war, the commercial war and the final allied assault on Canton in December 1857.

The campaign at Canton

As already mentioned, Admiral Seymour started to bombard Canton on 27 October. The next day parts of the city wall were destroyed and the houses outside the wall burnt down to pave the way for entry into the city. On 29 October, Seymour and Parkes went into the city. The Chinese soldiers retaliated unyieldingly, shooting from street corners and from inside houses, inflicting nearly thirty casualties on the enemy; but they were outgunned. The British, followed by the Americans, went straight to Yeh's deserted *yamen* and ransacked its rooms and harem, creating what has been described by Costin as scandalous scenes of vandalism.[39] Then they withdrew; but for the next three days, they continued to fire at the wall of the new city. However, all the breaches made during the day were quickly repaired at night. Therefore from 3 November onwards, the bombardment was extended to government buildings in the old city, such as those of the Tartar general and the governor.[40]

The Chinese, especially the military officers, were truly roused. 'Unless we deal them a deadly blow, they will never be curbed.'[41] Detailed plans and sketches as to how to attack the British and blow up their warships continued to flow into Yeh's *yamen*. Many of these plans were executed. One midnight, for example, a boat loaded with explosives went off near a house on the waterfront where 300 British soldiers were sleeping. Another night, four boats full of inflammable material floated downstream towards the British warships and started to burn, causing havoc on board. After this, Seymour barricaded his fleet with a circle of junks for protection. This did not prevent the determined Chinese from harassing their enemy with primitive hand-grenades, one of which destroyed a barricading junk on 12 November, and with underwater explosives, two of which went off prematurely beside a

British warship the next day. At 3 a.m. on 15 November, some war junks took advantage of the heavy fog to fire on two British gunboats for twenty minutes, and then disappeared quickly into the darkness. The following morning, another attempt was made to break the barricading junks. Eventually Seymour had to reinforce the boom with heavy iron chains.[42]

Once the Cantonese began to retaliate, the shortage of British soldiers became dangerously apparent. At one stage Parkes went to the extent of asking Bowring to despatch a task force of 200 Hakkas from Hong Kong because these people hated the Cantonese, but Bowring was sensible enough to decline such a request.[43] Instead, an alternative was planned. Large numbers of coolies in the colony were asked to join a labour force to relieve the pressure for manpower at Canton. These porters, however, refused to go.[44] The position of the British in Canton became indeed precarious. Perhaps sensing the danger to the factories, the small contingent of French marines withdrew.[45] This left the British even more vulnerable. As a defensive measure, they had already occupied the Hog Lane, which ran into the factories, and a clearance was made in front of this foreign settlement.[46] They also pulled down large numbers of Chinese houses at its back. Nevertheless, fires were started at 11 p.m. on 14 December among the demolished houses, and by 5 p.m. the next day, the whole of the buildings in the factories were a mass of smoking ruins, with the exception of only one house.[47] Consequently, Seymour found it necessary to barricade his countrymen by having an entrench-ment dug round the remains of the factories, and guarded with soldiers. However, the admiral had to abandon before long, on 14 January,[48] what was regarded by Bowring as an impregnable position in the gardens.[49] Although Parkes chose to call such a step a modification of position, a British soldier, Captain Bate, regarded it as a downright retrograde movement.[50] But this was not all. A month later, even the strongholds Seymour had occupied around Canton had to be deserted,[51] having had enough of 'the hundreds of junks that molest him', and 'the firerafts and most ingenious but most diabolic devices of the Chinese'.[52] However, Yeh would not let him withdraw peacefully. He sent a large body of war junks after him, but the fierce attack was said to have been repulsed.[53]

The war on the Pearl River

The campaign at Canton ended with Seymour's retreat, but the battle for the control of the Pearl River raged on. To obtain a full picture of this sector of the entire campaign, it is necessary to go back to 1 December 1856, when it was reported to Yeh that Captain Su, with his fleet of 35 junks, had scored a major victory near the second Barrier; conse-quently, Yeh rewarded Su and his men with $1,250.[54] Soon the British had to abandon Whampoa because even their men-of-war could not remain there in safety, and, in Bowring's own words, 'our forces are now confined to securing Hong Kong and our protection at Canton'.[55] Thus the Chinese were beginning to gain an upper hand in the control of the inner part of the Pearl River. At Fo-shan, for example, a steamer full of supplies for the British in Canton was captured. British gunboats were kept on a perpetual *qui vive* of apprehension,[56] and the forts they occupied were reduced to a state of siege. Captain Bate gave a vivid picture of life in the forts. There was very little to eat and to drink, and there was always something going on to rouse one in the night. He and his men were completely isolated, and he finally became so frustrated that he emphatically declared that 'Newgate and Pentonville must be pleasant abodes compared to this place.'[57] Eventually, Seymour became so painfully alarmed about being blockaded, and being unable to keep open his communications that he decided to retreat further down the river, to the Bogue.[58]

In all these operations, Yeh was directly involved. Among the Chinese papers later seized by the English, there was for example one in which Brigadier Huang K'ai-kuang wrote to a junior officer, saying that 'Yeh [had] desired him as well as the writer to proceed at once to P'ing-chou, there to wait for orders.'[59] Then there was a report by the same junior officer and others to Brigadier Huang on subsequent engagements with the English.[60] Reports from Yeh's informants in Hong Kong also gave details of British steamers returning to the colony with severe damage and casualties on board after engagements in the Pearl River.[61]

Waiting in vain for reinforcements to arrive, Seymour regarded it as pointless even to keep the forts in the Pearl River, harrassed as they were day and night by Chinese guerrilla tactics, and he withdrew to Hong Kong, which was the battleground for the third phase of the contest.

The campaign at Hong Kong

Once war had started, Yeh, like any capable military organiser, took into consideration all possibilities and the best way of winning the battle. One of his important tactics was to threaten the British base in Hong Kong after the enemy had invaded Canton. He sent Ch'en Kuei-chi, a member of the gentry of Hsin-an (Hong Kong was part of the magistracy of Hsin-an before it was ceded to the British), to carry out operations against the colony. Ch'en held a mass meeting of all the gentry of the district in a local Confucian temple (*ming-lun-t'ang*). In this meeting, they unanimously denounced British atrocities since the Opium War. They also passed resolutions calling for the stoppage of all supplies to

Hong Kong, the withdrawal of all natives of Hsin-an from the colony, and the elimination of all converts within the magistracy.[62] Ch'en reported the proceedings to Yeh and acted upon the resolutions. He received intelligence that some missionaries had once established themselves in a village, but had fled back to Hong Kong after the outbreak of hostilities. In case some Chinese converts might still be in hiding spying for the enemy, he secretly despatched some members of the gentry with militiamen to raid the house where the missionaries had stayed. No arrests were made, but the fugitives' property was seized.[63] His brother, who was specially invested with the charge of stopping supplies to Hong Kong, distributed his pickets along the communications between the magisterial city and Kowloon.[64] Flotillas of junks were also organised for the same purpose, and were so effective that Bowring was loud in his expression of annoyance.[65]

One step which Ch'en did not publicise was his plan to launch surprise attacks on the colony. On 19 January, for example, he sent a squad to Hong Kong. Moving about in disguise, they surprised and dispersed a British patrol, made good their escape and returned bearing a severed head.[66] This was by no means an isolated incident. 'Kidnapping, assassination and incendiarism', Bowring wrote to Lord Clarendon, 'keep us on the *qui vive*.'[67] To his son, Bowring confessed that these instruments of Chinese warfare made the colonists feel more than ordinary solicitude.[68] Consequently, he accepted the French admiral's offer to protect the least secure part of the colony.[69] Then came a plot of a far more serious nature. On 15 January, an attempt was made to poison the foreign community in the colony by secreting arsenic in one of the bakeries. However, there was too much arsenic in the loaves; vomiting came on speedily and there was a general panic leading to prompt and efficacious remedies.[70] Consequently, no lives were lost, but great sufferings were occasioned. The worst victim seems to have been Lady Bowring, who became very ill and was so considerably weakened as a result that she died prematurely in 1858.[71] It was with much anxiety that Sir John Bowring's aunt wrote to him: 'I was truly thankful on receiving your last note and deeply sympathise with you in all your trouble...I trust the power which protected you will still be with you and shield you from all harm. Should my life be spared I shall be thankful to see you all home again.'[72] The attempt at poisoning the whole colony increased the disquiet of the populace, who were daily expecting guerrilla attacks from the mainland.[73] Small wonder that the British community was in great consternation, and many were evacuating their families to Macao.[74] Ch'en's brother reported that 20 boats patrolled the harbour day and night, and the offices of foreign companies were guarded by troops; the cannon were always kept at the ready at dusk.[75] A measure similar to a curfew was imposed on the colony every day after six o'clock, when police and soliders would start to patrol in large groups. These were the major steps taken by Bowring 'for the preservation of the persons and property of Her Majesty's subjects, precautions which I hope will conduct us safely through our perils'.[76] Inevitably, these extra measures constituted a heavy financial burden. 'Our poor little colony's treasury is drawn dry', wrote Bowring, 'I have had to find steamers for the protection, to get troops from Singapore, to nearly double the police.'[77]

Yeh's guerrilla manoeuvres constituted the substance of his war effort during 1857. His best troops being away from Canton, he had no other option. His policy was set out in a proclamation to the gentry of the coast, undoubtedly in his *yamen* although in the name of the gentry of Tung-kuan. The crucial passage reads:

The British have attacked us without just cause and without declaring war...The governor-general is the best judge of whether to adopt an offensive or defensive strategy, but, for the protection of our own homes, the people should be exhorted to form militia...Our province is rich and is not dependent on foreign supplies, whereas the British have come from afar and rely on us for all their daily necessities. Hong Kong is their only base for operations and gunboats are their only means of tyrannising over us. We need not think of wiping them out in one battle, but we can do so in protracted warfare. If we concert our efforts to cut off their supplies, and if we concentrate the militia of the hinterland to take turns attacking them, it will not be difficult to root them out of their den for good. If we cannot achieve this in a day, we may achieve it in a year; if not in one year, then in two, or three, or five, or ten, or twenty years, until we have extirpated them.[78]

It is clear from this that Yeh was counting on a war of attrition, a kind of people's war, to force Bowring, who had absolutely refused to treat, to come to terms. Where he miscalculated was in discounting, as he was led to do by the misinformation he received about enormous British losses in the Crimea and in India, the possibility of British reinforcements with French allies. Nor did he seem to realise that his hundreds of war junks that menaced Hong Kong would face utter disaster once British gunboats of light draft arrived, as these junks could no longer take refuge in shallow waters inaccessible to large steamers.

Propaganda warfare

Meanwhile, brute force was not the only weapon with which the two men fought their battle. A fierce war of propaganda was going on continuously. In April 1857, for example, Bowring tried to weaken the Chinese war effort by sowing discord between the officials and the people. He printed and distributed 2,000 copies of a pamphlet in which he summarised the hostilities in 1856, shifting the responsibility of the war entirely on Yeh's shoulders and stressing that he was attempting only to reason with the Chinese officials and had no quarrel with the people.[79] In retaliation, Yeh employed his usual tactic of denouncing the enemy in the name of all the inhabitants of Kwangtung, aiming at convincing his subjects that it was largely a war between them and the foreigners, not just between the two governments. Here is a translation of part of his proclamation.

In the pamphlets they distributed, they described their action as an attempt to reason with the officials, while they had no quarrel with the people. May we ask, 'Are the destruction of forts and the bombardment of the city an act of reasoning? Is the burning of civilian houses and warehouses with goods worth millions of no concern to the people?'[80]

Again, when British marines fired on a village in Tung-kuan in June 1857, killing scores of unarmed inhabitants, the local gentry went to Hong Kong to confront Bowring with the discrepancy between his profession and his practice,[81] which Yeh had pointed out in this proclamation. This period was full of declarations of this kind, in which Yeh sought to direct the animosity of the populace against the British, and vice versa.

Commercial warfare

Yet another aspect of the contest was the stoppage of trade. Yeh believed that the aliens came to China solely to trade, which was true enough, and this served as a maxim of his diplomacy. On Sunday 26 October, after the British had attacked and occupied the Hai-chü Fort, Yeh closed the customs office,[82] hoping that the stoppage of trade, which meant so much to the British, would eventually force them to come to the conference table. This action was brought about by his experience during the Entry Crisis of 1849, about which he wrote, 'So much suffering was occasioned by the stoppage of trade that after just one month, the British merchants could not stand it any longer',[83] and the demand to enter the city was dropped. This may have been a misconception of the real situation, but Yeh was undoubtedly convinced that trade was the lifeline of the British, and once it was cut, the enemy would soon have to sue for peace. Unfortunately, the stoppage was, to say the least, ineffective. First, smuggling flourished in the Canton delta as a result. The export of tea and silk continued, illegally, on as large a scale as it would have done without the stoppage,[84] the only difference being that no customs duties were collected. It was difficult enough to stifle illicit traffic in peacetime. With his *corps d'elite* fighting away from Canton, and the rest of his subordinates busily engaged in the foreign war, it proved impossible to check smuggling. Some of his officers even collaborated in this lucrative business. There was the extreme example of an officer who, taking advantage of his appointment by the Foreign Affairs Office to sail to Hong Kong and Macao on an espionage mission, attempted to smuggle out large quantities of tea.[85] Even the police force of the customs office, who were supposed to patrol the waters of Canton, accepted heavy bribes and turned a blind eye to the contraband or even offered it convoy.[86] Consequently, 19,638,300 lb of tea were exported to England from Canton in 1857 (two-thirds of the export of tea of the previous year),[87] when theoretically no goods should have come out of Canton at all.

Secondly, the Manchu government, tottering under the weight of its financial difficulties, attached great importance to the foreign duties, and was anxious to preserve a peaceful state of affairs at the ports, apparently ignoring the position at Canton.[88] The intendant at Shanghai went so far as to assure Consul Robertson that under all circumstances the peace of the ports must be preserved; that the outbreak occurred with the people at Canton, and at Canton it must be settled.[89] In fact the emperor soon became impatient with the stoppage of trade at Canton and repeatedly urged Yeh to allay the hostility.[90] This was bad enough for Yeh's morale, but worse was yet to come. Bowring learnt about this imperial attitude before long and had the satisfaction of knowing that his opponent was in a very difficult if not impossible position.[91] Indeed, 'the rest of the empire remained neutral', wrote Morse, 'and even indifferent, and international relations even with the English remained undisturbed.'[92]

The Chinese nation had undoubtedly been unfair to Yeh by not giving him the necessary co-operation and support when he tried to stop foreign aggression, and then putting the entire blame on him after he had failed to do so. With good reason, Yeh wrote in one of his last poems,

> A general must make shift as best he can;
> His countrymen look on, and mock his fate.[93]

The rest of the story is fairly straightforward. Bowring had appealed to London for support. The British government decided that his proceedings should be approved.[94] Furthermore, they appointed Lord Elgin as Plenipotentiary Extraordinary with a force of 1,500 men from Britain, and 750 European and native Indian troops already in Hong Kong to back up Bowring's demands.

The final assault

Lord Elgin arrived at Hong Kong in July 1857, but he had diverted his troops to India to deal with the Mutiny.[95] Finding that he was unable to do anything without them, he too, left for Calcutta, and did not return to the colony until late in September. Meanwhile, an agreement had been reached with the French government for concerted action,[96] and the French High Commissioner, Baron Gros, arrived at Hong Kong on 15

October. These two men, together with their admirals, lost no more time in planning the capture of Canton.

During Lord Elgin's absence, Admiral Seymour had blockaded the Pearl River, causing much distress in the city, not the least part of which was the shortage of food.[97] In response to this new threat, Yeh consulted his advisers again and received many suggestions, for example, that the rural militia should be alerted, so that in case of war, those near Canton could quickly come to its defence, and those near Hong Kong could attack the colony. Furthermore, the local councils should be ordered to hire mercenaries ready for mobilisation, and the nearby magistracies to supply Canton with several hundred musketeers and with rice; cannon should be posted along the waterfront to prevent the British from landing, and large quantities of sand-bags, quick-lime, tiles and stones should be gathered on the city walls ready for battle.[98]

These would have been Yeh's main preparations for war before the final assault came four months later, by which time the Chinese alert would again have relaxed. Furthermore, the inaction of Elgin and Gros for months after their arrival until they were confident of their ability to occupy Canton can have given Yeh little warning of the coming attack. Moreover, his informants must have told him of the widespread opinion in Hong Kong that Elgin was seeking a peaceful settlement. Then suddenly came an ultimatum on 12 December, demanding, among other things, entry into the city and occupation of Ho-nan and the river forts pending a settlement with Peking. Yeh could not accede to the first demand for reasons discussed at length above; as for the second, he could not allow Canton to be stripped of its essential defence. He replied accordingly. On Christmas Eve, the allies notified him that they would proceed to military action.[99] Yeh had little time to build up his defence, because the attack came three days later. It will be remembered that this was the time of the Pearl River campaign against the rebels. The situation along the West River was particularly serious. As described above, there was great fear that the Kwangsi rebels might once more descend on Kwangtung. Less than a month before the *Arrow* incident, it was reported that a fleet of 70 war junks had been destroyed by the rebels at Wu-chou and Commander-in-chief K'un-shou was despatched there to conduct the campaign.[100] The following poem may give some idea of how critical the situation was in Kwangsi. Appealing desperately to Yeh for help, some gentry of the province wrote:

> With general's art and premier's Your Lordship is replete;
> The people's fortune you mete out from your judgement seat.
> Like the sweet tree,[101] by southern folk, Your Lordship's name is blest;
> Like timely rain your troops are sought by people of the west.[102]

To have recalled the troops to Canton would have meant the collapse of the government's campaign in Kwangsi. As for Kwangtung itself, it was never really free from rebel disturbances. Shortly after foreign hostilities broke out because of the *Arrow* incident, Yeh transferred to the provincial capital some of his troops. Immediately there followed horrible accounts of the destruction of life and property in the localities from whence the troops were withdrawn.[103] One of the nearby cities actually fell to the insurgents only two months before the British renewed their bombardment of Canton towards the end of 1857.[104] Therefore Yeh must have found it impossible, or at least unwise, to recall his troops to resist an attack which might turn out once again to be illusory.

Even if the troops were transferred back to Canton (which would have meant the abandonment of large food-producing areas), it would have been impossible to feed them there, because of the British blockade, which prevented the import of rice, and because the treasuries were empty. It was shown above how Yeh's government was desperately short of funds. The stoppage of trade meant the loss of one of the three main sources of revenue. Until 24 January, 528,307.553 taels had been spent on the foreign war alone, reducing the reserves of Canton to a total of only 17,076.600 taels.[105] From 26 January onwards, Yeh had to resort to the very risky step of drastically cutting the number of mercenaries and junks hired for the defence of Canton.[106] During the Entry Crisis of 1849, the normal garrison was reinforced by over 100,000 militiamen,[107] which made the defence of Canton in 1857 look even more miserly, because by the end of 1857 the militia movement had been very much crippled both in the city and in its vicinity. Yeh did recruit as many troops as he could afford by hiring mercenaries (see Table 23). The number of 15,248 mercenaries looks impressive, but they had to be thinned out, as is apparent from the table, to guard a hopelessly long line of defence. Furthermore, the Chinese weapons, as already mentioned, consisted only of muskets, swords, spears or even sand-bags, quick-lime, tiles and pieces of stone. With much contempt Bowring wrote, 'The strategy and the weapons of barbarism against consummate naval and military tactics with all the appliances which science has brought to experience could only lead to one result.'[108] The result was indeed predictable. Shells and rockets poured from the ships into the town without a shot being fired in return. It was only against the allies on land that the Chinese soliders had any chance of displaying resistance.[109] It is true that many of the Chinese soliders fought bravely and stubbornly, inflicting a total of 128 casualties on the enemies, but they were quickly overpowered and the city fell. Yeh was captured.

Table 23

Mercenaries hired to strengthen the defence of Canton in December 1857[a]

Place		Mercenaries		Leader	Number
1	*Old City*	1	Ta-li	—	400
		2	Hsiang-shan	Lin Fu-sheng	600
		3	Banners	—	200
2	*New City*	1	P'ing	Prefect Wu	500
		2	Ch'ao-chou	Magistrate-designate Mao	500
		3	Ch'ao-chou	Sub-Lieutenant Fang	500
		4	Ta-pu	—	700
		5	Marines	Lieutenant Su	500
3	*East outskirts*	1	Ch'ao-chou	Magistrate Ch'en	300
		2	P'an-yü (militia)	Magistrate Wang	2,000
		3	Tung-kuan	Lieutenant Chu Kuo-hsiung	800
		4	Tung-kuan	Hu Hsien-wei	200
		5	Tung-kuan	Chou Yüan-hsün	1,000
4	*South outskirts*	1	Tung	Chang Ching-hsiu	308
		2	Tung	Chang Hsing	100
5	*West outskirts*	1	Ta-li	—	2,100
		2	P'ing-lo (militia)	—	500
6	*North outskirts*	1	Hsiang-shan	Lin Fu-sheng	500
		2	An-liang (militia)	—	300
		3	Tung-kuan	Ho Jen-shan	140
7	14 strategic points north of Canton (total)				2,500
	Grand Total				14,648

[a] 137.6.53. Most of these so-called mercenaries, except perhaps those from Ch'ao-chou and those attached to the Banners, were ordinary peasants drafted into the militia, not professional soldiers.

Conclusion

It would have been madness to suppose that Yeh did not fight. Throughout the campaign, he showed the intelligence and flexibility of an experienced military organiser. In the absence of the main body of his troops from Canton, he adopted guerrilla tactics and waged protracted warfare with the ambitious aim of bringing the enemy to reason. However, guerrilla warfare needs to be mobile; if Canton were in danger of being captured, Yeh and his government should have moved into the hinterland to carry on the campaign. The difficulty lay in the law of the empire, which decreed that any official who lost his city should lose his head. Therefore Yeh had to remain at Canton and become a sitting target.

The resistance that he organised proved ineffective. All the capable field commanders who had served him had either died, disappeared or were no longer in the province: Fu-hsing was transferred to Hunan, Shen Ti-hui died in 1856, and K'un-shou he had despatched to fight in Kwangsi. As for the Tartar general, he was only an empty shell. Cooke gave a dramatic, though perhaps not entirely untrue, account of his behaviour in the war:

During the fight he never appeared upon the walls. After the fight he did nothing to gather his 7,000 men around him. When the French came he made no defence, but ran from room to room, and was dragged from a filthy closet. If he had been taken by Tai-pings instead of Europeans he would be howling at their feet.[110]

In the absence of good leadership, Yeh's troops were a mere armed mob. As for the people, whose wishes had been a guideline of his diplomacy, and who he expected would rise spontaneously to over-whelm the invaders with human waves, in the city they offered only passive resistance;[111] in the countryside, they did rise *en masse*, but too late to save Canton.[112] The war effort also suffered from lack of co-operation by Yeh's colleagues. As soon as they saw which way the wind was blowing, Governor Po-kuei and the Tartar general were quick to collaborate with the invaders. Well before Canton was captured, Seymour wrote to Bowring: 'You will hear of the probability of our shortly occupying a mode of treating with the authorities exclusive of Yeh...Pih Kwei and the Tartar General &c have expressed their willingness to denounce him to the emperor by memorial which is to be handed to us &c'.[113] One is reminded of Yeh's two lines quoted earlier:

A general must make shift as best he can;
His countrymen look on, and mock his fate.

The ballad-maker censured the man who had done his best to wage the war rather than those who collaborated with the enemy. Some clues as to why this injustice was done may be found in a local newspaper in Hong Kong: 'The question is whether the prestige of [Yeh's] memory will cause him to be subject of adoration by the Cantonese. His valour and determination there can be no doubt...the Cantonese must nevertheless feel proud of the champion.' The newspaper concluded, therefore, that the satisfactory solution of the difficult problem of occupying Canton involved: 'the necessity of the popular clamour being directed against Yeh, until his name and memory became execrated.'[114] This policy the allies readily adopted. It is thus quite possible that the ballad was written at the instigation of the English. The collaborators must have welcomed such an action because they were eager to divert public attention from themselves by blaming Yeh. Hence a distorted picture of the man was drawn and handed down to us.

Conclusion

The essence of the ballad is that Yeh did nothing during the crisis of the foreign war. This chapter has attempted to prove the fallacy of such an accusation. The pity is that this ballad, being in the popular idiom, has been taken as a true representation of the sentiments of all the Cantonese at that time. The allies, who set themselves the task of establishing a puppet government, experienced the force of Yeh's popularity, as the following letters reveal. Elgin wrote to Gros on 24 January 1858:

It has been represented to me by persons whose opinion on such a point I am not at liberty to disregard, among others by Mr. Parkes, who speaks with authority both by reason of his local knowledge and of his position as a member of the tribunal appointed by ourselves and the commanders-in-chief to aid in carrying on the government of Canton, that the presence of Yeh in the Canton waters tends to disquiet the public mind and to render the task of re-establishing order and confidence in that city more difficult of accomplishment.[115]

Therefore it was decided to remove Yeh to Calcutta. Requesting a naval vessel to transport him, Elgin wrote to Seymour, 'It would be manifestly objectionable to land him at any of the Straits Settlements where the Chinese form the bulk of the population.'[116]

Historians have taken the ballad seriously because there was a report, repeated in many contemporary writings, that during the final assault Yeh 'did nothing' as consultation of oracles revealed that the situation would return to normal after 30 December 1857.[117] Documentary evidence of this particular incident is lacking in Yeh's archive. Here, it will be useful to refresh our memories of the contents of Tables 2 and 3, and the discussion of them. The accusation that Yeh was ridiculously superstitious is undoubtedly grossly exaggerated. In fact, augury was as much a part of the cultural inheritance of the officials of the time as was Confucianism; examples are not wanting in the *Veritable Records* of the dynasty. Even if there is any truth in the story about the prophecy of 30 December, it is not dissimilar to the answer given by the oracle of Delphi to Croesus, king of Lydia. This prophecy was alleged to have emanated from Yeh's father, who was in the habit of consulting the oracle.[118] This is credible because Yeh's father, as described in chap. 1, was deeply interested in stone and bronze inscriptions, and those with such an interest were generally fond of divination. It is also reported that Yeh, being very dutiful, built a Taoist monastery called Ch'ang-ch'un hsien-kuan, where his father might live and pursue his hobby. This is also plausible, since there is a plan of such a building in Yeh's archive. The rumour was that Yeh's policy during the allied attack was governed by his father's auguries. Therefore after the capture of the city, Yeh's father was made a scapegoat for the disaster; the following poem appeared on the city wall:

> The sleet is falling, the wind is high,
> The winter vexes the yellow leaf;
> The wind is howling, the year must die –
> So must old Yeh, the whole world's grief.
>
> At the dawn of the year the sky is dun;
> The rain drops drearily all the day;
> Men curse the early spring, each one –
> They curse, each one, the aged Yeh.[119]

Even if Yeh the junior had believed in divination, in view of the practical and realistic measures he adopted throughout his career, it would be absurd to suppose that all his actions were governed by divination alone.

Another cause for the charge that Yeh was unduly inactive, as that suggested by the ballad, seems to have arisen from his apparent lack of response towards alarming reports of acts of aggression by the English.[120] However, most of the alarms were false ones, and the reports mere rumours. It is not surprising, therefore, that Yeh should have adopted an attitude not very different from that of his opposite number, Sir John Bowring, who wrote:

If I listen to everyday's romances, I should neither sleep by night nor rest by day. Too much rest I have not, but I have not yet lost my serenity and self-possession, and I think I can estimate at their fine value the rumours which run to the government offices from a hundred quarters.[121]

It should be noted that it was partly his 'serenity and self-possession' which enabled Yeh to become an efficient administrator and a successful military organiser. Yet the same qualities, because of his final defeat by the allies, were distorted in the worst possible manner, and consequently earned him nothing but the most severe rebukes. Table 21 gave a chronological account of the important steps Yeh took to resist foreign aggression and to restore peace. It should, in addition to the analysis provided in the foregoing pages, prove how wrong is the popular belief that Yeh neglected his duties as imperial commissioner for foreign affairs during the critical years of 1856–8. True, he lost the war, but it was not because 'he did not treat, nor made defence, nor yielded, nor showed fight', but because the cannon of the European gunboats were so formidable, and his own position had been so hopelessly weakened by the rebellions, as to make him look like a complete fool during the fateful days towards the end of 1857.

Yeh's firm foreign policy had won him wide acclaim from his countrymen in 1849; the emperor made him a peer, his colleagues showered him with congratulatory poems, the Cantonese set up monuments to commemorate his achievements. The same firm policy, which all his compatriots[122] strongly desired but to which they were able, to say the least, to contribute little, failed in 1857 and Yeh was denounced by high and low; the emperor stripped him of all his ranks and honours, his colleagues condemned him as the black sheep of the family, and some embittered Cantonese wrote defamatory ballads and poems like those cited. Finally, the fall of Peking, highlighted by the flight of the imperial family, and the burning down of the Summer Palace by the allies, inclined the whole empire to make Yeh a scapegoat for the national humiliation. Henceforth a distorted image of Yeh would begin to form itself in the minds of posterity.

Part six
Yeh's last days

11 Exile in India

Yeh was detained on board the *Inflexible* for 48 days, from 5 January to 23 February (when the gunboat eventually steamed out of the harbour of Hong Kong). Such a long period of confinement under the circumstances would have created tremendous nervous strains on anyone of less superior calibre than Yeh, but as we have seen, all sources agree that he was not in the least disturbed by his personal misfortune. All the officers of the ship were said to have great respect for him for the cool, dignified manner in which he bore his fall and imprisonment.[1] A reporter of the *Hong Kong Register* went to see him and wrote: 'Some gentlemen who happened to be on board deemed it proper to take off their hats to him, on which he half rose from his seat and courteously returned the salute, taking off his cap.'[2] Yeh left Hong Kong for Calcutta in apparently admirable spirits, and continued in a state of good humour until he was laid prostrate with sea-sickness. However, he rallied much more quickly than any of his attendants,[3] who consisted of his aide-de-camp Lan Pin, two servants, a chef, and a barber.[4] He also suffered greatly from the hot weather; but when his interpreter Alabaster fell ill, he took pains to look after him. In Alabaster's own words, 'His Excellency . . . has far from neglected me, coming in to see me and making his attendants bustle about to relieve my wants.'[5] The *Inflexible* arrived at Calcutta on 12 March in the evening, and arrangements were made for Yeh's landing three days later.

On Monday morning he was dressed and had finished his breakfast punctually at 7 and, on Major Herbert's arrival, he put on his official cap and led the way on deck, bowing to every one and descending (if Your Excellency can imagine such a quality in a Chinese) with much grace into the boat which was prepared to receive him.[6]

He was temporarily housed in Fort William, and having entered into possession of his rooms, he took a polite leave of Captain Brooker of the *Inflexible*, and gave him a short note saying that he had been under his care for so many days, but declined to affix his signature as he had not done so for Bowring.[7]

His confinement in Fort William lasted for over 50 days.[8] It is probably the striking similarity in some ways between that fortress and Chen-hai Tower (which marked the climax of his military career) that inspired him to write the following poem:[9]

> Above the lofty tower near the sea,[10]
> The moonlight glistens with an icy gleam;
> The star that once a pilot was to me
> Forlornly sinks into the ocean stream.
> I might have had a name as great as Fan;[11]
> But what avails it, howsoever great?
> A general must make shift as best he can;
> His countrymen look on, and mock his fate.
> Then why not end? Truly as ready I
> To sacrifice my life as was Hsiang Shu;
> Yet live I, when 'twere easier to die,
> And keep my wand of office whole, like Su.[12]
> Let artists come, if sport is to be had;
> But who could ever draw a face so sad?[13]

Here for the first time, Yeh revealed his true intentions for having willingly become a prisoner of war. The execution of his plans, however, started long before this. During the voyage, for example, he did not seem on the surface to take any notice of the lands he was passing through, declining to have a chair on deck or even to look out of the side ports so long as anyone was in the cabin. But when he was left alone, he was found seated up at the stern ports gazing at the country with great interest.[14] At Fort William and subsequently at his official residence in Tollygung,[15] he received large numbers of visitors every week. They ranged from military personnel, officials of the Indian government, judges, to professors and missionaries.[16] Every day he got up very early, and was said to be restless until the *Calcutta Englishman* was brought to him, whereupon he would request Alabaster to translate the news for him. He was described as miserable if the newspaper did not contain its usual modicum of Parliamentary eloquence. He was delighted to hear that Lord Palmerston had been turned out of office, and he chuckled all through his great body when he heard of Lord Derby's intention for a speedy peace with China. These readings were of course interspersed with explanations and inquiries, and Yeh was reported to be really beginning to acquire some glimmering notion of the British Constitution.[17]

'I am afraid I weary Your Excellency,' says the interpreter, himself weary with two hours' arduous translation.
'No, go on. I understand it now. It is much better than [what] I used to get from Hong Kong. I never could understand them.'[18]

However, Yeh was not given much opportunity to improve his understanding of the West, nor was his country ever going to benefit from the knowledge he had so painfully acquired. After the initial excitements were over, his presence in Calcutta ceased to be anything of special interest to the British community there. The number of visitors slowly declined. Major Herbert, who was the officer in charge of Yeh, was particularly bored because he had been instructed to visit him twice a day and make up a report every week. Subsequently, he requested permission to discontinue the routine reports. His request was granted on 2 April 1859. Yeh's death was announced eight days later.[19]

There were five parties who could have explained this rather sudden and mysterious development. First and foremost, the medical doctors. However, the conclusion of Dr Payne's report was that throughout his attention on Yeh – he was summoned for the first time on 2 April – and despite repeated examinations, he had not been able to recognise symptoms of any specific disease.[20] Nor could his colleague, Dr Scriven, who accompanied him twice to see Yeh, offer any explanation. A post-mortem examination was proposed, but was dropped when they found out from Alabaster that 'there were very serious objections to such'.[21]

Secondly, there was Major Herbert; but since the granting of his request to discontinue his weekly reports, he seems to have stopped visiting Yeh altogether and desired the Police Jemadar on duty[22] to send him a daily report every evening of all being well.[23] In any case Herbert's lack of interest is evident in that he made a mistake even about the number of servants in Yeh's suite after his death.[24] Thirdly, there was the interpreter. Alabaster was an energetic and adventurous young man who could hardly be expected to derive much satisfaction out of translating newspapers for Yeh every day. He soon took full advantage of the carriage hired for Yeh's benefit but which Yeh never used except for his journey from Fort William to Tollygung, to go on excursions for sight-seeing and visiting government officers. The horses were so grossly overworked as a result that the company, Silvery Hoblers, refused to renew the contract when it expired on 31 March 1859.[25] Anyway, Alabaster was unable to offer any explanation for the death of the man in his charge.

Fourthly, there were the Chinese servants. Their answer was:

On 24 March 1859, the provisions we brought with us ran out. We asked permission from our master to buy food locally, but he refused and said, 'I did not commit suicide because I heard that the British wanted to send me to England. Their Monarch should be a reasonable man, and I want to reason with him, to point out to him that he was wrong in breaching the peace. But here I am, waiting day after day, and nothing has happened. Is there any point in living any longer? I have eaten all that I brought with me, how do I have the face to eat alien food?'

The interpreter continued to bring him comestibles, but he absolutely refused to eat any. On 2 April he fell sick, but still refused to eat. Then in the evening of 10 April, he died. His last words were, 'I have disappointed His Imperial Majesty; I shall die with my eyes wide open [i.e. with a heavy burden on his mind].'[26]

The fact that Yeh brought his own provisions with him is confirmed by two British sources. Cooke wrote that before the departure of the *Inflexible*, Yeh sent for his Chinese cook who arrived, to Yeh's satisfaction, with 'great stores of Chinese comestibles'.[27] Major Herbert also reported after Yeh's death that 'the daily account is larger than formerly in consequence of its including the cost of rations to the Chinese servants subsequent to His Excellency's death, these having previously been given by him'.[28] Whereas the monthly bill used to be around 490 rupees,[29] that of April 1859 amounted to 3046.2.2 rupees.[30]

If Yeh began his hunger strike on 24 March, his weakness would have become too apparent by 2 April to escape the notice of Alabaster, who had been obliged to stay more in the house from 1 April onwards (the day he was first deprived of the use of the carriage). Dr Payne was summoned. Yeh was found to have suffered for some time from general languor, loss of appetite, constipation, and other dyspeptic signs, with evidence of some functional derangement of the liver. There was nothing specific in these indications, but Dr Payne observed in Yeh a debility far greater than could be explained by them. Dr Payne further remarked that Yeh 'retained his usual cheerfulness however and was inclined to concur in the opinion which I expressed that his ailments were due to the increasing heat'.[31] For the following days Dr Payne continued to attend to Yeh, whose condition seemed to improve with time. On 7 April, he thought that Yeh had sufficiently recovered for him to announce his intention of discontinuing his visits. The next morning he happened to be in the neighbourhood and called at Yeh's house. He found to his horror and astonishment that Yeh had suffered from great nausea and was quite unable to move.[32] Yeh died that very evening. It is clear that Yeh starved himself to death. This he did as quietly but determinedly as he directed the campaign against the rebels besieging Canton, or against the English in 1856 and 1857. He was capable of enduring great sufferings. During the voyage to Calcutta, which was the first sea journey he had ever made, 'sounds came through the cabin skylight like the strains and groans of Etna', wrote Cooke. 'Judging from the sounds, the Viceroy might by throwing up his two provinces of Quangsi and Quangtung. It must be admitted, however, that he struggled manfully...he manifested all a Chinaman's courage of endurance.'[33]

Finally, Yeh himself gave the explanation in a poem which he composed, possibly when he was lying on his death-bed:

Doleful the exile's drift across the foam
Of southern seas; now letters reach once more,[34]
Like wild geese winging from my far-off home,
My embassy beside the coral shore .
On foreign coasts, if one would keep one's pledge
Of fealty, food is hard to come upon;[35]
The envoy's raft, approaching the world's edge
Floats impotent into oblivion.
As at a tiger's leap trembles my heart;
A flute[36] insists a journey must be made;
In fading light I watch the crow[37] depart
Sadly, his debt of piety unpaid.
Only the spring returns; blushes anon
With cotton-flowers the garden at Canton.[38]

It was obviously extremely important to Yeh in exile to find examples in China's past to guide his conduct. As mentioned at the beginning of this book esteem for the force of example and reverence for the past were considered to be among the attributes of a good Confucianist, which Yeh tried to be. Hence he modelled himself during the first months of exile upon Su Wu but, when it became apparent that there was little point in keeping his wand of office whole, he decided to give up his life when his provisions ran out, like Po I and Shu Ch'i.

Conclusion

It is hard to resist the conclusion that Yeh Ming-ch'en has been too severely judged by posterity. The disastrous end of his career makes it all too easy to overlook the achievements of previous years. He was an administrator during a period of intense disorder, when it was an achievement to survive at all. The foregoing pages have attempted to show that as an administrator he took pains to foster a strong, efficient and loyal official hierarchy: he was not an innovator, but strove to make the existing system work. In a time of upheaval he secured its continued functioning by exercising great energy, resourcefulness and perseverance as a military organiser and financier. This required administrative talents of a high order as well as courage and ruthlessness. His military success was impressive. The effect of the suppression of the Sporadic Revolts and the Red Turban Rebellion was not only local but national. By preventing the rich province of Kwangtung from falling into the hands of the Taipings, he won a great strategic victory for the whole campaign of the empire, and was able to continue his function as paymaster general to the imperial troops in central China. In this respect Yeh helped to shape the history of his time.

Though his conduct of foreign affairs may seem in comparison a complete failure, even there some of his qualities were apparent. Having decided on a line of action, he stuck to it with great determination, and in the face of novel developments showed much of his old activity and intelligence. He used the limited resources at his disposal to wage war effectively in a variety of ways. In the absence of most of his troops, his attempted use of popular guerrilla warfare and a campaign of attrition is worthy of notice. The weakness of his diplomacy lay in the very fact that he was now dealing with foreigners. In common with all his compatriots of that period, he lacked knowledge and understanding of them and therefore could not cope with them as he had so successfully with the rebels. Even so, he continued to the last to show courage and perserverance. His readiness to suffer the humiliation of becoming a prisoner of war in order that he might perform a mission as useful as that of Su Wu, and finally his starving himself to death by refusing to eat foreign provisions, which would have meant a submission to the enemy, would have made him a public hero but for the fact that when his body was shipped back to Canton in the spring of 1859, public opinion was focused on the allied threat to Peking. To depict him, as the Chinese did, as supine and spineless in resisting invasion, or, as the British did, as a wilfully blind and obstructive mandarin, is inaccurate and unjust. His ultimate failure should not be allowed to overshadow his earlier success as an administrator, which did much to prevent the complete overthrow of the Manchu dynasty at that time.

There may be a lesson to be drawn from the too-ready condemnation of Yeh by his contemporaries and by historians. There is a fallacy in the assumption that all the servants of an admittedly declining state must in the nature of things be corrupt and inefficient. History is much concerned with individuals, and individuals vary greatly in character and capacity even within the same system. Historical characters were not wooden figures, but human beings with intelligence, sentiments, learning and judgement like ourselves, acting as they thought fit in the circumstances of their time, and ought not to be blamed or derided for not possessing the advantage of hindsight. Rather, they ought to be seen in the context of their own epoch and judged accordingly. It is only in this way that justice may be done to Yeh, and he may be given credit for his successes as well as censure for his failures. As it is, he has suffered a fate not uncommon in history:

> The evil that men do lives after them,
> The good is oft interred with their bones.

It may be illuminating to compare Yeh Ming-ch'en with Lin Tse-hsü. Both have been charged with 'obstinacy and lack of finesse in handling foreign affairs'.[1] It should be noted, however, that such charges have come mainly from western diplomats, merchants and historians. The Chinese attitude is somewhat different. In the last analysis, the two imperial commissioners are at worst loyalists who acted on instructions from Peking to preserve the status quo, and at best, national heroes who fought hard to stop foreign aggression. Elaboration on this Chinese attitude shows that Yeh was in fact regarded in quite a different light from Lin. Yeh's image as a loyalist, let alone a hero, has been, to say the least, greatly tarnished by his defeat, and still more by the subjugation of Canton, and by the burning of the Summer Palace. Lin Tse-hsü, on the other hand, became an object of adoration by his sensational burning of opium, and his virtues are lauded as much as Yeh's failures are exaggerated by popular literature.

Lin's biographer, Chang Hsin-pao, maintained that a major cause of Lin's failure at Canton was his pre-modern concept of foreign relations, in which he regarded England as a vassal state.[2] This may have been the case but was certainly not true of Yeh, who looked upon the British as a devious, greedy yet formidable enemy that had to be treated with extreme caution and firmness. Furthermore, Professor Chang took the view that it was this pre-modern concept of Lin's that prevented him from sitting down at a conference table with Elliot and ironing out their differences. In Yeh's case, it is of course not true that he was unwilling to negotiate a peaceful settlement. Rather, he was very anxious to do it, but all his attempts were foiled by Bowring's insisting on what he saw as an impossible condition, namely, that the Canton city question should be solved before all discussion could start.

Whereas Lin was wise after the event, conceiving a strategy of protracted warfare against the British when he was on his journey of exile to Ile,[3] Yeh not only envisaged such a possibility, but actually put it to practice. But such an advanced theory of warfare would never have worked within the framework of Ch'ing bureaucracy. Professor Chang did not think that a protracted war waged by Lin would have any chance of success because 'Neither the deteriorating Manchu regime, with its volatile and vacillating emperor, nor the fanatic but spineless court nobles shared any of the fortitude or wisdom of Lin Tse-hsü.'[4] Yeh was not counting on the support of Peking; he fought entirely on his own. Nevertheless, the law of the land was such that he was sacrificed because he had to remain in Canton and become a sitting target for the British. Because of his concept of guerilla warfare, Lin has been described as an idealist born a century too early, the same may indeed be said about Yeh.

In Professor Chang's estimation, Lin Tse-hsü was a profound thinker, Li Hung-chang a shrewd politician, and Tseng Kuo-fan excelled in the art of doing what was possible. In a similar vein, Yeh Ming-ch'en could be called a pragmatic statesman, and ingenious strategist, and a resourceful financier.

NOTES TO THE TEXT

ABBREVIATIONS

Any note not preceded by letters refers to the Canton Archive (part of F.O. 682)

B2; B4	Classifications in the Matheson Archive, University Library, Cambridge
Broadlands MSS	Palmerston Papers, National Register of Archives
Bulletin	*Bulletin of the John Rylands University Library of Manchester*
Bundle 2h	General Correspondence, India Office Library
CSLC	*Ch'ing-shih lieh-chuan*
F.O.	Foreign Office Archives, Public Record Office, London
HCFC	*Hui-chou fu-chih* (1881)
HF	*Ta-Ch'ing li-ch'ao shih-lu,* Hsien-feng period (Taipei, reprint, 1964)
HPTC	*Hu-pei t'ung-chih* (1921)
HYHC	*Han-yang hsien-chih* (1868)
IWSM	*Ch'ou-pan i-wu shih-mo*
KCFC	*Kuang-chou fu-chih* (1879)
KTTC	*Kuang-tung t'ung-chih* (1822)
L/PS/3	General Political Correspondence, India Office Library
L/PS/5	Secret Letters from Bengal, India Office Library
MSS Clar. Dep.	Manuscripts, Clarendon Deposits, Bodleian Library, Oxford
PG	Peking Gazette, British Museum. The numbers refer to the year, month and day in the Chinese calendar
Range 202–3	India Political and Foreign Proceedings, India Office Library
Ryl. Eng. MSS	Rylands English manuscripts, John Rylands University Library of Manchester
TK	*Ta-Ch'ing li-ch'ao shih-lu.* Tao-kuang period (Taipei, reprint, 1964)

Part One: Yeh's background and his time

Chapter 1 *Early career*

1 Yeh Chih-shen *et al.*, eds., *Yeh-shih tsung-p'u* (1873), 15. 14ff. and 16. 1ff. (the reference here, as in other Chinese works, is to chapter (*chuan*) and page numbers).

2 Whereas a *sheng-yüan* was an 'undergraduate', a *kung-sheng* was a 'graduate; see Ho Ping-ti, *The Ladder of Success in Imperial China* (New York, 1962), pp. 28–9.

3 The terms of Chinese offices in this and subsequent passages are translated according to H. S. Brunnert and V. V. Hagelstrom, *Present Day Political Organization of China* (Taipei, reprint 1963). There were 9 ranks in the official hierarchy, each divided into a and b. The rank of a secretary was 7b.

4 *HPTC*, 3408; *CSLC*, 72.50b; Fu Pao-shen, 'Yeh Chi-wen', in *Kuo-ch'ao ch'i-hsien lei-cheng ch'u-pien*, 138.21a; Yeh Chih-shen, *Yeh-shih tsung-p'u*, 16.7a and 20.28b.

5 One of his works, *P'ing-an Kuan ts'ang-ch'i mu*, was collected in the *Ts'ung-shu chi-ch'eng ch'u-pien* (Shanghai, 1963) and consequently is available in major libraries throughout the world.

6 *HYHC*, 18.51a; Fu Pao-shen, 'Yeh Chih-shen', in *Kuo-ch'ao ch'i-hsien lei-cheng ch'u-pien*, 138.21a; Yeh Chih-shen, *Yeh-shih tsung-p'u*, 20.1ff., 7a, 12a–b, 29b. The rank of an archivist was 8b and that of the director of a department, 5a.

7 A. W. Hummel, *Eminent Chinese of the Ch'ing Period* (Washington, D.C., 1943), p. 904.

8 The exalted status of officialdom was shown by symbolic distinction ranging from the style of garments, residence, horse carriage, sedan chair, and the number of guards and servants when travelling, down to minute specifications for funeral and burial rites. See Ho Ping-ti, *The Ladder of Success*, pp. 17–18. Cf. also Ch'ü T'ung-tsu, *Local Government in China under the Ch'ing* (Cambridge, Mass., 1962).

9 Hu Feng-tan, 'Yeh Ming-ch'en chia-chuan', in Miao Ch'üan-sun, ed., *Hsü pei-chuan-chi* (1910).

10 Cooke, *China*, p. 417; Hu Feng-tan, 'Yeh Ming-ch'en'; *CSLC*, 73.37b; TK 266.4–6, Imperial edict giving the list of newly selected bachelors, 1 June 1835.

11 TK 282.6b, Imperial edict, 2 June 1836.

12 A. W. Hummel, *Eminent Chinese of the Ch'ing Period*, p. 904. maintains that Yeh's first prefectship was held at Han-chung in the same province. This is contrary to *CSLC*, 40.44b and Hu Feng-tan, 'Yeh Ming-ch'en'. In fact Yeh never served at Han-chung, although at one time he was expecting to get that position (PG, Tao-kuang Period, 18.6.17), which probably gave rise to the confusion.

13 The exceptions were the provinces of Chihli, Kansu and Szechwan, where the post of governor was concurrently held by a governor-general. See note 14.

14 The title and number of governors-general changed from time to time, so did the number of provinces under their jurisdiction. For details, see Chao Erh-sun, ed., *Ch'ing-shih kao* (Mukden, 1937), 123.3b–5b.

15 There was always one provincial treasurer in each province, except in Kiangsu, where there were two after 1760 (*Ch'ing-shih kao*, 123.9a–b).

16 Ch'ü T'ung-tsu, *Local Government*, p. 14.

17 These translated terms of the Chinese official posts can be very misleading. Unlike the English magistrate, the Chinese *chih-hsien*, for example, was not only a judge, but the chief executive official, tax collector and high priest (in religious and ceremonial matters) of the district under his jurisdiction. He also looked after the postal service, salt administration, *pao-chia*, police, public works, granaries, social welfare and education (Ch'ü, *Local Government*. p. 16). In short, he was the general administrator in the lowest unit of the local government, but since his judicial function was regarded as his principal duty, he has always been referred to as a magistrate, and hence the territory under his jurisdiction as a magistracy. In this sense, the Chinese 'magistrate' was not unlike the Roman *magister* combining judicial and administrative functions.

18 Cooke, *China*, pp. 416–17.

19 It consisted of eight sections (hence the name eight-legged) of rhyming couplets. The word limit was set at 550 and later extended to 600. To express one's ideas efficiently in this rigid form and within the word limit required a high degree of scholarship and skill. See *Tz'u-hai* (1947), p. 147.

20 Cf. J. K. Fairbank, 'Meadow on China: A centennial review', *Far Eastern Quarterly* (*F.E.Q.*) 14.3 (1955), 365–71, suggesting the influence of China on the British civil service examination.

21 68.1. Provincial Judge Liang to Prefect Yeh, 10 Jan. 1839.
22 327.3.11. Governor Yü-ch'ien to Yeh, 7 Oct. 1840.
23 See Ch'ü, *Local Government*, chap. 6; K. E. Folsom, *Friends, Guests and Colleagues: The mu-fu system in the late Ch'ing period* (Calif., 1968), and Chang Ch'un-ming, 'Ch'ing-tai te mu-chih', *Ling-nan hsüeh-pao*, 9.2 (1950), 29–50.
24 HF 178.19b. Imperial edict, 3 Nov. 1855. Hsün-chou was a big city along the West River in Kwangsi.
25 Cf. 44.15.1. Chang's request for more military finance (17 Dec. 1856), and 44.15.2. Note transmitting Chang's request (17 Dec. 1856).
26 Chang Chin-chien, *Chung-kuo wen-kuan chih-tu shih* (Taipei, 1955), p. 154.
27 Cooke, *China*, p. 417.
28 Ch'ü, *Local Government*, p. 112.
29 *HPTC*, 3409.
30 His father died some years before his mother, and he observed the usual three years of mourning.
31 *CSLC*, 72.50b; Hu, 'Yeh Ming-ch'en'.
32 *Ibid.; HPTC*, 3408.
33 *HYHC*, 18.51b–52a; Yeh, *Yeh-shih tsung-p'u*, 20.2a–b.
34 *HYHC*, 18.59b–60a; Hu, 'Yeh Ming-ch'en'; Yeh, *Yeh-shih tsung-p'u*, 20.18b.
35 Cf. PG, Tao-kuang: 18.6.6–17, *passim*.
36 Hu, 'Yeh Ming-ch'en'.
37 391.3.2. Imperial edict, 29 Nov. 1848.
38 *IWSM* Hsien-feng period, 17.40b–41a, Imperial edict, 27 Jan. 1858. Cf. the fate of Hsü Kuang-chin (*CSLC* 48.14a–15b).
39 Cooke, *China*, p. 431.
40 *Ibid.*
41 *IWSM*, Hsien-feng period, 47b–48a, Censor Ho to emperor, 20 Feb. 1858.
42 *Ibid.* 42a and 49b, Imperial edicts, 27 Jan. and 21 Feb. 1858.
43 *Ibid.*
44 Cooke, *China*, p. 431.
45 Ch'ien Shih-fu, *Ch'ing-chi chung-yao chih-kuan nien-piao* (Peking, 1959).
46 378B.1.62. Yeh to Ch'i (1852).
47 137.5.12–13. List of persons to whom New Year presents were sent (26 March 1856).
48 Sources for Yeh's various posts are given in the footnotes to Table 1.
49 PG, Tao-kuang, 16.12.15–16.
50 Hu, 'Yeh Ming-ch'en'.
51 *HYHC* 18.60a.
52 *Ta-Ch'ing hui-tien*, 4.4a; *Ta-Ch'ing-hui-tien shih-li*, 25.7ff.
53 *Ibid.* 4.4b; *Ibid.* 25. 1b, 3a; *CSLC*, 40.45a.
54 TK 371.10a. Imperial edict, 17 May 1842; *Ch'ing-shih-kao, chih-kuan* 3.8.
55 327.3.35. Yeh's proclamation, 2 March 1843.
56 *CSLC*, 40.44b–45a.
57 TK: 309.8b–9a, 316.25b, 433.156a–b, Imperial edicts, 1848. It was Lin Tse-hsü who put down this particular rebellion, but conflicts between the Han and Moslem communities continued until they developed into the famous Mohammedan Uprising of 1856–73. See Wang Shu-hwai, *Hsien-T'ung Yün-nan Hui-min shih-pien* (Taipei, 1968).
58 According to one account, Yeh was reported to have acquired considerable popularity during his term of office in Yünnan (Range 203, no. 961, Alabaster–Beadon, 9 Aug. 1858).

59 Cf. TK 434.15b–16b. Imperial edict, 16 Nov. 1846.
60 See Chap. 4, pages 000–00.
61 *CSLC*, 40.44b.
62 It was not until 1861, after the disastrous defeat in the Second Opium War, that a foreign language school, the T'ung-wen Kuan, and something similar to a foreign office, called Tsungli Yamen, were established in Peking. See e.g. K. Biggerstaff, 'The T'ung Wen Kwan', *China Social and Political Science Review*, vol. 18, no. 3; I. C. Y. Hsü, *China's Entrance into the Family of Nations* (Cambridge, Mass., 1960); S. M. Meng, *The Tsungli Yamen* (Cambridge, Mass., 1962); and M. Banno, *China and the West, 1858–1861: the origins of the Tsungli Yamen* (Cambridge, Mass., 1964).
63 See O. Lattimore, *Inner Asian Frontiers of China* (Boston, 1962), and Lo Hsiang-lin, *Chung-kuo min-tsu shih* (Taipei, 1953). For edicts and memoranda concerning these conflicts in Yeh's time, cf. TK: 429.7–9, 433.17a, 425.11a, 12a, 17a, 16, 434.28a, 437.17a, 22a.
64 68.3.18. Yeh to the emperor, 12 Nov. 1842.
65 As mentioned, in 1843 he was appointed provincial treasurer of Kiangsu, in which Shanghai had recently been opened as a new treaty port. Then his mother died in 1844, and until 1846 he had to observe the customary three years' mourning. As soon as this was over, he was appointed to Canton.
66 A. Wright, 'Values, Roles, and Personalities', *Confucian Personalities* (Stanford, Cal., 1962), p. 8.
67 *Ibid.* p. 9.
68 Yeh, *Yeh-shih tsung-p'u*, 16.18a–b, 13b.
69 Chu's ideas are selected in his work *Ssu-shu chi-chu* (Taipei reprint, 1959). Cf. also Jung Chao-tsu, *Ming-tai ssu-hsiang shih* (Taipei, reprint 1962), p. 42.
70 Cooke, *China*, p. 401.
71 Ch'ien Mu, *Chung-kuo chin san-pai-nien hsüeh-shu shih* (Taipei, 1968), p. 167.
72 Cooke, *China*, p. 402.
73 Hu Shih, *Hu Shih wen-ts'un* (Shanghai, 1933), 3.2.113.
74 Cooke, *China*, p. 404.
75 Cf. e.g. Hsieh, 'Yeh-hsiang'; Ch'i-hsien-ho shang tiao-sou, 'Ying-chi-li Kuang-tung ju-ch'eng shih-mo'; *Ch'ing-ch'ao yeh-shih ta-kuan* (Taipei reprint, 1959): Ch'ing-jen i-shih, 7.312. The best known account is that of Hsieh, which specifically accused Yeh Chih-shen of extreme superstition. I shall treat this subject at some length because of its importance in later accusations concerning Yeh Ming-ch'en's handling of the *Arrow* War.
76 At the invitation of his son, Chih-shen had come to live in Canton since 1849 (Yeh, *Yeh-shih tsung-p'u*, 20.32b).
77 Lü was one of the eight legendary Taoist demigods. Li Po is an example of famous historical figures being deified by the Chinese.
78 Kuan-yin Shan, a hill at the back of the city of Canton.
79 Cooke, *China*, p. 336.
80 The British were provided with similar reports by their informants, Cf. e.g. F.O.17.277 Desp. 99, Incl. 7, Wade to Elgin, 24 Dec. 1857.
81 Cooke, *China*, p. 409.
82 Divination is very much a legacy of popular Confucianism of the Han dynasty, which was a constituent of neo-Confucianism (see above).
83 Cooke, *China*, p. 408.
84 See Table 2. The two queries in question were nos. 4 and 5. They were also written on the same day and about the same event.

85 'There was not one corner in the vast land of China where one did not find temples, shrines, altars and other places of worship...they stood as symbols of a social reality.' C. K. Yang, *Religion in Chinese Society* (Berkeley, 1961), p. 6.
86 Cooke, *China*, pp. 397-9.
87 L/PS/5 Vol. 167, Russel & Co. - Ashburner & Co. - Herbert, 7 May 1858; *Ibid.* Herbert-Beadon, 11 May 1858; *Ibid.* Jardine-Herbert, 10 May 1858.
88 Range 203, No. 271. Alabaster-Herbert, 18 April 1859. See chap. 7.
89 Cooke, *China*, p. 404.
90 *Ibid.* pp. 405, 409. It was alleged that he asked for some Taoist texts to be sent to him. Cooke, however, reported that his father sent him some Buddhist books. Cooke is wrong here. The interpreter, Alabaster, who read Chinese and who could tell what the books were, maintained that they were the Four Books (Ryl. Eng. MS 1230/146 Alabaster-Bowring, 2 March 1858).
91 Cooke, *China*, p. 411.
92 *Ibid.*
93 F.O. 17.285. Desp. 7, Incl. 1, Loch-Elgin, 5 Jan. 1858.
94 Cooke, *China*, p. 431.
95 Chang Hsin-pao, *Commissioner Lin and the Opium War* (Cambridge, Mass., 1964), p. 21.
96 *Ssu-kuo hsin-tang, Ying-kuo tang*, no. 1275, 7 August 1859.
97 The word lineage is used here, and by anthropologists generally, to denote the social unit commonly referred to by historians of China as the clan. For expert studies of Chinese lineages, see M. Freedman, *Lineage Organization in Southeastern China* (London, 1965) and *Chinese Lineage and Society* (London, 1966).
98 327.6. Booklet listing the property acquired under the name of *Yeh Chia-hui-t'ang*; the last date on this document was 14 Dec. 1842.
99 253A.8. Yeh Ming-feng to Yeh Ming-ch'en (1856).
100 Hu, 'Yeh Ming-ch'en'.
101 68.3.4. Yeh Ming-ch'en to the emperor, 2 July 1857.
102 Miao Ch'üan-sun, *Hsü pei-chuan chi*, 79.8a; Fu Pao-shen, 'Yeh Ming-feng', *Kuo-ch'ao ch'i-hsien lei-cheng ch'u-pien*, 138.21a-b; *CSLC* 73.37b; *HYHC* 18.6.
103 *HYHC* 18.52 and 60a; *HPTC* 3408-9.
104 378B.1.42. Anonymous official in Kiangsu to Yeh (1849).
105 Hu, 'Yeh Ming-ch'en'. This account gave only the alias of Yeh's father-in-law. Checking this alias in Ch'en Te-yün, *Ku-chin jen-wu pieh-ming so-yin* (Canton, 1937), he is identified as Wang T'ing-chen.
106 *Ch'ing-shih Kao, lieh-chuan*, 97.151.3-4; *CSLC* 34.26-9; Li Yüan-tu, 'Wang Wen-tuan kung shih-lüeh', *Hsü pei-chuan-chi*, 3.6-7; 'Wang T'ing-chen', *Hui-an fu-chih*, appendixed in *Hsü pei-chuan-chi*, 3.7-8; Li Yüan-tu, *Kuo-ch'ao hsien-cheng shih-lüeh*, 23.18-20.
107 279A.5.24. Wang Pao-jun to Yeh (1857).
108 Hu, 'Yeh Ming-ch'en'; Cooke, *China*, p. 402. Yeh En-i was said to be so deeply grieved by the deaths in rapid succession of his father and uncle in 1859, that he himself also died eleven years later, at the age of thirty. His biography may be found in Yeh, *Yeh-shih tsung-p'u*, 20.65b-67b.
109 This conclusion is arrived at after discussions with Mr Huang Chia-mu, fellow of Academia Sinica, Taiwan, when he was in London. He said that Emperor K'ang-hsi's poems were written in beautiful calligraphy, but the comments that he put down on the memoranda addressed to him were

written in a manner not unlike that of Yeh's corrections in the draft memoranda. Mr Huang pointed out that the habit of reading and correcting official despatches while lying in bed was not uncommon among Chinese officials.

110 J. Bowring, *Autobiographical Recollections of Sir John Bowring* (London, 1877), p. 217.
111 Hu, 'Yeh Ming-ch'en'.

Chapter 2 *The Canton period, 1847–58: a general survey*

1 Hsiao I-shan, *Ch'ing-tai t'ung-shih*, 2 (Taipei, 1963), 87–146, gives a detailed account of these campaigns.
2 *Ibid.* 2, 209–27, 261–70, 276–80. Ho-shen was alleged to have gathered 800 million taels through embezzlement and blackmail of junior officials throughout the empire. For a comprehensive biography of Ho-shen see A. W. Hummel, *Eminent Chinese of the Ch'ing Period*, pp. 288–90.
3 Chang Hsin-pao, *Commissioner Lin*, pp. 16–19; Morse, *International Relations*, 1, 556.
4 Teng Ssu-yü, *The Taiping Rebellion and the Western Powers: A Comprehensive Survey* (Oxford, 1971), p. 29. The outflow of silver was the most important but not the only cause of the devaluation of copper cash. For a fuller explanation, see F. H. H. King, *Money and Monetary Policies in China 1845–1895* (Cambridge, Mass., 1965); W. J. Peterson, 'Early nineteenth century monetary ideas on the cash-silver exchange ratio', *Papers on China*, 20 (1966), 23–53; and Wei Chien-yu, *Chung-kuo chin-tai huo-pi shih* (Shanghai, 1955).
5 Teng, *Taiping and Western Powers*, p. 20.
6 These are general statements derived from expert studies such as F. H. H. King, *op. cit.*; Ch'ü, *Local Government*; source materials on inflation of the period may be found in Nan-k'ai ta-hsüeh, *Ch'ing shih-lu ching-chi tzu-liao chi-yao* (Peking, 1959). The pressure of population and the shortage of arable land reduced the size of the average holding, forced up the price of land and rentals, and offered much better opportunities for large landowners to annex more land.
7 See chap. 6.
8 Ho Ping-ti, *Studies on the Population of China, 1368–1953* (Cambridge, Mass., 1959), Appendix 1.
9 Ho, *op. cit.* p. 270.
10 M. J. Elvin, *The Pattern of the Chinese Past* (Stanford, Cal., 1973).
11 W. Blythe, *The Impact of Chinese Secret Societies in Malaya* (Oxford, 1969), pp. 16–20, gives a comprehensive outline of the history of Chinese secret societies.
12 Full details of these revolts may be found in Hsiao I-shan, *Ch'ing-tai t'ung-shih*, 2, 246–351.
13 Hsiao, *Ch'ing-tai t'ung-shih*, 2, 289–93; Hu Ch'ang-tu, 'The Yellow River administration in the Ch'ing dynasty', *Far Eastern Quarterly* (*F.E.Q.*) 14.4 (1955), 505–13.
14 Ho, *Population of China*, p. 229.
15 Liang Jen-tsai, *Kuang-tung ching-chi ti-li* (Peking, 1956), pp. 1–5. The metric units of measurement have been converted into the British system by the present author.
16 *Ibid.* pp. 7–10.

17 J. A. G. Roberts, 'The Hakka–Punti War' (D.Phil. thesis, Oxford, 1968), p. 23, quoting M. Martini, *Histoire de la Guerre des Tartares Contre la Chine* (Paris, 1654), p. 155.

18 Hsieh Kuo-ching, 'Removal of coastal population in early Tsing period', *The Chinese Social and Political Science Review*, 15.4 (1932), 559–96.

19 See Hsiao, *Ch'ing-tai t'ung-shih*, 369–73.

20 Roberts, 'Hakka–Punti War', p. 26.

21 Teng, *The Taiping Rebellion and the Western Powers*, p. 16; T'ao Ch'eng-chang, 'T'ien-ti-hui yüan-liu k'ao', in Lo Erh-kang, *T'ien-ti-hui wen-hsien-lu*; Wakeman, *Strangers at the Gate*, pp. 117–25.

22 Ho, *Population of China*, p. 283.

23 *Ibid.* p. 52.

24 Roberts, 'Hakka–Punti War', pp. 37, 2. The Hakka, like the Punti, were migrants from northern China, but their migration 'had lagged behind the mainstreams of the southern movement, and the long periods they spent in areas of sparse population meant that by the time they reached Kwangtung, they had diverged rather widely from the general pattern of culture common to the southern Chinese' (*ibid.* p. 11). Special studies on southward migration of the Chinese include H. J. Wiens, *China's March towards the Tropics* (Hamden, Conn., 1954) and C. P. Fitzgerald, *The Southward Expansion of the Chinese People* (London, 1972). Lo Hsiang-lin *K'o-chia shih-liao hui-pien* (Hong Kong, 1965) is a very useful collection of historical sources for the study of the Hakka.

25 253A.3.109. Feng A-mou's deposition (spring 1851). Feng A-mou was Feng Yün-shan's brother. On the way to Kwangsi, Feng A-mou discovered what his brother was actually doing, and returned with the family to Hua-hsien, where he was eventually arrested.

26 Freedman, *Lineage Organization*, p. 1.

27 Freedman, *Chinese Lineage*, p. 115. Cf. also the two articles by Lang Ch'ing-hsiao, 'Chung-kuo nan-fang hsieh-tou chih yüan-yin chi-ch'i tsu-chih', *Tung-fang tsa-chih*, 30.10 (1933), 81–96, and 'Ch'ing-tai Yüeh-tung hsieh-tou shih-shih', *Ling-nan hsüeh-pao*, 4.2 (1935), 103–51.

28 Hsiao Kung-ch'üan, *Rural China: Imperial control in the nineteenth century* (Seattle, 1960), p. 365.

29 O. Lang, *Chinese Family and Society* (Hamden, Conn., 1968), p. 174.

30 Wakeman, *Strangers at the Gate*, p. 214, citing Makino.

31 M. J. Elvin, 'The Last Thousand Years of Chinese History', *Modern Asian Studies* (*M.A.S.*), 4.2 (1970), 97–114.

32 Ho, *The Ladder of Success*, pp. 209–12; Ch'en Han-seng, *Agrarian Problems in Southernmost China* (Shanghai, 1936), chap. 2.

33 Ch'ü Ta-chün, *Kuang-tung hsin-yü*, 17.5–6, cited and translated by Hsiao, *Rural China*, p. 329.

34 The proportion of tenants in Kwangtung in the nineteenth century has been quoted as 75 per cent by Hsiao, *Rural China*, p. 383.

35 The rents could be as high as half of the harvest: Hsiao, *Rural China*, p. 385, citing Wu Ju-lun, *T'ung-ch'eng Wu hsien-sheng jih-chi*, 15.48b.

36 Ch'en, *Agrarian Problems in Southernmost China*, p. 58. Their position was in fact not dissimilar to that of serfs, about which an excellent discussion is provided by Niida Noboru, *Chūgoku hōsei-shi kenkyū*, 3 (Tokyo, 1962), 217–26. His chapter on clan law (3, 283–364) is also illuminating.

37 Wakeman, *Strangers at the Gate*, p. 110, citing Hu Hsien-chin, *The Common Descent Group in China and its Functions* (New York, 1948), p. 90.

38 Wakeman's theory about the polarization of society 'into wealthy and poor by 1845, and that class interests were no longer 'softened' by the lineage' (*op. cit.*, chap. 10) is certainly well-founded.

39 Hsiao, *Rural China*, pp. 46–7. In Kwangtung, for example, the system was adapted to suit the lineages (i.e. villages) which were hence not divided, but were regarded as single units under the clan head.

40 *Ibid.* pp. 52, 59.

41 *Ibid*, p. 55.

42 Liang, *Kuang-tung ching-chi*, pp. 9–10. For the Co-hong System, cf. Liang Chia-pin, *Kuang-tung shih-san-hang k'ao* (Shanghai, 1937) and Ch'iang T'ing-fu, 'The Government and Co-hong of Canton, 1839', *Chinese Social and Political Science Review*, 15.4 (1932), 602–7.

43 Morse, *International Relations*, pp. 363–4.

44 Hsiao, *Rural China*, p. 381, quoting an edict of 1723.

45 By the eighteenth century, even the six major rice-producing provinces of Kiangsu, Anhwei, Chekiang, Kiangsi, Hupeh and Hunan had difficulty in sustaining their own inhabitants (Lo Erh-kang, 'T'ai-ping t'ien-kuo ke-ming ch'ien te jen-k'ou ya-p'o wen-t'i', *Chung-kuo she-hui ching-chi-shih chi-k'an*, 8.1 (1949), 49–52).

46 Liang, *Kuang-tung ching-chi*, p. 21.

47 Ho, *Population of China*, p. 203. Kwangtung was of course not the only place where large pieces of farmland were converted to grow commercial crops. In some magistracies in the neighbouring province of Fukien, for example, it was estimated that 'tobacco occupied some 60 or 70 per cent of the farmland'.

48 Wiens, *China's March towards the Tropics*, p. 11.

49 Ch'ien Chia-chü, *Kuang-hsi-sheng ching-chi kai-k'uang* (Shanghai, 1936), pp. 1–22.

50 Roberts, 'Hakka–Punti War', p. 82.

51 J. K. Fairbank, ed., *The Chinese World Order* (Cambridge, Mass., 1968), p. 4.

52 *Ibid.*, p. 261.

53 Cf. *Ya-p'ien chan-cheng shih-ch'i ssu-hsiang-shih tzu-liao hsüan-chi* (Peking, 1963).

54 Cf. e.g. Fairbank, 'The Manchu appeasement policy of 1843', *Journal of the American Oriental Society*, 59.4 (1939), 469–84 and *Trade and Diplomacy on the China Coast* (Cambridge, Mass., 1953), chap. 7.

55 See page 160.

56 *Ibid.*

57 HF 213.15. Imperial edict, 24 Dec. 1856.

58 See pages 178–80.

59 HF 222.29. Imperial edict, 23 April 1857.

60 In order to make the reading of ensuing chapters less cumbersome, this section is designed to provide for convenient reference a brief outline of the major events which will be examined subsequently in greater detail.

61 F.O. 682.1695, Yeh–Bowring, 25 April 1854.

62 Hu-men, a naval stronghold commanding the entrance to Canton River and Whampoa anchorage.

63 Cf. e.g. HF 217.10. Imperial edict ordering Yeh to send 1,000–2,000 soldiers into Kwangsi and supply them with provisions, 4 Feb. 1857; HF 233.8–9. Imperial edict ordering Yeh to send 2,000 soldies to Fukien and supply them with provisions, 29 April 1857. See chap. 5 for more details.

Part two: The administrator

Chapter 3 *The Administrator I: the scholar-gentry class*

1 Hu, 'Yeh Ming-ch'en'; Matheson Archive, B4/7, P. 352, D. Jardine – D. Matheson, 24 Feb. 1848.
2 See various correspondence of 1844–8 in the Canton Archive, e.g. 112.3.9–10; 327.5.54–94.
3 68.1. Hsü to governor-general's *yamen*, 24 June 1848.
4 Fu Tsung-mou, *Ch'ing-tai tu-fu chih-tu* (Taipei, 1963), is a specialised study on the system of governors-general and governors of the Ch'ing period.
5 B4/7, p. 352, D. Jardine – D. Matheson, 24 Feb. 1848; Hu, 'Yeh Ming-ch'en'.
6 Meadows, *The Chinese and their Rebellions*, p. 135.
7 See J. Nolde, 'The "False Edict" of 1849', *J.A.S.*, 20.3 (1960), 299–315.
8 112.3.25. Unsigned memorandum to the emperor (1850).
9 325.4.3. Imperial edict, 22 April 1849.
10 A combined term for the offices of governor-general and governor.
11 The dates on Hsü's letters to Yeh point to this conclusion.
12 Hsü meant Imperial Commissioner Sai-shang-a and Governor Chou of Kwangsi. The rebel Li Pei-she was active along the border of the two provinces, which hence made a joint effort to deal with him.
13 327.5.28; 253A.3.40–2; 279B.1; 112.4.2; 137.6.46. Hsü's letters to Yeh (21 Sept. 1851 – 10 May 1852).
14 253A.3.40; 324.4.4. Hsü's letters to Yeh (1852).
15 253A.3.9. Hsü to emperor, 2 June 1852.
16 253A.3.43. Hsü to Yeh (14 June 1852).
17 After his fall, Hsü escaped beheading but was relegated to a minor military post in the imperial army fighting in central China. Sir John Bowring later reported, when he was in Shanghai demanding treaty revision (see chap. 9). receiving from a junior Chinese official information to the effect that Hsü had charged Yeh in a letter to the emperor with failing to receive foreigners in Canton (F.O.17.215.107. Bowring–Clarendon, Incl. 1, 3 Aug. 1854). This seems unlikely. Most probably this information was deliberately supplied to Bowring in order to provide him with evidence of a change in Chinese policy at Canton and to forestall Bowring's intended visit to Peiho (and thence to Peking) which the emperor desired at all costs to avoid.
18 Hsieh, 'Yeh-hsiang', *hsü-pien*, 2.14–21.
19 279A.3.43. Yeh to the emperor (June 1852).
20 E.g. 253A.3.36. Copy of an imperial edict (May 1853), and 327.2.49 Po-kuei to Yeh (Spring 1854).
21 HF 167.23 Imperial edict, 20 Oct. 1855; HF 186.19 Imperial edict, 23 Jan. 1856.
22 137.6.34. Appendix to memorandum to the emperor, 12 Oct. 1857.
23 327.3.49. List of officials recommended for rewards (1855).
24 *CSLC* 43.29a.
25 The Hoppo was a member of the Imperial Household Dept sent by the emperor to Canton, then the only port trading with foreigners, to supervise the collection of customs revenue. For a detailed explanation of the Hoppo's office and function, see Liang T'ing-nan, *Yüeh hai-kuan chih* (Taipei reprint, 1968).

26 For a detailed account of the allocation and collection of tax quotas, consult Ch'ü, *Local Government*, pp. 130–47. See also Wang Yeh-chien, *An Estimate of the Land-Tax Collection in China, 1753 and 1908* (Cambridge, Mass., 1973).
27 327.3.29. Confidential report (1847).
28 253A.5.6. List of fines imposed upon Yeh (1855).
29 279A.6.6 and 23; 327.3.14 and 57. Balance sheets of the provincial treasury (14 Aug. 1853 – 8 Nov. 1856).
30 279A.6.19. Report from magistrate of Ssu-hui (1852).
31 Generally speaking, the titles of Chinese officials were merely indications of their positions in the official hierarchy but their functions were, as will be seen, non-specific. Cf. also chap. 1, pages 4–6.
32 68.4.41; 112.4.24; 253A.3.59 and 61; 289.3A.4. Reports on the trial of rebels (1854–6).
33 253A.3.79. Report on a robber arrested in Shun-te (n.d.).
34 Cooke, *China*, p. 407.
35 Chou, *Yen-fa t'ung-chih*, 14.19b; Cf. also *KTTC* 43.711.
36 137.5.21; 279A.6.41; 138.5.1,9,15–16. Reports from salt comptrollers (1850s).
37 325.3.3; 121B.7.6. Reports from deputy salt intendant (1850s).
38 In addition to land tax, landowners had to pay a form of tribute in grain to the emperor. It was collected by magistrates and then transferred to the prefectural offices of the grain intendant. At the end of the Ch'ing period, when this grain tax was converted into cash payments, the grain intendant was free from the task of having to handle grain physically. See Wang, *Land-Tax 1753 and 1908*, p. 16.
39 In Ming and Ch'ing times there were colonies, military, convict, commercial and civilian in nature, with the function of opening up virgin land in south China for cultivation. See Wiens, *China's March towards the Tropics*.
40 *KTTC* 43.7–3–4.
41 Briefly, the grain composed 80 per cent of the cargo, and the owner of the ship was permitted to fill the remaining space with duty-free goods. A fixed amount of the grain was also set aside to meet the miscellaneous expenses of the voyage. Vigorous inspection was necessary because many merchants absused these privileges. -
42 253A.5.1. Report to Yeh about regulations of grain tribute (*c.* 1853).
43 See e.g. 327.5.56. Notification to high officials of the maritime provinces from Ch'i-ying, 28 Feb. 1848.
44 Table 5, which gives the official salaries and subsidies, shows that the Hoppo did not have a salary which generally indicated rank, but only received a subsidy, presumably because he was appointed directly by the Imperial Household and was therefore outside the official hierarchy.
45 112.3.46; 137.5.20; 138.5.17,20–1; 279A.6.27; 327.3.32. Reports from the Hoppo (1854–5).
46 The last edition of the provincial gazetteer of Kwangtung, published in 1842, listed these circuits as Kuang-shao-nan-lien, Hui-ch'ao-chia, Chao-lo, Kao-lien and Lei-ch'iung, each part of the name representing a prefecture which constituted part of that particular circuit (*KTTC* 43.712). The name of the first circuit that appears in Yeh's archive was slightly different. It was called Nab-shao-lien; the 'Kuang' (Kuang-chou-fu, of which Canton was the capital) was missing (68; 112; 137; 145; 253A; 279A series, *passim*). Probably what happened was that in Yeh's time, or immediately before, Kuang-chou-fu became a separate entity. This was a

sensible decision, as Canton was the centre of activity not only of the province, but of the empire so far as foreign relations were concerned, and therefore too important and complicated to be governed by an intendant stationed in the extreme north of the province, at Shao-chou (see Map 4).

47 112.3.5 Hsü and Yeh to emperor, 24 Jan. 1851.
48 112.3.44. Hsü and Yeh to emperor (c. 1848–9).
49 68.3A.24. List of memoranda to be sent to Peking (1850).
50 327.2.60. Tsung Yüan-shun to emperor, 28 July 1851.
51 138.5.2; 279A.6.1. Reports from prefect of Kuang-chou to Yeh (1847–8, 1853).
52 327.2.55. Report on threat posed by piracy (1856).
53 327.5.46. Hsü and Yeh to the emperor, 27 Nov. 1850.
54 137.6.7e–1. Report from acting prefect of Ch'ao-chou to Yeh, 9 June 1853.
55 253A.5.6. List of fines imposed on Yeh since 1847 (1856).
56 Cf. e.g. 138.3.9; 378B.1.2 and 11; 279A.3.16. Various reports to Yeh (1852–5).
57 Cf. e.g. HF 168.16; 378B.5.7. Imperial edicts, 5 July and 6 Oct. 1857.
58 279A.3.35. List of cities fallen during the rebellion (1855).
59 HF (e.g. 1852–6) passim.
60 Ho-shan belonged to the prefecture of Chao-ch'ing, not Kuang-chou; but as mentioned before, the prefect of Kuang-chou was often involved in politics at the provincial level, hence the order.
61 138.5.10. Yeh to Ministry of Personnel (1856). 253A.5.49. Hua T'ing-chieh to Yeh (1856).
62 112.8. Hsü and Yeh to emperor, 12 May 1850.
63 325.3.10. Anonymous letter, 5 Jan. 1852.
64 253A.3.8. Hsü and Yeh to emperor, 18 Feb. 1852.
65 327.3.48. Report on salt administration (1853). For details, see chap. 5.
66 Fu, Ch'ing-tai tu-fu, p. 103.
67 Cf. also chap. 1, pages 6–8, 'Friends at court'.
68 279A.6.56. Wang Han-ch'iao to Ch'i Chün-tsao (1852); 378B.1.62. Yeh to Ch'i Chün-tsao (1852).
69 In fact the number of government students (sheng-yüan) increased in Kwangtung from 39,116 in the pre-Taiping period to 53,309 in the post-Taiping period, which time corresponds roughly with Yeh's service at Canton. See Chang Chung-li, The Chinese Gentry: Studies on their Role in nineteenth-century Chinese Society (Seattle, 1955), Tables 20 and 22.
70 See Liang Ou-ti, 'Sung-tai te shu-yüan chih-tu', Chung-kuo she-hui ching-chi-shih chi-k'an 8.1 (1949), 20–80; and his 'Ming-tai te shu-yüan chih-tu', Hsien-tai shih-hsüeh, 2.4 (1935), 1–20.
71 Liu, Kuang-tung shu-yüan, pp. 2, 7, 70–2, 78.
72 For details about the hsiang-yüeh, see Hsiao, Rural China, pp. 184–208.
73 Liu, Kuang-tung shu-yüan, p. 80.
74 137.5.2; 138.5.9. Financial reports (1854).
75 121B.7.4. Report of military finance of Nan-hsiung in 1854–5.
76 112.6. Salaries paid out to various academies of Kwangtung for 1857.
77 Liu, Kuang-tung shu-yüan, p. 309.
78 Ibid. pp. 157–8, 306, gives an excellent account of these details.
79 Hsieh, 'Yeh-hsiang', hsü-pien, 2.14–21; cf. also Cooke, China, pp. 340–1.
80 Liu, Kuang-tung shu-yüan, pp. 80, 437–8.
81 Ssu, districts into which a magistracy was subdivided. The official responsible for each district was the sheriff (hsün-chien, rank 9b), who was usually stationed at a key point of communication to check offenders.
82 253A.3.105. Report from sub-magistrate of P'an-yü (1855).

83 68.3a.24. List of matters of which the emperor is to be informed (1850).
84 Chang, *The Chinese Gentry*, Table 6.
85 For a comprehensive survey of the history of Chinese examination system, see Teng Ssu-yü, *Chung-kuo k'ao-shih chih-tu shih* (Taipei reprint, 1967), and Shang Yen-liu, *Ch'ing-tai k'o-chu k'ao-shih shu-lu* (Peking, 1958). Cf. also J. M. Menzel, ed., *The Chinese Civil Service, Career Open to Talent* (Boston, 1966). The system was officially abolished towards the end of the Ch'ing dynasty; for details see W. Franke, *The Reform and Abolition of the Traditional Chinese Examination System* (Cambridge, Mass., 1960).
86 325.3.3. Report from acting deputy salt intendant of Ch'ao-chou (1850s).
87 137.6.35. Yeh and Po-kuei to emperor, 7 Nov. 1856.
88 HF 167.1. Imperial edict, 14 June 1855; *KCFC* 46.15.
89 112.3.44. Yeh to the emperor (1848–9).
90 *KCFC* 46, 10–19. It was customary during the first year of a new emperor's reign to grant an extra provincial examination in order to give candidates a further opportunity to qualify.
91 279A.1.1. Procedure for military examination of 1852; 179B. 10.1–2. List of 10 examiners and memorandum on examination procedure (1856).
92 68.3a.8. Cases of corruption, cheating etc. in provincial examinations (1849).
93 J. G. Keer, 'Description of the Great Examination Hall at Canton', *Journal of the North China Branch of the Royal Asiatic Society*, N.S. 5.3 (1866), 63–9, has provided us with an excellent contemporary account not only of the building but of the administration and procedures of the provincial examination.
94 63.3A.8. Cases of corruption, cheating etc. in provincial examinations (1849).
95 Specialist studies on the Chinese gentry include Chang, *The Chinese Gentry*; Ho, *The Ladder of Success*; and Ch'ü, *Local Government;* for a very simple introduction to this class, see beginning of previous chapter.
96 Chang, *The Chinese Gentry*, Table 32.
97 253.3.5. Hsü and Yeh to emperor, 31 Jan. 1850.
98 253A.3.5. Hsü and Yeh to emperor, 31 Jan. 1850.
99 327.2.45. Proclamation prohibiting Hakka–Punti feuds (1855); 253A.5.30. Report on Hakka–Punti feud in En-p'ing (1856).
100 68.4.29 and 44. Intelligence reports (1855).
101 279A.3.37 and 15. Reports on rebels (1854, 1855).
102 253A.3.58. Military intelligence report on Ssu-ma village (1853).
103 378B.1.31. Instruction for arrest of Kuan Chü (1856).
104 253A.3.56. Regulations against banditry, etc. (1855).
105 121B.7.3 and 16; 279A.3.8; 378B.1.48 and 49. Reports on rebels, etc. (1855).
106 279A.3.28. Report to Yeh concerning rebellion in Kwangsi (1854).
107 137.6.7d and 7e. Reports to Yeh from Chang Ch'ung-k'o (1855); 279A.3.35. List of cities fallen during the rebellion (1855).
108 378B.1.21–4; 378B.5.1. Documents concerning the loss of Po-lo (1855); 378B.5.7 and HF 168.16. Imperial edicts, 6 Oct. and 5 July 1857.

Chapter 4 *The Administrator II: the non-scholar-gentry class*

1 *KTTC* 72a.
2 HF 34.5. Imperial edict, 15 June 1851.
3 137.5.2. Financial report, 1854; HF 67.19. Imperial edict, 11 Sept. 1852.

4   B4/6–15, p. 707, A. Percival – D. Jardine, 12 June 1852.
5   279A.3.31; 279A.6.2; 253A.5.14. Reports on the condition of dykes, and
    funds allocated for their repair (1852, 1853).
6   391.2.100. Hsü to Yeh (4 Oct. 1851).
7   391.4.46. Songsheet (n.d.).
8   68.3A.24. List of matters to inform the emperor (1850).
9   378B.1.16. Report on bandits (1851–2).
10 279A.6.44. A detailed report on granaries of Kwangtung (1853).
11 279A.3.36. Report on magisterial granary of Tseng-ch'eng (1855).
12 See Table 5 and note.
13 Cf. E-tu Zen Sun, 'The Board of Revenue in nineteenth-century China',
    Harvard Journal of Asiatic Studies (*HJAS*), 24 (1963), 176.
14 378B.1.21. Report from prefect of Hui-chou (1855).
15 Literally, it should be translated as 'under the present government', but the
    then government at Canton was that of Yeh.
16 137.6.12. Justification of war against secret societies (1854). The poem, of
    course, hardly constitutes an objective record of social welfare under Yeh,
    nor, as will be seen, should it be regarded wholly as government-inspired
    propaganda. Translation by present author.
17 137.5.21; 121B.7.11; 138B.5.1 and 9; 121B.7.4; 137.5.2. Financial Reports
    (1850s).
18 112.4.24; 68.4.7–8, 37 and 41; 253A.3.59; 325.3.25. Reports from the special
    court (1854–7).
19 In the Chinese calendar, the month was divided into three periods (*hsün*) of
    ten days each, regardless of the month. The third *hsün* could, in fact, be ten
    or nine days.
20 68.4.7 and 41; 253A.3.59; 289.3A.4; Verdicts of trials (1854). 3 Sept. 1854
    corresponds to the first day of the middle *hsün* of the intercalary month of the
    fourth year of Emperor Hsien-feng's reign.
21 253A.3.66. Awards recommended to officials of the Military Supply Bureau,
    etc. (*c.* 1857).
22 137.5.2. Financial report, 1854.
23 253A.3.77. Report from the district court of Shao-chou about the condition
    of captured rebels (May 1855).
24 279A.3.8. Report on execution of rebel suspects at Fo-shan (1855).
25 137.6.62–3. Report on captured rebels (1855).
26 253A.3.35. Militia report on captured rebels (n.d.).
27 *Ibid.* 325.3.26. Number of captured rebels delivered to Canton from various
    local councils (1855); 378B.1.48. Intelligence report on rebel activities
    (1850s).
28 Jung Hung, *Hsi-hsüeh tung-chien chi* (Taipei reprint, 1961), p. 36.
29 F.O.17.231, Desp.208, Incl., Morrison's report, 8 June 1855.
30 S. M. Fang, *Ti-erh-tz'u ya-p'ien chan-cheng shih-hua* (Shanghai, 1956), p.
    20.
31 279A.3.8. Report on three rebel suspects executed at Fo-shan (1855).
32 112.4.19. Report on exhumation of bodies of ancestors of a rebel leader, 1
    May 1856.
33 325.3.2. Report on the location of ancestral graves of Hung Hsiu-ch'üan and
    Liu Heng-t'ai (1850s).
34 279A.3.8. Report to Yeh by the provincial judge, etc. (1855); 121B.7.3 and
    378B.1.14. Reports on three executed rebels at Fo-shan (June 1855).
35 See Hsiao, *Ch'ing-tai t'ung-shih*, for details of organisation of the Eight
    Banners and the Green Standard.

36 Obviously because of the lack of primary documents such as those in the Canton Archive, even Fu Tsung-mou, in his published thesis entitled *Ch'ing-tai tu-fu chih-tu* (Taipei, 1963), made such an assumption.

37 318.5.38. Hsü and Yeh to emperor, 30 Jan. 1850.

38 325.3.15. Deposition of Ch'en Chao-ch'ing (1855).

39 378B.5.6. Imperial edict, 24 Sept. 1857.

40 112.3.23 and 41; 325.4.1–2; Correspondence between Canton and Peking during the Entry Crisis, 1849.

41 279A.6.16. Account of supplies to Banners at the gates (1855).

42 378B.3.5. Shuang-ling to Yeh (29 Dec. 1857).

43 279A.6.3; 327.3.13; 68.4.28; 137.5.2. Reports on the pay and victuals of regular troops in Kwangtung (1851–6).

44 A pension was a favour by grant not by right, and officials did not contribute to it during service.

45 Apart from the general inflation, there were two important reasons for this decline. The number of Bannermen continued to multiply, but since the status was hereditary and the number of soldiers in each Banner was fixed, and since the surplus manpower was forbidden by law to engage in anything other than artillery and archery, those who were employed had to share their fixed wages with those who were not.

46 253A.3.22. Five proposals for the defence of Canton (1854).

47 It would be interesting to find out whether Yeh did actually adopt this policy or not. Lin Tse-hsü tried unsuccessfully to do the same during the Opium War but that was fifteen years before Yeh, when, as was to be expected, the Manchus were still in a very strong position. Furthermore, Yeh had served at Canton for a much longer period of time and enjoyed absolute command over practically everything in the province. He might have succeeded where Lin had failed. In fact, there is documentary evidence (137.6.53. Register of troops in and around Canton [1857]) which states that mercenary units were attached to the Banners in 1857, but it is not clear whether these were recruited from among the Bannermen or from an external source.

48 289.2.10, 17–19, 22–6, 35, 38–44, 52, 60 and 61. Military maps and documents relative to them (n.d.).

49 137.5.5. Report on a case of maladministration in Na-fu battalion (1853).

50 318.5.38. Hsü and Yeh to the emperor, 30 Jan. 1850.

51 137.1.20. Report from naval forces at She-t'ou Bay (Oct. 1856).

52 For details, see Fu, *Ch'ing-tai tu-fu*, p. 104.

53 138.3.10. Entry book of comments on officials and officers (n.d.).

54 391.3.3. Report on vacant army positions and officers qualified to fill them (12 April 1855).

55 327.3.39–40. Notifications of appointment of first-captain (3 June 1855).

56 769.1. Hsü to Yeh (n.d.).

57 327.2.61. Memo to emperor (1854); 378B.1.16. Letter from Kwangsi (1856–7).

58 378B.1.66. Yeh to Hui-ch'ing (19 June 1855). Hui-ch'ing would have found the last sentence most reassuring, but in fact Yeh lied: Kwangtung was herself in extreme financial difficulties and the provincial treasury was more or less empty (see chap. 7).

59 112.4.30. Letter from Hung to unspecified destination (1855).

60 279A.3.10. Report on tensions between garrisons of Hu-men and local population (1854).

61 HF 162.10. Imperial edict, 28 April 1855.

62 253A.3.94. Report on unruly soldiers (n.d.).

63 279A.3.10. Report on tensions between garrisons of Hu-men and the local population (1854).

64 Cf. *Ibid.*

65 It is not clear how widespread drug addiction was among the soldiers, but Fig. 4, which shows the estimated consumption of opium in China in this period, may give some general idea of its extent. Also Sir John Bowring, writing to the Foreign Office, said, 'It is likely the general disorganization will tend to promote rather than diminish its sale' (F.O.17.214, Bowring–Clarendon, Desp.52, 5 June 1854).

66 279A.3.8. Case of three rebel-suspects executed at Fo-shan (1855).

67 137.6.6. Note on rebellious societies along the coast of Kwangtung (*c.* 1855).

68 Cf. 253A.3.98. Deposition of an ex-mercenary (*c.* 1855).

69 Cf. 327.2.38. Report on allocation of troops at Ling-shan (Dec. 1851).

70 378B.1.45; 121B.7.23. Reports on certain mercenaries (1855).

71 HF 52.6–8. Imperial edict, 8 March 1852. Cf. 327.2.53. A note from Kwangsi to Yeh transcribing the edict (1852).

72 Cf. 325.3.9. Depositions of three rebel-suspects (1853).

73 327.3.19. Order by provincial government of Kiangsi to investigate an excessive claim for military funds (1856).

74 325.3.15. Deposition of Ch'en Chao-ch'ing (Sept. 1855).

75 279A.3.38. Anonymous intelligence report (n.d.).

76 253A.3.50. Proclamation of Lin Fu-sheng (1854).

77 325.3.15–17. Depositions concerning a case of salt smuggling (Sept. 1855).

78 138.3.20. Report on deposition of Feng Chung-ju (1853).

79 For a cogent analysis of the role of militia in the history of China, especially in the late Ch'ing period, see P. A. Kuhn, *Rebellion and Its Enemies in Late Imperial China*. While Kuhn deals mainly with the militia in the Yangtze region, this section concentrates on events in Kwangtung.

80 121B.7.17; 253A.3.105; 112.4.9; 327.2.3; 378B.1.49. Reports on the organisation and activities of militia (1855).

81 378B.1.30 and 52. Reports on organisation of militia (1855–6).

82 112.4.26. Report from three gentry leaders on their battles with rebels from Fo-shan (Aug. 1854).

83 44.12. Ch'üan-ch'ing to Yeh (1856). Translation by the author.

84 327.3.46; 279A.6.19. Reports on tax collection (1848 and 1853).

85 121B.7.6; 112.4.16. Reports from acting deputy salt intendant of Ch'ao-chou, 4 and 14 Oct. 1856.

Part three: The military organiser

1 Wakeman, *Strangers at the Gate*, pp. 126–256, using mainly consular reports, has given us the first general account in English of the uprisings of 1850–6. This part, with its abundant additional documentation from the Canton Archive and its individual treatment of each incident, aims to provide a more detailed description.

Chapter 5 *The revolts, 1850–3*

1 325.4.3. Imperial edict, 22 April 1849.

2 A short form for Ch'ing-yüan and Ying-te.

3 TK 17.3 and TK 20.16. Imperial edicts (5 Oct. and 25 Nov. 1850). 391.3.25. Hsü and Yeh to emperor, 25 Dec. 1850.

4 391.3.29. Hsü to emperor (Oct. 1850); 391.3.64. Imperial edict, 20 Oct. 1850.
5 391.4.13 and 33. Hsü and Yeh to emperor, 24 Sept. and 19 Dec. 1850.
6 112.4.1. Hsü to Yeh (25 Feb. 1851); TK 23.16. Imperial edict, 12 Jan. 1851.
7 289.2.11, 29, 32, 33, 50, and 52. Military maps (1850s).
8 1371.39. File giving complete details of the campaign of Ch'ing-ying, Jan.–Feb. 1852; TK 23.16. Imperial edict, 12 Jan. 1851.
9 HF 48.22. Imperial edict, 18 Jan. 1852.
10 TK 23.16. Imperial edict, 12 Jan. 1851.
11 253A.3.42. Hsü to Yeh (10 May 1852).
12 327.2.38. Report on allocation of troops at Ling-shan, Dec. 1851.
13 HF 61.34. Imperial edict, 30 June 1852.
14 HF 33.7–9 and 28, Imperial edicts, 1 and 12 June 1851.
15 HF 39.28. Imperial edict, 10 Sept. 1851.
16 HF 61.34. Imperial edict, 30 June 1852.
17 HF 38.17–18. Imperial edicts, 18 Aug. 1851; 769.1. Hsü to Yeh, 8 Sept. 1851.
18 HF 37.5–6 and HF 34.1–3. Imperial edicts, 29 July and 15 June 1851.
19 Jen Yu-wen, *The Taiping Revolutionary Movement* (New Haven, Conn., 1973), p. 73.
20 68.4.14. Three documents about rebel Ling Shih-pa (1850); 327.2.35. Hsü and Yeh to emperor, 10 April 1850; HF 32.11. Imperial edict, 25 May 1851.
21 391.3.10. Hsü and Yeh to emperor, 7 Aug. 1852.
22 HF 45.16, HF 46.11, HF 47.3. Imperial edicts, 3, 15 and 13 Dec. 1851.
23 HF 56.1–6. Imperial edicts (5), 29 April 1852; 253A.3.9. Hsü to emperor, 2 June 1852.
24 279A.3.43. Yeh to emperor (June 1852); 253A.3.8. Hsü and Yeh to emperor, 18 Feb. 1852.
25 391.3.1. List of gentry leaders and militiamen recommended for awards (late 1852). 289.2.17, 22, 25, 60 and 61. Military maps (n.d.).
26 *Ibid.*; 391.3.9–10. Yeh to emperor, 16 July and 7 Aug. 1852; 378B.1.33 and 39. Letter from intendant of Kao-lien circuit to Yeh (1851); 769.1. Letters from Hsü to Yeh (5) (1851–2). Despite claims by Wakeman (*Strangers at the Gate*, p. 133) that Ling Shih-pa committed suicide, the documents of the Canton Archive prove that he was killed by one of Yeh's officers.
27 HF 38.7–8. Imperial edicts, 13 Aug. 1851.
28 HF 66.5 and HF 67.11. Imperial edicts, 25 Aug. and 5 Sept. 1852. The only other detailed account of Ling Shih-pa and his rebellion may be found in Jen Yu-wen, *T'ai-p'ing-t'ien-kuo ch'üan-shih* (Hong Kong, 1962), I, 247–62. However, Jen Yu-wen, using secondary sources and local histories, seems to think that Hsü Kuang-ch'in had done most of the hard fighting and was about to achieve complete success when Yeh took over. Far from Yeh simply giving the finishing touch to the task, the Canton Archive shows that Yeh's victory was by no means easy to come by.
29 Kuo T'ing-i, *T'ai-p'ing t'ien-kuo shih-shih jih-chih* (Taipei reprint, 1965), p. 182.
30 Kuo, *Jih-chih*, p. 192.
31 Cf. Chien, *Ch'üan-shih*, p. 390.
32 *Ibid.* p. 389.
33 Kuo, *Jih-chih*, p. 186.
34 Chien, *Ch'üan-shih*, p. 390
35 Kuo, *Jih-chih*, p. 185.
36 253.3.99. Deposition of a captured Taiping spy (1850).
37 112.4.3. Depositions of captured Taiping infiltrators (1852–3); HF 68.14–15 and 19–20. Imperial edicts, 19 Sept. 1852.

38 137.1.1c Yeh–Bonham, 24 Oct. 1852.
39 112.4.3 Depositions of captured Taiping infiltrators (1852–3).
40 HF 66.12. Imperial edict, 29 Aug. 1852; 391.3.13 and 7, Yeh to emperor, 3 Oct. and 5 Nov. 1852.
41 289.2.17, 22 and 35. Military maps (n.d.).
42 HF 74.8. Imperial edict, 1 Dec. 1852.
43 279A.3.17. Yeh to emperor, 7 Jan. 1853; HF 93.4. Imperial edict, 8 June 1853.
44 253A.3.45. Chang Fei to Yeh (1853).
45 The fact that the Taipings moved north from Kwangsi is not disputed; but their reasons for so doing have never been closely examined. Jen, *Ch'üan-shih*, is perhaps the fullest account of the Taiping movement, but the author treats the Taipings' northern expedition almost as a matter of course. Possibly Jen Yu-wen's passion for details, in itself a very necessary and useful thing, has tended to obscure the more apparent questions. Had Kwangtung been undefended and accessible, Hung Hsiu-ch'üan would hardly have risked the march from Chin-t'ien to Nabking as he did, since Nanking would have made no better a capital than would Canton. Its only advantage from the Taiping point of view was its greater proximity to Peking, a dubious one in the event of defeat. See my review article on Jen Yu-wen's books, in *Modern Asian Studies* 9.4 (1975), 557–66.

46 HF 142.11. Imperial edict, 8 Oct. 1854.
47 HF 31.16–17; 36.5; 38.5–6. Imperial edicts, 13 May, 17 July and 13 Aug. 1851.
48 391.3.19. Yeh and Po-kuei to emperor (1854); 112.4.17. Report on suppression of banditry (1855).
49 Translated in F.O.17.226, Bowring–Clarendon, Desp.18, 9 Jan. 1855. This translation is misquoted by Wakeman (*Strangers at the Gate*, p. 139) who refers to 'the fall of the Ming dynasty'. Furthermore, the dynasty only ended in 1644.

Chapter 6 *The general insurrection, 1854–8*

1 HF 104.25. Imperial edict, 26 Sept. 1853.
2 HF 67.19. Imperial edict, 11 Sept. 1852.
3 112.4.16; 121B.7.6. Reports from acting deputy salt intendant of Ch'ao-chou, 14 and 4 Oct. 1856.
4 391.2.10. Hsü and Yeh to emperor (1851).
5 391.2.6. Imperial edict (1853).
6 68.4.46. Note concerning interrogation of Kan Hsien (1855).
7 137.6.50–1. Intelligence report (1853).
8 68.4.35. Proclamation of Yeh and Po-kuei (1854).
9 Cf. F.O.17.203. Bonham–Clarendon, Desp.63, 6 July 1853.
10 253A.3.92. Deposition of a rebel leader (*c.* April 1855).
11 F.O. 17.215, Desp. 122, Incl. 1, Morrison's report, 20 July 1854; B4.6–15, P.788, Joseph Jardine–David Jardine, 13 July 1854.
12 *Ibid.*; 253A.3.35. Report by militia organisation (n.d.).
13 Chien, *Ch'üan-shih*, pp. 830–8.
14 Most recently by Wakeman (*Strangers at the Gate*, Chapter 14).
15 Chien, *Ch'üan-shih*, p. 838.
16 253A.3.92. Deposition of a rebel leader (*c.* April 1855).

17 Cf. 327.3.19. Order by provincial government of Kiangsi to investigate excessive demands for military funds (1856); HF 161.7. Imperial edict, 17 April 1855; HF 142.13. Imperial edict, 8 Oct. 1854; Chien, *Ch'üan-shih*, p. 852.

18 391.3.13. Yeh to emperor, 3 Oct. 1852; cf. F.O. 17.217. Desp. 59, Incl., Morrison's report, 9 Nov. 1854.

19 391.2.6. Imperial edict (1853).

20 378B.1.66. Yeh to C.-in-C. of Kwangsi, 19 June 1855.

21 Chien, *Ch'üan-shih*, p. 842.

22 F.O. 17.215, Desp. 122, Incl., Morrison's report, 31 July 1854. The Banners in fact consisted of only 4,158 soldiers and 106 officers (279A.6.3. Report on annual payments to Banners, n.d.). For other details, see Table 9.

23 253A.3.46. Recommendation for a number of meritorious militiamen to be rewarded (1854); *Tung-kuan hsien-chih* 72.4a; 253A.3.50. Proclamation by Lin Fu-sheng (1854–5).

24 325.3.8. Report from C.-in-C. of Kwangtung marine forces (1854); HF 98.24. Imperial edict, 29 July 1853; cf. similar edicts in HF 105.15 (5 Oct. 1853), HF 164.8 (19 May 1855), HF 176.10–11 (15 Oct. 1855), HF 176.16 (17 Oct. 1855).

25 *KCFC* 108.22–3.

26 Cooke, *China*, p. 343.

27 253A.3.22. Five proposals for the defence of Canton (late 1854); 279A.6.16. Account of supplies issued to troops at Canton city gates (1855).

28 279A.3.22. Report on defence of the new city of Canton (late 1854).

29 Chien, *Ch'üan-shih*, p. 843.

30 If Governor Po-kuei and the Tartar General 'shook at the sound of his [Yeh's] footsteps', observed Cooke (*China*, p. 344), it is not surprising that both played a very unimportant role in the military government.

31 253A.3.66. Awards recommended for officials of the Military Supply Bureau, etc. (*c*. 1857).

32 253A.3.22. Five proposals for the defence of Canton (late 1854).

33 253A.3.53. Writ from Yeh, 30 Jan. 1857.

34 253A.3.54. Report from Military Supply Bureau, 2 Feb. 1857.

35 112.4.5, 8 and 10; 327.3.53. Security measures at Kuei-lin (n.d.).

36 112.4.14. List of leaders and officials of militia stationed in the New City of Canton (late 1854).

37 F.O. 17.215, Desp. 122, Incl., Morrison's report, 31 July 1854.

38 *Ibid.*

39 391.3.52. Additional regulations for the organisation of militia in Canton (Jan. 1855).

40 112.4.23. Contributions to the defence of Canton, 1855–7.

41 F.O. 17.217, Desp. 59, Incl., Morrison's report, 10 Nov. 1854.

42 325.3.22; 378.1.7 and 9. Intelligence reports (1854–5).

43 325.3.22. Report on abduction of Ch'en Sung (1854). Unfortunately it has not been possible to find out more about the background of this man. Chien, *Ch'üan-shih*, pp. 822–8, describes how a leader of a certain secret society called Ch'en Sung-nien led his followers to besiege the magisterial city of Hsin-hui, but his account of the man and his associates differs entirely from the document and probably refers to a different person.

44 253A.3.32; 279A.3.25 and 48. Reports on manufacture, stocking and distribution of ammunition, 1847–54.

45 137.6.9. Report on cost of manufacture of gunpowder (n.d.).

46 327.2.52; 137.6.7b. Reports on recasting and inspection of ordnance (1854).

47 137.6.56–7; 253A.3.27; 253A.4.15, 16 and 18; 327.56. Reports on the production of munitions and on stocks at the arsenals (1850s).
48 279A.6.45 and 46. Reports on the sale of surplus military supplies and on materials in stock at *chün-ch'i-chü* (1850s).
49 137.6.9; 253A.3.32; 279A.3.25 and 48. Reports on the cost, manufacture, stocking and distribution of ammunition, 1847–54.
50 253A.3.106. Account of distribution of cannon, Aug. 1854.
51 289.3A.5; 327.3.37. Inventory of ammunition (1854).
52 253A.3.34. Intelligence report on rebels (late 1854).
53 T. T. Meadows, *The Chinese and their Rebellions* (reprint, 1954), p. xxii.
54 137.1.16. Report on possibility of import of rice (n.d.).
55 F.O. 17.227. Bowring–Clarendon, Desp. 73 (& Incls. 1–4), 3 Feb. 1855.
56 325.4.27. Report on cargo of three foreign ships (n.d.).
57 378B.1.3. Report on an American merchant (Endacott) (1855).
58 327.2.25. Report from Hsiao Ting-an in Hong Kong (14 April 1855).
59 E.g. 138.5.20; 279A.6.27; 327.3.31. Reports on imports of rice (1854–5).
60 253A.3.39. Intelligence report (1854); F.O. 17.215, Desp. 122, Incl., Morrison's report, 20 July 1854.
61 Both Jen (*Ch'üan-shih*), using mainly local histories, and Wakeman, using mainly consular reports, have given us a general picture of the campaign, but not a satisfactory answer to why the government won and the rebels failed. Yeh's personal role in the campaign, as described here, is of course an important factor, and his preparations for war, as detailed in the previous section, is indeed decisive.
62 112.4.26. Report from three leaders of the gentry on campaign against rebels near Fo-shan (Aug. 1854); cf. Chien, *Ch'üan-shih*, p. 832.
63 F.O. 17.215, Desp. 122, Incl., Morrison's report, 20 July 1854. (Also cf. B4.6–15, P.792, James Whittal to Joseph Gardiner, 23 July 1854.)
64 *Ibid.* 31 July 1854.
65 Cf. *ibid.* 20 July 1854.
66 F.O.17.216, Desp.142, Incl., Morrison's report, 11 Sept. 1854; Chien, *Ch'üan-shih*, p. 842.
67 *Ibid.* pp. 842–3.
68 137.6.25. Deposition of a captured rebel (Jan. 1855); 121B.7.15. Report on campaign north of Canton (Jan. 1855).
69 Chien, *Ch'üan-shih*, pp. 859–60; 68.4.12; 253A.6.37; 279A.6.37; 327.2.32; 391.3.54. Lists of captured rebels and proposed recipients of rewards (1855).
70 Chien, *Ch'üan-shih*, p. 844.
71 F.O. 17.218, Desp. 226, Incls., Robertson–Bowring, 2 and 5 Dec. 1854.
72 F.O. 17.218, Desp. 230, Bowring–Clarendon, 11 Dec. 1854; Kuo T'ing-i, *Chin-tai Chung-kuo shih-shih jih-chih* (Taipei, 1963), p. 224.
73 F.O. 17.218, Desp. 231, Incl., Morrison's report, 9 Dec. 1854.
74 Chien, *Ch'üan-shih*, p. 844.
75 F.O. 17.218, Desp. 231, Incl., Morrison's report, 9 Dec. 1854.
76 Wakeman, *Strangers at the Gate*, p. 148.
77 F.O. 17.218, Desp. 230, Incl., Bowring–Yeh, 11 Dec. 1854.
78 F.O. 17.218, Desp. 237, Bowring–Clarendon, 25 Dec. 1854.
79 Hua T'ing-chieh, 'Ch'u-fan shih-mo', in *Chin-tai-shih tzu-liao*, no. 2 (Peking, 1956).
80 *KCFC* 108.26–7.
81 F.O. 17.218, Desp. 226 (8 Dec. 1854), Incl., Translation of a communication from gentry and merchants of Canton to Bowring (n.d.).

82 *Ibid*. Incl., Bowring–Robertson, 5 Dec. 1854.
83 F.O. 17.218. Desp. 230, Incl., Yeh–Bowring, 7 Oct. 1854.
84 See chap. 7.
85 This suspicion is reinforced by a consular report which reads:
'There is one thing consequent of the altered position of affairs at Canton which strikes me forcibly; I refer to the change in public opinion with regard to foreigners: the firm attitude they have assumed there, their known determination to resist any attack on the Factories, and the naval force anchored off the settlement, ready, as they believe, to act with terrible effect should the necessity arise, impress the minds of the Chinese with a feeling of respect for us that at no other time to the same extent has been observed: men who but the other day were indifferent and even contemptuous in their bearing, assume now a far different attitude; they speak openly and unreservedly of the weakness of their government, the uncertainty which clouds the future, and their desire to see life and property guaranteed at the expense even of foreign intervention, rather than remain as they now are in peril of both. There must be some great influence at work therefore to cause so total a change in the sentiments of a class of the people whose opposition has hitherto been the great bar to the extension of the privileges of foreigners.
'These men composed the middle, moneyed and influential class of traders.' (F.O. 17.216, Robertson–Hammond, Desp. 17, 10 Oct. 1854.)
86 F.O. 17.217, Robertson–Hammond, Desp. 60 (and Incls.), 10 Nov. 1854.
87 Wakeman (*Strangers at the Gate*, pp. 147–8) has come to the same conclusion after reading the same documents.
88 F.O. 17.218, Bowring–Clarendon, Desp. 237, 25 Dec. 1854.
89 137.6.16. Deposition of a member of the gentry suspected of rebel connections, 21 April 1855.
90 253.3.24; 279A.3.6. Lists of proposed recipients of awards (1855).
91 F.O. 17.228, Desp. 130, Incl., Robertson–Bowring, 8 March 1855.
92 *Ibid*.
93 289.2.2–6, 8–9, 13, 21, 30, 34, 48; 324.3.5. Military maps (1854–5).
94 378B.1.14, 48–53, 67. Intelligence reports (1854–5).
95 HF 33.7–9, 28. Imperial edicts, 1 and 12 June 1851.
96 378B.1.26. Copy of imperial edict condemning Sai-shang-a (late 1852).
97 137.6.39. Hsü to emperor, 26 Sept. 1852, concerning imperial edict of 7 Sept. 1852.
98 *CSLC* 44.22b–23a.
99 Cooke, *China*, p. 396.
100 F.O. 17.218, Bowring–Clarendon, Desp. 235, 23 Dec. 1854.
101 Cf. 68.3a, 10. Captured rebel correspondence (1854); 253A.3.34. Intelligence report on disagreement among rebel leaders (1854).
102 F.O. 17.218, Desp. 231, Incl., Morrison's report, 9 Dec. 1854.
103 F.O. 17.218, Bowring–Clarendon, Desp. 235 (and Incls.), 23 Dec. 1854.
104 F.O. 17.228, Desp. 108, Incl., Robertson–Yeh, 23 Feb. 1855.
105 F.O. 17.228. Bowring–Clarendon, Desp. 108, 28 Feb. 1854.
106 279A.5.19; 325.4.20. Reports on construction of light war junks (1855).
107 F.O. 17.229, Woodgate–Hammond, Separate no. 15, 15 April 1855.
108 *Ibid*.
109 F.O. 17.231, Desp. 208, Incl., Morrison's report, 8 June 1855.
110 B4.6–15, P.954 and 977. J. Jardine, 1 and 28 July 1855.
111 Cf. 289.2.28. Military map of East River (1854–5); 378B.1.20 and 48–9. Intelligence reports (July 1856).

112 Chien, *Ch'üan-shih*, pp. 873–5.
113 Cf. *Ibid.* pp. 888–93.
114 F.O. 17.231, Desp. 208, Incl., Morrison's report, 8 June 1855.
115 B4.6–15, P.962. James Whittal–Joseph Jardine, 16 July 1855.
116 327.2.5. List of proposed recipients of awards for defence of Shao-chou (1855); 378B.1.13, 20, 48 and 49. Notes and reports on rebels (1855); 253A.3.100. Report on travelling expenses of C.-in-C. K'un-shou from Shao-chou to Hui-chou (Aug. 1855). Cf. also Chien, *Ch'üan-shih*, p. 893.
117 68.4.21 and 47. Notes on the rebels and their property in Hai-feng (1855); 137.6.35. Yeh and Po-kuei to emperor (25 Nov. 1857); 289.2.47. Map of area around Hui-chou (n.d.); 3781.11. Letter containing account of rebel attack on Hui-lai (1854). 378B.1.21–4. Reports concerning the loss and recovery of Po-lo (1855). Cf. also *HCFC* 30.3; *Shao-chou fu-chih* 30.5–6; and Chien, *Ch'üan-shih*, pp. 883–4.
118 279B.12.1. Citation (probably by one of Yeh's private secretaries) from an unidentified work regarding methods of rebel suppression in Ming times.
119 Chien, *Ch'üan-shih*, p. 920.
120 *Ibid.* p. 921; 378B.1.19, 50–1, 53. Intelligence reports (1855–7); F.O. 17.250, Bowring–Clarendon, Desp. 280, 11 Sept. 1856.
121 289.2.31. Military map (1856).
122 378B.1.16. Anonymous letter to Yeh (1857); 378B.1.17. Report to Yeh on military situation in Kwangsi (1856–7). Cf. Chien, *Ch'üan-shih*, pp. 818–29.
123 137.6.34. Yeh and Po-kuei to emperor, 12 Oct. 1857; cf. Chien, *Op. cit.*, pp. 903–4.
124 Jao Tsung-i, *Ch'ao-chou chih*, pp. 35–59.

Part four: The paymaster general

1 This part concentrates on Yeh's financial policies in Kwangtung; for the general administration of finance in China in this period, see E-tu Zen Sun, 'The Board of Revenue in nineteenth-century China', *HJAS*, 24 (1963), 175–228, and two articles ('Tao-kuang shih-ch'i te yin-kuei wen-t'i' and 'Wang Mao-yin yü Hsien-feng shih-tai te hsin-pi-chih'), both in *Chung-kuo chin-tai-shih lun-ts'ung*, 3, 9–39 and 49–70. Cf. also note 4, p. 206.

Chapter 7 *Conventional management of finances*

1 391.3.34. Hsü and Yeh to emperor (1850).
2 137.1.39; 253A.4.20. Reports concerning rebel suppression (1852).
3 378B.1.62. Yeh to Ch'i Chün-tsao (1852).
4 *Ibid.*
5 Wang, *Land-Tax, 1753 and 1908*, p. 16
6 Canton Archive, *passim.*
7 Wakeman, *Strangers at the Gate*, pp. 134–5. His account of the same incident is incomplete and misleading. The new emperor did not, as Wakeman suggests, remit the land tax of 1851 but cancelled all arrears of the tax up to the end of 1850 (see 137.5.1. Report to Yeh on investigation into the case of gentry refusal to pay taxes, 1851; and 391.2.10. Hsü and Yeh to emperor, 1851). Wakeman's error arises from a misinterpretation of a

consular report (F.O. 228.126, Bowring–Bonham, Desp. 57, 17 March 1851) which distinctly refers to 'an imperial edict remitting such *outstanding debts* to the government'. Moreover, the edict to this effect was publicised and not kept secret as the consular reports suggest (see 137.5.1 and 391.2.10 *op. cit.*).

8 The sum deducted had originally been earmarked for stocking a state granary against famine, but, for some unknown reason, had been transferred to the Academy. It as now redirected to its original purpose.

9 391.2.10 and 137.5.1 *op. cit.*; HF 30.22–3. Imperial edict, 29 April 1851. Also see notes 10 and 11 below.

10 F.O. 17.193, Bowring–Malmesbury, Desp. 157, 11 Nov. 1852; HF 33.20. Imperial edict, 8 June 1851.

11 HF 37.4. Imperial edict, 29 July 1851.

12 378B.1.49. Intelligence report (1855–6).

13 279A.6.23. Financial report, 1853; 279A.6.50. Report on aspects of land tax collection, 1854.

14 279A.6.50. *Op. cit.*

15 279A.6.50. *Op. cit.*

16 Chou, *Yeh-fa t'ung-chih*, 14.7b.

17 327.3.54–5. Reports on tax receipts for 1851–2.

18 279A.6.26. Account of money borrowed by intendant of Kao-lien from various sources to pay the marines in his circuit (1831–54).

19 279A.2.2. Arguments against changes of salt administration in Hunan (*c.* 1856).

20 253A.5.37. Report on salt administration in Kwangtung (n.d.). The number of *pu* in Kiangsi given in this document as included in the Han River region is 9, which, when added to the 14 in Kwangtung and the 8 in Fukien, exceeds 29. In Chou, *Yen-fa t'ung-chih* 6.18a–b, the numbers quoted are: Kwangtung 14, Kiangsi 7 and Fukien 8, totalling 29.

21 327.3.54. Report on Kwangtung tax receipts for 1852.

22 327.1.1. Report on the development of salt administration (n.d.).

23 325.3.15–18. Depositions concerning a case of salt smuggling (1855).

24 Cf. 327.5.27. Intelligence report on conditions in Hong Kong (1855); 327.1.4. Report on arrival of salt junks (at Hong Kong), 1–30 May 1851; Hansard, *Parliamentary Debates*, Series 3, 144, pp. 1167ff.

25 F.O. 17.267, Bowring–Clarendon, Desp. 169, 8 April 1857.

26 The master of the lorcha *Arrow*, Thomas Kennedy, for example, was one of the Britons thus employed. 'He was a young man of 21, who had been put on board, as he very candidly admits in his deposition, as nominal master of the vessel; and he literally knew so little about the vessel that he did not know who was the owner, but had always understood that it was Mr. Block's comprador at Canton' (Hansard, *op. cit.* p. 1165). During the month previous to the notorious *Arrow* incident, the boat was acting as a receiver of stolen goods for pirates (F.O. 17.267, Bowring–Clarendon, 8 April 1857). We have little record of her activities before this. It is quite possible that, like so many similar lorchas, she had also been engaged in the lucrative business of salt smuggling (Hansard, *op. cit.* pp. 1167).

27 253A.6.6. Report on decline of salt monopoly in Kwangtung (*c.* 1853).

28 Report on merchant and gentry contributions toward costs of salt shipment (n.d.).

29 253A.6.7. Draft regulations for salt administration at Canton (n.d.).

30 Cf. F.O. 682.1757. Bowring–Yeh, 21 Nov. 1855; F.O. 682.1777, Yeh–Bowring, 12 Dec. 1855; F.O. 228.212, Bowring–Winchester, Desp. 62, 26 May 1856.

31 279A.2.4. Report on quantities of salt handled in 6 localities (1855).
32 Cf. E. G. Beal, *The Origin of Likin, 1853–64* (Cambridge, Mass., 1958), and Lo Yü-tung, *Chung-kuo li-chin shih* (Shanghai, 1936).
33 279A.2.3. Arguments against changes of salt administration in Kwangsi (*c.* 1856).
34 Hansard, Series 3, 144, pp. 1167–8.
35 The salt regime was reformed at the turn of this century. See S. A. M. Adshead, *The Modernization of the Chinese Salt Administration, 1900–20* (Cambridge, Mass., 1970).
36 137.1.42. Report on the decline of trade at Canton since the opening of the five ports (1848).
37 137.1.23. Report from the Hoppo on collection of customs duties for the period 1 Feb. 1848 to 15 Nov. 1854.
38 F.O. 17.231, Desp. 208, Incl., Morrison's report, 9 June 1855.
39 F.O. 17.231. Desp. 242, Incl., Alcock–Bowring, 6 July 1855.
40 253A.5.2–3. Report on malpractices of junior officials in the customs service, and proposals for its reform (1856).
41 F.O. 17.230, Bowring–Clarendon, Desp. 155, 15 May 1855.
42 68.4.20. Proclamation to Chinese and English merchants (n.d.).
43 112.3.46; 137.5.20; 138.5.17; 279A.6.27; 327.3.32. Financial reports and tax receipts from the Hoppo (1854–5).
44 F.O. 228.212, Desp. 18, Alcock–Bowring, 2 Feb. 1856.
45 Hansard, Series 3, 144, p. 1167.
46 Hansard, *op. cit.*, p. 1160.
47 The ordinance of course meant Chinese residents in Hong Kong; but as pointed out by the Attorney General, 'of the 60,000 Chinese in that colony, hardly one could be legally called British subjects' (*ibid.* p. 1161). Furthermore, the majority of these 60,000 Chinese had their homes in China, and they went to Hong Kong only for purposes of trade. Thus, the ordinance was in effect granting the right to fly the British flag and claim British protection to Chinese subjects in Chinese waters.
48 *Ibid.* p. 1167.
49 *Ibid.* p. 1314. Cf. also *ibid.* pp. 1160ff.
50 *Ibid*, p. 1167.
51 F.O. 17.277, Desp. 68, Incl., J. Jardine–Elgin, 1 Oct. 1857.
52 F.O. 17.251, Desp. 321, Incl., Parkes–Bowring, 6 Oct. 1856.
53 F.O. 228.212, Alcock–Bowring, Desp. 20 (4 Feb. 1856), Incl., Morrison's translation of a proclamation by Yeh and Po-kuei, 22 Jan. 1856.
54 See Fig. 5. There was no customs revenue in 1857, as Yeh had closed Canton to foreign trade at the end of 1856 because of the outbreak of hostilities with Great Britain.
55 279A.6.23 and 40; 253A.4.9; 253A.5.16; 253A.6.6. Reports on government loans to merchants and the arrears in payment of the interests (1815–55).
56 *Ibid.*
57 B3/16 and B4/7 series (both 1847), and B4/6–15 series (1848), *passim.*
58 Cf. 253A.3.107. Report on a raid on a pawn-shop (1855).
59 Cf. 253A.3.9. Report on a robber arrested in Shun-te (n.d.).

Chapter 8 *Yeh's innovations*

1 112.2.4. Report on military expenditure (1850).
2 327.2.14. Report on military expenditure (1851).
3 137.1.39. Report on suppression of rebellion and expenditure incurred (1852).
4 253A.5.34–5 and 38; 327.2.58–9. Reports on military expenditure (1851–5).
5 378B.1.38. Letter from an intendant regarding military finance (1851).
6 324.3.2. Reasons for rejecting the second financial report prepared by Prefect Li (1852).
7 138.1.14. Petition to Yeh concerning the sanctioning of expenditure (n.d.).
8 Hsü Ta-ling, *Ch'ing-tai chüan-na chih-tu* (Peking, 1950), pp. 13–22.
9 The practice was, of course, familiar in *ancien régime* Europe.
10 TK 22.4.5. Imperial edict, 20 Dec. 1850.
11 The year when his father died, 1850, and when he came to the throne, was not considered the first official year of his reign.
12 Hsü, *Ch'ing-tai chüan-na*, p. 60.
13 The national quota of land tax has been given as 30,419,000 taels. See Wang, *Land tax, 1753 and 1908*, Table 27.
14 Cf. E-tu Zen Sun, 'The Board of Revenue in nineteenth-century China', *HJAS*, 24 (1963), 177–9.
15 391.4.44. Ch'i to emperor, 28 Nov. 1851; 378B.1.62. Yeh to Ch'i (1852).
16 Hsü, *Ch'ing-tai chüan-na*, p. 60.
17 279A.6.56. Draft letter from Wang Han-ch'iao to Ch'i Chün-tsao (1852). 112.4.5. Regulations concerning contributions in Kwangsi (1853). 138.5.11. Ministry of Revenue to Yeh (1857).
18 327.3.44. Yeh to emperor, 7 Sept. 1852; 391.4.39. Hsü and Yeh to emperor, 5 May 1852.
19 112.5.2; 253A.3.112; 279A.6.9, 22 and 53; 327.3.45. Various reports concerning financial contributions by officials 1852–3.
20 253A.7.3. Ministry of Revenue to Yeh *et. al.*, 10 Jan. 1854.
21 112.4.11; 137.5.2; 138.5.8 and 11; 279A.6.10, 11, 21, 24 and 51. Various documents concerning gentry contributions (1851–7).
22 378B.1.27. Suggestion for raising military funds (1855).
23 279A.6.38; 253A.5.9 and 40. Reports on merchant contributions (1855–6).
24 137.6.7c. Note on two merchants avoiding contributions (1856–7).
25 327.2.27. Intelligence report from Hsiao Ting-an (12 June 1855).
26 112.4.16. Report from acting deputy salt intendant of Ch'ao-chou, 14 Oct. 1856.
27 378B.5.8. Proposals concerning gentry contributions (1855–6).
28 378B.1.30. Orders for collection of extra taxes in coastal areas (1856).
29 279A.6.43. Report on contributions by villages (1855–6).
30 68.4.21, 33 and 47; 112.4.4 and 27; 327.2.15. Documents on confiscation of rebel property and fines imposed (1854–7).
31 Cf. e.g. HF: 98.1; 105.15; 106.50; 111.12–13; 125.10; 128.6; 131.6; 140.28; and 141.12. Imperial edicts, 26 July 1853 to 25 Sept. 1854.
32 Cf. e.g. HF: 121.4; 125.18 and 53–4; 136.16; and 136.23. Imperial edicts, 10 March 1854 to 9 Aug. 1854.
33 Cf. e.g. 137.6.7m–n. Letter describing conditions in Kiangsi (June 1853). 137.6.60. Newsletter from Fukien, 16 Oct. 1856; and 279A.6.17. Report on military expenses incurred on behalf of Hunan and Hupeh (n.d.).
34 HF 128.3. Imperial edict, 17 May 1854.
35 253A.3.93. Chang Fei to Yeh, 11 March 1855.

36 279A.5.24. Wang Pao-jun to Yeh (22 March 1857).
37 HF 77.2. Imperial edict, 31 Dec. 1852.
38 378B.1.36. Anonymous letter (incomplete) to Yeh (n.d.).
39 378B.6.2–3. Instructions from ministers of the Imperial Household to Kwangtung, 27 March and 25 April 1856.
40 See J. M. Norris, *Shelburne and Reform* (London, 1963), and W. G. Beasley, *The Meiji Restoration* (Stanford, Cal. 1973). Apart from the vicissitudes of Yeh, one might briefly mention the fact that the inability of the traditional tax structure to meet 'extraordinary' expenditures was not an exclusively Chinese phenomenon. Nor were Yeh's methods unique. Interesting comparisons may indeed be made with contemporary Japan, and European monarchies in the sixteenth and seventeenth centuries.
41 Cf. Cooke's classic eye-witness account that both the Tartar General and Governor Po-kuei 'shook at the sound of his footsteps ' (*China*, p. 344), and L/PS/5, Vol. 164, Secret letters from India, 1858.

Part five: The imperial commissioner for foreign affairs

1 This section is concerned with only one aspect of the Second Anglo-Chinese War, namely, Yeh's role in it. This, to some extent, has been dealt with by Hsieh, 'Yeh-hsiang', and Huang Yen-yü, 'Viceroy Yeh Ming-ch'en and the Canton Episode (1856–61)', *HJAS*, 6 (1941), 37–127. A fuller analysis of the origins of the war still needs to be written, and it is on this subject that the present author is at present engaged in research and writing.
2 Hsieh, 'Yeh-hsiang'.

Chapter 9 *A survey of Yeh's activities as Imperial Commissioner for Foreign Affairs*

1 B2/16. D. Jardine–D. Matheson, p. 1395, 3 April 1847. Macgregor was British Consul at Canton.
2 *Ibid.* p. 1396, 4 April 1847.
3 *Ibid.* p. 1397, 5 April 1847.
4 *Ibid.* p. 1402, 12 April 1847.
5 Wakeman, *Strangers at the Gate*, pp. 86–9, using the British Consular reports, gives a detailed description of the incident. The present account seeks to throw new light on it by using the Jardine and Matheson papers as well.
6 B4/7. D. Jardine–D. Matheson, pp. 306–7, 6–7 Dec. 1847.
7 *Ibid.* Cf. also *ibid.* p. 311, 11 Dec. 1847.
8 F.O. 228.73, Desp. 261, Incl., Ch'i-ying's announcement of the arrests and execution, 10 Dec. 1847.
9 B4/7. D. Jardine–D. Matheson, pp. 316 and 326, 14 and 21 Dec. 1847.
10 112.3.4. Yeh to emperor (Sept. 1847).
11 112.3.19. Yeh to emperor (1849).
12 He was later promoted to the post of brigadier of Shao-chou and then commander-in-chief of the land forces in Kwangtung.
13 On this occasion, Howqua was appointed Commissioner Extraordinary for Foreign Affairs (*wei-pan i-wu*) because of his experience in dealing with foreign merchants.

14 112.3.41. Hsü to emperor (1849).
15 325.4.1. Note to Yeh, 11 March 1849; 325.4.2. Imperial edict, 28 June 1849.
16 Cited in J. Nolde, 'The "False Edict"', *JAS* 20 (1960), 299–315.
17 *Ibid.* The original declaration in Chinese may be found among the Broadlands MS GC/BO/85 (by permission of the Trustees of the Broadlands Archives).
18 F.O. 17.154, Desp. 45, Incl. 4, Bonham–Hsü, 18 April 1849.
19 They regarded Bonham's communication as an abandonment of the claim to enter the city, perhaps through no fault of theirs, because the communication in the Chinese version could be read as such.
20 Ryl. Eng. MS. 1228/162. Bowring–Edgar Bowring, 12 Nov. 1856.
21 CSLC 40.44b–50a and 48.10b–15a.
22 378B.1.42. Letter from an official in Kiangsu to Yeh (1849). Translation by the author.
23 112.2.7. Letter to Yeh (anon. 1849). Translation by the author.
24 112.3.3. Hsü and Yeh to emperor, 24 Sept. 1849.
25 112.3.15. Hsü and Yeh to emperor, 2 June 1850.
26 112.3.24. Hsü and Yeh to emperor (June–July 1850).
27 112.3.6–7. Hsü and Yeh to emperor, 24 Sept. and 19 Dec. 1850.
28 For the life of Sir John Bowring before he went to the Far East, see G. F. Bartle, 'The Political Career of Sir John Bowring (1792–1872) between 1820 and 1849' (M.A. thesis, London, 1959).
29 F.O. 682: 1698, 1684 and 1701. Correspondence between Yeh and Bowring on 7 May, 11 May and 26 May 1854.
30 F.O. 17.231, Bowring–Clarendon, Desp. 241, 9 July 1855.
31 F.O. 17.216, Bowring–Clarendon, Desp. 165, 5 Oct. 1854.
32 *Ibid.* Incl., Memo of conference between Chinese, British and U.S. authorities in Shanghai, 3 Oct. 1854. For a comprehensive account of this episode, see G. F. Bartle, 'Sir John Bowring and the Chinese and Siamese Commercial Treaties', *Bulletin*, 44.2, 286–308.
33 F.O. 17.215, Desp. 128, Incl., Medhurst–Bowring, 2 Sept. 1854.
34 *Ibid.* Bowring–Medhurst, 22 Aug. 1854.
35 *Ibid.* Medhurst–Bowring, 2 Sept. 1854.
36 F.O. 17.216, Bowring–Clarendon, Desps. 160, 164–9, Oct. 1854.
37 F.O. 17.218, Bowring–Clarendon, Desp. 237, 25 Dec. 1854.
38 *Ibid.*
39 F.O. 682.1759, Bowring–Yeh, 22 Nov. 1855.
40 F.O. 682.1776, Yeh–Bowring, 12 Dec. 1855.
41 F.O. 17.230, Bowring–Clarendon, Desp. 150, 14 May 1855.
42 For details, see G. F. Bartle, 'Sir John Bowring and the Chinese and Siamese Treaties', *Bulletin*, 44.2, 286–308; N. Tarling, 'The Mission of Sir John Bowring to Siam', *The Journal of the Siamese Society*, 50.2, 92–118.
43 F.O. 17.250, Bowring–Clarendon, Desp. 303, 27 Sept. 1856.
44 F.O. 17.251, Bowring–Clarendon, Desp. 317 and Incl., 3 Oct. 1856.
45 See my article, 'The *Arrow* Incident: A Re-appraisal', *MAS* 8.3 (1974), 373–89.
46 See my article, 'Harry Parkes and the *Arrow* War in China', *MAS*, 9.3 (1975), 303–20.
47 See S. Lane-Poole, *The Life of Sir Harry Parkes*, Vol. 1 (London, 1894), and chap. 1 of G. Daniels, 'Sir Harry Parkes, British Representative in Japan, 1865–1883' (D.Phil. thesis, Oxford, 1967).
48 See Parkes' despatches and inclosure to Bowring since 8 Oct. 1856.

49 Ryl. Eng. MS 1228/161. Bowring–Edgar Bowring, 16 Oct. 1856. See my article, 'Sir John Bowring and the Canton City Question', *Bulletin*, 56.1 (1973), 219–45.
50 Ryl. Eng. MS 1228/165. Bowring–Edgar Bowring, 29 Nov. 1856.
51 *Ibid.* 15 Dec. 1856.
52 *Ibid.* 12 Nov. 1856.
53 Bowring was fully aware of the fact that the Cantonese were violently opposed to any foreigner entering their city; at one time he even proposed to bring his own troops for self-protection should Yeh agree to see him in the city (F.O. 17.267, Desp. 168, Incl., Bowring–Yeh, 18 Nov. 1856), but Yeh would not risk an armed conflict between the citizens and the British troops, and declined (*ibid.* Yeh–Bowring, 19 Nov. 1856).
54 It is not surprising that Bowring should be constantly accusing Yeh of ignoring his communications, but it is extraordinary that the Chinese historians should have made the same remark, which shows beyond doubt their bias against him. However, Huang Yen-yü's research has led him to conclude that, 'There is enough evidence in the English and French documents to show that Yeh practically replied to every letter he received and often very promptly' (*HJAS* 6 (1941), 52).
55 Parkes papers, Bowring–Parkes, 29 Oct. 1856; cf. *ibid.* 18 Oct. 1856.
56 MS Clar. Dep. C71, Bowring–Clarendon, 21 May 1857.
57 *Ibid.* Parkes–Cavendish, 25 May 1857.
58 *Ibid.* Bowring–Clarendon, 24 July 1857; Ryl. Eng. MS 1228/190. Bowring–Edgar Bowring, 25 July 1857.
59 *Ibid.* Bowring–Edgar Bowring, 11 June 1857.
60 *Ibid.* 21 Oct. 1857.
61 Cf. HF 144.5. Imperial edict, 23 Oct. 1854.
62 Indeed, constant foreign demands were very much a source of irritation and resentment to the emperor. Cf. HF: 131.39–40; 133.8–9; 134.1–2; 136.15–16; 143.8–12, 15, 24, 28–9, 39; 144.2, 5, 11, 21–2; 145.1. Imperial edicts, 23 June–1 Nov. 1854.
63 Hua T'ing-chieh, 'Ch'u-fan shih-mo', in *Chin-tai-shih tzu-liao*, no. 2 (Peking, 1956).
64 Hu, 'Yeh-hsiang'.
65 MS Clar. Dep. C71, Bowring–Clarendon, 27 Aug. 1857.
66 Cooke, *China*, p. 399.
67 *Ibid.*
68 F.O. 17.285, Desp. 7, Incl., Loch–Elgin, 5 Jan. 1858.
69 Cooke, *China*, p. 400.
70 Ryl. Eng. MS 1230/68. Alabaster–Bowring, 7 Jan. 1858.
71 *Ibid.* 8 Jan. 1858.
72 Ryl. Eng. MS 1230/76. Seymour–Bowring, 9 Jan. 1858.
73 MSS Clar. Dep. C85. Bowring–Clarendon, 11 Jan. 1858.
74 Lane-Poole, *The Life of Sir Harry Parkes* (London, 1894), p. 274.
75 Cooke, *China*, p. 344.
76 Cooke, 'Yeh's Portrait', *The Times*, 10 May 1858.
77 Correspondance de Napoléon Ier, publiée par ordre de l'Empéreur Napoléon III (Paris, 1858–69), xxviii, 348–9.
78 Cooke, *China*, p. 400.
79 Hsieh, 'Yeh-hsiang'.
80 A famous general of the kingdom of Sung in the Eastern Chou period (*c.* 770–474 B.C.).

81 Su Wu was an envoy sent by Emperor Wu (reg. 140–86 B.C.) to make an
   alliance with a northern tribe against the Hsiung-nu. While he was travelling
   through the territory of the Hsiung-nu, *en route* to the said tribe and spying
   out the land at the same time, he was captured, and detained for 19 years
   without submitting but keeping the staff given him by the emperor as a sign of
   his unswerving loyalty to the emperor and his mission. Eventually he was
   released and was received by the Chinese with acclamation. See chap. 11 for
   the full text of the poem.

Chapter 10 *A reappraisal of Yeh's ' do-nothing' policy during the ' Arrow' War*

1 F.O. 17.251, Desp. 350, Incl., Parkes–Yeh, 21 Oct. 1856.
2 68.3A.7. Warrent for arrest of the three second-captains for having failed to
   do their duty, 24 Nov. 1856.
3 Hua T'ing-chieh, 'Ch'u-fan shih-mo', in *Chin-tai-shih tzu-liao*, no. 2
   (Peking, 1956).
4 *Ibid.*
5 *Ibid.*
6 *Ibid.*
7 F.O. 17.267, Desp. 168 (7 April 1857), Incl., Yeh's proclamation (27 Oct.
   1856), translated by present author.
8 137.1.46b. Proclamation of merchants organising urban militia (1856).
9 MS Clar. Dep. C71. Bowring–Clarendon, 15 Feb. 1857. See pages 173–4
   for details.
10 112.4.23. Report of contributions by various streets to defence in 1855–7.
11 MS Clar. Dep. C71, Lay–Bowring, 14 Jan. 1857.
12 112.4.23. Report of contributions by various streets to defence in 1855–7.
13 253A.3.91. Ten suggestions for the defence of Canton (1857).
14 44.15. Eleven documents concerning the war with the British (1856–7);
   112.3.35. Report on the allocation of funds to the river forts (1857).
15 68.4.18. *Yamen* register of documents (1856).
16 137.6.7b. Note concerning recasting of cannon in 1854.
17 378B.1.40. Report on British troops occupying forts at the Bogue (15 Nov.
   1857).
18 391.3 (extra). Peking Gazette extracts for 1857–8.
19 137.6.14–15, 17, 19, 23, 26–8, 30, 59. Depositions by captured collaborators
   with the British (1856–7).
20 MS Clar. Dep. C71. Elgin–Clarendon, 16 Dec. 1857, Incl., a memo, 9 Dec.
   1857.
21 F.O. 17.267, Bowring–Clarendon Desp. 179 (and Incl.), 11 April 1857; *ibid.*
   Desp.
22 Ryl. Eng. MS 1228/179. Bowring–Edgar Bowring, 14 April 1857.
23 *Ibid.* 8 May 1857. Cf. also *ibid.* 17 May 1857.
24 *Ibid.* 6 June, 8–9 July, 24 Sept., 5 and 16 Oct. 1857.
25 MS Clar. Dep. C71. Bowring–Clarendon, 25 Sept. 1857.
26 112.3.6. Hsü and Yeh to emperor, 24 Sept. 1850.
27 324.4.3; 327.2.25–7; 327.5.27, 36–9; 378B.3.6. Intelligence reports from
   Hsiao Ting-an (1854–7).
28 E.g. 340B.3.5–7. Translations of Hong Kong newspapers (1855–6).
29 391.2.106; 279B.4; 325.4.33. Intelligence reports (1857).
30 E.g. 68.3.29. Intelligence report (1857).
31 112.4.20. Evidence given in a case of tea-smuggling, April 1857.

32 112.2.8–9. Intelligence reports, 7 Sept. 1856 and 1857. For other reports of this kind, see 253A.4.10a–d, 12; 325.4.12; 327.2.25–7; 327.5.47–8; 327B.3.1–2; 391.2.107.

33 Hua, 'Ch'u-fan shih-mo'.

34 327.5.40. Gentry proclamation (1856); 279B.9.3. Printed proclamation of a local council in Canton (1857).

35 327.5.48. Intelligence report (1857); 378B.3.2. Intelligence reports from Hong Kong, 4 Sept. 1857.

36 See e.g. Bowring's letters to his sons (Ryle, Eng. MS 1228 and 1229) and Captain Bate's letters to Mrs Parkes (Parkes Papers).

37 One may get some idea of the belief in the weakness of the British prevalent among the Chinese in Hong Kong from the eye-witness account of Lord Elgin's private secretary: 'The Chinese continued to kidnap, assassinate, seize steamers, and annoy us in sundry cunningly-devised methods... never before since the abolition of the monopoly had Englishmen made so poor a figure in the eyes of the Chinese populace. If one went into a curiosity shop at Hong Kong, he was the object of the quiet irony of the sleek vendor of carved ivory behind the counter, who informed him his choice collection was at Canton, and asked, "why you no can come my shop Canton?" The very urchins in the street considered a Briton a fit subject for "chaff", while their respectable parents took a mercenary view of his head. Hong Kong was neither a safe nor agreeable abode in those days.' (L. Oliphant, *Narrative of the Earl of Elgin's mission to China and Japan in the years 1857, '58, '59* [London reprint, 1970], p. 24.)

38 F.O. 17.277, Elgin–Clarendon, Desp. 78, 10 Dec. 1857.

39 Costin, *Great Britain and China*, p. 211.

40 Chiang Meng-yin, *Ti-erh-tz'u ya-p'ien chan-cheng* (Peking, 1965), p. 58.

41 279A.5.9. Proposal to attack British warships (1856).

42 Chiang, *Ti-erh-tz'u*, pp. 57–8. Similar incidents were also recorded in D. Bonner-Smith and E. W. R. Lumby, *The Second China War 1856–60* (London, 1954).

43 Parkes Papers, Bowring–Parkes, 2 Nov. 1856.

44 *Ibid.* 5 Nov. 1856.

45 MS Clar. Dep. C57. Bowring–Clarendon, 20 Nov. 1856.

46 *Ibid.* 14 Nov. 1856.

47 Morse, *International Relations*, pp. 430 and 435.

48 MS Clar. Dep. C71. Bowring–Clarendon, 15 Jan. 1857.

49 Ryl. Eng. MS 1228/169. Bowring–Edgar Bowring, 22 Dec. 1856.

50 Parkes Papers, Bate–Mrs Parkes, 30 Dec. 1856.

51 MS Clar. Dep. C71. Bowring–Clarendon, 15 Feb. 1857.

52 Ryl. Eng. MS 1228/173. Bowring–Edgar Bowring, 24 Jan. 1857.

53 *Ibid.* 15 Feb. 1857.

54 44.15. Eleven documents concerning the war with the British (1856–7).

55 Ryl. Eng. MS 1228/170. Bowring–Edgar Bowring, 15 Jan. 1857.

56 *Ibid.*

57 Parkes Papers, Bate–Mrs Parkes, 30 Nov. 1856, 31 Jan., 23 Feb., 30 March 1857. Newgate and Pentonville were two large prisons in Britain.

58 *Ibid.* Wednesday night (n.d.).

59 Ryl. Eng. MS 1230/23. Wade's report on Chinese papers captured on 1 June 1857.

60 *Ibid.*

61 253A.4.10A, 10B, 10D; 327.5.31; 138.3.24. Intelligence reports (1857).

62 137.1.3. Proclamation by all the gentry of Hsin-an, 19 Dec. 1856.

230 Notes to pages 181–5

63 112.3.22. Ch'en Kuei-chi to Yeh (1857).
64 F.O. 17.267. Desp. 181, Incl. Wade–Bowring, 14 April 1857.
65 *Ibid.* Desp. 178, 11 April 1857.
66 112.3.22. Ch'en Kuei-chi to Yeh (1857).
67 MS Clar. Dep. C57. Bowring–Clarendon, 30 Dec. 1856.
68 Ryl. Eng. MS 1228/170. Bowring–Edgar Bowring, 10 Jan. 1857.
69 MS Clar. Dep. C71. Bowring–Clarendon, 11 Jan; *ibid.* 12 Feb. 1857.
70 Ryl. Eng. MS 1228/172. Bowring–Edgar Bowring, 20 Jan. 1857.
71 *Ibid.*; cf. also *ibid.* 16 and 24 July, 1 and 7 Aug., 9 Sept., 13, 16 and 25 Oct.,
   25 Nov. 1857; also *ibid.* 14 Jan. 1858. MS Clar. Dep. C85, Bowring–
   Clarendon 19 May 1858. Ryl. Eng. MS 1230/262. Draft biography of Sir
   John Bowring.
72 Ryl. Eng. MS 1230/211. Lane–Bowring, 30 March 1857.
73 Parkes Papers, Winchester–Parkes, 20 Dec, 1856.
74 325.4.12. Intelligence report from Hong Kong (1857).
75 F.O. 17.267, Desp. 181. Incl., Ch'an Tsz to Ch'an Kwei-tsik [sic]
   5 Feb. 1857.
76 F.O. 17.267, Bowring–Clarendon. Desp. 181, 14 April 1857.
77 Ryl. Eng. MS 1228/175. Bowring–Edgar Bowring, 15 Feb. 1857.
78 137.1.2. Proclamation of the gentry of Tung-kuan (1857).
79 F.O. 17.267, Bowring–Clarendon. Desp. 168, 7 April 1857. A copy of the
   pamphlet was enclosed in Bowring's despatch.
80 279A.5.8. Proclamation of the population of Kwangtung (1857).
81 327.5.97. Intelligence report, 19 June 1857.
82 Chiang, *Ti-erh-tz'u*, p. 56.
83 112.3.30. Two memoranda from Hsü and Yeh to the emperor (1849).
84 112.5.7; 253A.4.17; 279A.5.6, 10, 12; 378B.3.2. Documents concerning
   smuggling (1856–7).
85 112.4.20. Evidence given in a case of tea smuggling (April 1857).
86 279A.5.10. A proposal to halt smuggling (late 1856).
87 Morse, *International Relations*, p. 336.
88 F.O. 17.267, Desp. 183, Incl., Robertson–Bowring, 1 April 1857.
89 F.O. 17.268, Desp. 277, Incl., Robertson–Bowring, 28 April 1857.
90 Cf. IWSM HF 15.11a. Imperial edict, 23 April 1857 and IWSM 16.35
   Imperial edict, 13 Sept. 1857.
91 Ryl. Eng. MS 1228/184. Bowring–Edgar Bowring, 17 May 1857.
92 Morse, *International Relations*, pp. 436–7.
93 See chap. 7.
94 MS Clar. Dep. C69. Cabinet, Jan.–April. The subsequent debate in
   Parliament and election are deliberately omitted here because they bear no
   direct relevance to Yeh's conduct in the war.
95 MS Clar. Dep. C71, Elgin–Clarendon, 22 June 1857.
96 Costin, *Great Britain and China*, pp. 234–5.
97 The French ground for intervention was the killing of a missionary, Père
   Chapdelaine, in Kwangsi (see Huang, 'Viceroy Yeh', *HJAS*6.1, Appendix
   4). Legally this was a breach of extraterritorial rights, but the victim had
   disobeyed treaty stipulations by having gone into the interior of China.
   Furthermore, according to the Chinese case, he was disguised as a Chinese,
   captured in the company of rebels, and had been involved in a revolt.
98 253A.3.91. Ten suggestions for the defence of Canton (1857).
99 Costin, *Great Britain and China*, pp. 235–9.
100 F.O. 17.250, Bowring–Clarendon Desp. 280, 11 Sept. 1856.
101 Kan-t'ang tree.

102 327.2.3. Two letters from gentry members in Kwangsi to Yeh (1856). Translation by present author.
103 MS Clar. Dep. C57. Bowring–Clarendon, 13 Dec. 1856.
104 Ryl. Eng. MS 1228/199. Bowring–Edgar Bowring, 14 and 15 Oct. 1857.
105 253A.4.13. Financial report for an unspecified period of three months (1857).
106 253A.3.71 and 253A.5.53. Reports on savings of defence expenditure (1857).
107 112.3.30. Hsü and Yeh to emperor (1849).
108 MS Clar. Dep. C85. Bowring–Clarendon, 9 Jan. 1858.
109 MS Clar. Dep. C71. Bowring–Clarendon, 28 Dec. 1857.
110 Cooke, *China*, p. 343.
111 Morse, *International Relations*, p. 501.
112 Chiang, *Ti-erh-ts'u*, pp. 100–3.
113 Ryl. Eng. MS 1230/62. Seymour–Bowring, 3 Jan. 1858.
114 Ryl. Eng. MS 1230/67. *The Daily Press*, 6 Jan. 1858.
115 Bundle 2h (India) General Correspondence 1858, Admiralty, 29 March 1858, Incl., Elgin–Gros, 24 Jan. 1858. (Cf. also L/PS/5. Vol. 164, Secret Letters from India.)
116 *Ibid.* Elgin–Seymour, 11 Feb. 1858. The year before, there was a great scare of a massacre of the English communities by the Chinese in the Straits Settlement (MS Clar. Dep. C71. Elgin–Clarendon, 19 June 1857).
117 Hsieh, 'Yeh-hsiang'.
118 *Ibid.*
119 *Tung-kuan hsien-chih* 35.11a. The Chinese version is cited in Huang, 'Viceroy Yeh', *HJAS* 6.1 (1941), 73. The translation is by the present author. The original contains a double pun; the character *yeh* can mean either the family name Yeh or leaf, and 'early spring' is a literal translation of a supposed alias of Yeh's father.
120 Cf. Hsieh, 'Yeh-hsiang'; Lu Ch'in-ch'ih, 'Ying-Fa lien-chün chan-chü Kuang-chou shih-mo', *Chung-kuo chin-tai-shih lun-ts'ung* 1 (1958), 74–109.
121 Ryl. Eng. MS 1228/175. Bowring–Edgar Bowring, 15 Feb. 1857.
122 Except perhaps the small appeasement group led by Ch'i-ying and Mu-chang-a.

Part six: Yeh's last days

Chapter 11 *Exile in India*

1 Ryl. Eng. MS 1230/84. *The Hong Kong Register*, 16 Feb. 1858.
2 *Ibid.*
3 *Ibid.* 146, Alabaster–Bowring, 2 March 1858.
4 IWSM 41.27. Imperial edict, 7 Aug. 1859.
5 Ryl. Enf. MS 1230/147. Alabaster–Bowring, 17 March 1858.
6 *Ibid.*
7 *Ibid.*
8 L/PS/5, Vol. 167, Herbert–Beadon, 3 May 1858.
9 This poem is recorded in Hsieh, 'Yeh-hsiang'. Translation by the present author.
10 This is a literal translation of the name Chen-hai Tower, which in the text can be an allusion to the one at Canton or Fort William.

11 Fan Chung-yen, a famous scholar-general of the Northern Sung dynasty (960-1126), who successfully curbed the aggression of a neighbouring state called Hsi Hsia.
12 See notes to the same verse cited on p. 168.
13 During Yeh's imprisonment at Fort William, and artist came to draw his portrait (L/PS/5, Vol. 167, Herbert–Beadon, 5 April 1858).
14 Ryl. Eng. MS 1230/147. Alabaster–Bowring, 17 March 1858; Cooke, *China*, pp. 425–6.
15 Yeh was moved in May 1858 to a two-storied building in Tollygung in the suburbs of Calcutta (L/PS/5, Vol. 167, Herbert–Beadon, 3 May 1858).
16 Range 202–3, Herbert's reports, *passim.*
17 Cooke, *China*, pp. 429–30.
18 *Ibid.*
19 L/PS/5, Vol. 164, Herbert–Beadon, 15 March 1858; Range 203, Herbert–Simson, 14 Feb. 1859; Range 203, Payne–Herbert, 10 April 1859.
20 Range 203, Payne–Herbert, 10 April 1859.
21 Range 203, Herbert–Beadon, 11 April 1859.
22 A police guard of five had been planted at the gate of Yeh's residence since he moved in (L/PS/5, Vol. 157, Herbert–Beadon, 19 March 1858).
23 Range 203, Herbert–Beadon, 12 Nov. 1858. This happened for a month in Nov.–Dec. 1858. when Herbert had a surgical operation.
24 Range 203, Herbert–Beadon, 15 April 1859.
25 Range 203, Herbert–Beadon, 29 March 1859.
26 *Ssu-kuo hsin-tang, Ying-kuo tang*, no. 1275, 7 Aug. 1859.
27 Cooke, *China*, p. 401.
28 Range 203, Herbert–Beadon, 1 May 1859.
29 Range 202–3, *passim.*
30 Range 203, Simson–Herbert, 5 May 1859.
31 Range 203, Payne–Herbert, 10 April 1859.
32 *Ibid.*
33 Cooke, *China*, p. 405.
34 Letters, clothes and money were sent to him by his relatives and Howqua in Canton by steamer. Cf. L/PS/5, Vol. 167, Russel & Co.–Ashburner & Co.–Herbert, 7 May 1858; *ibid.* Herbert–Beadon, 11 May 1858; *ibid.* Jardine–Herbert, 10 May 1858.
35 The original makes allusion to the two brothers, Po I and Shu Ch'i, who refused to eat the grain of the new dynasty, Chou (1122–255 B.C.), and consequently died of hunger.
36 The original means an alien wind instrument, probably an Indian flute.
37 A particular kind of crow which, according to legend, feeds its parents when they become too old to go and search for food by themselves.
38 The poem is recorded in Hsieh, 'Yeh-hsiang'. Translation by the present author.

Conclusion

1 Chang, *Commissioner Lin*, p. 216.
2 *Ibid.* p. 214.
3 *Ibid.* p. 215.
4 *Ibid.* p. 216.

GLOSSARY[1]

A-niang-hsieh　阿娘鞋
Amoy　廈門
An-ho Chü　安和局
An-liang Chü　安良局
Anhwei　安徽
Anking　安慶

Ch'an-tsung　禪宗
Chang　張
Chang Chin-chien　張金鑑
Chang Ching-hsiu　張敬修
Chang Ch'ung-k'o　張崇恪
Chang Fei　張芾
Chang Pai-k'uei　張百揆
Chang-yüan hsüeh-shih　掌院學士
Ch'ang-chou　長洲
Ch'ang-ch'un hsien-kuan　長春仙館
Ch'ang-lo　長樂
Ch'ang-ning　長寧
ch'ang-p'ing-ts'ang　長平倉
Changsha　長沙
Chao　趙
Chao Ch'ang-ling　趙長齡
Chao-ch'ing　肇慶
Chao-lo　肇羅
Ch'ao-ch'iao　潮橋
Ch'ao-chou　潮州
Ch'ao-liang-t'ing　潮糧廳
Ch'ao-yün-t'ung　潮運同
Ch'e　車
Ch'e Jen-chung　車任重
Chekiang　浙江
chen　鎮
Chen-hai (Tower)　鎮海（樓）
Chen-k'ou　鎮口
Ch'en Chao-ch'ing　陳肇慶
Ch'en-chou　郴州
Ch'en Chi　陳吉
Ch'en Chin-kang　陳金缸
Ch'en Erh　陳二
Ch'en Hsien-liang　陳顯良
Ch'en K'ai　陳開

Ch'en Kuei-chi　陳桂籍
Ch'en Kuo-hui　陳國輝
Ch'en Mei-hsiu　陳梅脩
Ch'en Niang-k'ang　陳娘康
Ch'en Sung　陳松
Ch'en-ts'un　陳村
Cheng Ch'eng-kung　鄭成功
Cheng Hsi-ch'i　鄭錫琦
cheng-kao-fang　正稿房
cheng-pen-fang　正本房
Ch'eng　程
Ch'eng Chao-kuei　程兆桂
Ch'eng-hai　澄海
Ch'eng-hua　成化
chi-mi　羈縻
Ch'i Chün-tsao　祁寯藻
Ch'i-shui　蘄水
Ch'i Su-tsao　祁宿藻
ch'i-t'ou　旗頭
Ch'i-ying　耆英
chia　甲
Chia-ch'ing　嘉慶
Chia-ho　嘉禾
Chia-hui-t'ang　嘉會堂
　p'ing-an chia-hsin　平安家信
Chia-ying-chou　嘉應州
chiang-chiang chih ts'ai　將將之材
chiang-chün　將軍
Chiang-hua　江華
Chiang Kuo-lin　江國霖
Chiang-men　江門
chiang-ping chih ts'ai　將兵之材
Chiang-ts'un　江村
Chiang Wen-ch'ing　蔣文慶
chiao-lu　教錄
chiao-yü　教諭
Chieh-yang　揭陽
chien-sheng　監生
ch'ien　錢
ch'ien-liang kao-fang　錢糧稿房
Ch'ien-lung　乾隆
chih-fu　知府

[1] The transliteration follows the Wade–Giles system except for well-known Post Office spellings, e.g. Kwangtung, Nanking. In the case of historical figures of the Ch'ing period, I have adopted the form of a name used in A. W. Hummel, *Eminent Chinese of the Ch'ing period*, e.g. I have used the form Wu Ch'ung-yüeh, rather than Wu Ch'ung-yao. When in doubt over the pronunciation of a character, I have checked this against the version given in *Kuo-yü tz'ŭ-tien*.

chih-hsien　知縣
chih-kuan-chih　職官志
chih-kuan chih kuan　治官之官
chih-li chou　直隸州
chih-shih　值事
chih-shih chih kuan　治事之官
chih-ying-so　支應所
Chihli　直隸
chin-shih　進士
Chin-t'ien　金田
Ch'in-chou　欽州
Ch'ing　清
Ch'ing-p'ing　青平
Ch'ing-Ying　清英
Ch'ing-yüan　清遠
Chiu-chiang　九江
Ch'iu Ta　邱大
Ch'iung-chou　瓊州
Cho Ping-t'ien　卓秉恬
chou　州
Chou　周
Chou Ch'un²　周春
Chou T'ien-chüeh　周天爵
Chou Tou-p'i-ch'un²　周豆皮春
Chu Hsi　朱熹
Chu Kuo-hsiung　朱國雄
Chu-liao-hsü　竹料墟
chu-shih　主事
Chu Tzu-i　朱子儀
Chu-tzu wai-chi　朱子外紀
chü　局
chü-jen　舉人
Ch'ü-chiang　曲江
Ch'üan-ch'ing　全慶
Ch'üan-chou　全州
Chuang　壯
chün　軍
chün-cheng　軍政
Chün-chi Ch'ü　軍機處
chün-ch'i-chü　軍器局
chün-chuang-chü　軍裝局
chün-chuang-so　軍裝所
chün-hsü-chü　軍需局
Ch'ün-tai-lu　裙帶路
Chung Ju-ch'i　鍾汝騏
chung-shu　中書

Fan Chung-yen　范仲淹
Fang Wan　方晚
fei-shou　匪首
fei-wu　匪屋
Feng　馮
Feng A-mou　馮阿茂
Feng-ch'uan　封川
Feng Chung-ju　馮仲儒
Feng-shun　豐順
Feng Yün-shan　馮雲山

Fo-kang　佛岡
Fo-ling-shih　佛嶺市
Fo-shan　佛山
fu　府
Fu-chou　福州
Fu-hsing　福興
fu-kao-fang　副稿房
fu-pen-fang　副本房
fu-piao　撫標
fu-ping　府兵
fu-tu-t'ung　副都統
Fukien　福建

Hai-chu (Fort)　海珠（砲台）
　i.e. Dutch Folly
Hai-feng　海豐
Hai T'ing-ch'en　海廷琛
Hai-yang　海陽
Hakka　客家
Han　漢
Han　韓
Han (River)　韓（江）
Han-chung　漢中
Han-lin　翰林
Han Shih-wen　韓師文
Han-yang　漢陽
Heng-chou　橫州
Heng-tang　橫檔
Ho Ch'ang-chü　何長琚
Ho Liu　何六
Ho Ming-k'o　何名科
Ho-nan (Island)　河南（島）
Ho-p'ing　和平
Ho Po-fen　何博份
Ho-p'u　合浦
Ho-shan　鶴山
Ho-shen　何珅
Ho Ying-ch'un　何應春
Ho-yüan　河源
Ho Yüan-hsün　何元勳
Hoppo　粤海關監督
Howqua　伍崇曜
　(Wu Ch'ung-yüeh)
Hsi Hsia　西夏
Hsi-hsiang　西鄉
Hsi-hu (Academy)　西湖（書院）
Hsi-nan　西南
Hsi-ning　西寧
Hsia　夏
Hsiang Chiang　湘江
Hsiang Jung　向榮
Hsiang-lin　祥麟
Hsiang-shan　香山
hsiang-shih　鄉試
Hsiang Shu　向戍
hsiang-yüeh　鄉約
Hsiao Ch'ao-kuei　蕭朝貴

---

² Chou Ch'un and Chou Tou-p'i-ch'un are probably the same person.

Hsiao-heng-tang　小橫檔
Hsiao-lan　小欖
Hsiao Ting-an　蕭定安
hsieh　協
Hsieh Fu-ch'eng　薛福成
Hsieh Hsiao-chuang　謝效莊
hsieh-li chih-shih　協理值事
Hsieh San　謝三
Hsieh Yü-han　謝玉漢
hsien　縣
Hsien-feng　咸豐
hsin　汛
Hsin-an　新安
Hsin-chou (Shansi)　忻州（山西）
Hsin-hsing　新興
Hsin-hui　新會
Hsin-i　信宜
Hsin-ning　新寧
Hsin-p'u　新鋪
Hsin-tsao　新造
　(Blenheim Reach)
Hsing-an　興安
Hsing-jen　興仁
Hsing Pu　刑部
Hsiu-jen　修仁
hsiu-ts'ai　秀才
Hsiung-nu　匈奴
Hsü A-mei　許阿梅
Hsü Hsiang-kuang　許祥光
Hsü Kuang-chin　徐廣縉
Hsü-wen　徐聞
Hsü Yen-ku　許延毂
hsüeh-cheng　學正
hsüeh-hsiao　學校
hsün　旬
Hsün-chou　潯州
hsün-fu　巡撫
Hu　胡
Hu Feng-tan　胡鳳丹
Hu Huang-mao-wu　胡黃毛五
Hu-men　虎門
　(The Bogue)
Hu Pu　戶部
Hu Shih　胡適
Hua-hsien　花縣
Hua T'ing-chieh　華廷傑
Huai-an　淮安
Huai River　淮河
Huang Chia-mu　黃嘉謨
Huang Hsien-piao　黃賢彪
Huang K'ai-kuang　黃開廣
Huang Ta　黃大
Huang Ta-jung　黃大榮
Hui-ch'ao-chia　惠潮嘉
Hui-ch'ing　惠慶
Hui-chou　惠州
Hui-lai　惠來
hui-shih　會試

Hui-tien Kuan　會典館
Hunan　湖南
Hung Hsiu-ch'üan　洪秀全
Hung Ming-hsiang　洪名香
huo-yao-chü　火藥局
Hupeh　湖北

Jen-hua　仁化
Jen Wei-ch'i　任爲奇
Ju-chia　儒家
Ju-chiao　儒教
Ju-yüan　乳源
Jui-chou　瑞州

K'ai-chien　開建
K'ai-p'ing　開平
Kan Hsien　甘先
Kan-t'ang (tree)　甘棠（樹）
K'ang-hsi　康熙
k'ang-liang　抗糧
Kansu　甘肅
Kao-chou　高州
Kao-lan　高欄
Kao-lien　高廉
Kao-ming　高明
Kiangsi　江西
Kiangsu　江蘇
Ku Ping-chang　顧炳章
kua-hao　掛號
Kuan　關
(Emperor) Kuan　關帝
Kuan-ch'iao　官橋
Kuan Chü　關巨
Kuan-yin Shan　觀音山
Kuan-yin-t'ang p'u　觀音堂鋪
Kuang-chou　廣州
Kuang-chou-fu　廣州府
Kuang-liang-t'ing　廣糧廳
Kuang-ning　廣寧
Kuang-shao-nan-lien　廣韶南連
Kuei-hsien　貴縣
Kuei-lin　桂林
Kuei-shan　歸善
K'un-shou　崑壽
kung-chü　公局
kung-sheng　貢生
kung-t'ien　公田
kung-yüan　貢院
K'ung Chi-an　孔繼安
Kuo　郭
Kuo-shih Kuan　國史館
Kuo-tzu Chien　國子監
Kwangsi　廣西
Kwangtung　廣東
Kweichow　貴州

Lai-ts'un　來存
Lan-chou　蘭州

Lan Pin 藍鑌
lao-ch'eng 老城
Lei-ch'iung 雷瓊
li 里
Li 李
Li (Hai-nan Island) 黎
Li Chang-yü 李章煜
Li Ch'eng-tung 李成棟
Li Fan 立凡
Li-hsüeh 理學
Li Hung-chang 李鴻章
Li Pei-she 李北社
Li Po 李白
Li Pu 吏部
Li Pu 禮部
Li Shih-ch'ing 李士青
Li Shih-k'uei 李士奎
Li-shui 溧水
Li Tan-yen-jen 李單眼壬
Li Tun-yeh 李敦業
Li Tzu-hua 黎子驊
Li Wen-mao 李文茂
Li Yüan-pao-k'o 李元寶壳
Liang 梁
Liang Chiang 兩江
Liang Chien-fu 梁建富
Liang Erh-shih-pa 梁二十八
Liang Kuang 兩廣
Liang Kuo-ting 梁國定
Liang Ming-t'ai 梁明太
liang-t'ing 糧廳
Liang Yüan 兩院
lieh-chuan 列傳
lien-chieh t'uan-lien 聯街團練
Lien-chou (north Kwangtung) 連州
Lien-chou (west Kwangtung) 廉州
Lien-p'ing, 連平
Lien-shan 連山
Lien Ssu-hu 練四虎
likin 釐金
Lin-chiang 臨江
Lin-ch'ing 臨清
Lin Fu-sheng 林福盛
Lin Kuang-lung 林洸瀧
Lin Tse-hsü 林則徐
Ling-shan 靈山
Ling Shih-pa 凌十八
Liu Heng-t'ai 劉恆泰
Liu-ho ts'ung-t'an 六合叢談
Liu Hsün 劉潯
Liu Pa 劉八
Liu Ping-yüan 劉炳垣
Liu Sheng 劉陞
Liu T'ing-chang 劉廷章
Lo-ch'ang 樂昌
Lo-ching 羅鏡
Lo-ting 羅定
Lü Tung-pin 呂洞賓

Lung-ch'uan 龍川
Lung-men 龍門

Ma Pin 馬斌
Mei-ling 梅嶺
Miao 苗
mien-szu chih-chao 免死執照
ming-lun-t'ang 明倫堂
mou 畝
Mu-chang-a 穆彰阿
mu-pin 幕賓
Mu-te-li (*ssu*) 慕德里（司）
mu-yu 幕友

Na-ch'in 那芹
Na-fu 那扶
Na-p'eng 那彭
Nan Mountains 南山
Nan-ch'ang 南昌
Nan-hai 南海
Nan-hsiung 南雄
Nan-ling 南嶺
Nan-shao-lien 南韶連
Nanking 南京
Nei Ko 內閣
Nei-t'ing 內廷
Nei-wu Fu 內務府
ni-shou 逆首
Ninety-six Villages 九十六鄉
Ningpo 寧波
Niu-lan-kang 牛欄岡

o-cheng 額征
Ou Yang-ch'üan 歐陽泉

pa-ku-wen 八股文
p'ai 牌
p'ai-chüan 派捐
P'an-yü 番禺
pao-chia 保甲
Pao-ho Tien 保和殿
Pao-te 保德
P'eng 彭
P'eng Wen-chang 彭蘊章
pin 稟
ping-fang 兵房
ping-mu 兵目
ping-pei-tao 兵備道
Ping Pu 兵部
P'ing-nan 平南
P'ing-ting 平定
Po I 伯夷
Po-kuei 柏貴
Po-lo 博羅
Po-pai 博白
pu 埠
P'u-chi T'ang 普濟堂
Punti 本地

Sai-shang-a 賽尚阿
San Fan 三藩
San-shui 三水
San-yüan 三遠
Seng-ko-lin-ch'in 僧格林沁
Sha-chiao 沙角
Sha-wan 沙灣
Shan-t'ou 汕頭
 (Swatow)
Shansi 山西
Shao-chou 韶州
she-hsüeh 社學
She-t'ou (Bay) 蛇頭（灣）
Shen Ti-hui 沈棣輝
sheng-ho 省河
sheng-se-k'o 聲色科
sheng-tz'u 生祠
sheng-yüan 生員
Shensi 陝西
shih 石
Shih-ch'i 石歧
Shih-ching 石井
shih-ch'üan wu-kung 十全武功
Shih-feng-pao 石峰堡
Shih-hsing 始興
Shih-lung 石龍
Shih P'u 史樸
shih-tu 侍讀
Shou 壽
shu-chi-shih 庶吉士
Shu Ch'i 叔齊
shu-yüan 書院
Shuang-ling 雙齡
shui-li 水利
Shun-te 順德
Shun-t'ien fu-yin 順天府尹
Shuo-p'ing 朔平
ssu 司
Ssu-hui 四會
Ssu-ma 司馬
Ssu-pao 四堡
Su 蘇
Su A-ch'eng 蘇阿成
Su-chou 蘇州
Su-ch'ung-a 蘇崇阿
Su Ning-san 蘇凝三
Su Wu 蘇武
Sun 孫
Sung 宋
Sung Ch'i-ta 宋七大
Swatow 汕頭
Szechwan 四川

ta-chi 大計
Ta-heng-tang 大橫檔
ta-hsüeh-shih 大學士
Ta-kang 大岡
Ta-li 大瀝

Ta-liang 大良
Ta-pu 大埔
Ta-shih 大石
Ta-t'ung 大同
Ta-yu Ts'ang 大有倉
Ta-yü 大庾
Tai-chou 代州
T'ai-p'ing-hsü 太平墟
Taiwan 台灣
Tan-chou 儋州
t'ang 堂
T'ang 唐
tao 道
Tao-chia 道家
Tao-chiao 道教
Tao-chou 道州
Tao-hsüeh 道學
Tao-kuang 道光
tao-li 道理
tao-t'ai 道台
T'ao An-jen 陶安仁
T'ao Yü-wen 陶煜文
Te-ch'ing-chou 德慶州
Teng Shih-fu 鄧十富
Ti Huo-ku 翟火姑
ti-pao 地保
T'i-jen Ko 體仁閣
t'i-tiao-chü 提調局
t'i-tu 提督
tien-shih 殿試
T'ien-li Chiao 天理教
t'ing 廳
Ts'ai-t'ang(*hsin*) 彩堂（汛）
Ts'ao-ch'ang (*hsin*) 草場（汛）
Ts'ao Li-t'ai 曹履泰
Tseng-ch'eng 增城
Tseng Ch'i 曾琪
Tseng Kuo-fan 曾國藩
Tseng T'ing-hsiang 曾廷相
Tseng-tzu 曾子
Ts'ui 催
Tsung-jen Fu 宗人府
tsung-pan i-wu 總辦夷務
tsung-tu 總督
Tsung Yüan-shun 宗元醇
Ts'ung-hua 從化
Tsungli Yamen 總理衙門
Tu-ch'a Yüan 都察院
tu-liang-tao 督糧道
tu-piao 督標
Tu Ta-chiang 杜大降
tui-chang 隊長
t'un 屯
Tung-an (*hsien*) 東安（縣）
Tung-an (Fort) 東安（砲台）
tung-chüan-fang 東卷房
tung-kao-fang 東稿房
Tung Ko 東閣

Tung-ku 東固
Tung-kuan 東莞
T'ung-jen she-hsüeh 同仁社學
t'ung-p'an 通判
t'ung-sheng 童生
T'ung-sheng 同昇
t'ung-shih 童試
T'ung-wen Kuan 同文館
tzu 咨

Wan 萬
Wang 王
Wang Chün 王浚
Wang Han-ch'iao 王漢橋
Wang Hsi-ts'ung 王錫從
Wang-hsia 望廈
Wang Pao-jun 汪報潤
Wang T'ing-chen 汪廷珍
Wei Cheng 韋正
wei-pan i-wu 委辦夷務
Wei Tso-pang 衛佐邦
wei-yüan 委員
wen (ch'ien) 文（錢）
Wen-ch'ing 文慶
Wen-hua Tien 文華殿
Wen-yüan Ko 文淵閣
Weng-yüan 翁源
Wo-jen 倭仁
Wu A-jen 吳阿認
Wu-ch'ang 武昌
Wu Ch'ang-shou 吳昌壽
Wu-chou 梧州
Wu Chün 吳均
Wu Chung-shu 吳忠恕
Wu Ch'ung-yüeh 伍崇曜
  (Howqua)
Wu Hsien-shih 吳顯時
Wu-hsüan Ssu 武選司
Wu San 吳三

Wu-ying Tien 武英殿
Wu Yüan-yu 吳元猷

Yang Ch'ang-ssu 楊昌泗
Yang Mou-chien 楊懋建
Yang-shan 陽山
Yao 瑤
yeh 葉
Yeh Chi-wen 葉繼雯
Yeh Chia-hui-t'ang 葉嘉會堂
Yeh Chih-shen 葉志詵
Yeh En-i 葉恩頤
Yeh Ming-ch'en 葉名琛
Yeh Ming-feng 葉名灃
Yeh T'ing-fang 葉廷芳
yen-chü 讞局
Yen P'in-yao 顏品瑤
Yen-p'ing 雁平
Yen-t'ang 燕塘
yin 蔭
ying 營
Ying-te 英德
ying-yü 盈餘
yu-shih-lang 右侍郎
Yü-ch'ien 裕謙
Yü-tieh Kuan 玉牒館
Yüan-chou 袁州
Yüeh Hai-kuan 粵海關
Yüeh hai-kuan chien-tu 粵海關監督
Yüeh-hsiu 粵秀
Yüeh-hua 越華
Yüeh-yen hsiao-ti 粵鹽銷地
Yung-an 永安
Yung-cheng 雍正
Yung-feng Ts'ang 永豐倉
Yünnan 雲南

Zen (sect of Buddhism) 禪宗

BIBLIOGRAPHIC ESSAY

In this bibliographic essay I shall first describe the sources I have used, and then make some remarks about the previous historiography of the subject of this book.

A major consignment of documents from the British Legation in Peking was deposited in the Public Record Office in 1958, in the manner described in the Foreword. A preliminary list of all the documents was drawn up in 1963 by Chang Hsing-pao and Eric Grinsted. Since 1966, David Pong has been engaged in separating Yeh's papers, known collectively as the Canton Archive, from the rest, and cataloguing them. My work since 1968 has in many respects complemented his. However, for the analysis I have made of the authorship, dates and significance of the documents, I must take full responsibility, as on certain points they differ from Dr Pong.

Many of the documents of the Canton Archive are in bad repair, but they are for the most part readily legible. They are written on rice-paper; official documents are written in formal Chinese script, but private letters and draft letters and reports are in 'grass' or 'cursive' script, i.e. in hastily written and highly simplified characters, the deciphering of which requires a high level of expertise in Chinese calligraphy. Some of the documents require a knowledge of the peculiarities of the Cantonese dialect. In some cases, geographical references in the documents will cause problems for those without an intimate knowledge of the Canton delta. The Archive comprises all manner of Yeh's papers: memoranda and reports from subordinate officials, military officers and intelligence agents, proposals from his private secretariat, petitions from the gentry, letters and instructions from the emperor and courtiers and Yeh's draft reports to them, official and private letters from colleagues in other provinces and Yeh's draft replies; drafts and copies of communications to British authorities, correspondence with his family and friends.

I have also made use of the 'Peking Gazette', copies of which accompanied the Canton Archive in the papers from the British Legation, but which are now in the British Museum. This Gazette appeared periodically, usually once or twice a month, from the 1820s onwards, and consisted of the emperor's edicts to and memoranda from all his high officials. Until mid-century they were hand-written by the imperial clerks, then they were printed on wooden blocks. They were originally distributed to high officials, as a sort of newsletter of what was happening in the empire. This near-complete set of Gazettes is a source superior to the 'Veritable Records', which were edited and selective compositions made by official scholars to describe the reign of an emperor after his death. The 'Veritable Records' of the Ch'ing dynasty were rarely available until reprinted in Taiwan in the 1960s, but they are now a convenient compendium of more important official documents. The *Chou-pan i-wu shi-mo* ('A Complete Account of the Management of Foreign Affairs'), also reprinted recently in Taiwan, contains edicts and memorials on foreign affairs which were often not included in the 'Veritable Records'. I have used the far more extensive Peking Gazette to supplement these printed collections.

Contemporary local histories, written by the gentry and usually sponsored by the local government, have illuminated the activities of local officials and gentry. I have found the *Ssu-kuo hsin-tang* ('New Archives concerning Our Relations with England, Russia, France and America'), a collection of foreign policy documents by Taiwan scholars, a convenient compilation.

Apart from the well-known Foreign Office documents in the Public Record Office (F.O. 17, 228, 233), I have used hitherto untouched documents in the India Office Library, which bear on Yeh's captivity in India. I have drawn on the following private collections.

Bowring Papers. Letters to his sons in England, letters to Bowring from his superiors, and Bowring's press-cuttings from Hong Kong newspapers about the *Arrow* War and its aftermath in China and Hong Kong (1849–60).

Clarendon Papers. Correspondence with Palmerston, with his permanent Under-Secretary Hammond, and letters from Bowring and other parties interested in the Far East (1854–7).

Davis Papers. Letters to Sir Francis Davis, and his miscellaneous papers (1830s–1860s).

Matheson Papers. An incomplete collection of correspondence between the Hong Kong management and representatives in the five treaty ports of the firm of Jardine, Matheson and Company. The most important letters for this study were those passing almost daily to and from the representative in Canton (1840–60).

Palmerston Papers. Private letters from Bowring (1849–53).

Parkes Papers. Letters from Captain Bate, Bowring, Clarendon and others (1840–60).

These are the major sources, Chinese and British, which have been used to supplement and interpret the Canton Archive.

Most books on the *Arrow* War and Anglo-Chinese relations in this period have tended to ignore the domestic context in which Chinese officials responsible for foreign affairs were operating, and which heavily influenced their decisions. This is true of books by well-known scholars such as H. B. Morse, W. C. Costin, E. Holt, and D. Hurd, and by Chinese historians such as Wei Chien-yu, Fang Shih-ming and Chiang Meng-yin (see bibliography). Indeed, the only Chinese account of conditions in Kwangtung in this period is given by Chien Yu-wen in connection with the Red Turban Rebellion in his book on the Taipings, *T'ai-p'ing t'ien-kuo ch'üan-shih* ('A complete History of the Taiping Rebellion'). The only attempt to relate China's foreign relations to her domestic situation was made by Frederick Wakeman in *Strangers at the Gate*. Wakeman, however, relied heavily on Foreign Office records, which give a very incomplete and sometimes misleading picture of developments in South China; and in several instances this has led to serious errors in his account of diplomatic relations too.

By using the combination of sources described above, and by studying the interplay of domestic and foreign policy, I have tried to present a more complete and balanced account of Chinese history and Anglo-Chinese relations in this period.

As for Yeh the man, we have to be contented with inferences because he has left us with no written work of his own (except the two poems translated in chapter 11).

BIBLIOGRAPHY

Archives

Foreign Office Archives: Public Record Office, London
1. F.O. 682 (Canton Archive and others), papers in the Chinese language
2. F.O. 17 General correspondence, China.
3. F.O. 228 Embassy and Consular Reports.

India Office Archive: India Office Library, London
1. Political General Correspondence, Bundle 2h.
2. L/PS/5 Secret letters from Bengal, 1858.
3. L/PS/3 General Political Correspondence.
4. Range 202–3 India Political and Foreign Proceedings.

Matheson Archive: University Library, Cambridge
1. B2 General correspondence.
2. B4 Personal letters.

Peking Gazette: British Museum
1. Tao-kuang period.
2. Hsien-feng period.

Private papers

The Bowring Papers: The John Rylands University Library of Manchester Ryl. Eng. MSS 1228 Bowring's letters to his son Edgar. 1229 Bowring's letters to his son Lewis. 1330 Letters to Bowring, newspaper cuttings, miscellaneous.

The Clarendon Papers: Bodleian Library, Oxford
MSS Clar. Dep.
C9 China (1854).
C37 China (1855).
C57 China (1856).

The Davis Papers: in the possession of a descendant of Sir Francis Davis who wishes to remain anonymous

The Palmerston Papers: National Register of Archives (temporary)
Broadlands MSS GC

The Parkes Papers: University Library, Cambridge

Selected bibliography of published works

Anderson, M. A., 'Edmund Hammond: Permanent Under-Secretary of State for Foreign Affairs, 1854–73', unpublished Ph.D. thesis, University of London, 1956.

Banno, M., *China and the West, 1858–1861: the origins of the Tsungli Yamen*, Cambridge, Mass., 1964.

Kindai Chūgoku Gaikōshi Kenkyū (A study of modern Chinese diplomatic history). Tokyo, 1970.

Bartle, G. F., 'The Political Career of Sir John Bowring (1793–1872) between 1820 and 1849', unpublished M.A. thesis, University of London, 1959.

'Sir John Bowring and the *Arrow* War in China', *Bulletin of the John Rylands Library*, 43, no. 2 (1961), 293–316.

'Sir John Bowring and the Chinese and Siamese Commercial Treaties', *Bulletin of the John Rylands Library*, 44, no. 2 (1962), 286–308.

Bary, W. T. de, 'A reappraisal of Neo-Confucianism', in A. F. Wright, ed., *Studies in Chinese Thought*, pp. 81–111. Chicago, 1953.

Beal, E. G., *The Origin of Likin, 1853–64*. Cambridge, Mass., 1958.

Beasley, W. G., *The Meiji Restoration*. Stanford, Cal., 1973.

Bendix, R. and Lipset, S., eds., *Class, Status and Power: A Reader in Social Stratification*. London, 1954.

Biggerstaff, K., 'The T'ung Wen Kuan', *China Social and Political Science Review*, 18, no. 3 (1934), 307–40.

Blythe, W., *The Impact of Chinese Secret Societies in Malaya*. Oxford, 1969.

Boardman, E., *Christian Influence upon the Ideology of the Taiping Rebellion, 1851–1864*. Madison, Wis., 1952.

Bowring, Sir John, *Autobiographical Recollections of Sir John Bowring*. London, 1877.

Brine, L., *The Taiping Rebellion in China: A narrative of its rise and progress*. London, 1862.

Bruce, J. P., *Chu Hsi and his Masters*. London, 1923.

Brunnert, H. S. and Hagelstrom, V. V., *Present Day Political Organization of China*, tr. A. Beltchenko and E. E. Morgan. Taipei (reprint), 1963.

Buxbaum, D., 'Some aspects of civil procedure and practice at the trial level in Tanshui and Hsinchu from 1789 to 1895', *Journal of Asian Studies*, 30, no. 2 (1971), 255–80.

Cady, J. F., *The Roots of French Imperialism in Eastern Asia*. New York, 1954.

Callery, M. M. and Yvan, *The History of the Insurrection in China*, tr., John Oxonford. London, 1854.

Chang, Carson, *The Development of Neo-Confucian Thought*. New York, 1957.

Chang, Chin-chien, *Chung-kuo wen-kuan chih-tu shih* (The institutional history of China). Taipei, 1955.

Chang, Chung-li, *The Chinese Gentry: Studies on their Role in nineteenth-century Chinese Society*. Seattle, 1955.

The Income of the Chinese Gentry. Seattle, 1962.

Chang, Ch'un-ming, 'Ch'ing-tai te mu-chih' (Private secretaries of the Ch'ing period), *Ling-nan hsüeh-pao* (Ling-nan Journal), vol. 9, no. 2 (1950).

Chang, Hsin-pao, *Commissioner Lin and the Opium War*, Cambridge, Mass., 1964.

with Grinstead, E., *see* Grinstead.

Chang, P'ei-kang, *Kuang-hsi liang-shih wen-t'i* (The food problem in Kwangsi). Ch'ang-sha, 1938.

Chang, Shun-hui, *Chung-kuo li-shih yao-chi chieh-shao* (An introduction to important works on Chinese history). Wu-han, 1956.

Chang, T'ien-tse, *Sino-Portuguese Trade from 1514–1644: A Synthesis of Portuguese and Chinese Sources*. Leyden, 1934.

Chao, Erh-sun, *Ch'ing-shih kao* (A draft history of the Ch'ing dynasty). Mukden, 1937.

Chao, Tang-li, 'Anglo-Chinese Diplomatic Relations, 1858–70', unpublished Ph.D. thesis, University of London, 1956.

Ch'ao-chou fu-chih (Local history of Ch'ao-chou prefecture). 1775.

Chen, Chün, *Kuo-ch'ao shu-jen chi-lüeh* (Short biographies of Ch'ing calligraphers). 1908.

Chen, Han-seng, *The present Agrarian Problem in China*. Shanghai, 1933.

Agrarian Problems in Southernmost China. Shanghai, 1936.

Landlord and Peasant in China. New York, 1936.

Ch'en, Po-ta, *Chin-tai Chung-kuo ti-tsu kai-shuo*. Peking, 1949. (The English version, *A Study of Land Rent in Pre-liberation China*, was published in Peking in 1958.)

Ch'en, Te-yün, *Ku-chin jen-wu pieh-ming so-yin* (Index of aliases). Canton, 1937.

Chesneaux, J., *Secret Societies in China in the Nineteenth and Twentieth Centuries* (tr. G. Wettle). London, 1971.

ed., *Popular Movement and Secret Societies in China 1840–1950*. Stanford, Cal., 1972.

Peasants' Revolts in China 1840–1849 (tr. C. Curwen). London, 1973.

Chi, Ch'ao-ting, *Key Economic Areas in Chinese History*. London, 1936.

Ch'i-hsien-ho shang tiao-sou, pseud. 'Ying-chi-li Kuang-tung ju-ch'eng shih-mo' (A complete account of the British entry into the city of Canton), in *Yang-shih ch'ien ch'i-pai erh-shih-chiu ho-chai ts'ung-shu*, 1929.

Chia, Chih-fang, *Chin-tai Chung-kuo ching-chi she-hui* (The economy and society of modern China). Shanghai, 1949.

Chiang-hsi t'ung-chih (Local history of Kiangsi province), 1732.

Chiang, Meng-yin, *Ti-erh-tz'u ya-p'ien chan-cheng* (The Second Opium War), Peking, 1965.

Chiang, Pei-huan, 'Anglo-chinese Diplomatic Relations, 1856–60', unpublished Ph.D. thesis, University of London, 1939.

Chiang, T'ing-fu, 'The Government and Co-hong of Canton, 1839', *Chinese Social and Political Science Review*, 15, no. 4 (Jan., 1932), 602–7.

Chin-tai Chung-kuo wai-chiao shih-liao chi-yao (Selected materials on modern Chinese diplomatic history), 2 vols. Taipei (reprint), 1966.

Chien, Yu-wen, 'Yeh Ming-ch'en fou-hai chi' (A translation of W. Cooke's 'Yeh's Portrait'), *Ta-feng hsün-k'an* (Ta-feng Journal), nos. 57–9. Hong Kong, 1939–40.

T'ai-p'ing t'ien-kuo ch'üan-shih (A complete history of the Taiping Rebellion), 3 vols. Hong Kong, 1962.

The Taiping Revolutionary Movement. Yale, 1973.

Ch'ien, Chia-chü, *et. al.*, *Kuang-hsi-sheng ching-chi kai-k'uang* (The economic situation in Kwangsi). Shanghai, 1936.

Ch'ien, Mu, *Chung-kuo chin san-pai-nien hsüeh-shu shih* (A cultural history of China in the past three hundred years). Taipei, 1968.

Ch'ien, Shih-fu, *Ch'ing-chi chung-yao chih-kuan nien-piao* (Chronological table of important officials of the Ch'ing period). Peking, 1959.

Chin-tai-shih tzu-liao (Sources on modern history), compiled by the Modern History Research Institute of the Chinese Academy of Sciences, no. 2. Peking, 1956.

Ch'ing-ch'ao hsü wen-hsien t'ung-k'ao (Supplements to the Encyclopedia of the Historical Records of the Ch'ing dynasty). Shanghai, 1901.

Ch'ing-ch'ao wen-hsien t'ung-k'ao (Encyclopedia of the Historical Records of the Ch'ing dynasty). Shanghai, 1901.

Ch'ing-ch'ao yeh-shih ta-kuan (An unofficial history of the Ch'ing dynasty), by an anonymous compiler. Taipei (reprint), 1959.

Ch'ing-shih lieh-chuan (Biographies in Ch'ing history), ed. by Chung-hua shu-chü. Shanghai, 1928.

Chou, Ch'ing-yün, *Yen-fa t'ung-chih* (Salt administration). Peking, 1918.

Chou, Yü-chin, *Chung-kuo tsu-shui shih* (A history of Chinese taxation), Taipei, 1963.

Ch'ou-pan i-wu shih-mo (A complete account of the management of foreign affairs). Peiping, 1930.

Chu, Hsi, *Ssu-shu chi-chu* (Commentaries on the Four Books). Taipei (reprint), 1959.

Chu, Shih-chia, *A Catalogue of Local Histories in the Library of Congress.* Washington D.C., 1942.

Ch'ü T'ung-tsu, 'Chinese Class Structure and its Ideology', in J. K. Fairbank, ed., *Chinese Thought and Institutions*, pp. 235–50. Chicago, 1957.

Local Government in China under the Ch'ing. Cambridge, Mass., 1962.

Ch'ü, Ta-chün, *Kuang-tung hsin-yü* (New words about Kwangtung). 1700.

Chung-hua min-kuo fen-sheng hsing-shih ch'üan-t'u, ed. by the Board of Education. Peking, 1914.

Chung-kuo ts'ung-shu tsung-lu (Index to Chinese collections of books) 3 vols., compiled by Shang-hai t'u-shu kuan. Shanghai, 1959.

Cohen, P. A., 'The anti-Christian tradition in China', *Journal of Asian Studies*, 20, no. 2 (1960), 169–80.

Commercial Press, *Chung-kuo kuo-chi mao-i shih* (A history of China's foreign trade). Taipei (reprint), 1961.

Cooke, G. W., 'The Capture of Canton', *The Times*, 27 February 1858.

'Yeh's Portrait', *The Times*, 10 May 1858.

'Ex-Commissioner Yeh', *The Times*, 17 May 1858.

China: being 'The Times' special correspondence from China in the years 1857–8, with corrections and additions. London, 1858.

Costin, W. C., *Great Britain and China, 1833–1860.* Oxford, 1937.

Cranmer-Byng, J. L., *Lord Macartney's Embassy to Peking in 1793, from official Chinese documents.* Reprinted from the *Journal of Oriental Studies*, vol. 4, nos. 1–2. Hong Kong, 1961.

Downing, C. T., *The Fan-Qui in China in 1836–1837*, 3 vols. London, 1838.

Elvin, M. J., 'The Last Thousand Years of Chinese History', *Modern Asian Studies* 4, no. 2 (1970), 97–114.

'The High-level Equilibrium Trap: the Causes of the Decline of Invention in the Traditional Chinese Textile Industries', in W. E. Willmott, ed., *Economic Organization in Chinese Society.* Stanford, 1972.

The Pattern of the Chinese Past. Stanford, Cal., 1973.

Endacott, G. B., *A History of Hong Kong.* Oxford, 1958.

Fairbank, J. K., 'The Manchu Appeasement Policy of 1843', *Journal of the American Oriental Society*, vol. 14, no. 4 (1939).

'Tributary Trade and China's Relations with the West', *Far Eastern Quarterly*, 1, no. 2 (1942), 129–49.

Trade and Diplomacy on the China Coast: The opening of the treaty ports, 1842–1854. Cambridge, Mass., 1953.

'Meadow on China: A centennial review', *Far Eastern Quarterly*, 14, no. 3 (1955), 365–71.

ed., *Chinese Thought and Institutions.* Chicago, 1957.

ed., *The Chinese World Order.* Cambridge, Mass., 1968.

and Teng, Ssu-yü, 'On the Ch'ing Tributary System', *Harvard Journal of Asiatic Studies*, 6, no. 2 (1941), 135–246.

Reischauer, E. O., and Craig, A. M., *East Asia: The Modern Transformation.* Boston, 1965.

Fang, Shih-ming, *Ti-erh-tz'u ya-p'ien chan-cheng shih-hua* (The Second Opium War). Shanghai, 1956.

Fei, Hsiao-t'ung, *China's Gentry: Essays on rural-urban relations*, rev. and ed. by M. P. Redfield. Chicago, 1953.

'Peasantry and Gentry: An interpretation of Chinese social structure and its changes', in R. Bendix and S. Lipset, eds., *Class, Status and Power: A reader in social stratification*, pp. 631–50. London, 1954.

Feuerwerker, A., 'From "Feudalism" to "Capitalism" in recent historical writings from mainland China', *Journal of Asian Studies*, 18, no. 1 (1958), 107–16.

Fevour, Edward Le, *Western Enterprise in Late Ch'ing China: A selective survey of Jardine, Matheson and Company's Operations, 1842–1895.* Cambridge, Mass., 1968.

Fishbourne, Capt. E. G., *Impressions of China and the present Revolution: Its progress and prospects.* London, 1855.

Folsom, K. E., *Friends, Guests and Colleagues: The mu-fu system in the late Ch'ing period.* Berkeley, 1968.

Fortune, R., *A Residence among the Chinese: Inland, on the coast, and at sea: being a narrative of scenes and adventures during a third visit to China, from 1853–1856.* London, 1957.

Fox, G., *British Admirals and Chinese Pirates, 1832–1869.* London, 1940.

Franke, W., *The Reform and Abolition of the Traditional Chinese Examination System.* Cambridge, Mass., 1960.

Freedman, M., *Lineage Organization in Southeastern China.* London, 1965.
Chinese Lineage and Society: Fukien and Kwangtung. London, 1966.

Fu, Chen-lun, *Chung-kuo fang-chih-hsüeh t'ung-lun* (A critical study of Chinese local histories). Shanghai, 1935.

Fu, Ch'i-hsüeh, *Chung-kuo wai-chiao shih* (A history of Chinese diplomacy). Taipei, 1966.

Fu, I-ling, *Ming-Ch'ing nung-ts'un she-hui ching-chi* (Rural society and economy in the Ming and Ch'ing periods). Peking, 1961.

Fu, Pao-shen, 'Yeh Chih-shen', in Li Huan, ed., *Kuo-ch'ao ch'i-hsien lei-cheng ch'u-pien* (Eminent scholars of the Ch'ing period).
'Yeh Chi-wen', in Li Huan, ed., *Kuo-ch'ao ch'i-hsien lei-cheng ch'u-pien.*
'Yeh Ming-feng', in Li Huan, ed., *Kuo-ch'ao ch'i-hsien lei-cheng ch'u-pien.*

Fu, Tsung-mou, *Ch'ing-tai tu-fu chih-tu* (The system of governors-general and governors in the Ch'ing period). Taipei, 1963.

Gerson, J. J., *Horatio Nelson Lay and Sino-British Relations, 1854–1864.* Cambridge, Mass., 1972.

Greenberg, M., *British Trade and the Opening of China, 1800–1842.* Cambridge, 1951.

Grinstead, E. and Chang Hsin-pao, 'Chinese Documents of the British Embassy in Peking, 1793–1911', *Journal of Asian Studies* 22, no. 3 (1963), 354–6.

Gulick, E. V., *Peter Parker and the Opening of China.* Cambridge, Mass., 1973.

Han-yang hsien-chih (Local history of Han-yang magistracy), 1868.

Hao, Yen-p'ing, *The Comprador in Nineteenth Century China: Bridge between East and West.* Cambridge, Mass., 1970.

Hinton, H. C., *The Grain Tribute System of China, 1845–1911.* Cambridge, Mass., 1970.

Ho, A. K. L., 'The Grand Council in the Ch'ing Dynasty', *Far Eastern Quarterly*, 11, no. 2 (1951), 167–82.

Ho, I-k'un, *Tseng Kuo-fan p'ing-chuan* (A critical biography of Tseng Kuo-fan). Taipei, 1964.

Ho, Ping-ti, 'The Salt Merchants of Yang-chou: A study of commercial capitalism in eighteenth-century China', *Harvard Journal of Asiatic Studies*, 17 (1954), 130–68.
Studies on the Population of China, 1368–1953. Cambridge, Mass., 1959.
The Ladder of Success in Imperial China. New York, 1962.
Holt, E., *The Opium Wars in China.* Pennsylvania, 1964.
Hsia Hsieh, *Chung-hsi chi-shih* (Records of Sino-Western affairs), contained in *Chin-tai Chung-kuo shih-liao ts'ung-k'an*, 106 (Collections of Chinese historical works). Taipei (reprint), 1967.
Hsiao, I-shan, *Chin-tai mi she-hui shih-liao* (Materials on secret societies). Peiping, 1935.
Ch'ing-tai t'ung-shih (A general history of the Ch'ing period). 5 vols. Taipei, 1962, 1963.
Hsiao, Kung-ch'üan, *Rural China: Imperial control in the nineteenth century.* Seattle, 1960.
Hsiao Yüan, 'Yüeh-k'e t'an Hsien-feng ch'i-nien Kuo-ch'ih' (A Cantonese recalling the national disgrace of 1857), *Kuo-wen chou-pao* (National News Weekly), Vol. 14, nos. 24, 26, 28, 30, 32, 40 (1937).
Hsieh, Fu-ch'eng, 'Shu Han-yang Yeh-hsiang Kuang-chou chih pien' (Grand Secretary Yeh and the Canton episode), *Yung-an ch'üan-chi hsü-pien* (Yung-an Collection). Shanghai, 1897.
Hsieh, Kuo-ching, 'Removal of coastal population in early Tsing period', *Chinese Social and Political Science Review*, 15, no. 4 (1932), 559–96.
Hsieh, Ting-yu, 'Origin and Migrations of the Hakkas', *Chinese Social and Political Science Review*, 13 (1929), 202–27.
Hsü-hsiu Nan-hai hsien-chih (A revised local history of Nan-hai magistracy), 1872.
Hsü, I. C. Y., *China's Entrance into the Family of Nations: the diplomatic phase, 1858–1880.* Cambridge, Mass., 1960.
The Ili Crisis. Oxford, 1966.
The Rise of Modern China. Oxford, 1970.
Hsü, Ta-ling, *Ch'ing-tai chüan-na chih-tu* (The system of purchasing offices and titles by contributions during the Ch'ing period). Peking, 1950.
Hu, Ch'ang-tu, 'The Yellow River administration in the Ch'ing Dynasty', *Far Eastern Quarterly*, 14, no. 4 (1955), 505–13.
Hu, Feng-tan, 'Yeh Ming-ch'en chia-chuan' (A commemorative biography of Yeh Ming-ch'en), in Miao Ch'üan-sun, ed., *Hsü pei-chuan-chi* (Additions to the collection of obituaries). 1910.
Hu, Hsien-chin, *The Common Descent Group in China and its Functions.* New York, 1948.
Hu-nan t'ung-chih (Local history of Hunan province). 1934.
Hu-nan t'ung-chih (Local History of Hunan), 1887.
Hu-pei t'ung-chih (Local history of Hupeh province). 1921.
Hu, Sheng, *Ti-kuo chu-i yü Chung-kuo cheng-chih.* Peking, 1952. (The English version, *Imperialism and Chinese Politics*, was published in Peking in 1955.)
Hu, Shih, *Hu Shih wen-ts'un* (The collected works of Hu Shih), 3 vols. Shanghai, 1933.
Hua, T'ing-chieh, 'Ch'u-fan shih-mo' (A complete account of contacts with foreigners), in *Chin-tai-shih tzu-liao* (Sources of modern history) no. 2. Peking, 1956.
Huang, Yen-yü, 'Viceroy Yeh Ming-ch'en and the Canton Episode (1856–61)', *Harvard Journal of Asiatic Studies*, 6 (1941), 37–127.
Hucker, C. O., *China: A Critical Bibliography.* Tucson, Ariz., 1962.

Hudson, G. F., *Europe and China: A Survey of their relations from the earliest times to 1800*. London, 1931.

Hui-chou fu-chih (Local history of Hui-chou prefecture). 1881.

Hummel, A. W., *Eminent Chinese of the Ch'ing Period*. Washington D.C., 1943.

Hunter, W. C., *The 'Fan-Kwae' at Canton before Treaty Days, 1825–1844*. London, 1882.

   Bits of Old China. London, 1885.

Hurd, D., *The Arrow War: An Anglo-Chinese Confusion, 1856–60*. London, 1967.

Jao, Tsung-i, *Ch'ao-chou chih* (Local history of Ch'ao-chou). 1946.

Jen, Yu-wen, *see* Chien Yu-wen.

Jung, Chao-tsu, *Ming-tai ssu-hsiang shih* (A history of philosophy of the Ming period). Taipei (reprint), 1962.

Jung, Hung, *Hsi-hsüeh tung-chien chi* (The coming of Western learning). Taipei (reprint), 1961.

Kao-chou fu-chih (Local history of Kao-chou prefecture). 1889.

Keer, J. G., 'Description of the Great Examination Hall at Canton', *Journal of the North China Branch of the Royal Asiatic Society*, New series, 5, no. 3 (Dec. 1866), 63–9.

King, F. H. H., *Money and Monetary Policy in China, 1845–1895*. Cambridge, Mass., 1965.

Koa, Shiaw-chian, 'British Opinion and Policy on China between the First and Second Anglo-Chinese Wars, 1842–1857', unpublished M.A. thesis, University of Leeds, 1967.

Krone, R., 'Eine Missionsreise in Sanon-Kreise', *Berichte der Rheinischen Missionsgesellschaft*, No. 7 (1853), pp. 97–110.

   'Die chinesischen Mandarinen', *Berichte der Rheinischen Missionsgesellschaft*, No. 21 (1853), pp. 321–33.

   'Der Besuch in der Ngamun zu Fukwing', *Berichte der Rheinischen Missionsgesellschaft*, No. 21 (1853), pp. 333–6.

Kuang-chou fu-chih (Local history of Kuang-chou prefecture), 1879.

Kuang-hsi t'ung-chih (Local history of Kwangsi province), 1802.

Kuang-tung t'ung-chih (Local history of Kwangtung province), 1822.

Kuang-tung yü-ti t'u-shuo (The geography of Kwangtung), compiled by Liao T'ing-hsiang and others. Taipei (reprint), 1967.

Kuhn, P. A., *Rebellion and Its Enemies in Late Imperial China: Militarization and social structure, 1796–1864*. Cambridge, Mass., 1970.

Kuo, Pin-chia, 'Hsien-feng ch'ao Chung-kuo wai-chiao kai-kuan' (A general survey of Chinese diplomacy during the reign of Emperor Hsien-feng), *Wu-ta she-hui k'o-hsüeh chi-k'an* (Wu-han University Journal of Social Sciences), 5, no. 1 (1835), 81–126.

Kuo, T'ing-i, *T'ai-p'ing t'ien-kuo shih-shih jih-chih* (A chronicle of the Taiping Rebellion). Taipei (reprint), 1965.

   Chin-tai Chung-kuo shih-shih jih-chih (A chronology of historical events of modern China). Taipei, 1963.

Kuo-yü tz'u-tien (A dictionary of Chinese terms), 4 vols. 2nd edn., Shanghai, 1948.

Lane-Poole, S., *Sir Harry Parkes in China*. London, 1901.

Lang, Ching-hsiao, 'Chung-kuo nan-fang min-tsu yüan-liu k'ao' (A study of the origin of the people in south China), *Tung-fang tsa-chih* (Tung-fang Journal), 30, no. 1 (1933), 88–100.

   'Chung-kuo nan-fang hsieh-tou chih yüan-yin chi ch'i tsu-chih' (The causes and organization of armed conflicts in south China), *Tung-fang tsa-chih*, 30, no. 10 (1933), 81–96.

'Ch'ing-tai Yüeh-tung hsieh-tou shih-shih' (Armed conflicts in Kwangtung during the Ch'ing period), *Ling-nan hsüeh-pao* (Ling-nan Journal), 14, no. 2 (1935), 103–51.

Lang, O., *Chinese Family and Society*. Hamden, Conn., 1968.

Lattimore, O., *Inner Asian Frontiers of China*. Boston, 1962.

Leavenworth, C. S., *The Arrow War with China*. London, 1901.

Lee, Kuo-chi, *Chang Chih-tung te wai-chiao cheng-ts'e* (The foreign policy of Chang Chih-tung). Nan-kang, 1970.

Li, Chien-nung, *The Political History of China, 1840–1928* (tr. S. Y. Teng and J. Ingalls). Princeton, 1956.

Li, En-han, *Tseng Chi-tse te wai-chiao* (The foreign policy of Tseng Chi-tse). Nan-kang, 1966.

Li, Huan, ed., *Kuo-ch'ao ch'i-hsien lei-cheng ch'u-pien* (Eminent scholars of the Ch'ing period), n.d., Taipei (reprint), 1966.

Li, T'ai-fen, *Fang-chih hsüeh* (On the technique of writing local histories). Shanghai, 1935.

Li, Yüan-tu, 'Wang Wen-tuan kung shih-lüeh' (A brief biography of Wang T'ing-chen), *Hsü pei-chuan-chi* (Additions to the collection of obituaries), 3.6a–7b. (1910).

Kuo-ch'ao hsien-cheng shih-lüeh (Short biographies of righteous men of the Ch'ing dynasty). 1866.

Liang, Chia-pin, *Kuang-tung shih-san-hang k'ao* (The Hong merchants of Canton). Shanghai, 1937.

Liang, Jen-ts'ai, *Kuang-tung ching-chi ti-li* (The economic geography of Kwangtung). Peking, 1956.

Liang, Ou-ti, 'Ming-tai te shu-yüan chih-tu' (The academy system of the Ming period), *Hsien-tai shih-hsüeh* (Modern History), 2, no. 4 (1935), 1–20.

'Sung-tai te shu-yüan chih-tu' (The academy system of the Sung period), *Chung-kuo she-hui ching-chi-shih chi-k'an* (Journal of Chinese social and economic history), 8, no. 1 (1949), 20–80.

Liang, T'ing-nan, *Yüeh hai-kuan chih* (The Canton Customs Office). Taipei (reprint), 1968.

Lieh-ch'iang ch'in-lüeh (The encorachment by the Powers). Taipei, 1964.

Lin Ch'ung-yung, *Lin Tse-hsü chuan* (Biography of Lin Tse-hsü). Taipei, 1967.

Liu, Po-chi, *Kuang-tung shu-yüan chih-tu* (The system of academies in Kwangtung). Taipei (reprint), 1958.

Liu, Yat-wing, 'The Ch'ing Grand Council: A study of its origins and organizations to 1861', unpublished M.A. thesis, University of Hong Kong, 1966.

Lo, Erh-kang, ed., *T'ien-ti-hui wen-hsien-lu* (A collection of documents about the Heaven and Earth Society). 1943.

'T'ai-p'ing t'ien-kuo ke-ming ch'ien te jen-k'ou ya-p'o wen-t'i' *Chung-kuo she-hui ching-chi shih chi-k'an* (Journal of Chinese social and economic history), 8, no. 1 (1949), 20–80.

Lo, Hsiang-lin, *Chung-kuo min-tsu shih* (A history of the Chinese people). Taipei, 1953.

1842-nien i-ch'ien Hsiang-kang chi ch'i tui-wai chiao-t'ung. Hong Kong, 1963. (The English version, *Hong Kong and its external commercial communications before 1842*, has also been published.)

K'o-chia shih-liao hui-pien (Historical sources for the study of the Hakka). Hong Kong, 1965.

Lo, Yü-tung, *Chung-kuo li-chin shih* (A history of *likin*). Shanghai, 1936.

Lu, Ch'in-ch'ih, 'Ying-Fa lien-chün chan-chü Kuang-chou shih-mo' (A complete account of the Anglo-French occupation of Canton), *Chung-kuo chin-tai-shih lun-ts'ung* (Articles on Modern China), 1, 74–109. Taipei, 1958.

Lu, Shih-ch'iang, *Chung-kuo kuan-shen fan-chiao te yüan-yin* (Reasons for the anti-Christian acts of Chinese gentry). Taipei, 1966.

Lu, T'ung, *Ta Chung-hua min-kuo tao-hsien hsing-shih ch'üan-t'u* (Atlas of Chinese circuits and magistracies). Peking, 1914.

Ma, Shao-ch'iao, *Ch'ing-tai Miao-min ch'i-i* (The Miao uprisings during the Ch'ing period). Wu-ch'ang, 1956.

Mao-ming hsien-chih (Local history of Mao-ming magistracy). 1888.

Meadows, T. T., *Desultory Notes on the Government and People of China, and on the Chinese Language*. London, 1847.

The Chinese and their Rebellions. Stanford, Palo Alto, Cal. (reprint), 1954.

Menzel, J. M., ed., *The Chinese Civil Service, Career Open to Talent?* Boston, Mass., 1966.

Meng, Hsien-chang, *Chung-kuo chin-tai ching-chi-shih chiao-ch'eng* (Economic history of modern China). Shanghai, 1951.

Meng, S. M., *The Tsungli Yamen*. Cambridge, Mass., 1962.

Miao, Ch'üan-sun, *Hsü pei-chuan chi* (Additions to the Collection of obituaries). Peking, 1910.

Michael, F., *The Taiping Rebellion*. Seattle, 1966.

Min, Erh-ch'ang, *Pei-chuan chi-pu* (Supplements to the collection of obituaries). Peking, 1931.

Morse, H. B., *The International Relations of the Chinese Empire*. 3 vols. London, 1910–18.

Myers, R. H., 'The usefulness of local gazetteers for the study of modern Chinese economic history: Szechwan during the Ch'ing and Republican periods', *Ch'ing-hua hsüeh-pao*, N.S., Vol. 14, nos. 1–2 (1967).

Nan-k'ai ta-hsüeh li-shih-hsi, *Ch'ing shih-lu ching-chi tzu-liao chi-yao* (Collection of economic materials extracted from the Ch'ing Shih-lu). Peking, 1959.

Napoléon, B., *Correspondance de Napoléon Ier*, publiée par ordre de l'Empéreur Napoléon III. Paris, 1858–69.

Niida Noboru, *Chūgoku hōsei-shi kenkyū* (Studies in Chinese legal history), vol. 3, 'Dorei nōdo-hō, kazoku sonraku-hō' (Laws of serfdom, family and village). Tokyo, 1962.

Nolde, J. J., 'The "False Edict" of 1849', *Journal of Asian Studies*, 20, no. 3 (1960), 299–315.

Norris, J. M., *Shelburne and Reform*. London, 1963.

Oliphant, L., *Narrative of the Earl of Elgin's Mission to China and Japan in the years 1857, '58, '59*. London (reprint), 1970.

Owen, D. E., *British Opium Policy in China and India*. New Haven, Conn., 1934.

P'an-yü-hsien hsü-chih (Local history of P'an-yü magistracy). 2nd edn., 1931.

Pao, Cheng-ku, *Ya-p'ien chan-cheng* (The Opium War). Shanghai, 1954.

P'eng, Yü-hsin, *Ch'ing-tai kuan-shui chih-tu* (The customs system in the Ch'ing period). Wu-han, 1956.

Peterson, W. J., 'Early nineteenth century monetary ideas on the cash-silver exchange ratio', *Papers on China*, 20 (Cambridge, Mass., 1966), 23–53.

Pong, D., 'The income and military expenditure of Kiangsi province in the last years (1860–1864) of the Taiping Rebellion', *Journal of Asian Studies*, 26, no. 1 (1966), 49–65.

'The Kwangtung provincial archives at the Public Record Office of London: a progress report', *Journal of Asian Studies*, 28, no. 1 (1968), 139–43.

Pritchard, E. H., 'Anglo-Chinese relations during the seventeenth and eighteenth centuries', *University of Illinois Studies in the Social Sciences*, Vol. 17, nos. 1–2 (1930).

'The crucial years of early Anglo-Chinese relations, 1750–1800', *Research Studies of the State College of Washington*, Vol. 4, nos. 3–4 (1936).

Roberts, J. A. G., 'The Hakka–Punti War', unpublished D.Phil. thesis, University of Oxford, 1968.

Sasaki, Masaya, *Shimmatsu nō himitsu kessha, zem-piem* (Secret societies at the end of the Ch'ing dynasty). Tokyo, 1970.

Ahen Sensō zen Chū-Ei kōshō bunsho (Anglo-Chinese relations before the Opium War). Tokyo, 1967.

Schlegel, G., *Thian Ti Hwui, the Hung League or Heaven-earth-league*. Batavia, 1866.

Shan-hsi t'ung-chih (Local history of Shansi province). 1811.

Shang, Yen-liu, *Ch'ing-tai k'o-chü k'ao-shih shu-lu* (A Description of the Civil Service Examination of the Ch'ing period). Peking, 1958.

Shang-wu yin-shu kuan, *see* Commercial Press.

Shao-chou fu-chih (Local history of Shao-chou prefecture). 1873.

Shen-hsi t'ung-chih (Local history of Shensi province). 1735.

Shen Wei-t'ai, 'T'o-niao cheng-ts'e' (The ostrich policy), *Lieh-ch'iang ch'in-lüeh* (The encorachment by the Powers), 2, 167–77. Taipei, 1964.

Shih, V. Y. C., *The Taiping Ideology: Its Sources, Interpretations, and Influences*. Seattle, 1963.

Shun-te hsien-chih (Local history of Shun-te magistracy). 1929.

Shun-t'ien fu-chih (Local history of Peking). 1884.

Skinner, G. W., *et. al.* (ed.), *Modern Chinese Society: An Analytical Bibliography*. 3 vols. Stanford, Cal., 1973.

Spector, S., *Li Hung-chang and the Huai Army, a study in nineteenth century Chinese regionalism*. Seattle, 1964.

Ssu-kuo hsin-tang (New archives concerning our relations with England, Russia, France and America). Nan-kang, 1966.

Stanley, C. J., 'Chinese Finance from 1852–1908', *Papers on China*, 3, 1–23. Cambridge, Mass., 1949.

Stanton, W., *The Triad Society or Heaven and Earth Association*. Hong Kong, 1900.

Sun, Chin-ming, *Chung-kuo ping-chih shih* (A history of Chinese military systems). Taipei, 1960.

Sun, E-tu Zen, 'The Board of Revenue in nineteenth-century China', *Harvard Journal of Asiatic Studies*, 24 (1963), 175–228.

and Francis, J. de, *Chinese Social History: translations of selected studies*. Seattle, 1965.

Ta-Ch'ing hui-tien (Collected statutes of the Ch'ing period). Kuang-hsü period.

Ta-Ch'ing hui-tien shih-li (Collected statutes of the Ch'ing period: with precedents). Kuang-hsü period.

Ta-Ch'ing li-ch'ao shih-lu (Veritable records of the successive reigns of the Ch'ing dynasty). Taipei (reprint), 1964.

Taga, Akigorō, *Sōfu no kenkyū: shiryōhen* (An analytic study of Chinese genealogical books). Tokyo, 1960.

T'an, Cho-yüan, *Chung-wen tsa-chih so-yin* (Index to Chinese learned articles). Canton, 1935.

T'ang, Hsiang-lung, 'Tao-kuang shih-ch'i te yin-kuei wen-t'i' (The problem of the rising price of silver in the Tao-kuang period), *Chung-kuo chin-tai-shih lun-ts'ung* (A collection of articles on Modern China), 3, 9–39. Taipei, 1958.

Tao-kuang Hsien-feng liang-ch'ao ch'ou-pan i-wu shih-mo pu-i (Supplements to *Ch'ou-pan i-wu shih-mo*, Tao-kuang and Hsien-feng periods). Nan-kang, 1966.

T'ao, Ch'eng-chang, 'T'ien-ti-hui yüan-liu k'ao' (The evolution of Heaven and Earth Society), Lo Erh-kang, ed., *T'ien-ti-hui wen-hsien-lu* (A collection of documents about the Heaven and Earth Society). 1943.

Teng, Ssu-yü, *Chung-kuo k'ao-shih chih-tu shih* (A history of the Chinese examination system). Taipei, 1967.

The Taiping Rebellion and the Western Powers: A comprehensive survey. Oxford, 1971.

and Fairbank, J. K., *China's Response to the West.* New York, 1963.

Tsang, Li-ho, *Chung-kuo jen-ming ta-tz'u-tien* (A dictionary of Chinese names). Shanghai, 1934.

Tso, Shun-sheng, ed., *Chung-kuo chin-pai-nien-shih tzu-liao ch'u-pien* (Source materials for the study of modern Chinese history). Taipei (reprint), 1966.

Tu, Lien-che, and Fang, Chao-ying, eds., *San-shih-san chung Ch'ing-tai chuan-chi tsung-ho yin-te* (Index to thirty-three collections of Ch'ing biographies). Peking, 1932.

Tung-kuan hsien-chih (Local history of Tung-kuan magistracy). 1919.

Twitchett, D. C., 'Problems of Chinese biography', in A. F. Wright and D. C. Twitchett, eds., *Confucian Personalities.* Stanford, 1962.

Tz'u-hai (A Chinese dictionary). Shanghai, 1947.

Vincent, J. C., *The Extraterritorial System in China: Final Phase.* Cambridge, Mass., 1970.

Wakeman, F., Jr, *Strangers at the Gate, Social Disorder in south China, 1836–1861.* Berkeley, 1966.

Walrond, T. ed., *Letters and Journals of James, Eighth Earl of Elgin.* London, 1872.

Wang, Erh-min, *Huai-chün chih* (History of the Huai Army). Nan-kang, 1967.

'Wang Mao-yin yü Hsien-feng shih-tai te hsin pi-chih' (Wang Mao-yin and the fiscal changes in the reign of Hsien-feng), author unknown, *Chung-kuo chin-tai shih lun-ts'ung*, 3, 49–70. Taipei, 1958.

Wang, Shu-hwai, *Hsien-T'ung Yün-nan Hui-min shih-pien* (The Mohammedan Uprising in Yünnan, 1856–1873). Nan-kang, 1968.

Wang, S. T., *The Margary Affair and the Chefoo Convention.* New York, 1939.

Wang, Y. C., *An Estimate of the Land-Tax in China, 1753 and 1908.* Cambridge, Mass., 1973.

Weber, M., *The Religion of China, Confucianism and Taoism*, tr. and ed. H. H. Gerth. Glencoe, Ill., 1962.

Wei, Chien-yu, *Chung-kuo chin-tai huo-pi shih* (A history of the monetary system in modern China). Shanghai, 1955.

Ti-erh-tz'u ya-p'ien chan-cheng (The Second Opium War). Shanghai, 1955.

Wiens, H. L., *China's March towards the Tropics.* Hamden, Conn., 1954.

Wong, J. Y., 'Sir John Bowring and the Canton City Question', *Bulletin of the John Rylands University Library of Manchester* (formerly *Bulletin of the John Rylands Library*), 56, no. 1 (1973), 219–45.

'The *Arrow* Incident: A Reappraisal', *Modern Asian Studies*, 8, no. 3 (1974), 373–89.

'Harry Parkes and the Arrow War in China', *Modern Asian Studies*, 9, no. 3 (1975), 303–20.

'The Taiping Revolutionary Movement; a review article', *Modern Asian Studies*, 9, no. 4 (1975), 557–66.

'The Role of Peter Parker in the Opening of China; a review article', *China Quarterly* (1975) no. 63, 539–42.

Wright, A. F., ed., *Studies in Chinese Thought*. Chicago, 1953.
   'Values, Roles, and Personalities', in A. F. Wright and D. C. Twitchett, eds., *Confucian Personalities*, pp. 3–23.
   and Twitchett, D. C., *Confucian Personalities*. Stanford, 1962.
Wu, Ch'eng-ch'iao, *Ch'ing-tai li-chih ts'ung-t'an* (Discussions on Ch'ing bureaucracy), contained in *Chin-tai Chung-kuo shih-liao ts'ung-k'an*, 12 (Collections of Chinese modern historical works). Taipei (reprint), 1968.
Wu, Ju-lun, *T'ung-ch'eng Wu hsien-sheng jih-chi* (The diary of Mr Wu of T'ung-ch'eng). 1928.
Ya-p'ien chan-cheng shih-ch'i ssu-hsiang-shih tzu-liao hsüan-chi (A collection of essays reflecting the attitude of the Chinese during and after the Opium War), compiled by the Modern History Research Institute of the Chinese Academy of Sciences. Peking, 1963.
Yang, C. K., *Religion in Chinese Society*, Berkeley, 1961.
Yang, Chia-lo, *Li-tai jen-wu nien-li t'ung-p'u* (Index of dates and places of birth of figures in Chinese history). Taipei, 1963.
Yeh, Chih-shen, *P'ing-an kuan ts'ang-ch'i mu* (Catalogue of antiques in the P'ing-an Kuan), contained in *Ts'ung-shu chi-ch'eng ch'u-pien* (A collection of Chinese miscellaneous works). Shanghai, 1963.
   et al., eds., *Yeh-shih tsung-p'u* (Genealogy of the Yeh family). 1873.
Yü, Ping-ch'üan, ed., *Chung-kuo shih-hsüeh lun-wen yin-te* (Index to learned articles on Chinese history: 1902–62). Hong Kong, 1962.

INDEX